This vivid book opens with a shipload of convi driven ashore at Wreck Bay, south of Sydney.

How had their lives in Ireland brought them to this place? How did they make their way in Australia afterwards? In following them down the years, Babette Smith presents us with a bracing set of conclusions about Australia—and about Ireland.

Barrie Dyster, University of NSW

A fascinating interpretation of the many roles that the Irish played in Australia's development in the nineteenth century. Rigorously researched, this story covers the many facets of the early growth of New South Wales in which Irish immigrants, from convicts to Governor, played a shaping role. Their impact is with us yet.

Robert O'Neill, former Chichele Professor of the History of War,
All Souls College, University of Oxford

It's Babette Smith's best. Deeply researched and vividly written, it's a terrific new and up-to-date account of the convict experience, mainly from the bottom up. There's balance and judgement, and an easy grasp of a penal system which was very complex and continuously changing. I'm impressed.

Emeritus Professor Alan Atkinson FAHA, University of Sydney

OTHER BOOKS BY BABETTE SMITH

NON-FICTION

A Cargo of Women: Susannah Watson and the convicts of the Princess Royal
Australia's Birthstain
Mothers and Sons
Coming up for Air

FICTION

A Cargo of Women, the novel

THE LUCK OF THE IRISH

HOW A SHIPLOAD OF CONVICTS SURVIVED THE WRECK OF THE *HIVE* TO MAKE A NEW LIFE IN AUSTRALIA

BABETTE SMITH

ALLEN&UNWIN

SYDNEY·MELBOURNE·AUCKLAND·LONDON

First published in 2014

This project has been assisted by the Australian
Government through the Australia Council,
its arts funding and advisory board.

Allen & Unwin
83 Alexander Street
Crows Nest NSW 2065
Australia
Phone: (61 2) 8425 0100
Email: info@allenandunwin.com
Web: www.allenandunwin.com

Cataloguing-in-Publication details are available
from the National Library of Australia
www.trove.nla.gov.au

ISBN 978 1 74237 812 1

Map by Janet Hunt
Set in 11.4/14.7 pt Adobe Garamond Pro by Bookhouse, Sydney
Printed and bound in Australia by Griffin Press

10 9 8 7 6 5 4 3 2 1

For Carl Harrison-Ford, editor, whose contribution to my work has always been helpful and significant

Contents

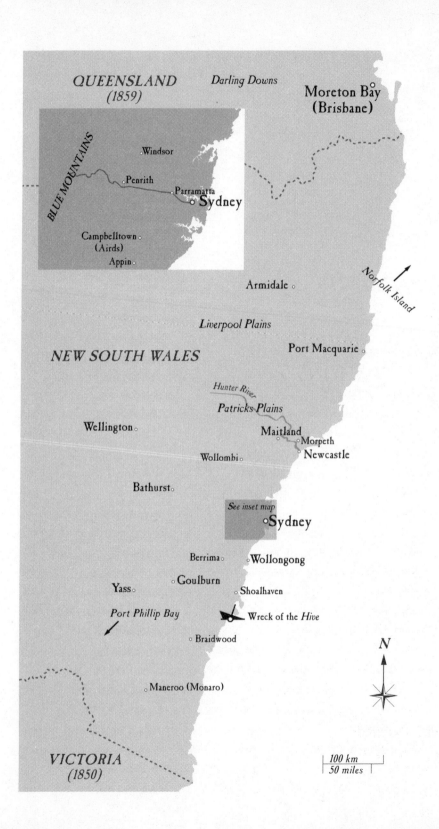

QUEENSLAND
(1859)

Darling Downs

Moreton Bay
(Brisbane)

BLUE MOUNTAINS

Windsor

Penrith

Parramatta

Sydney

Campbelltown
(Airds)

Appin

Armidale

Liverpool Plains

NEW SOUTH WALES

Port Macquarie

Norfolk Island

Hunter River

Patricks Plains

Wellington

Maitland

Morpeth

Wollombi

Newcastle

Bathurst

See inset map
Sydney

Berrima

Wollongong

Yass

Goulburn

Shoalhaven

Port Phillip Bay

Wreck of the Hive

Braidwood

Maneroo (Monaro)

N

VICTORIA
(1850)

100 km
50 miles

Introduction

The idea that the Irish convicts were helpless victims of poverty who stole sheep is one of the truisms of Australian history. When we do acknowledge that they committed other crimes, such as stealing sugar, for example, or clothes, they are categorised—my previous research indicates rightly—as urban thieves who were no different to the English or Scots. Indeed, many were convicted in England and Scotland.

More disturbing, however, is how we regard violent crimes, such as assault, committed by Irish convicts. Traditionally, any violent crimes are assumed to be a consequence of English oppression and therefore justified, the violence itself being disregarded. In the 1960s, Lloyd Robson detected their significance, writing in *The Convict Settlers of Australia* that 'There was a nightmare of violence in Ireland that was no dream, and to which the population had become accustomed.' He acknowledged the extraordinary situation in which where 'warfare existed between Irish and English, Roman Catholic and Protestant, landlord and tenant, tenant and sub-tenant, and sub-tenant and sub-sub-tenant, not to mention feuds between families that had been going on for so long that no one remembered why they had started.'[1] Unfortunately, like many others, he explored no further than a brief summary of what this meant. Nor did anyone else. The tragic circumstances were apparently enough to explain everything. Combined with the fact that a bomb destroyed many legal records in 1922, it ensured that, one way or another, we preserve an image of the Irish convicts which is bland, even boring.[2]

Meanwhile, the Irish themselves were asking questions about the historical roots of the violence that permeated their society in modern times. A.T.Q. Stewart, who seems to stand in relation to Irish history as A.G.L. Shaw does to Australian, explored this question in *The Narrow Ground*. Like Shaw, he was an empirical investigator, rigorously uncompromising in his analysis and courageous in his argument, all on display when he wrote that a constant feature of the Irish people throughout their history 'is their capacity for very reckless violence, allied to a distorted moral sense which magnifies small sins and yet regards murder as trivial. Their kindness and hospitality are legendary, but so too is their reputation for hypocrisy and cruelty'.[3] Now this is definitely not part of Australians' image of the Irish. Have we missed something?

Hard on our idea of Irish prisoners as helpless victims driven to crime has been our acceptance that they suffered gross discrimination from the moment of their arrival in Australia. This has often been accompanied by a puzzled, perhaps more accurately a disappointed, question: why didn't they rebel? The Castle Hill Rebellion of 1804, which spluttered and died so swiftly, was no answer. After all, the Irish are famous for flinging themselves passionately into nationalist causes. In Australia, they had a chance of success. Why didn't they try again?

The dull, virtuous picture of the Irish should have made me realise there would be more to discover. Researching my earlier books, *A Cargo of Women* and *Australia's Birthstain*, taught me that Australian history of this era was full of surprises which had been buried either by ignorance or due to propaganda by anti-transportationists who were making a case to stop the flow of prisoners. It is not as though I was entirely unacquainted with Irish convicts—approximately 20 per cent of men and women who sailed from England were Irish, after being caught in England or Scotland. I had researched them as assiduously as I did the English, the Scots and the Welsh.[4] They weren't dull. However, I had never looked at the Irish in their own terms. Quite an oversight since they made up more than one-third the total number of convicts transported to Australia.[5] To round out my understanding of the Australian penal colonies, I decided it was time I investigated some of the most cherished assumptions and favourite stereotypes. The outcome has been surprising, to say the least.

The timeframe covered in *The Luck of the Irish* concentrates on the two decades from 1825 to 1845, although its broad spread reaches further in both directions. Convict transportation was at its peak during this period, although ending officially in 1840 to New South Wales after recommendations by the Molesworth Committee in London. It was a time when the so-called 'slave' colony would have been at its height, when the landholding tyrants, the lash and the chain gang were said to rule. And in this setting, all the convicts were imagined as the cowed and cowardly scum of the earth, men and women with neither morals nor backbone. Investigating the Irish meant I must explore their experience in context, in particular that of the colonial workforce of which they were part. This, too, produced a surprising outcome, revealing some legacies of real substance and long-lasting significance.

While I was pondering the subject of the Irish I was invited to speak at a conference of the Professional Historians Association on Norfolk Island in 2010. Maritime archaeologist Tim Smith, from Heritage New South Wales, was also one of the speakers and it was he who first told me details of the wreck of the convict ship *Hive*. Carrying a cargo of 250 male prisoners from Ireland, she ran aground on the New South Wales south coast in 1835. When maritime archaeologists first confirmed the site of the wreck in the mid-1990s, it was a one-day wonder for the media. But I was gripped by the idea of the unremarked shipwreck, a sensation in its day but essentially now lost to all but specialists. It was a story worth telling.

My knowledge of the *Hive* was scanty. I had mentally lumped it with other convict shipwrecks and assumed that, as with many of them, everybody on board had perished. Discovering from Tim Smith that all the prisoners survived but that, as far as he knew, no one had ever asked what happened to them, set my curiosity alight. The 'luck of the Irish', it seemed, had played out with all its traditional irony in the catastrophe of the wreck but the survival of those on board. The shipwreck became my pretext for investigating the Irish factor in the later decades of convict New South Wales and this, in turn, led me to explore the colonial male working culture. It also provided a broad cross-section of people in addition to the prisoners who were linked through their arrival on the *Hive* and who, in their various ways, contributed to the development of Australia.

BABETTE SMITH

CHAPTER 1
Beached

For thousands of years the bay that now fringes Booderee National Park was a significant and abundant place for Aboriginal people. They had fished there from time immemorial, 'riding' the winds that reflected the changing moods of the bay. In Aboriginal lore Tootawah created the winds but the people named them: Yilarm from the north, Murrawaddi who blew in from the east, Dulamar who gusted from the south and Curragama, the dry, west wind.[1] On the night of 10 December 1835 Murrawaddi was blowing, fresh but not gusty, by no means in a stormy mood, just steadily and persistently compelling flotsam and jetsam towards land. Cloud covered the moon but the white foam of a low surf could be faintly detected as it broke against land's edge. The bay was peaceful.

When darkness fell, the traditional owners of the bay had hauled in their nets and gone home to their community behind the dunes, out of reach of Murrawaddi. They were not watching when the wooden ship loomed up. They did not hear her keel scrape as it slanted along the bottom. She was a prey to Murrawaddi who pushed and pushed until the ship wedged deep in the soft sand where the waves took possession, breaking repetitively against their prize, intent on destruction. After a voyage of 109 days, across 13,000 miles of ocean, with Sydney Town only a day's sail away, the convict ship *Hive* was beached.

To that point it was just an ordinary night at sea. Two hundred and fifty Irishmen were locked, as usual, in their prison deck. Their guard, numbering 29 soldiers from the 28th Regiment, were mostly relaxing below, a lucky few (eight in all) with their wives and children.[2] The commander of the guard, 25-year-old Lieutenant Edward Lugard, was in his cabin. Calling at Sydney, indeed leading this detachment, was an interlude for him; his eventual destination was to rejoin his regiment in India after recovering from wounds sustained there three years earlier. Sailing on the *Hive*, however, did offer time with his younger brother Henry who had just been gazetted second lieutenant in the Royal Engineers and whose first posting was the penal colony of New South Wales.[3] The surgeon Dr Anthony Donoghoe was busy updating documents he must hand to officials in Sydney. It had been an uneventful voyage: no extreme weather; no attempted mutinies; few people seeking medical attention and those just as likely to be soldiers as prisoners. Just one death—a young lad named Michael Desmond from Limerick of pulmonary disease that Donoghoe blamed on his time as an apprentice glassblower, although a second, James Harding, was ailing with dysentery and would die before reaching Sydney.[4] The master, Captain John Thomas Nutting, was also below, indulging in some mysterious activity which later evidence suggests was linked to the contents of a bottle.

In this relaxed atmosphere, the shock of running aground was magnified. 'The confusion and terror that prevailed at this time is not to be described,' wrote one of the passengers. Women screamed and kept screaming. Children wailed in fright. On the prison deck, men, at risk of death, yelled and swore mutiny if they were not released. Desperation and panic would have given them strength to break out; fear of drowning made them careless of death from gunshot. Some convicts had their young sons hidden among the ship's crew. As parents, they must have been mad with anxiety when they could do nothing to protect them from danger. Fortunately, Pat Maloney, who had been a seaman, saved the day. Accurately assessing they were in no immediate danger, he somehow convinced that large group of fearful men to calm down. Someone overheard him and recorded: 'owing to the intrepidity of one of the prisoners the spilling of human blood was prevented'.[5]

Confusion below was matched by confusion and strife above. When land was sighted earlier in the day chief officer Edward Canney had warned the captain that the course he was setting from Montagu Island might bring them too close in during the night. Captain Nutting, who had been out in his reckoning several times during the voyage, resented Canney's advice. 'Mind your own business. One person is sufficient to navigate the ship,' he snapped. When third mate Thomas Morgan took over for the night watch Canney again expressed concern but the captain was insistent. After posting lookouts, he ordered the ship be kept under full sail, then retired to his stateroom.[6]

Canney too went below but he remained uneasy. Unable to sleep, he went on deck again at 9.30 p.m. Talking with Ensign Waldron Kelly and a prisoner named Joseph Tweeble, who were on deck, did nothing to allay his anxiety. Both men had experience at sea. Ensign Kelly had been in the naval service of the East India Company before purchasing a commission in the British Army. Sixty-year-old Tweeble was being transported for bigamy but he had once been master of an American vessel.[7] Before he left the deck, Canney tried to convince Morgan, as officer of the watch, to trim the sails but he refused, fear of disobeying the captain outweighing any doubts of his own about their course. With Canney again below, it was Tweeble who urged Kelly to tell Morgan about the land they could now see on the starboard bow.[8] Morgan's first reaction was denial. 'It's only cloud. I've been watching it for some time,' he said. But the other two were right. Shortly after, an alarmed Morgan hurried to Canney's cabin, blurting out dire news: 'There's something white on the port bow. It looks like breakers.'

Canney rushed on deck yelling, 'Hard-a-port!' On a vessel like the *Hive* this would turn her to starboard, away to clear water. But it was too late to manoeuvre. Under full sail and carried forward by the swell, the *Hive* began running through sand. As she started to wedge, Canney's attempt to swing her round created a hard jolt that shocked everyone on board into realising something was wrong.[9]

Edward Canney was, as the saying goes, 'born to the sea'. Raised in Kent where the Thames meets the English Channel, his family had been seafarers for centuries, his father a pilot of the Cinque Ports, like his father before him. Growing up on the broad sands near Deal, Canney learned the joys and the dangers of water from an early age. The sea was his playground, his challenge and adventure. Twenty-two years old when the *Hive* struck, he had first sailed the globe at thirteen and spent five years as an apprentice under his uncle Captain Canney on the *Katherine Stewart Forbes*. Since then he had served several masters as mate and had been with the *Hive* as chief officer the year before, but under a different captain.[10]

By the time Captain Nutting appeared on deck, Canney had ordered the topsail furled and the mainyards back. The master was furious. 'Who the Hell ordered the foretop clued-up?' he demanded. 'I did, sir. I was trying to make her turn off,' Canney replied. When Nutting countermanded what he had done, Canney forced the issue by asking formally for orders. But the master suddenly tired of the argument. 'Do what you think best,' he shrugged. At this point, surgeon Donoghoe asked Nutting what he intended to do. The master could not answer him. 'He appeared confused and unequal to giving the necessary directions,' Donoghoe later told the inquiry. Meanwhile, with Nutting brooding silently on the poop deck, Canney organised the crew to furl all sails fore and aft, heave the spars overboard and clear the longboat ready for hoisting. The surgeon was so concerned by the captain's condition that he sounded out Canney about taking command. The chief officer refused, 'not knowing by what authority it was done'.[11]

Canney would have been very conscious that he risked a charge of mutiny by opposing the captain. He could hang for it. Only one man on board had sufficient power to take action against the captain and survive this fate. The presence of a surgeon superintendent on each convict ship had been mandatory since 1815 (when the war with France ended). It was designed to ensure there was no repetition of the terrible death toll caused by captains who had neither care nor interest in the fate of the prisoners their ships carried. Consequently, Dr Donoghoe, like other surgeons, had over-riding responsibility from the British government for the safety of the 250 prisoners under his care. Over the years, ships' masters had become used to this split command and few surgeons had found it necessary to pull rank against a captain. Most incidents were minor and related to rations or insisting that convicts spend more time on deck or the decision to disembark someone too ill to travel. It was, however, awesome power in an emergency and events gave Donoghoe no choice.[12]

At first light, Canney reported to Nutting that the longboat was ready for launching. To his dismay the captain instead ordered the jolly boat should be lowered from the starboard quarter, the side of the ship that was being lashed by surf. Canney had no choice but to obey. Unable to convince the captain to lower the longboat, Canney chose to join Ensign Kelly and one of the experienced hands on the jolly. Predictably, she could not survive the violence of the waves. As soon as she touched water, she capsized and was smashed against the ship. Flung into the surf, Canney managed to grab hold of a rope thrown him. Simultaneously, however, he realised that Kelly, dressed in the heavy red uniform of the British army, was in danger of drowning. With what Henry Lugard described as 'the most extraordinary presence of mind' Canney somehow got the rope round Kelly and 'had him hauled on deck in a very exhausted state, thereby saving his (Ensign K's) life, which he has since repeatedly acknowledged'.[13] Meanwhile the third man had surfed to the beach by clinging to the upturned boat. Edward Canney then followed him ashore with the hawser line, which he made fast on land before returning to the *Hive*.

Back on board, he found the captain intended that everyone make their way individually through the surf by clinging to the hawser. Again Canney remonstrated, proposing the longboat as a safer way to get them to the beach. The potential loss of life using the hawser alone was immense. Many on board could not swim. There were eight women who, whatever their personal strength, would have been hampered by the clothing of the day and by intense anxiety for their children, who numbered eleven, some of them infants. Bridget Tierney, for example, wife of Private Patrick Tierney of the 28th, had two children on board. Margaret, the eldest, was nine years and Michael only three. And Bridget herself was pregnant.[14] The captain's idea was dangerous even for those who were young, unencumbered and confident in the water. The surf was high. And darkness made it entirely unpredictable. Even as Nutting over-rode Canney's suggestion, a youth from the crew got into difficulties when he tried to swim ashore. Jumping overboard to help him, the boatswain struck his head against the ship's stern and drowned in the turbulent waters before anything could be done to rescue him. One observer estimated that at least half the 300 people would have drowned if Nutting's plan had been allowed to stand.[15]

When the captain peremptorily refused to use the longboat, Dr Donoghoe intervened. Canney's initial refusal to accept command had reminded him to step carefully. With the formal support of Edward

Lugard as commander of the guard, the surgeon deposed Captain Nutting and gave organisational control to Canney, who, this time, accepted. Donoghoe justified his action on two grounds. First, the captain's repeated errors in navigation during the voyage: 'I consider him an unfit man from his repeated mistakes in the reckoning.' Second, his responsibility to care for 250 prisoners: 'My anxiety to save the lives of those under my charge on board.'[16]

Near dawn, they finally got the longboat clear and hoisted out. Her first load was women and children accompanied by some of the guard, men who would have been chosen because they could swim. Just descending from the ship into the boat was a challenge for the passengers. Very likely some were slung over the shoulders of experienced seamen. Next they must successfully ride the surf to shore in conditions none had encountered before. Even with the bigger boat, there was a risk of capsizing. Determined to avoid a tragedy, it seems Canney personally escorted each boatload to the beach. On the deck of the *Hive*, Henry Lugard watched with admiration: 'Thus with almost indescribable difficulties, up to his neck in water all the time, did Mr Edward Canney safely land and save the lives of 300 men, women and children without one single accident,' he wrote.[17]

As the first beams of the sun rose out of the ocean the *Hive*'s passengers could see they were in a wide bay with the headland, mistaken for cloud, rising steeply to the north. In more exact terms, the ship had grounded 'south of Jervis Bay in a deep bight between Cape St George (to the north) and Sussex Haven'.[18] Looking around they could see a long shallow curve of white sand stretching as far as the eye could see. The ship was almost exactly in the centre of the curve. Daylight also revealed that the *Hive* was no more than her own length—120 feet—from shore with about four to five feet depth around her. At low tide it would be possible to wade out.[19]

During the night, Henry Lugard had been forced to stand by while his brother and the surgeon took charge. Once on shore, however, his engineering skills could be put to use to design a camp. There were no trees to fell, just dense low scrub which offered neither building material nor protection from the weather. One document describes the shelters that were built as 'bowers', which suggests that pieces of sailcloth were stretched over scrubby bushes to create makeshift tents. Under Lugard's direction, teams of prisoners also dug latrines, built campfires and brought up provisions from the beach.

As the operation ferrying people to shore wound down, Captain Nutting recovered his voice and his senses. He resumed giving orders as though there had been no interruption. Relieved of anxiety about the lives of the passengers, nobody challenged his authority and he was left to order the salvage of stores and supplies and to direct the crew in futile attempts to float her off.[20]

Dr Donoghoe and Lieutenant Edward Lugard now had another worry: they had only the vaguest idea of where they were. 'A day's sail from Sydney' was no help when confronted with a vast scrubby wilderness with no sign of human habitation, no people or houses, no vehicles or discernible tracks or any of those markers that made Europeans feel safe. Sydney lay to the north, but what lay in between and how were they going to get there? The answer appeared, walking along the beach towards them.

Emerging at sunrise from their settlement at the northern end of the bay, the indigenous people were intent on catching early morning fish—the wattle was blooming, which meant bream would be travelling along the beach.[21] They must have been shocked to find over 300 men, women and children milling around on their land. But over nearly 50 years, even in the remote Booderee bush, they had become used to Europeans and their strange habits. Anyway, the scene before them told its own story. The Aborigines knew what to do. They approached in friendship, offering help.

The Europeans would have been equally shocked when they first saw the Aborigines. And frightened. As well as carrying their nets, they had spears for fishing. Would they attack? Were they friendly? Soldiers reached for their muskets. Women nervously called their children to them. Fortunately, Edward Lugard, who would later be described by his commanding officer as 'cool and intrepid', held his nerve until the goodwill of the indigenous people became obvious. By sign language and broken English they offered to guide someone to the nearest European who, their gestures indicated, was 'up the hill'. There was no way of estimating how far that meant. As the most junior officer, Ensign Waldron Kelly was again given the hard job.[22] Before he plunged into the bush with his escort, Donoghoe scribbled a note: 'Sir, I beg leave to report this vessel on shore, as the Master states, to the Westward of Jarvis bay in heavy breakers, where she ran last night at 10 o'clock. Every exertion is being made to get the women, guard and convicts onshore.'[23]

It was 8.30 a.m. when Kelly set out. Approximately two hours later he was at *Erowal*, the 2600 acre farm of John Lamb Esquire, which spanned the ridge between St George's Basin and Jervis Bay. Lamb was one of those free immigrants who had been tempted to the penal colony in the 1820s by the promise of land grants if they brought capital to develop them. Earlier in life, he had been a naval officer and twice sailed to New South Wales as master of the convict ship *Baring*.[24] From his point of view, the ramifications of a stranded convict vessel were alarming. The danger of so many prisoners on the loose, with so few guards, was bad enough, let alone the difficulty ahead for a rescue operation that would deliver everyone securely to Sydney.

Captain Lamb took Kelly another fifteen miles north to an estate named *Coolangatta* on the banks of the Shoalhaven River. It was owned by 56-year-old Alexander Berry, one of the most prominent settlers in the colony, who had also arrived in the twenties. With his partner Edward Wollstonecraft, Berry had developed a highly successful business in Sydney on the north side of the harbour. Through land grants and purchases he had also created a large and prosperous farm in what was then called the Illawarra.[25] Lamb and Kelly reached it at 8 p.m., almost exactly twelve hours after Kelly set out.

Berry knew the south coast well and cross-examined the ensign until he was confident he understood exactly where the ship lay—which was not in the location described by Donoghoe's note which quoted Captain Nutting. While Kelly slept, Mr Berry wrote to the colonial secretary Alexander Macleay giving more precise directions and warning that the *Hive* was 'in a situation of great danger and most likely . . . will go to pieces in the first southerly gale'. He had been particularly alarmed to learn some previously secret information that the *Hive* was carrying treasure. Forty thousand pounds in coin was the figure Berry quoted, although official documents state it was ten thousand. To Berry's horror, it seemed to have been overlooked and was still in the hold of the *Hive*.[26] Both letters were despatched 'express' that night to the police magistrate at the small cluster of buildings called Wollongong. From there, they were sent by steamer to Sydney. The next morning Berry and Captain Lamb accompanied Ensign Kelly back to the *Hive* encampment. When he returned to Coolangatta two days later, Berry wrote again to Macleay.

The treasure had still been afloat when he got to the wreck, and visions of coins scattered across the seabed made him very agitated. 'I urged Captain Nutting to land it immediately,' he told the colonial secretary. He gave details of the location and condition of the ship—'I consider she might again be got afloat under the direction of an <u>Able</u> commander' (underline in original)—but emphasised the difficulties of the site for evacuating people and supplies and recommended, as did Lamb, that any rescue be made from Jervis Bay which was within walking distance, for the prisoners and soldiers, at least. 'No prudent commander would risk his vessel in that Bight.'

Having finished the official version, Berry then wrote the colonial secretary a private note in which he passed on what could only be whispered. 'From Mr Kelly's account, the Captain of the *Hive* has already lost two ships and is not a very competent person,' he confided. 'The Surgeon Superintendent . . . suspended the Captain and put the Ship under the charge of the Chief Mate—taking to himself an awful responsibility . . . but he [the Captain] appears afterwards to have recovered himself and resumed command. On my arrival, Ensign Kelly introduced me first to the Surgeon and the latter immediately after introduced me to the Captain. [When] I observed that I thought the vessel might still be saved—the Surgeon looked towards the Captain and replied, "This will be a point for the <u>after</u> consideration of the Captain." From all I saw, I do consider that the Captain was exercising his usual authority.'[27] Thus was the ground laid for face-saving Captain Nutting while simultaneously protecting Donoghoe and Canney from a charge of mutiny. It also meant that Canney's outstanding behaviour must be downplayed, which was almost more than Henry Lugard could bear. Once in Sydney, he drafted a letter for publication in the *Sydney Herald* which told the inside story about the captain's conduct and Canney's heroism. He never sent it. Elder brother Edward probably dissuaded him by pointing out that such a tribute would also put Canney at risk. Seventy years later, Canney's eldest son sent a copy to the Mitchell Library in Sydney.[28]

News that the *Hive* was wrecked caused a sensation in Sydney. The press were competing for every last detail and anxious residents devoured everything the papers could tell them. Some were worried about relatives or friends who might be on board. Others feared that mail had been lost which might include letters for them. Merchants who were expecting cargo began to calculate their potential losses. Donoghoe's and Berry's letters arrived early Sunday. On Monday morning, 14 December, the *Sydney Herald* broke the news of the wreck and Governor Bourke's response. '[T]he ship *Hive* from Ireland is on the coast near Jervis' Bay,' it reported. 'Orders were immediately given to despatch HM brig *Zebra* and the Revenue Cutter to the assistance of the unfortunate people on board. In the course of the afternoon yesterday, the *Tamar* steam-packet was sent on the same errand.' People concerned about relatives would not have been reassured. News of the treasure had reached the paper's ears—'It is reported there was £40,000 in specie for the Commissariat on board'—but there was no mention of whether lives had been lost. 'On the coast' could mean wrecked on rocks. Fortunately the paper added a postscript which mentioned the involvement of Messrs Berry and Lamb and claimed that 'the vessel has lost all her boats and . . . the prisoners are being landed in Mr Berry's schooner; it is not stated that any lives have been lost.'[29]

Five days later the *Tamar* was back carrying four soldiers of the 28th Regiment, eight women, eleven children and 106 prisoners. Dr Donoghoe and Henry Lugard were also on board. Before she left the site of the wreck, the revenue cutter *Prince George*, which had a shallow draught, had ferried the specie round to Jervis Bay where it was loaded on the naval vessel *Zebra*. When word got out that the *Tamar* had returned, the press besieged the passengers for information. Some officials quietly passed on details of the wreck site and activities of the other rescue vessels, but Henry Lugard was the only person who could speak with some freedom. Within limits, he did his best to satisfy their desire for detail. In the lengthy article that followed, the *Herald* assured its readers that it obtained the information from 'a gentleman passenger'. But if Lugard was frustrated by the need for discretion, the newspaper was piqued at his reticence. 'We have now given every particular that we could give on this "mistake", as it is called, [and are] waiting the explanation of Captain Nutting when he reaches Sydney.'[30]

At the end of the week the *Zebra* entered the harbour carrying 94 prisoners and ten more soldiers, leaving 48 convicts (James Harding had died on the beach) and the remainder of the regiment to continue transferring luggage, cargo and stores from the ship and to help in efforts to get her afloat. Three days later Captain McCrea of the *Zebra* was still waiting for instructions where to land the men. The authorities had sent the first group of convicts to Hyde Park Barracks and were now rapidly assigning them to make room for the next batch.[31] The colonial architect was asked to test the competence of some of the mechanics whose skills had been revealed in the emergency. They included 34-year-old Patrick Brien from Cork, who was a blacksmith, four carpenters and a plasterer.[32]

The shipwreck had revealed that Patrick Brien had a secret. A muster of the ship's crew on the beach had to be done twice to establish exactly how many sailors there were and who they were. The second count was supervised by Captain McCrea, who uncovered the overall youth of the crew and the high proportion classified as lads and boys—eighteen out of a crew of approximately 33. The ship sailed from England to collect her prisoners from Dublin and then Cork. Most crew would have signed on for the voyage in England, yet two of the boys had surnames similar to prisoners. G. Cavenagh, age eighteen, occupation in the crew 'boy', may have been related to Patrick Cavenagh aka Kavenagh who was a prisoner. Also on board was W. Keys, aged fourteen, who earned ten shillings for the voyage in the role of 'boy' and who may have been the son of the prisoner Patrick Keys, something only their descendants could prove. There may have been desertions from the crew that created space. It may have been coincidence. It may also have been that someone decided not to press the issue about Cavenagh and Keys. Two boys, however, were too young to ignore. Eleven-year-old Daniel who was described as 'working his passage' and nine-year-old Michael were the sons of blacksmith Patrick O'Brien.[33] Captain Nutting denied all knowledge of their existence, but took care to assert that neither was 'a charge on the public purse'. No one questioned whether Canney was complicit in this unauthorised immigration, but given his significance in the crew he almost certainly was. The surgeon said he discovered the boys after the ship sailed, which is very likely true since he would otherwise have been obliged to disembark them. It is also possible he simply turned a blind eye to what was going on. Once the boys' presence was exposed, their fate was in the hands of local authorities. Both were taken away to the newly established Roman Catholic Orphan School.

On 7 January Alexander Berry's schooner *Edward* brought in the remainder of the stores, the ship's crew of 28 and Captain Nutting.[34] Within days, Nutting had persuaded the enterprising local owner of a schooner called the *Blackbird* that it would be in his interests to help salvage what was left of the *Hive*. They sailed for the wreck on 14 January and the following day anchored about two miles out from the beach. On 25 January the *Herald* reported the farce that ensued. The *Blackbird*'s boats made 22 trips ferrying goods from the shore. Then the wind changed. That night a strong southerly turned into a violent gale. The *Blackbird* started to drift. Not even a second anchor would hold her as she began to drive towards the shore. The longboat broke away. Everything that had been carefully loaded during the day was now thrown overboard and full sails ordered up in the hope she would run up the beach and thus save everyone's lives. In this the little schooner obliged. After striking the sand several times, with the surf breaking over her and the crew frantically throwing out the very last of the rescued goods, she 'carried up high on the beach', out of danger. At daylight, the ship's owner and Captain Nutting returned to Sydney by land.[35]

Nutting was just in time to give evidence to the official inquiry into the wreck of the *Hive*. It was conducted at the office of the Harbour Master, John Nicholson, RN, at the dockyard. A panel of five had been assembled consisting of Nicholson, a second naval officer Lieutenant Lefebre of the *Zebra*, L.C. Bailey, a ship's master, and John Robson and John Moncrieff who were masters of the convict transports *John Barry* and *Royal Sovereign*. Nutting was the first witness. He took credit for what Canney had done and denied handing over the ship to anyone, claiming that the surgeon and Lieutenant Lugard had 'attempted to take it out of my hands'. He also denied ordering out the jolly boat. 'There was a Boat lowered down but not by my orders . . . I gave orders to hoist out the longboat for the purpose of saving the lives, the landed Guard, Women, Children and Prisoners.' And he denied that Canney had warned him about the course they were steering. In diplomatic but frank testimony Canney contradicted virtually everything Nutting said. He was followed by the combined weight of evidence from surgeon Donoghoe, Edward Lugard and Ensign Kelly, who between them testified to the captain's navigational incompetence and his dependence during the voyage on the chief officer, to his orders regarding the jolly boat, the course and the sails and his condition (unnamed) which demonstrated his incapacity to direct the rescue operation. Nobody ever uttered the word 'drunk'. On the contrary, he was said to be bewildered and 'to have lost all presence of mind'. Donoghoe referred to his over-riding responsibility for the prisoners but with two masters of convict ships on the panel it was unnecessary for him to give great detail.[36]

On 11 February, the panel's verdict was sent to Governor Bourke. They granted Nutting some small leeway on his navigation: 'the course steered . . . would have taken the *Hive* clear of Cape St George had it not been a strong indraught the existence of which the Master appears to have been ignorant of.' But there was no ambiguity about the criticism that followed, which upheld Canney's evidence in particular: 'We cannot help expressing our surprize, at the inefficient manner the *Hive* was conducted out; particularly the Master's conduct in going to bed when the Mate had noticed to him that the Ship was kept too near the land, himself [the mate] remaining up fearful of danger.'

The panel also gave Donoghoe their support: 'We also feel it our duty to state we do not consider the Master used any exertions after the *Hive* struck to extricate her from her situation or save the lives of those on board; which caused Mr Donahue [*sic*] Surgeon Superintendent to divest him of his command; the Mate then gave the necessary directions until daylight when the Master again took charge.'[37]

The loss of the *Blackbird* had made Nutting even more anxious to get out of Sydney, but he had been denied permission to attend the rest of the inquiry and he wanted a copy of the report. It took three letters before the governor released a copy to him on 14 March. Responding that 'a more malicious, groundless and false accusation, could not possibly be made', he nevertheless pressed for permission to leave the colony, which was granted. Despite the loss of the *Hive*, Nutting was hired as master of the barque *Avon* carrying oil after a season of hunting sperm whales. The *Herald* duly reported his departure for London on 2 April, noting that he 'carried no passengers'.[38]

Surgeon Donoghoe left for England as soon as he could. He had made two previous voyages to the penal colony and would return once more in 1837 as surgeon superintendent on the *Calcutta*.[39] Edward Canney, too, made haste for home. He had no problem getting a berth for London as first mate under Captain Chalmers on the barque *Auriga*. If he didn't know Chalmers already, the surgeon Dr Patrick McTernan would have recommended him to the master. They had sailed on the *Katherine Stewart Forbes* together when Edward Canney was an apprentice and his uncle was master of the ship. When the *Auriga* sailed on 17 March Canney must have been thankful to put the *Hive* behind him and with it anxiety that the wreck and its aftermath would damage his career.[40]

With the prisoners and guards spread widely across the colony, the bonds between the castaways now dissolved. The soldiers of the 28th were stationed in detachments around New South Wales: the Tierney family spending a month in barracks at Parramatta before Patrick was posted to Moreton Bay. Ensign Waldron Kelly had begun his career in the naval service of the East India Company before buying a commission as ensign in the British Army in 1834. Following the wreck of the *Hive*, he was promoted to lieutenant and became adjutant to the commander of the 22nd Regiment which was then stationed in the colony. On returning to England with the regiment in 1837, Kelly married Ann Edith Roper with whom he had four children. Despite being the son of Major General Thomas Julius Waldron Kelly, his military career was not spectacular. He moved up through the ranks to first lieutenant and had achieved captain by October 1844. Shortly after, however, he was injured and spent the next three years on half pay. He died on 12 April 1847 at his home in Sligo aged only 34.[41]

Like the other young men connected with the wreck of the *Hive*, the Lugard brothers were following in their father's footsteps. Captain John Lugard was influential in the British Army not just because he served in foreign parts. In mid-career, he became adjutant in charge of the Duke of York's School for the Children of Soldiers in Chelsea, not far from the Hospital for Army Pensioners.[42] The Lugard children grew up at Chelsea when it was still a rural hamlet. Members of the royal family would stop the night at the village on their way to the palace at Hampton Court and the Duke of York, who took a personal interest in his charges, called frequently. When they reached the necessary age, both Edward and Henry followed their brother John to Sandhurst, from where Edward graduated in 1828. Henry was marked out by the college as someone with the potential to be an engineer. He spent time at the Royal Artillery at Chatham before graduating in 1834.[43]

After the shipwreck, Edward Lugard lingered in Sydney for several months while Henry began his duties with the Ordnance Office under colonial engineer, Colonel Barney. Edward may have been waiting for a ship for India, and possibly sailed with the 17th Regiment when it embarked in June. Both intent on global careers, the brothers may have sensed that this separation would be final. There is no indication they ever met again. Their careers took them in such different directions that each time it was likely they would meet in England, they were on opposite sides of the world. In June 1836, Edward finally sailed to rejoin the 31st Regiment to pick up what became a glorious military career. He took part in the war on the North-West Frontier (modern Afghanistan) and in various campaigns in India. Later he served in Persia, then returned to India to take up appointment as adjutant-general and distinguished himself particularly in the relief of Lucknow during what was called the Indian Mutiny of 1857. Knighted in 1858, he became under secretary of state for war in 1861, a position he held for a decade. His private life was less successful. Within a year of returning to India he married Isabella Mowbray Hart. Their first child Eliza was born in May 1838 but she died in October 1840, only months after her infant brother Travers. Isabella also died in India. Although Edward later remarried, he died divorced and childless in 1898 at the age of 88.[44]

None of the prisoners ever forgot the unusual way they arrived. Among a fascinated audience of convicts and emancipists who were landed without any such drama, it became almost a badge of honour. Something to boast about. Something to entertain. They never missed an opportunity to mention it. In the convict records for Port Phillip, the clerk recorded the full catastrophe quite unnecessarily against the name of Bartholomew Williams 'per *Hive* ran aground just south of Jervis Bay, picked up by *Prince George*, landed Sydney Jan 1836'. For young Nicholas White, all of sixteen when he was unceremoniously dumped on the beach, the record notes, 'arrived per *Hive* at Jervis Bay'. On Norfolk Island, John Black told the clerk who was taking his details that he arrived on the *Hive*, adding 'she was wrecked going into Sydney, no lives lost'. These men had a tale to tell and, beyond official records, we can be sure they enjoyed recounting every detail for the rest of their lives.[45]

The wreck of the *Hive* has broader significance to Australians beyond its personal impact. Not just entertainment. Nor a cautionary tale. Its fate raises a question: Why didn't the convicts seize the opportunity the shipwreck created? Why didn't they escape into the bush? Or flee in the longboat? Some men could have made rafts from the ship's timbers. There were seamen among the prisoners skilled enough to navigate the vast sea to unknown places. Given the disproportion between 250 convicts and 29 guards, they could have risked bloodshed to overwhelm the soldiers, killing them if necessary, then taken over the camp while they planned their next move. None of these options were even attempted.

CHAPTER 2
A Capacity for Violence

The Irish convicts have traditionally been presented to Australians as rural innocents. Missing from this legendary tale is their violence. Bloody, brutal, personally inflicted violence was the reality of crimes for which many Irish prisoners were transported. Yes, they included thieves, like John Sheill on the *Hive* who was caught picking pockets, or Martin Ryan, an errand boy who stole sugar, but a very large proportion were all too familiar with hands-on violence, enough for us to be sure that it was not fear of bloodshed that stopped the prisoners on the wrecked ship from attacking their guards. In Ireland, these men were enmeshed in a culture that historian Roy Foster has called 'an underworld of dissent by violence'.[1] However, assuming that violence was caused only by the British occupation and laws about land or the payment of tithes is far too simple. And too romantic. It disguises the bloody reality as effectively as the emphasis on sheep stealing. A.T.Q. Stewart, for example, noted that research into agrarian crime in 1836 'did not bear out the traditional view of Irish peasants as a feckless and volatile race, degraded by poverty and turning to violence through sheer desperation'.[2] Closer scrutiny of the Irish convicts brings violence confrontingly to the foreground, where it can be found in four loosely grouped categories of tribal, political, religious and sexual violence.

Some of the most brutal acts arose from traditional feuds between neighbours. Tribal riots could be sparked by nothing more than a trivial slight or altercation. The trigger might be an argument in a pub which flared like fuel on a bonfire into a fight involving hundreds, sometimes thousands, from the surrounding district and which could last for several days. Other riots might have a longstanding territorial quarrel or a family grievance at their heart, an issue which had been fought over many times during centuries. They were usually preceded by a build-up of insults and tension that culminated in an explosion of violence.[3]

Maurice Leehy (sometimes named Thomas) who sailed on the *Hive* was no hotheaded youngster. Aged 37, he was married with five children and employed as a farm servant in Kerry. Some tradition in his life had made him hate the community across the river and he took an active part in what was described as 'a savage atrocity'. It occurred in the summer of 1834 after the races on the strand at Ballyeagh beside the River Cashen not far from Trahlee in County Kerry. At the Milltown fair on Monday, 24 June, hostility and threats were being hurled around publicly between members of the Lawlor/Mullvihill clan and representatives of the Coolheens from across the river. By Wednesday, the authorities were sufficiently alarmed to send a detachment of the 69th Regiment to keep order at the races. A magistrate even read the Riot Act to the crowd who had gathered for what was meant to be a festive day. It had no effect. The clans and their supporters had come primed for battle. With the race run and the prize of a saddle awarded to the winner, they set to.

If the tale stopped there, the event might be dismissed as nothing more than an outbreak of fisticuffs, a harmless opportunity for old enemies to let off steam. But a foreshortened version would overlook the terrible brutality to the point of massacre that actually occurred. In the hours that followed the races, a crowd of more than one thousand fought 'furiously engaged in mortal strife and no quarter given on either side'. This was not a neighbourhood spat. It was a bloody war between the Irish. The weapons on both sides were, as usual, sticks and stones, too easily underestimated. These were hurling sticks made of blackthorn, some weighted with lead, and they were wielded by men expert in creating maximum damage. Women were also active in the fight, loading up their aprons with stones to ensure their menfolk did not lack ammunition for even a moment. And they were not just onlookers in these battles, sometimes throwing the stones themselves, or using them to 'finish off' the wounded.[4] At Ballyeagh, people were knocked down, then mercilessly battered. 'From the number of ghastly wounds inflicted, there can be no doubt that a great number of lives have been lost,' an onlooker wrote. 'The Coolheens were at length defeated and, the tide having risen to the full, the fugitives were driven into the water where many of them were barbarously massacred.' The *Kerry Evening Post* reported: 'The most melancholy part of this horrible story is still to be told. A vast number of the defeated party crowded into boats which they found afloat at high tide, in order to escape across the river but being overladen, the boats sunk and all on board perished.' At the subsequent trial, a horrified judge described how 'their brains were beaten out while struggling in the deep water of the river'. Rumour had it that four bodies were picked up near the Cashen ferry and a further twelve, both male and female, elsewhere. The official death toll was put at sixteen. No one died from gunshot. Indeed throughout the afternoon the British troops had been reduced to bystanders, helpless to check strife involving so many people and spread across such a wide battlefield. All the soldiers could do was arrest individuals as the opportunity arose. Altogether, eighteen men were crowded into the Trahlee gaol for trial, one of whom was Maurice Leehy.

As with other mass tragedies in Ireland at this time, Maurice Leehy was apparently a test case for everyone else. Perhaps he was the only one for whom there was enough evidence to convict, or he may have agreed to take the rap for others. It is impossible to be sure because legal records that could have supplied the answer were destroyed by a bomb at the Four Courts building in Dublin in 1922. Press reports of the trial indicate that Leehy pleaded not guilty to murder and was convicted of manslaughter, whereupon another sixteen people then pleaded guilty to manslaughter. Leehy was sentenced to transportation for life but those who had pleaded guilty received prison terms ranging between a few months and two years of hard labour. Leehy was not resigned to his sentence. Six weeks later he was one of several prisoners who broke out of Kerry County gaol in a violent attempt to avoid being moved to Cork. Armed with stone hammers and sledges they tried to get firearms from the guardroom but were driven back and placed in leg irons. Notorious through his association with Ballyeagh, Maurice Leehy was described as 'the most desperate' of the group.[5]

The British occupation did directly spawn violence, probably the most famous response being from the secret societies that operated across Ireland, beginning with the Whiteboys in Tipperary in 1761. Another society, the Defenders of Ireland, whose activities culminated in the attempted rebellion of 1798, delivered some of Australia's most famous middle-class convicts from Ireland, men such as Michael Dwyer, Joseph Holt and Philip Cunningham. Individual acts of arson, assault, cattle-maiming and threatening letters were part of the protest mix carried out by underground societies which were the most organised means by which Irish fought back against their conditions. A convict newly arrived in Australia gave an insider's description of Ribbonism.[6]

> Ribbon sects are illegal combinations sworn to obey their chief, to take the arms of the Protestants and turn them out of the country. County delegates travel over Ireland giving the Ribbon men new signs and making appointments to meet at certain times. They also travel through England and Scotland. The members of the Society choose their delegates by polling. They assemble every quarter. The oldest delegate is appointed chairman and has the general superintendence of the delegates. Each guardian is over twelve men. One parish master is over them and one delegate over all the parishes in the county.

Once again, any mention of violence is missing. Yet, according to Stewart, the Ribbonmen were motivated by outrage over ill-usage or interference relating to land, but 'the motives and tactics of outrage were then, and still are today, often far removed from the idealistic conceptions of nationality associated with them in the popular mind'. He contrasts the ruthless pragmatism of the societies with the 'traditional picture of an impulsive, feckless peasantry living in a mythical world of ancestral glories'.[7]

Twenty-two-year-old Fanton Delaney from Queen's County was involved in a Whiteboy group who tried to force a farmer named Maurice Kelly to give up his land. In the early stage of the group's campaign, accompanied by Michael Phelan, and 'bearing arms', Fanton posted a threatening notice on Kelly's harrow which explicitly warned him to get off the farm. Somebody informed on them and the local constable organised a determined pursuit for miles across the fields and in nearby mountains. Fanton took refuge in the Killenure mountain but must have been betrayed because he was finally caught asleep at the house of a farmer named Dooley. He was sentenced to seven years transportation at the Kildare Assizes in Maryborough in 1835.[8]

Three men named Daniel Fitzgerald, Timothy Connors and Michael Leeny were convicted of a crime called 'assaulting habitation', which was not an offence that appeared in the calendars for prisoners on trial in England or in Scotland. In Ireland it was usually deployed by the secret societies and a description by one of the victims, in this case William Jackson junior, reveals typical features: 'I was sitting at my father's fireside,' he told the court. 'Four armed men entered the house, one of them stamped his foot and cried out "fire". They then pelted a volley of stones at the whole family. One of the stones hit my uncle and knocked him into the fireplace. They attacked my brother and sister also. Two of them attacked my father who cried out to me for help. Leeny hit me with the butt of his pistol which threw me against the partition.' An all-out brawl developed as the family fought back vigorously. Young Jackson struck Fitzgerald and managed to knock him down. The combined force of his father and uncle and his siblings then overcame their attackers and tied them up while Jackson's brother went for the police.

'Assaulting habitation' was usually a Whiteboy attempt to redress some agrarian injustice. In this case there was reference under cross-examination to '12 acres of land at 40s per acre' but not enough information survives to understand fully the grievance that caused Fitzgerald, Connors and Leeny to risk transportation for life. Connors and Leeny were in their twenties and still single but Fitzgerald was 30 years of age and married with three children.[9]

There was no mistaking the Whiteboy nature of the crime for which Patrick Lawler (sometimes Lalor) was convicted. Together with James Carthy he was indicted for having administered an unlawful oath to a farmer named William Dunphy who was approvingly described by the *Kilkenny Moderator* as 'a respectable farmer at Scart'. The enforced oath bound Dunphy to relinquish an acre of land to a man named James Quirke and to provide a house to a woman named Mrs Lannan. The two men were also indicted with the crime of 'appearing in arms'.

Dunphy testified that 'after using threatening language and ill-treating his person', Lalor held a pistol to his breast while Carthy hit him, then they forced him to kneel. 'I promised to perform all they demanded,' he said. Dunphy's servant John Sealy had been called as a witness by both parties, but the defence succeeded in getting him to testify for Lalor and Carthy. *The Kilkenny Journal* described him as 'very uneasy and hesitated often while giving his evidence'. Obviously fearing retribution, Sealy confirmed that he had seen a pistol and that the men who invaded the house swore and beat him but he insisted that neither Lalor nor Carthy were among them. He was 'quite positive' that Carthy, whom he had known for four years, was not present that night. The local community turned out in numbers to give character references but the contradictory, implausible or dubious alibis they offered were quickly dismissed. Both Lalor and Carthy were sentenced to transportation for life but only Lalor sailed on the *Hive*.[10]

Agrarian injustice was a consequence of the discrimination of the British Penal Laws relating to land and inheritance. Brothers James, Patrick and Timothy Maloney, all in their twenties, were convicted in Kilkenny of assaulting a farmer who had taken over land from which they were ejected. They caught him in a country lane, dragged him from his horse and Tim Maloney held him by the neck on the ground while the other two beat his head with stones. He was found unconscious on the road the following morning, his right ear nearly cut off, most of his teeth knocked out and his tongue split in two. Tim Maloney escaped but Pat and Jim were brought to trial where they were convicted of violent and grievous assault and sentenced to seven years transportation.[11]

Patrick, John and James Connery became notorious in their day and legendary in history for the battle they waged against dispossession from their family's land.[12] The Connerys' father had been a tenant on the lands of Bondoon under Lord Yarborough from which they were ejected by his agent, a Thomas Foley. According to the press, the Connerys' fierce reputation made the sheriff afraid to enforce the order to eject them so he took many police with him to force the Connerys off the land. Mr Foley then transferred the tenancy to someone else but before he could take possession the Connerys took their cattle back to the land and erected a hut there. Then they wrote to Foley threatening that if he didn't change his mind his woods would be reduced to ashes and his life would be in danger every time he left his house. 'Bally Lemmon Woods is our object,' they warned. Several witnesses supported Foley's version of events and the two brothers were found guilty of resisting a legal decree. Erupting with anger, John Connery struck the front of the dock, yelling 'I'll return to you again, Foley.'

The authorities pursued every avenue. An attempt was made to convict John for the murder of David Tobin in March 1834, and when that failed he was tried with eight others for manslaughter of Patrick Brien. The witnesses collapsed one after another as they had done in the Tobin trial and, with his co-accused, John was again acquitted. Early in 1835, however, James and John were indicted for the manslaughter of Maurice Hackett in 1831. Lawrence Crotty, an approver as informers were called, swore that he had frequently heard the Connerys speak resentfully of Hackett who replaced one of the brothers in a job as wood ranger. Crotty also testified that the Connerys owned firearms. 'I saw two men with their faces blackened and dressed in women's clothes,' he added. 'They crossed the field where I was planting cabbages. They went to where Hackett was working. I heard a shot.' Another witness confirmed that two men fired at Hackett, and when he ran they beat him down. Hackett died two days later. A third witness, who may have been related to the land agent Thomas Foley, gave evidence that he had heard James Connery saying: 'Hackett won't survive what I gave him.'

James was found guilty of manslaughter and sentenced to life transportation, but John was acquitted. In July 1835, however, John and Patrick were convicted of 'taking forcible possession' of five acres of land and sentenced to seven years transportation. According to a newspaper reporter who watched the trial, they put up a good front. 'These worthies were well acquainted with the Court and showed by their nonchalance that they were careless of their situation.' In fact, the Connerys may have been well satisfied. Earlier, their lawyer had tried to cut a deal with the Crown that all the brothers would leave the country if James, who had not yet sailed on the *Hive*, was pardoned. But Thomas Foley was outraged: 'You want to have a man transported for felony, pardoned?' Later that day, John again shouted threats from the dock at their relentless prosecutor.[13] In 1836 they staged a spectacular escape from Cork County gaol, incidentally triggering a major inquiry into conditions there. It was two years before they were recaptured by police. This time they followed James to Sydney, each with a sentence of seven years.[14]

In what must have been a discomforting twist, Lawrence Crotty was charged with perjury the week after James Connery was sentenced because the evidence he gave against James was different from what he originally told a magistrate. Sentenced to seven years transportation, he sailed on the *Hive* with the man he helped convict.[15]

Political violence pervaded the culture from which the men on the *Hive* came. In addition to the longstanding grievances over land, the 1830s in Ireland were a time of violent clashes around campaigns by the great Irish reformer Daniel O'Connell. During the 1820s O'Connell, a Catholic lawyer from Kerry, had mobilised the people to overturn the Penal Laws by which the British oppressed the Irish. By these rules, Catholics were prevented from owning land for more than 31 years. Catholic deceased estates had to be split in equal shares unless the eldest child took an oath of conformity to the Church of Ireland. Under the laws, Catholics were prevented from educating their children, bearing arms, joining the army, even from owning a horse worth more than £5. Over time, some aspects were not enforced—for example, the British Army was riddled with Irish soldiers—but Catholics were also disenfranchised. They could not vote and no Catholic could hold public office unless they took the oath. All professions except medicine were closed to Catholics unless they conformed, which some did. O'Connell was helped by a newly energised Catholic Church which by the 1820s had been weakened by more than a century's discrimination under the Penal Laws. Despite a shortage of priests and of churches, individual priests became rallying points for involvement by the people. The people were given a sense of engagement in support of O'Connell by joining the Catholic Association for a penny a month, known colloquially as 'the Catholic rent'.[16] When emancipation was achieved in 1829, ordinary people understood for the first time that victory could be theirs. O'Connell and others such as Anglo-Irish landholder Thomas Spring Rice became members of parliament which, since the Act of Union in 1800 abolished the Irish one, meant the parliament in London.

Catholics were no longer forced to educate their children surreptitiously at hedge schools. In 1831 a system of national schools began with the aim of teaching all children everything but religion, which they would be taught separately.[17] One of the architects of the national scheme was a Limerick landholder named Richard Bourke. A friend of Thomas Spring Rice (later Lord Monteagle), Bourke believed passionately that it was the responsibility of government to educate the public in order 'to raise a people from ignorance and misery to knowledge and comfort'.[18] Over many years the two men had imagined a system of education that might work to achieve this while also breaking down the sectarian divide in Ireland. When Spring Rice became secretary of the treasury in

London, he called on Bourke for input into the regulations that would make their dream a reality.

Bourke had already put his ideals into practice on his own estate, *Thornfield* in County Limerick. Keen to establish a school for the mainly Catholic children of local tenant farmers, he sought endorsement from the bishop of Killaloe to employ a Catholic couple as teachers. When the bishop demanded Protestant teachers in return for a contribution to funding, Bourke rejected him and turned to the Kildare Place Society which claimed to educate without religious bias. By 1823, 48 boys and 31 girls were enrolled, some of their tuition subsidised from Bourke's own pocket. His wife, Elizabeth, paid the fees of eighteen girls to ensure that neither lack of parents nor poverty would deprive them of education too.[19]

Early in 1831 Richard Bourke was appointed governor of New South Wales, succeeding Ralph Darling, who had been recalled. Then aged 54, Bourke had been born to a Protestant family in Dublin but much of his education took place in England at Westminster School and at Oxford. During this time he stayed frequently with his relative Edmund Burke in Buckinghamshire. The eminent Irish-born parliamentarian, orator, political theorist and philosopher significantly influenced young Richard's thinking and attitudes. As a parliamentarian and in his personal life, for example, Edmund Burke practised the kind of ecumenical Christianity that Richard Bourke would display throughout his life and which shaped actions he later took as governor. After taking his degree at Oxford in 1798, Bourke joined the Grenadier Guards and served in the Netherlands, where he was wounded in the jaw, which caused him lasting pain and self-consciousness. He also served in South America before taking part in the Peninsular War. An appointment as military resident in Galicia, Spain, drew attention to his administrative and negotiating skills and he served a successful term as acting governor of the Cape Colony before being appointed to New South Wales.[20]

In the intervening years, Bourke acted as a magistrate in Limerick. He recognised that discrimination against the Irish was the major reason behind Ireland's problems, that 'lack of basic civil rights such as religious freedom and a fair and impartial system of justice, was a cause of much social unrest', but it did not blinker him to the brutality of Irish society. Sentencing a Limerick man to transportation for seven years after a conviction for aggravated assault, Bourke remarked 'to us, who have sat for days listening to the recital of acts of the most barbarous violence, it is quite clear that an example of severe punishment is necessary for this species of crime.'[21]

The first two decades of the nineteenth century were in a sense a regrouping period in Ireland after the failed armed rebellion of the United Irishmen in 1798. Daniel O'Connell was a rare Irish nationalist. Unlike his predecessors, the United Irishmen and his successors, the Young Irelanders, he did not believe in force to achieve the goals they all shared. Instead, he urged non-violent means as the way to gain concessions from the British and put his faith in parliamentary membership, legislation and negotiation. With that approach it is not surprising that his relationship with the Ribbon societies was uneasy.[22] An important part of his strategy was mobilising on the ground support from the labouring class (usually referred to in Ireland then and now as 'the peasants') but their ready resort to brutal violence troubled him, as it did Bourke and the growing Catholic middle class who were his supporters.

The case of brothers Philip and Michael Ryan provides a glimpse of this tension. The Ryans' crime arose from a fight about who owned 100 acres of the lands of Ardaloe in County Kilkenny. Multiple loans and mortgages and rights to title were exchanged over four to five years before a Mr Neary finally got possession. Michael Ryan then alleged that he had made an earlier deal to purchase the land from one of the two original owners. Furthermore, he had paid £60 for it. A campaign of harassment began against Neary and his workers. Threatening notices were posted. Property was damaged. Workers were assaulted and some left Neary's employ. Despite threats, one of them, James Roe, continued to plough the land and he became the focus for the Ryans' revenge. A local man named Michael Brennan had 'potato ground' on their farm and in May 1835 they hired him to be their hit man. After plying the victim with whiskey and drinking several glasses himself, Brennan walked him up the road past the Ryans' house, stopping to talk to Philip Ryan on the way. He then escorted his befuddled victim into a field where Michael Ryan identified him as James Roe before handing Brennan a gun. Brennan fired, but Roe was only wounded. He escaped after a fierce chase through the fields with Michael Ryan and Brennan on his heels.

On the face of it, this crime stemmed from anger about a broken contract and the loss of £60. No case papers survive, however, and doubt lingers about the motive for attempting to kill James Roe. The Ryans were not poverty-stricken. At their trial the judge referred to their 'rank and situation' pointing out they could have sought redress for their grievance through the law, but chose instead to take retribution by violence. We can dismiss an underlying sectarian dispute: everyone in this matter was Catholic. In court, the prosecutor cast it as 'one of that public character which has so long disgraced and distracted this and neighbouring counties and which grew out of the feelings indulged by the peasantry respecting the possession of lands'. But the Ryans were not victims of ejectment, nor acting on behalf of others who had been driven off their land. The hint of a subtext arises in their lawyer's attempt to discredit James Roe. Under cross-examination he was forced to admit that he had been a member of the Whitefoot, and 'gone out' with them several times although he would not say how often and claimed he did not stay with them long. He admitted to being held on suspicion of beating a Mr Saunders but denied another charge of 'breaking ploughs' and denied that he had ever taken a leadership role or been called 'Captain Roe'. These questions suggest the Ryans were hostile to Whiteboys. In fact, they may have been examples of Catholics who supported Daniel O'Connell and felt the factional feuds and traditional violence of secret societies were detracting from his efforts.[23]

Whatever their motive, evidence against the accused had substance. Michael and Philip Ryan were found guilty of conspiracy to murder James Roe, after which Michael Brennan pleaded guilty to shooting him. All had death sentences recorded against their names, which were commuted to transportation for life.[24]

The violence of Irish crimes contradicts the traditional image of Irish convicts as mainly rural innocents whose offences were justifiable reaction to poverty and politics: they 'only' stole sheep; they were 'only' fighting the British.[25] To an Australian researcher familiar with these images, the brutal details of Irish crimes is confronting. It is vividly displayed in the calendars or lists of people to be tried at the assizes of which the following are examples from the 1830s.

Reported in the *Clare Journal*, 19 March 1835, City of Cork Calendar
Murder 1; rape 1; attempting to drown a child 1; injuring with vitriol 2; assault on a female 1; perjury 1; forgery 1; cow stealing 2; sheep stealing 1; coining 2; highway robbery 7; burglary 4; felony 11; receiving 3; being concealed 2; embezzling 2

County Cork Calendar
Murder 22; burglary and robbery 85; rape 15; child murder and deserting
infants 6; sheep stealing 26; cow stealing 8; horse stealing 4; pig stealing
3; highway robbery 1; passing base coin 3; vagrants 16; embezzlement
3; taking forcible possession 8; fraudulently obtaining goods 2; violent
assaults 7; larcenies 57

**Reported in the *Roscommon Gazette*, 7 March 1835, in Roscommon
Gaol awaiting trial**
Murder 12; rape 21; abduction and robbery 3; violent crimes 27; assaulting
habitation 8; stealing livestock 9; theft 16

Fifteen men on the *Hive* had killed someone. In addition to those
detailed above, they included Joseph Ryan, who hit his victim with a
hammer for calling him 'a whitefoot' and who, according to the *Leinster
Express* (25 March 1835), seemed pleased when he was sentenced to
transportation. Edmond (sometimes Edward) Breen was one of a gang
of four who pelted a man with stones until he died (*Clonmel Advertiser*,
8 August 1835). Twenty-one-year-old Timothy Cleary was convicted of
murder for pointing out the victim to another man who struck him with
a stick. Evidence revealed that the Cleary family had lost their land to the
man that was killed (*Leinster Express*, 25 March 1835). Nine men were
transported for manslaughter. No details survive for six of them. Very
likely they were participants in a riot and there was enough evidence to
prove they contributed to someone's death. In March 1835, the *Limerick
Chronicle* listed sentences at the assize which reveal the wide range of
sentences for manslaughter.

Limerick Chronicle, 14 March 1835
manslaughter: seven years transportation
manslaughter: twelve months prison
manslaughter: two months prison
manslaughter: six months hard labour
manslaughter: twelve months hard labour
manslaughter: two months prison, etc.

Religious violence was always a feature of Irish life but politics certainly
aggravated it. Evangelicalism had reinvigorated Protestant Christianity

in the eighteenth century, giving rise, for instance, to the anti-slavery movement, but evangelicalism was also explicitly anti-Catholic. Daniel O'Connell's high profile campaign in the 1820s coincided with the influential Pastorini prediction that the downfall of Protestantism would occur between 1821 and 1825. Hostility between the two major branches of Christianity increased with the start in the mid-1820s of a concerted evangelical challenge to Catholicism dubbed the Second Reformation. Evangelicals saw conversion to Protestantism as the solution to Ireland's problems rather than the Catholic emancipation that was being advocated by O'Connell. Feeling threatened by his program, they increased their attempts to convert Catholics.[26]

The most blatant symbol of the Protestant crusade was the Orange Order, which was founded in 1795. One of the older men on the *Hive*, 47-year-old James McCabe, was from Monaghan, an area which would later be the fracture line between Northern Ireland and the Republic. Even in the 1830s it was a volatile centre of sectarian clashes. Each July, Orangemen would celebrate the Protestant conquest of King William of Orange by parading through the town. This occurred elsewhere in the country as well, but Monaghan became a centre for Protestant display. Marchers could be mistaken for a group of strolling players, with orange flags waving and drums beating time, until it was realised that some carried firearms, others swords. Their leaders led the way mounted on horseback. More often than not it ended in a brawl. Catholics protested with sticks and stones. And their fists. Sometimes one or more people were killed. James McCabe, who was a Protestant, was caught in the middle of an affray like this at Monaghan. No specific details survive about his crime but he was convicted of malicious assault. Sentenced to transportation for seven years, he left behind a wife and five children.[27]

In the 1830s Daniel O'Connell turned his focus to repealing the hated Act of Union by which England forcibly absorbed Ireland into Great Britain. He also continued the struggle for justice over landholding and, in the immediate term, to redressing the situation where Catholics were forced to pay tithes for the support of Protestant clergymen. Many men were transported for crimes committed in the war against tithes that raged between 1831 and 1835. O'Connell drove the fight against what he called 'this bloodstained impost', stirring his countrymen in an election speech which was widely distributed as a pamphlet:

[Tithes] have caused more dissatisfaction—they have stimulated to more crime—they have produced more oppression and misery—they have incited more hatred and rancour—they have been more emphatically condemned, than any other mischief's and grievances under which poor Ireland has suffered during ages of misrule. Unfeeling landlords are bad enough—extorting and pitiless absentee agents are worse; but tithes, tithes—bloodstained tithes—are beyond any comparison the worst of all . . . If the result of the next elections should give the Tories a majority . . . then tithes will be collected and enforced at the point of the bayonet. If the Tories are defeated by the anti-Tories, then tithes must be abolished by law in name and in nature.[28]

Anger about tithes trapped Daniel Kennedy, his son Pat and a friend Cornelius Neill, who were all convicted of violent assault at Rathkeale, County Limerick. On 14 May 1834 they joined thousands of people who stormed the Rathkeale courthouse where a barrister named Croker was conducting the annual tithe session. Claiming they had been given no receipts for tithes paid, they overpowered police who were guarding the door with fixed bayonets. Once inside, the angry crowd destroyed Mr Croker's papers and demolished every table and chair they could lay their hands on. Dragoons had to escort Mr Croker to the tithe session at the next town.[29] Once again, Richard Bourke was ahead on the issue. Unlike other landlords, he paid tithes for the Protestant clergyman on behalf of his tenants who were then spared demands for payment. Finally, in 1838, the Tithe Act took direct grievance out of the issue by transforming tithes into rent, which was then paid by the landlord into a fund for clerical costs. This wider compromise, however, was too late for men who sailed on the *Hive*.[30]

Unions of trades emerged in Ireland during the 1820s and were active during the campaign for emancipation. Riots caused by the United Trades reveal the clergy's control of the populace was circumscribed at this time. Certainly some clergy could and did defuse a riot, but historian John McGrath argues that 'open, public and, at times, ostentatious loyalty to the Catholic Church and clergy' should not be taken at face value. 'The riots engaged in by the United Trades perhaps showed the most blatant disregard for clerical authority and disdain for authority at all levels . . . Even round denunciations by the Catholic Bishop of the day did not stop the disturbances.' Actively supporting O'Connell in the 1835 elections, the United Trades could be brutal. Working men who did not pay their dues or openly opposed the unions risked having vitriol thrown in their face. By mid-February 1835, for example, surgeons at the North Infirmary at Cork had treated eight men who had been attacked in this way. Two cases were particularly serious. A man was blinded in one eye. A second had lost his sight entirely. *The Cork Constitution* described him as 'in great agony. His head is kept in continual motion from the acute pain of the eyes. [He] presents a most wretched and heart-rending spectacle.'[31]

Twenty-four-year-old Dan Herlihy was a sawyer who had served his seven-year apprenticeship in the trade in Cork. He was also literate, which increased his value as a union official. At the March Assizes 1835 he was indicted for throwing vitriolic acid at John Carroll who was a fellow sawyer. Carroll had signed up for membership of the union but never paid his dues. He told the court that in mid-January he was instructed by a man named Collins to call at the committee room, which he failed to do. About a week later, he was confronted in the street by Herlihy and two others. Herlihy was holding something behind his back. 'As I turned to run, he threw something at me from a goblet. It burned me dreadfully on the head and neck.' Cross-examined at length by Herlihy's lawyer, he was unshakeable. 'I've known him for sixteen years. I couldn't possibly be mistaken. I thought he would be the last man in the world to do anything to me.' Despite claims from one witness that it was not Herlihy who threw the acid, and despite two character references, the jury found Herlihy guilty. He received a sentence of death recorded which was preceded by a homily from the judge, who described the crime as 'most dreadful and heinous' and added, 'It is a lamentable thing to see a man of your apparent rank in life brought to the bar of a criminal court to answer to an indictment of this nature.' Pointing out that Herlihy was fortunate Carroll had not died, he added, 'I will take it upon myself to recommend the sentence be commuted to . . . perpetual banishment from this land.'[32]

Among O'Connell's campaign managers in 1835, was John Hubert Plunkett, a friend of his eldest son Maurice O'Connell. While still a law student, Plunkett had signed up as a member of the Catholic Association soon after it was conceived in 1823. Analysing an early portrait, Plunkett's biographer described the young barrister as 'a wiry fellow of medium height. Aside from the ruddy complexion and shock of sweptback hair, the portrait suggests a sensitive intelligence with a tight-lipped humour and also, perhaps, in the eyes, a gleam of the steady fortitude' that he displayed throughout his life. Like O'Connell, Plunkett came from the Catholic middle class with all the disadvantages that entailed. The Catholic Relief Act of 1793 had allowed him to study for a university degree without compromising his Catholic faith, but he still had to take the Oath of Allegiance to the Crown. And his future was circumscribed before Emancipation in 1829, because Catholics could not be sheriffs, nor senior barristers, nor judges in senior courts and neither attorney nor solicitor-general.[33]

Like other Irish lawyers, Plunkett was based in Dublin but developed a practice around the circuit court for his native province of Connaught which included the assize towns of Roscommon, Carrickshannon, Sligo, Castlebar and Mayo. He also appeared at quarter sessions and other lesser, local courts. He was well placed to be a conduit for information and persuasion for O'Connell's campaigns. In New South Wales years later he would recognise many faces he had met, in some cases defended, in Connaught.

After the success of the Catholic Association in O'Connell's campaign for emancipation, an Anti-Tory Association was created as the rallying organisation for the 1835 elections but it had some detrimental repercussions for people at the coalface. At Youghal in County Cork for example, speeches by local candidate Dominick Ronayne stirred strong feelings that were exacerbated by a small but active Orange Association in the town. Recently married, twenty-year-old Patrick Murray was caught up in the furore around Ronayne's visit. On the face of it, his offence seems a straightforward common law crime of 'robbing a store' but an anguished petition from his wife Mary suggests something more complex. Having walked 26 miles barefoot to deliver it, she pleaded that her husband be returned to her. He was found guilty 'on no other proof than being in a state of intoxication near the Coal Store' and having a pen knife which the prosecutor swore was his, she claimed. Furthermore the stolen money was found some days later. Patrick Murray was a butcher which means he would have been involved in the political tactic of 'exclusive trading' during the election in Youghal. Under this scheme devised by the Anti-Tory Association, Catholics undertook to buy only from Catholic shopkeepers and ostracise those who were Protestants. Sentries were placed at the door of Protestant stores to enforce the ban. One farmer who bought two casks of herrings from a Protestant was pursued and the casks destroyed. The violence and the bans did not end after the election was over. A Protestant with a grudge against Patrick Murray may have taken the opportunity for revenge.[34]

And finally to sexual violence. According to Patrick O'Farrell, 'studies on pre-Famine sexuality in Ireland . . . show a traditional society, healthily non-repressive, demonstrating a balance between respect for sexuality and a lack of sexual prurience.'[35] And yet the crime of 'abduction' appeared frequently in Irish calendars although it was rare in the English or Scottish lists at the time.[36] The calendars indicate there were also more rapes in Ireland. Any conclusion this was behaviour of a society coerced by religion is questionable. Although highly influential before 1850, the Catholic Church was not yet the controlling force it became later in the nineteenth century. Did sectarian issues explain some of these cases? Unlikely, since the participants were overwhelmingly Catholic.[37] Or did the poverty of some families mean men and women could not afford to marry and their despairing suitors forced the issue? Was any of this explicable as an Irish courtship romp of the kind celebrated in the film *The Quiet Man*? And last, what was meant by abduction? Did it involve two individuals or many people? Was sexual violation, that is, rape, part of it? Or were the women returned unharmed? I found a multitude of answers, only some of which support the legendary Irish courtship which has allowed us to romanticise such behaviour.

In a typical outcome, two men on the *Hive*—John Burke and Murtagh Gorman—with a third named William O'Shaunessy, were transported for rape after their death sentence was commuted. No descriptions of their crime exist, but the involvement of a gang of men was a common feature of rape in Ireland. Sometimes they all raped the victim. Often they were helping one man with a personal or economic motive. Remarks by a judge give some details of a rape case. On handing down sentence, he said: 'You have been found guilty after a long and fair trial of collecting a large gang of ruffians for purpose of committing the crime . . . you broke into the house of a peaceable man and carried away his only daughter, a young girl of 15, whom you violated.'[38]

With abduction there was a formula to what some might describe as just a rough-and-ready courtship. The abductors came by night, very late, in a gang that could range in size from three or four men to twenty, but with one of them intent on taking a particular woman. Sometimes the woman told the court she had refused to marry her abductor. Sometimes she insisted there had been nothing between them or she had never seen him before. The defence usually questioned a woman from the assumption she had flirted with her abductor, 'led him on' we would call it today. Sometimes there was evidence a prospective dowry had enhanced the woman's attraction. At least two men later admitted their motive was mercenary: 'She possessed some land—I wanted to marry her', and from the second, 'I suppose she had a good deal of money'.[39] Frequently a woman's family was roughed-up in the process of her abduction. On many occasions the gang would put the woman in the care of one of their wives or mothers, with whom she would stay until her family and/or the police recovered her. Sometimes she was raped by one or, occasionally, by many of them.[40] This may explain why there were fifteen men on trial for rape in County Cork in March 1835 and 21 in Roscommon gaol for rape the same month (see calendars above). On the other hand, it may not. In the summer of 1835 five men were in gaol charged with rape. Having married their female prosecutors while waiting to be tried, they were discharged by proclamation.[41]

Allowing for inaccurate or partisan newspaper reports, the behaviour that resulted in charges of abduction and rape raises questions about Patrick O'Farrell's conclusion that there were no idiosyncratic features to Irish sexuality. Romanticising, let alone normalising abduction, for instance, has concealed the significant violence, in particular, violence against women that occurred. For example:

> On Saturday night . . . a large body of men amounting to between 40 and 50 persons went to the house of a farmer named Edmond Kelly . . . and demanded admittance which, being refused, they burst in the door. Some of the party then entered and dragged out a daughter of Kelly by the hair of her head; on examining her by moonlight she was found not to be the person they sought and she was allowed to return. Some of the men then searched for and brought out her sister whom they placed on a horse behind one of the party . . . Then some men went back into the house and severely beat Farmer Kelly and another man. Hearing her father's cries, the girl escaped their grip and tried to reach him but, again, they forced her onto the horse, with someone behind to keep her there.[42]

According to Kiera Lindsey, who specialises in the topic, abduction or bride theft in Irish society was embedded in ancient Gaelic custom which can be traced as far back as the fourth century and was probably a highly ritualised part of Irish society that existed among all classes. Sometimes abductions occurred *en masse* at particular times of the year, which suggests these were collusive or romantic abductions performed with the woman's consent in order to marry the man of her choice. This aspect of abduction continued into the nineteenth century.[43] With the introduction of the penal code in the eighteenth century, however, Irish gentry who were disadvantaged as Catholics began to use abduction as a means of redress for land and property. Initially, they were personally involved, but by the 1830s they sometimes used labourers and servants to act on their behalf.[44] In the last decade of the eighteenth century abduction also became a political act. During the United Irishmen's rebellion in 1798, for example, rape was used as a deliberate act of terror and revenge as abduction became enmeshed in war.[45]

During the first half of the nineteenth century, abduction often formed part of the Whiteboys crime of 'assaulting habitation' and many detailed examples exist which combine these elements. For example, James Dalton on the *Hive* had his sentence of 'death recorded' commuted to seven years for abduction, but his crime may have been part of an assault on habitation aimed at redressing an agrarian grievance. Press reports of Dalton's crime variously label it 'aiding and assisting the abduction of Catherine Hartney' or 'rape' or 'abduction' but it is abduction which appears on the ship's indent and to which he pleaded guilty. Research by descendants revealed that Dalton's 60-year-old father-in-law, James Ryan, was transported nine months earlier after leading a group to force a farmer named Redmond Connors to relinquish land at Keelogues in County Limerick. His crime contained familiar Whiteboy characteristics. Redmond Connors was forced outside in the middle of the night where a large group of men were waiting. They wanted to know why he had not left the farm in accordance with the notice they served on him. 'I told them it was a bad time for me to leave, especially as my potatoes were not dug out of the ground,' Connors testified. The group argued among themselves, some in favour of giving him more time, others refusing to accept what he said as an excuse. Eventually he was told to go back to bed.[46]

James Ryan's 28-year-old son, Daniel, evaded the police for nearly a year until they found him in 1835, hidden in a disguised cellar at what had been his father's house. At his trial, Redmond Connors testified how he saw the younger Ryan setting fire to his house. 'He had no arms nor took no part in the transaction but I am certain he was one of the party.' Connors' son and daughter supported their father's evidence but identified no one. Daniel offered no defence except a character reference from Reverend Thomas Hewett. With his death sentence commuted, he sailed on the *Hive* with his brother-in-law James Dalton.[47] Lack of records makes it impossible to be sure but some reports indicate that it was Daniel Ryan who raped Catherine Hartney during this crime. Despite this, he was charged with arson at the same assizes in Limerick when James Dalton was tried.[48] Very likely Dalton and young Ryan with their convictions for abduction and arson were 'left overs' from the central crime of assaulting habitation. No more was said about rape.

The Ryan/Dalton case confirms the ambiguity around abduction in Ireland and how mistaken it is to assume the crime was romantic. Of interest to Australia are Kiera Lindsey's findings for the period 1800–50, which indicate that '146 cases were brought before the courts relating to incidents which probably involved a further 1000 or so conspirators, of whom many were never brought to trial. Of those for which we have some form of primary evidence at least seventeen defendants were acquitted, twenty-three executed, twenty-one imprisoned and *a further 134 transported to the Australian colonies*' (emphasis added).[49] The Ryan/Dalton case demonstrates how the description did not always fit the crime, so there may well have been more.

A.G.L. Shaw analysed the crimes of all 945 men transported from Ireland during 1835, a period which included the 250 men on the *Hive*. Shaw found that approximately 25–30 per cent stole livestock, mostly sheep, and most had no prior conviction, indicating they stole from need.[50] John Williams put the percentage as high as 31 per cent but his research included the Famine years when sheep stealing was particularly high. His sample was also skewed by the cessation of transportation for two years.[51] In 1850, in a glimpse of what might be guilt about the Famine, the lord lieutenant of Ireland argued that 'the Irish convicts . . . are not hardened offenders . . . [Their] offences . . . are usually theft to which they are often driven by distress.'[52] On the *Hive*, 51, or 20 per cent of the men, stole sheep, cows and pigs (five who stole horses are excluded).

This figure was lower than Shaw's overall percentage for 1835 so other ships that year must have had more livestock thieves. Their crime and its circumstances fulfil our traditional expectations about Irish convicts.

There was little difference in thefts of livestock regardless of where they were committed. Whether in England or Ireland, stolen animals were difficult to hide and slow to move as 26-year-old John Buckley, sometimes known as John Denahy, found out. He was caught near the lands of Sleveen in County Cork with two sheep that the landowner swore were his. This claim was supported by a constable who found Buckley trying to move them along a nearby road. Like most of the livestock thieves on the *Hive*, Buckley was sentenced to transportation for life. Fortunately he was single, although his family may have lost his contribution to their welfare. He was a stocky young man, dark haired, with a ruddy freckled face, who had a record for one previous offence. Although illiterate, Buckley was enterprising. He described himself as 'a carter', an occupation he would turn to again in the future.[53]

To avoid the harsh penalty for stealing living stock, a youthful gang led by Owen Singleton aged 50 stole wool off the sheep's back rather than the animal itself. Singleton's co-offenders were three brothers named Kelly—Michael aged 24 and two teenagers, Dennis aged fifteen and Tom aged only thirteen. James Hanrahan aged 28 completed the group. According to the *Connaught Journal*, their crime injured poor people who depended on their wool to pay rent. As a strategy for avoiding a life sentence it worked. All five received seven years transportation.[54]

And then there were the thieves, burglars, robbers, highway robbers, coiners, receivers and embezzlers. Lumped together they amount to 119 of the 250 who sailed on the *Hive*.[55] In most cases there is little difference in crime to those you would find in this category in England and Scotland. Young boys like the fifteen-year-olds Martin Ryan stealing sugar, and Peter Ryan stealing a watch with his friend Nicholas White. Blacksmith Patrick Brien who joined with four others to steal 300 barrels of oats from the stores of the proprietor of the Cork mail coach, plus £12 from a shop in Fermoy. Veteran burglars like Paddy Cavenagh, his nephew James Byrne and Paddy's sister Catherine who was James' mother. Accompanied by Catherine's friend John Tuhy, they broke into a house to steal money and clothes. John McVey who stole £6 from Lieutenant Knox of the 89th Regiment. Thirty-five-year-old Robert Millar, convicted of false pretences for pretending he was still employed as a clerk and collecting rent when he had in fact been sacked. In Queen's County two boys, John Sheill aged thirteen and Lawrence Synott aged fourteen, were caught picking pockets. John Horgen, 29, described as 'an unpopular man who voted for Conservatives at the recent election', who bought his own farm but 'didn't turn anyone out', was charged with perjury for what was in effect insurance fraud. On the strength of his affidavit, he was paid £70 for outbuildings destroyed by fire when their true value was subsequently revealed to be £10. 'Dressed respectably in a suit of black', he crumbled 'much affected' when he was sentenced to transportation for life.[56]

The 250 men who sailed on the *Hive* were victims of poverty and hunger caused by a pernicious system of landholding and threat of dispossession, but like all convicts to New South Wales and most to Van Diemen's Land they never experienced the Famine. Although Catholic and generally respectful of their religion and its priests, they left before the reorganisation and dominance of the Catholic Church, which began in the 1820s, took full effect. Their forcible departure reflected the political turbulence and poverty of life in Ireland in the 1830s, particularly the war on tithes and the elections of January 1835. In this they were similar to prisoners transported from England during the thirties, many of whom were suffering poverty exacerbated by bad harvests. They too were caught in a mix of hope and disappointment, protest and despair surrounding the passage of the Reform Bills. Many prisoners were transported for murder and assault from England too but it is the greater direct experience of violence that most vividly differentiates the Irish from other convicts. They came from a tradition of violence around politics, religion and education and sexual relationships, over land and in workers' unions, all of which contradicts the romanticised version of feisty Irish protest in which somehow a fist, let alone a stick or a stone, never quite connected with anything that might bleed.

CHAPTER 3
Settling to the Task

With brother Edward on his way to India, Henry Lugard's family context dissolved into the background of his life. At 22, he was no longer someone's younger brother, or the baby of four sons, or a fledgling engineer, but a fully qualified professional soldier who must find the maturity to put the skills he had learned at the Royal Artillery College into practice.

In Sydney, Henry joined a detachment of Royal Engineers and Royal Sappers and Miners most of whom had arrived over the previous twelve months. Some of them were involved in the biggest engineering project then under way in Sydney—designing and supervising the construction of a tunnel to bring reliable water supply to town from the Lachlan Swamp (later dignified by the name Centennial Park). Command was vested in Colonel George Barney, who had arrived with his family in December 1835. He was responsible for all ordnance activities in the colony. On his recommendation, Henry was promoted to the rank of first lieutenant and in October 1836, with induction into the local detachment completed, he was ordered to Newcastle to superintend the construction of military barracks there.[1]

Until 1823, Newcastle had been the feared secondary punishment place for prisoners who committed a crime after they arrived. Even those from Van Diemen's Land were sentenced there until 1824 when the southern penal colony received a Supreme Court, and a secondary punishment settlement at Macquarie Harbour. Convicts sent to Newcastle experienced hardship of the most brutal kind as they laboured in lime pits and coalmines. But they also kept escaping and many made their way back to Sydney. In 1823, after Commissioner John Bigge reported on his investigation into the penal colonies, Newcastle was opened to free settlers and new distant punishment settlements were established at Port Macquarie, Moreton Bay and Norfolk Island. In Van Diemen's Land, Port Arthur replaced Macquarie Harbour in 1830.

When Henry Lugard arrived in Newcastle in 1836 it was a small town of approximately 700 people. While many were emancipists, there was also a handful of free immigrants who worked as servants or tradesmen or labourers and an even smaller group of gentry officials. One way or another, everyone was involved in guarding, disciplining or servicing the needs of the workforce which consisted of over 400 prisoners, some in irons as punishment. Their major activity was working for government on the breakwater that would link Nobby's Island to the mainland or as miners for the Australian Agricultural Company which, despite its name, took over the coal deposits from government in 1830.

At a glance it might seem a highly stratified society of guards and slaves, but there were too many undercurrents for that, too many emancipists in positions of power, some now themselves employers of convicts, and too many prisoners who knew these masters were former transportees. Friction was commonplace between convicts and free citizens and police constables who were ex-convicts also. Mobility between prisoner and ex-prisoners, master and servant, official and worker prevented the development of a 'respectable' group and a 'depraved' class of citizens, however much some desired it. The consequence was a community permeated by a criminal ethos in all its corners. Perjury, bribes, lies and aggression were commonplace. Respect for office was non-existent and often undeserved anyway. In such an ill-defined egalitarian mix there was often a subtext to the immediate issue. An example can be seen in the exchange between native-born Joseph Eckford who drank so much at Mrs Mary Beattie's public house that he was charged with drunkenness and 'violent conduct towards Constable Rourke in the execution of his duty'. The constable had history with Eckford, having confined him in the watch-house for two months for being disorderly in the street. When he approached with the latest warrant, he was greeted by Mrs Eckford, 'Here he comes,' she jeered. 'He wants five pounds more.' That brought out Henry Eckford who yelled at the constable: 'Bill Rourke you are a bloody rascal. You took a false oath today for fifty shillings.'[2]

Culturally, Newcastle was a working-class community with only a tiny gentry drawn from the upper echelons of the military, the medical staff, a clergyman, local magistrate and a handful of settlers from nearby farms. Regardless of class, everyone knew everyone else and much of their business and their history as well. Settler and magistrate Robert Scott described the mixture of intense scrutiny and gossip with which he was daily regaled by one of his travelling companions. 'Talk of any person in the Colony of NSW and their deficiencies,' he wrote in his journal, 'and it is ten to one but B. [Bowman] can tell you the whole private and publick history of that individual.'[3]

In this climate it was not unusual for rules to be bent to convenience. For example, Michael Moran, a convict assigned to construction of the breakwater, was a skilled carpenter. Theoretically restricted to government work, Moran operated a thriving sideline making and repairing whatever was needed for Newcastle's leading citizens. He was aggrieved when told that he could not do private work in his own time. And doubly so because he claimed that he did the extra work with his overseer James Pumpfrey's permission. Pumpfrey and the town gentlemen, including Dr George Brooks and James Reid Esquire, who had been utilising Moran's services, went into meltdown trying to explain their complicity. Under investigation, Pumpfrey told the bench, 'It has been my practice to give the good men leave to work in their [own] time such as Saturday—they seem to work better for Government from these indulgences.'[4] In other words, the prisoners had convinced their masters that a carrot was more effective than a stick.

The tradition of prisoners having time to work for themselves dated back to the early days of settlement when Governor Phillip negotiated with convict agricultural gangs over the amount of work they would complete. At the same time, his second in command, John Hunter, found it necessary to negotiate with his prisoner workforce on Norfolk Island about setting taskwork they felt was realistic. Later when he was governor, Hunter 'confronted a gang of sawyers at the Hawkesbury settlement who had apparently set their own taskwork. They had set this at a level which was, in his opinion, too low, for it gave them half a day free.' But his real concern, according to historian William Robbins, was the way they openly bargained with government officials over their reward for any extra labour above their taskwork. They also negotiated directly with free settlers on a contract basis. Hunter tried to regain some control by formalising the hours of work for all gangs and curtailing the prisoners' ability to influence the subject. His lack of success can be seen by the fact that Governor King was still grappling with the problem of a standardised working day in 1801.[5]

In those pioneering years when every person's effort was required to establish a foothold, when the colony was little more than a camp—and the prisoners hugely outnumbered their guards—it seemed wise to work by cooperation rather than coercion. But the practice of convicts combining servitude with private enterprise became a tradition, and over the years prisoners like Moran and his ex-convict overseer resisted or ignored attempts to change it. In 1819 Commissioner Bigge aimed to make the punishment of transportation fit the crime and recommended that 'indulgences' such as this should end. It continued even in a somewhat underground fashion (even on Norfolk Island) because, as overseer Pumpfrey revealed, it was the way colonial leaders extracted some effort from their recalcitrant workforce.[6]

Major Druitt, chief engineer in Governor Macquarie's time, was responsible for work gangs. Giving evidence to Commissioner Bigge in 1819, he said that he used the taskwork system because he found 'it the best mode of securing the performance of *a Fair Days work*'.[7] Nearly two decades later, giving evidence about working conditions on a Hunter Valley property, convict James Brown mentioned what might be called penalty rates. 'It is not a practice to work the men on Sunday, not latterly. I have known wheat to be cleaned and bagged on a Sunday about 18 months ago, for which the men were to be paid extra. This occurred three or four times.' When interrogated, he was less assertive, 'I do not know [for sure] whether they were paid or not.' And Sir Edward Parry, who ran the Australian Agricultural Company which had a large labour force, said that in his experience, 'A convict, unless he is well watched, will not perform the same amount of labour [as a free worker] except in the case of what is called task work . . . that is the only case in which convict labour is really valuable labour at all.'[8] As a newly arrived master

in 1830, Parry turned to the colonial secretary for guidance after he
had tried in vain to obtain information about the exact productivity
which could be expected from prisoners employed on taskwork. 'In this
endeavour, I have entirely failed,' he wrote, 'the various accounts differing
in some instances almost by one-half.'[9] As he discovered, there was no
colony-wide regulation of labour, a situation which allowed the prisoners'
view of how they should work to prevail.

The cost of trying to force the convicts to work and the probability
of a drop in productivity contributed to the prisoners' success in keeping
the taskwork system alive.[10] Not to mention the gentry's need for special,
personal jobs which could not have been performed if the prisoners'
working hours and their free time were circumscribed. And life for the
masters could have been costly and very unpleasant if they were required
to enforce it with whips and chains and close supervision, as James
Macarthur pointed out to a British parliamentary committee in 1837.
'The system of forcing labour on a private establishment I conceive would
not be a very profitable one; at all events, it would be an exceedingly
disagreeable one.'[11] Regardless of official policy, taskwork continued on
the Macarthur estate, where servants could work in their own time and
were paid either in kind or with credit at the estate's store.[12]

'Time of their own' did not just mean an hour or two after the day's
work was done but soon extended to the men having one whole day off
per week. In this, their expectation was always assisted by official policy
that prisoners should receive the benefit of religion on the Sabbath. In
practice, however, the day off could be Saturday or Sunday but the former
was preferred by the men because musters and church services tended to
disrupt Sundays. In the men's minds, time to themselves took precedence
over religious observances. For example, Thomas Stewart, a free-settler
official who was left on Norfolk Island to manage a 'handover team'
of nine convicts in 1855, was bluntly told by a ticket-of-leave constable
that the men preferred to spend Sundays doing their washing and other
personal chores rather than go to church. 'It leads me to think that some
would more readily approve if no religious observances were attended at
all,' Stewart wrote in his journal.[13]

With the right to a day off established, negotiations occurred over
time to entrench two refinements of this entitlement. By 1828 the men
constructing the Great Northern Road officially worked only until
2 p.m. on Saturdays and then 'were conducted to a pond or river in the

neighbourhood to bathe and wash their clothes.'[14] Sunday remained their day off. In *Convict Workers,* Stephen Nicholas summarised his findings as follows: 'The convicts in New South Wales generally laboured 5½ days per week to perform an average 56 hours of work . . . convicts worked fewer hours than most coerced, contract and free workers. [By comparison] a six-day working week was the standard for bonded Indians and Spanish and American slaves as well as free labourers in Britain.'[15] Of great significance to Australian history, however, is recognising the extent to which this work structure was achieved by negotiation and pressure from the workers themselves.

By the 1830s prisoners were testing the idea of 'time in lieu' which, they thought, should take effect if a master's need for his servant's work intruded on his free time. In explaining his refusal to work on a Monday, prisoner Edward Gill spoke as though it was a commonplace assumption. 'I had been working all week like the rest of the men and took out the sheep on Sunday to oblige my master. On Monday when I told Mr Free [the overseer] I would not work, I thought I had a right to half of that day having been at work [also] all day Saturday.'[16]

Try as it might the government never succeeded in ending the day off, in attitude or in fact. It may have begun as a necessity—or a privilege—but as time passed it was regarded as an entitlement. The practice was still common enough nearly 50 years after the Europeans arrived for the colonial secretary to make enquiries of officials, such as engineer John Busby who was in charge of building the tunnel from Lachlan Swamp. Following incidents where his convict miners were picked up drinking in town pubs and had proffered the traditional explanation of being on their own time, Busby was asked to report 'if it is the practice for prisoners of this department to be allowed the whole of Saturday to themselves?' Busby replied, 'It is not the practice here.'[17] Almost certainly he, like James Pumpfrey and many employers in the colony, had taken the line of least resistance and turned a blind eye.

In addition to the challenges of a convict workforce, Henry Lugard would have discovered that Newcastle was full of brawling soldiers. Detachments of the 28th Regiment were stationed in the town and surrounding areas. As well as Newcastle itself, some were based at the recently gazetted town of Maitland which sprawled on either side of Wallis Creek inland from Newcastle. Some were at the Hunter River port of Morpeth, others at Harper's Hill on the road north from Maitland where there was a large stockade. Some of these soldiers had been shipwrecked with Henry on the *Hive*. Others had been sent out as guards on earlier transports during 1835. Their job was to control the prisoners who were working on building projects which included not only the breakwater but the military barracks that Henry had specifically come to supervise, a courthouse and other official buildings at Maitland as well as roads in all directions: between Newcastle and Maitland, north-west up through the Hunter Valley and from Morpeth to Maitland. The Great North Road from Wiseman's Ferry through Wollombi to Patrick's Plains (later named Singleton) had been completed approximately five years earlier but needed constant improvement and repair.[18]

The local commander of the 28th was Major James Crummer, an Irishman in his mid-forties. Arriving in the colony in October 1835, he had been sent to the Newcastle area where he combined his role of guarding the prisoners with acting as one of the local magistrates. Crummer was a veteran of the Napoleonic wars including the Battle of Waterloo, who subsequently spent time at the Royal Military College at Sandhurst which coincided with the cadetship of Henry Lugard's older brother John. No doubt this family acquaintance and the shared experience of Sandhurst helped the two military men bridge the age gap. In 1836, both men probably expected their time in New South Wales would be short, but in fact Crummer would long outstay Henry Lugard. Increasingly disabled from leg wounds sustained during the war, he decided in 1839 to sell his commission and settle permanently in Australia. He served as police magistrate in the Maitland area until he was 'old and shaky as well as ill' when, in 1858, he was persuaded to retire to a less demanding post at Port Macquarie.[19]

Among the rank and file of the 28th in the Hunter area was Private Patrick Tierney. On landing in Sydney, Patrick and his family had been quartered at the regiment's base at Parramatta, but only briefly. Obliged by army regulations to follow their man, Bridget and the children took the steamer north when Patrick was ordered to Port Macquarie for three months, then back to Parramatta for a short period. By April 1836 they were based at Maitland and it was here that Bridget's baby was born. Did they name him Henry after the young engineer they had come to know so well? It is tempting to think so but no evidence remains to confirm it. In any event, baby Henry did not survive long enough to meet his namesake. Safe within his mother's body, he had survived the rough surf and alarm of a shipwreck, but once outside he faltered, then tragically died aged only seven weeks.[20]

Patrick Tierney's military comrades kept the local bench occupied almost as much as the convicts.[21] The worst event involving the 28th took place at Morpeth where Private John Lestle died as a result of a punch from another soldier when both men were in the lock-up for drunkenness. His assailant was acquitted because a prisoner assigned to pastoralist William Spark testified that he had moved two drunken soldiers in a cart to their quarters and on the way, one of them fell out and hit his head.[22]

There was nothing unusual in Private Lestle's behaviour. Similar incidents occurred elsewhere with the 28th and with all regiments that spent time in the penal colonies. Soldiers stationed in Australia as guards came from the same socioeconomic group as the prisoners. Many of them were Irish. Furthermore, soldiers knew what it was like to be flogged and far more brutally than convicts. It was not uncommon for court-martialled soldiers who were transported as convicts, to arrive in the penal colonies having already experienced 600, 800, 1000 lashes. Despite this background, it was often soldier prisoners who volunteered to be scourgers, that is, floggers, risking retribution from their fellow prisoners in return for what they judged an easier life. Private Edward Robinson, who was one of two soldiers transported as convicts on the *Hive*, made this choice. A 21-year-old private in the 60th Regiment of Foot, he and three others were convicted of 'acting in a most riotous, violent and unsoldierlike manner' on parade and 'in the line of march'. In fact, they were drunk. The court-martial, however, summarised the charge as mutiny and sentenced Robinson to transportation for life. In New South Wales he was initially based with magistrate Thomas Moore at Liverpool but subsequently administered the lash in Bathurst and Parramatta.[23] Presumably, he shared the experience of another scourger who claimed, 'my name is branded all up the country and I am pointed at and abused wherever I go'.[24] Later in the century Alexander Stewart, who was a boy at the time, remembered details about punishment in the 1820s. 'The floggers at Wollongong were Maddell, Roach, Francis (a black savage), and Davey Mott. They used the cat-o'-nine-tails, a military sergeant counted the strokes. The sergeants were usually very exacting.' Retribution, he recalled, could be merciless. 'On one occasion a flogger—a savage—was waylaid on Seven Mile Beach, murdered, and the body left for the dingoes . . . What else could be expected from men who, after a severe flogging, had to sleep on their bellies for weeks?' For a similar crime, three men were hanged at Wollongong.[25] As the use of flogging declined, Edward Robinson merged this role into being a turnkey or gaoler. In 1845 he married Margaret Donolon, with whom he had several children.[26]

By joining the British Army, soldiers had chosen the legal route for survival, but with a background of poverty and disadvantage, their attitudes, interests and recreation were similar to the prisoners'. In their role as guards, ethnic discrimination was not an issue because many of them were Irish. Furthermore, drunkenness, gambling and brawling were shared characteristics, all of which could put the official differentiation between military and criminal at risk. Soldiers escorting prisoners long distances, from Bathurst to Sydney for example, would stop at pubs for a drink and allowed prisoners to quench their thirst too. Frequently they would all end up drunk. Small acts of sympathy occurred, which occasionally surface in the records. For example, a prisoner in the Illawarra stockade for punishment recounted how he was 'up late reading the *Sydney Gazette* newspaper', adding, 'We often get pieces of newspapers from the military.'[27] As we shall see, sometimes soldiers and prisoners even escaped together.

During its years in New South Wales, the 28th (North Gloucestershire) Regiment of Foot consisted of 23 detachments which were spread around the colony. Its soldiers were stationed in Sydney and Parramatta, at Hassans Walls stockade on the Great Western Road, at the Illawarra where the *Hive* ran aground, at Towrang which would one day be called Goulburn and at the new settlement of Port Phillip. In 1839, the regiment's Major Sydney Cotton was the last commandant of Moreton Bay, followed consecutively by two lieutenants of the 28th who oversaw the penal settlement's closure. Among its many colonial activities, the 28th is given credit for founding the Australian Jockey Club because shortly before the last detachment left the colony in June 1842 one of the regiment's officers, Captain Hunter, attended a meeting of the Australian Race Committee. At the meeting, he proposed that since the public so enthusiastically flocked to race meetings at Homebush, the committee should resolve itself into a club to be called the Australian Jockey Club. They settled on an annual subscription of £10 which entitled members to run a horse at each race meeting.[28]

Whenever a regiment prepared to leave the colony, there was a spate of desertions. The 28th was no different. A significant number of men went on the run as their departure date drew near.[29] The mounted police, many of them former soldiers themselves, were tasked with rounding up those who were trying to stay illegally. Other members of the 28th settled in New South Wales on condition of joining the mounted police, while some men from the rank and file bought their way out of the army. Officers were entitled to land grants if they settled in the colony and some, such as Major Crummer, sold their commissions in order to stay.

Private Patrick Tierney was among those who saw opportunity in New South Wales. In December 1839 he paid the large sum of £15 to buy himself out of the army. He and Bridget and the family settled in Maitland where for the next decade he operated a business as a shoemaker and, as we shall see, was active in community affairs.[30] It took two further years for the last of Tierney's colleagues in the 28th Regiment to depart for service in India.

A major attraction for settlers like the Tierneys was the egalitarian culture that permeated the colonies. The contrast between the class-ridden society from which they came tempted working people to stay. A significant contributor to the creation of this unusual community had been the practice in both New South Wales and Van Diemen's Land of assigning convicts to employers who had themselves been prisoners, some of whom were wealthy. Born out of the numerical dominance of emancipists in the community, this practice continued the cultural levelling ashore which had begun on the voyage out when gentlemen convicts were transported along with thieves from the slums of Dublin or London. In 1819, when Commissioner Bigge investigated the penal colonies, he disapproved of the way that many ex-convict employers shared their living arrangements with their convict servants.[31]

No such lack of distinction existed between master and servants in Henry Lugard's household, where the master came from a personal and occupational background that assumed power, deference and obedience were his right. When first ordered to Newcastle, Henry was allocated a convict to act as personal servant and butler. Over time he also acquired several labourers for his farm on Ash Island between Maitland and Newcastle. However, not all was as it seemed. Birthright and privilege cut no ice in the convict colony. And as masters from James Pumpfrey to John Busby had discovered, the trappings of office, or a management culture of 'command and control' from above, produced neither deference, nor a cooperative workforce. Like other colonial masters, Henry Lugard ruled in a community which was intent on making it plain that no man was better than anyone else. Its gatekeepers took pride in refusing to defer and were creative in the ways they undercut a master's authority. Dumb insolence was a well-tried tactic. Derogatory nicknames another. Among themselves, for example, Henry's men referred to him as 'The Lobster'. Still feeling his way towards self-confidence, he must have been embarrassed when their lack of respect was published for all to see in the *Sydney Herald*.[32] And exasperated by Edward Black and Patrick Kenny who were before the Newcastle bench for 'disorderly conduct' in January 1838. News in March that he was ordered to Norfolk Island to superintend the public works may well have been a relief although it was August before he sailed. His men soon took advantage of his absence. Barely two months later four walked off the farm in search of recreation. An eagle-eyed constable charged them with 'being absent' but it was not a deterrent. Early in the new year, three left the farm without a pass and were caught drinking in a public house on the Maitland Road for which each received 50 lashes.[33]

Meanwhile down on the Illawarra, Alexander Berry had seized the opportunity presented by the shipwrecked *Hive* to find some good men. Berry had learned a thing or two as a pastoralist in the colony. He must have been watching the unloading at Bherwerre beach, mentally noting the quality of the prisoners. Conversations with surgeon Donoghoe doubtless amplified his own opinion about which men would serve him best. The three Berry kept for himself included two with life sentences, which meant it would be eight years before they were entitled to a ticket-of-leave. Excellent labour force continuity from an employer's point of view. The lifers were 30-year-old Daniel Thomas aka Thomas Daniel who had been convicted of highway robbery in Waterford and young John Cormack, aged 24, who had stolen calves in Queen's County. The third man was Patrick Murray, a butcher from Youghal in County Cork who is recorded as arriving at the Berry estate on 7 January 1836—in other words, straight off the beach.[34]

Despite his seven-year sentence, Patrick Murray was a real prize: only twenty years of age, but possessing the skills of a butcher which were so valuable on a farm. Berry kept Murray for himself but appears to have lent him to other settlers when requested. His estate records show that

Murray 'transferred' to William Nairn Gray, the police magistrate at Wollongong, six months after he arrived but was returned a few weeks later.[35] He would have had a small farm with some cattle and Murray was just the man to help him maximise their value by slaughtering them.

When he received his ticket-of-leave in 1840, Patrick Murray chose to stay in the Illawarra. For a while he continued working on the Berry estate but was probably also hiring himself out to other people in a similar pattern to that established when he was an assigned servant. Later he hired himself to the Terry estate at Dapto before settling in his own right at Albion Park. He was one of the fortunate few to be reunited with his wife, Mary, who did not wait for him to become eligible officially for reunion. Having walked barefoot from Youghal to Cork to present her petition to save him from transportation, she did not give up when Murray sailed away. Somehow she got herself a passage to New South Wales, probably as a free settler on a convict ship. She had arrived by 1840 because in 1841 they had their first child Catherine, and two years later a son, James.[36] The family prospered in the Illawarra. We get a glimpse of how well they were doing by Murray's involvement in a court case in 1843. Travelling back overnight from Sydney on the steamer, he was robbed by the steward of £21 when he fell asleep. There was some debate about whether he was drunk, which he refuted indignantly: 'I had one glass of rum after I went on board and then lay down. I remained in my berth until the steamer arrived at Wollongong when I missed the notes.' Despite his denial, there was contradictory evidence that everyone in the forecabin was drunk and they had been gambling at cards. Mary Murray was sworn to give evidence that identified the notes he was carrying: 'Patrick, it turned out, had gone to town to buy cattle but had not bought any after all. The ship's captain testified that he knew Patrick traded 'largely in potato and cabbage-tree plat [*sic*]' and might have had the money (for that reason rather than gambling). Evidence either way was contradictory and slight. The defendant Smeaton's barrister played the ethnic card, arguing, 'All that could be said was a drunken Irishman and a sober Scotchman had been playing at cards for money, which had been won by the latter.' Patrick recovered £16 which had been found clutched in the hands of a sleeping Smeaton but the jury decided he had lost the rest at cards. Smeaton was acquitted and Patrick severely rebuked by the judge, who told him 'he had himself alone to blame for being drunk and gambling'. Sadly, the Murrays' life together was short. Only three years later, in 1846, Patrick died at Wollongong aged 33.[37]

By all appearances, Patrick Murray's career as a convict was straightforward and benign, with an outcome that healed the emotional trauma of separation and produced material prosperity. But for once we have information that reveals the dark side of being an assigned prisoner, however lucky. Detailed records kept by the Berry estate reveal that Murray did not escape a flogging. In February 1837 he received 50 lashes on the orders of the visiting magistrate, A. Holden Esquire, for hitting Mr Coloun, the overseer at Berry's Numba property. Murray felt Coloun was interfering in his work.[38] Flogging was not indiscriminate on the Illawarra coast, however. Punishment records for the Illawarra Stockade 1827–44 cover the peak servitude period for the *Hive* men but none of them appear in it.[39]

As a master, Alexander Berry could be tough with those prisoners who crossed him or who reoffended, but as we shall see he had an approach to managing his men which explains the stability among his workforce over many years and which, in essence, treated his assigned men 'as ordinary workers'. Furthermore, when the men transitioned from servitude to freedom, Berry's managers often negotiated new terms for the relationship, including wages or leasing them land to farm. Looking back he was proud of the stable and productive workforce that resulted. 'Some of these Government men are still in my service till the present day, and some are my tenants.'[40]

For his settler friends on the Illawarra, Berry chose Patrick Maloney, whose experience as a seaman and his courage in standing up to his fellow prisoners had been vital in keeping them calm when the *Hive* ran aground. Aged 23, he had been convicted of stealing a hat in Cork City. In New South Wales he was allocated to John Ritchie senior who, like Berry, had settled on the Illawarra in the early 1820s, in his case at Jamberoo about halfway between the later site of Wollongong and Berry's estate on the Shoalhaven River.[41]

George Wood, who also farmed at Jamberoo, took eighteen-year-old William Rawson who had been sentenced to seven years for stealing a book in Dublin. Rawson received his ticket in 1840 for the Illawarra district but by 1847, after he was officially free, he moved to Armidale where he married.[42]

James Stares Spearing, who spent a decade as a pastoralist at the Illawarra between 1825 and 1836, makes an interesting contrast to Berry. He had two grants of 1000 acres each which he called *Paulsgrove* on land which is today occupied by the Wollongong University campus and the Botanic Gardens. With the tactical thinking of a man on the make, Spearing and the woman he intended to marry emigrated separately so she too could obtain a nearby grant of 1920 acres before they were officially linked.[43] Like Berry, he wrote numerous letters but while Berry's were always civil and, if he was seeking a favour, strategically smart in their timing, the subject matter and the choice of recipient, Spearing's were not. Historian Lorraine Neate describes Spearing as, 'a vexatious correspondent, with governors, the surveyor-general, the postmaster and the principal superintendent of convicts falling foul of his pen. He was constantly outraged by his treatment from local military commandants and magistrates. Some of his neighbours even became the subjects of his letters and litigation.' Local magistrate, Lieutenant John Fitzgerald of the 39th Regiment, wrote at the time that he was 'a very troublesome and litigious character'. Fitzgerald was sufficiently intimidated to wait until he could sit with a second magistrate so that Spearing 'should have no opportunity of saying that I acted precipitately or malevolently towards him'.[44]

As we shall see, Spearing was in direct conflict with his convict workers, whose rejection of his authority took several forms including a strike. He was also afraid of them, particularly the Irish. In this atmosphere it was probably no coincidence that life at *Paulsgrove* also contained a vicious example of prisoners turning on one another. Greed, brutality, betrayal and stupidity all followed convict Thomas Austin's attempt to bribe the overseer. He was overheard by another prisoner, John Stephenson, who spread the word about Austin's stash of sovereigns among the workforce. When Austin vanished, foul play was suspected but no body could at first be found. Next the prisoner John Hutton was seen splashing about new-found wealth. Further searching uncovered Austin's body. Hutton was hanged for the crime but not before he claimed Stephenson did it while Hutton only watched.[45] The incident is a reminder that surviving convict life was no picnic: a man must be wary and give nothing away, opportunism must be matched by cunning.

Shortly after the *Hive* was wrecked, Spearing sold up and returned home but his workers remained. Some were passed on to the new owner of *Paulsgrove*. Others, whose sentence had expired, settled into citizenship with varying degrees of success, mainly as small farmers, small businessmen or independent contractors. Most of the men from the *Hive* assigned to the Illawarra, either at Berry's behest or later, made their lives there. Meanwhile their shipmates were being scattered far and wide across the land.

CHAPTER 4
'The O'Connellite Tail'

The prisoners from the *Hive* disembarked at Sydney into a society unlike any they had experienced before. They would quickly have spotted that British expectations of hierarchy, control and orderliness were turned upside down. Three years earlier, the newly arrived governor's daughter, Anne Bourke, noticed it too, writing in her diary that the people were 'not tractable' and 'there is a spirit of equality and independence amongst them.'[1] But a management problem for the governor was opportunity for his subjects. The community the *Hive* men saw before them lacked the traditional barriers of class and privilege. Their own kind were included in every occupation, in all aspects of society, the prosperous as well as the poor. As we shall see, they would discover that, generally speaking, being Irish was no great impediment. Indeed, some of them must have taken heart at the news that the highest office in the land was occupied by Richard Bourke, whom they knew not only as a magistrate but as chairman of the Limerick branch of the Irish Relief Association and as a champion of education for Catholics.

Bourke had arrived in the colony in December 1831. After turning down other offers suggested by his friend Thomas Spring Rice, he finally accepted what looked like an interesting challenge as governor of New South Wales, whose climate was also good for the delicate health of his wife, Elizabeth. However, despite Bourke's personal care for her she died in May 1832, less than six months after their arrival. Bourke was devastated and his grief weighed heavily throughout his time as governor. His daughters, Fanny and Mary, had been left behind in London where they would marry, but Anne and his son, Dick, were with him, as was his second son, John, who had been left both blind and lame after an attack of hydrocephalus when he was a toddler. The Bourkes brought out a Mr Marsh who was related to the governor's aide, Captain Robert Marsh Westmacott, to care for John in an unknown environment.[2]

Unlike his two predecessors, Bourke wasted no time in exploring his new domain, approaching the task with the same enthusiasm and curiosity as Governor Macquarie had done years before. But Bourke's terrain was much larger.[3] In 1832, the settled areas stretched north to Port Macquarie, south to Wollongong and Shoalhaven on the Illawarra, west over the mountains as far as Wellington, and to the south-west where settlers were moving beyond the fast-developing town of Goulburn. Punishment outposts existed at Moreton Bay and Norfolk Island. By the time the *Hive* arrived Bourke had traversed most of the colony. In that year, however, new pressures arose about the spread of settlement. Bourke believed settlement should be extended but he had been instructed by London to contain it within the boundaries established by Governor Darling. Nevertheless, when he heard that settlers from Van Diemen's Land were crossing Bass Strait to establish themselves on New South Wales territory he despatched surveyor-general Thomas Mitchell to explore further south to the area known as Port Phillip.

Like his daughter, Bourke must have been struck by the egalitarian culture of the colony, which by the 1830s was well entrenched. Furthermore, the citizens, whether free or bond, made it plain they intended to keep it that way. One means of doing so was to ram home the message that no one should think they were better than anyone else. Well aware that the local gentry's status often rested on uncertain foundations, working men used this vulnerability to deadly effect. For example, Thomas Kenny, who may have been a free immigrant rather than an emancipist, objected to the terms of his contract as a servant and was brought before the Newcastle bench consisting of civilian magistrate Alexander Scott and Major Crummer of the 28th Regiment. Sentenced to one month's hard labour in gaol for refusing to combine the duties of clerk *and* butler, Kenny was furiously aggrieved by what he regarded as unfair treatment. 'It's a dammed shame,' he shouted in the courtroom, 'a bloody shame that a bloody set of magistrates should ". . . orf" a poor fellow. Mr Scott is a bloody vagabond. By God I will report the Bench to Horseguards.' Into the dumbfounded silence, he demanded, 'Well have you got any more to say, Scott?' Then he let fly a deadly public barb, pronouncing to one and all, 'Mr Scott wants to prove himself a gentleman in this colony but he cannot do so at home.'[4]

Richard Bourke, as we have seen, was a liberal, with deeply considered views on issues such as education and ecumenical religion. He also believed that emigration was the way to remedy poverty in Ireland. Described by some as a radical, his views were increasingly shared by members of the British parliament including Daniel O'Connell and Thomas Spring Rice, who became secretary of the Treasury and later secretary of state for the colonies. Bourke's reputation as a progressive preceded him to the colony. On his arrival, the colonists did everything that was proper to welcome him but their reaction was coloured by where they had stood regarding his conservative predecessor, Ralph Darling. A measure of the partisanship that had developed around Darling is the contrast between his official farewell from conservative landholders, merchants and government officers with the derisive crowds and celebratory barbecue hosted by William Charles Wentworth in the grounds of his Vaucluse home. In town, the *Sydney Monitor* displayed an illumination of glass lanterns which announced bluntly, 'He's off!'[5] This opposition group was more laudatory about their new governor: 'He is the individual from whom the people have a right to expect good government. We know of General Bourke that he is a man who has been educated in liberal principles . . . and we find that he has taken an active part in the support of those principles in his native country . . . [and] at the Cape, where by his wisdom, he introduced, if not a perfect feeling of unanimity, at least a strong tendency to it.'[6]

An Austrian diplomat, Baron Charles von Hugel, met Bourke about eighteen months after he arrived and found him very unforthcoming. 'He does not appear to be happy. The death of his wife a year ago in Sydney and the pain from an old wound in his right jaw may perhaps explain his withdrawn manner, which makes conversation on subjects not connected with official business difficult.' Of course the governor may not have warmed to the baron, not least because he was close to the colonial secretary Alexander Macleay who was proving obstructive to Bourke. And von Hugel's expectations were considerable. 'General Bourke is reputed to be a deep thinker,' he wrote. 'He was brought up by his uncle, the celebrated Bourke [Edmund Burke] and takes a keen interest in intellectual pursuits. He is said to be engaged in writing a work on the history of New South Wales.' Disappointed not to find common ground, the baron resorted to criticism. 'His conversation tends to be disconnected and saying little himself, his ideas follow a direction different from that indicated by his questions.' Perhaps conscious that he had been ungracious, Bourke invited von Hugel to dinner a few weeks later.[7]

Slavery was an issue about which Bourke felt strongly. Like other campaigners against it, he assumed that New South Wales had all the elements of a slave colony, in particular brutal treatment of the convicts and consequent degradation of the masters who inflicted it. One of his reasons for supporting a gradual end to transportation was 'the pernicious effects of the use of convicts, which is slave labour, upon the character of the masters'.[8] It was the same argument vigorously prosecuted by those in Britain who campaigned to end slavery worldwide. However, at the House of Commons Select Committee into Transportation in 1837–38 Sir Francis Forbes, who had just retired as chief justice after many years in the colony, disagreed emphatically with the suggestion that the convicts in New South Wales were slaves. He would not accept the proposition that assigned service was slavery, telling the committee instead that the extent to which an employer had right of property in the services of a convict assigned to him was similar to how a master had rights over his apprentice and definitely not similar to a master and slave relationship.[9]

It is true that when they were highly aggrieved, prisoners could be heard describing themselves as 'nothing but bloody slaves'. More often, however, their behaviour and attitudes contradicted any idea they actually saw themselves that way. Brutalised slaves, for example, don't risk their lives to save others, as convicts did in countless individual and collective incidents even in places such as Norfolk Island. Close scrutiny of thousands of convict archives supports Sir Francis Forbes' description of an apprentice-style contract. Most records contradict suggestions that New South Wales was a slave colony. Furthermore, the fact so many prisoners continued to work for their former master after they were free, or settled nearby, gives the lie to describing their servitude as slavery.

Most of the time that was not how they saw it. At best, the description might apply to sections of the secondary punishment regime—on the roads, or at Newcastle and Macquarie Harbour or, later, Moreton Bay and Norfolk Island. Or in Van Diemen's Land when the probation system replaced assigned service for convicts.

In the colony, Governor Bourke occasionally referred to the prisoners as 'slaves' or 'slave labour', especially when he was castigating their masters or restricting their excesses, such as the limitation he placed on flogging. Advertisements which were placed when a pastoralist was selling his property sometimes publicised that the assets of the farm included, say, 22 assigned men. Such notices would have confirmed Bourke's opinion that, whatever the legal niceties, convicts were owned, like slaves, by their masters. Or at least that the masters regarded them as property. There were also examples of egregious behaviour by employers. In mid-1832, for example, Bourke learned that John Bingle had arranged for one of his servants to receive 100 lashes at his own farm. In a cosy arrangement by two landowners, magistrate John Pike visited Bingle's farm to satisfy the legalities. Bourke rebuked Bingle for 'irregular and reprehensible' conduct and he told Pike in no uncertain terms that 'a more unnecessary, indiscreet and unseemly exercise of such jurisdiction cannot be imagined'.[10]

Only months later, the governor introduced the Summary Jurisdiction Act of 1832 which was designed to curtail the settlers' ability to punish their assigned servants. The 100 lashes inflicted by John Bingle on his servant were not typical. The most common punishment was 25 or 50 lashes, but Bourke's changes meant they were now limited to 50 lashes where previously they go could as high as 150. Also two magistrates were now required for sentence to an iron gang. Furthermore, the legislation specified what kind of lash could be used, effectively outlawing the more painful cat-o'-nine-tails. Bourke's Act was also designed to confront magistrates with the consequences of their decisions. Henceforth, they had to be present when the flogging occurred and to report the suffering of the prisoner then and over the subsequent month.[11] The settlers were angry and resentful at these changes. Some alleged the governor was to blame for a rise in 'insubordination'. In the Goulburn district one claimed the convicts were becoming 'every day more reckless and daring than before, and bushranging more rife'.[12]

The *Hive*'s arrival coincided with the final stage of this dispute. Just as the prisoners were being distributed to assigned service in January 1836,

Bourke dispensed with 33 magistrates by choosing not to renew their appointments. Well-known gentlemen who had previously been justices of the peace, were missing from his list. Although the unpaid workload was sometimes onerous, being appointed a justice of the peace by the governor conferred status as well as power on its holder. The office replicated a role performed by the gentry, including aristocrats, in England which made it doubly prized by those aspiring to similar rank in the colony.

Bourke's announcement caused an outcry. Meetings were held. Letters written. In the Hunter Valley, more than 200 settlers put their names to an indignant petition. Started by James Webber of the *Tocal* estate at Paterson and Robert Scott of *Glendon* near Patrick's Plains, the petition was sent directly to the King arguing that Bourke's actions put the settlers in danger.[13] Among the signatories were John Bingle, mentioned above, and also James Mudie of *Castle Forbes*, about whom we shall hear more later. Their opponents nicknamed their plea to the King as the 'Hole and Corner Petition', mocking their attempt to be discreet by labelling their behaviour as secretive like 'men who crept into holes and corners like rats' without the courage to stand up publicly and be counted. The issue created tremendous public debate and enhanced existing stereotypes of ruthless, brutal and wealthy masters. His Majesty took no action. Bourke, however, was left with a divided community with Emancipists and Exclusives in opposite camps reminiscent of the days of Governor Macquarie nearly twenty years earlier.[14] It was not an atmosphere conducive to the introduction of other reforms.

Bourke was not without allies. The 'opposition' press, as it had been labelled in Governor Darling's day, supported him, led by *The Australian* which was founded by William Charles Wentworth but now owned by native-born George Robert 'Bob' Nichols, who was descended from convicts. The *Sydney Monitor* was actively engaged on the side of the settlers while the *Sydney Herald* published a barrage of criticism about the governor. Bourke was not helped by an eloquent speech against slavery by Daniel O'Connell in the House of Commons, in the course of which he damned the tyranny of Governor Darling and praised the appointment of Governor Bourke.[15]

By 1834, the *Sydney Herald* was regularly sneering at what it called 'the O'Connellite tail'.[16] This was a reference not just to Bourke but also to a coterie of Irish gentry who held influential positions in the colony. The superintendent of convicts, Frederick Hely, and the attorney-general, John

Kinchela, were both Irish but were already in New South Wales by the time O'Connell rose to fame with his campaign for Catholic emancipation. Like the governor, they were Protestant. First of the newcomers to whom the *Sydney Herald* was referring was Roger Therry, who had been a student at Trinity College with John Hubert Plunkett and shared the disadvantages of being Catholic in Ireland. He disembarked at Sydney in 1829 having been appointed commissioner for the Court of Common Requests. As a civil court for disputes less than £10 in value, the job situated Therry at the core of the local community. He also developed a private practice and by the time Bourke arrived was one of the colony's leading barristers. With the ill-health and imminent retirement of chief justice Sir Francis Forbes with whom Bourke was close friends, Therry quickly became a confidant of the governor.

Bourke and Therry were joined in 1833 by John Hubert Plunkett as solicitor-general, an appointment arranged after lobbying in London by Daniel O'Connell and others. Plunkett brought with him a retinue of people, including his bride Marie Charlotte who was his cousin and only nineteen years old to the groom's 30 years. If rumour is correct, Plunkett had married on the rebound following a broken engagement, but this might have been no more than a family tale to justify the speed of his wedding and emigration. Other evidence indicates he was very much in love with her.[17] In fact Plunkett, like Therry, had recognised the limitations that still existed for Catholic lawyers in Ireland. When the appointment of solicitor-general was offered he accepted with alacrity, which required swift decisions on other issues as well.[18] Plunkett's youngest sister, Kate Amelia, came with him to the colony. In 1841 she was married in Sydney to Francis Merewether, an ecumenical relationship that encompassed two wedding ceremonies, one at St James' for the groom's Protestant faith and the other at St Mary's Roman Catholic chapel beside Hyde Park.[19]

Plunkett was also accompanied to the colony by a priest, Father John McEncroe, who was at the dock at the Cobh of Cork seeking to console prisoners who were about to be transported. Having already spent time in America, McEncroe was keen to go to New South Wales but had not yet received permission from the British government. He and Plunkett had met previously through shared enthusiasm for Catholic emancipation. When Plunkett's clerk providentially decided not to travel, it was easy for the young lawyer to agree to Father McEncroe's request to take his place. They sailed without official permission. Plunkett's letter to the Colonial

Office informing them of what he had done was despatched in January. Despite what must have been a tense delay for the two conspirators, the *Southworth* left unimpeded with Father McEncroe on board.[20] Many years later, the *Sydney Herald* entertained its readers by recalling Plunkett at the time he arrived as 'a slashing Irishman, as fine a young chap as ever set foot on these shores, and full of the wildest opinions of what were the rights of people'.[21] Well, that was the *Herald*'s point of view. According to Plunkett's biographer, 'Catholic Emancipation was the single most significant event in Plunkett's life. Not only did it make his subsequent career possible but the campaign which led up to it inculcated values and methods that he carried with him throughout his life . . . the fundamental principle of the Catholic Association—civil rights through just law was to be the touchstone of his career.[22]

The age difference between Plunkett and Daniel O'Connell was bridged by Plunkett's friendship with his son. There was no such conduit to Richard Bourke. Plunkett would have been well disposed towards him by reputation, however, and when they met in the colony Bourke liked the younger man. Plunkett and Marie Charlotte soon became regular visitors for weekends at Government House in Parramatta which would have been enlivened by her skill as a pianist as well as Plunkett's talent as a violinist and his love of Irish folk music.[23] Throughout Bourke's governorship, the two men worked increasingly together to implement shared goals symbolised most of all by changes Bourke proposed and Plunkett sought to implement for equality of religion and non-denominational education in the colony. Not long after he arrived, Bourke, who was a Protestant, wrote to Roger Therry, a Catholic, that 'I have set my heart on laying a good foundation whilst I am in office. I dread much even in this reforming age, the blighting influence of religious intolerance.'[24] Plunkett agreed. He knew first hand what it was like to be a Catholic under a Protestant ascendancy. As an active member of the Catholic Association he would have applauded when it unanimously passed a resolution consisting of five principles, the first of which announced forthrightly, 'The State should have no established religion. It should preserve neutrality between them all.'[25] On this subject Bourke and Plunkett were kindred spirits. Twenty years later, soliciting popular votes in the heat of an election campaign, Plunkett publicly described himself as 'the confidential and bosom friend of Sir Richard Bourke'.[26]

In 1835 Plunkett assisted Bourke in his attempt to set standards for the magistracy by publishing *The Australian Magistrate*, which set out principles of practice for the jurisdiction. It played an important role in standardising the administration of justice at a local level.[27] Another early task was to implement a decision authorised in Bourke's final discussions before leaving London, that trial by jury should be extended more widely and civil juries should replace the military ones which had predominated since 1788. In a turn-up for the many former criminals in the community, emancipists would henceforth be entitled to sit on juries. Plunkett drafted the new legislation which Bourke submitted to the Legislative Council in 1833. There had been no opposition from the judiciary but some councillors were fiercely opposed and Bourke had to exercise his casting vote. Even then, the bill only survived by an amendment that allowed military juries to be used if the defendant chose.[28]

John Kinchela was still attorney-general when Plunkett arrived but age—and deafness—had caught up with him. Combined with the absence of crown solicitor, William Henry Moore, who had been sacked for 'fecklessness and incompetence', this meant the colonial government's law office was a mess. Bourke wanted to promote Plunkett to attorney-general immediately, but slow communications delayed this appointment for four years. Meanwhile Plunkett, in effect, carried the workload of both solicitor-general and attorney-general and, by default, of crown prosecutor too.[29] Soon after his arrival, Plunkett's multitasking responsibilities created a heartrending clash of duty, principle and personal feeling when he was obliged to prosecute one of his own servants for murder. The accused, Bryant Kyne, who had been a magistrate in Ireland before being transported, was well liked by both Plunkett and Marie Charlotte. But feelings had to be set aside when, late on Boxing Day 1833, Kyne who was Plunkett's overseer killed another servant and, for lack of anyone else, Plunkett had to act as the Crown's prosecutor. He played his role all too well. Despite pleading 'not guilty', Kyne was convicted. Three days later Plunkett, who was opposed to capital punishment, had to stand by while he was hanged.[30]

As attorney-general, Plunkett would have advised on the case of George Comerford, a former soldier who was transported on the *Hive*. Comerford was one of two court-martialled soldiers embarked at the last minute. Twenty-two years old, he was a private in the 29th Regiment who had been convicted in Cork of desertion, but in circumstances so slight that the sentencing panel described it as 'not deserving of capital punishment nor of corporal punishment'. Instead they sentenced him to seven years transportation, which they thought was doing him a favour.[31]

In New South Wales this apparently inoffensive young man was convicted of a series of horrific murders. Assigned on arrival to Ambrose Wilson at Penrith, he absconded from there after six months. For the next year he was incredibly successful at passing himself off as a native of the colony named William Cooper. Employed under that name by a Mr Ebden, he was sent to Port Phillip as a shepherd. In May 1837 he absconded from Mr Ebden's Port Phillip station with two assigned servants named Dignum and Smith. The trio soon joined up with other assigned convicts but as they headed towards Portland Bay, one of the group called 'the Shoemaker' told Dignum and Comerford that the others intended to murder them. At this, Dignum, Smith and Comerford reversed the plan. According to Comerford, Dignum and Smith killed four men with an axe as they slept beside the camp fire. Two others, who woke up, were shot. The trio then burned the bodies in a gigantic fire. Two nights later, Comerford woke to see Dignum murdering the Shoemaker as he slept. When he realised Dignum was priming a pistol to shoot him he ran for miles to the police magistrate at Yass, where he confessed. He was despatched to Sydney where the authorities at first doubted his story. Finally, he was sent back to Melbourne and under instructions took two constables to the sites of the murders and the fire where he proved his story to their satisfaction. Not long after, when one of the constables was distracted, Comerford suddenly grabbed his musket and shot him. It was this death for which he hanged.

At the Sydney gaol, a grave was prepared for Comerford in the north-west corner of the yard. On the day of his execution many invited spectators were in the yard and big crowds gathered on the hill behind, which overlooked it. The press were also there, the *Monitor* reporting that Comerford 'walked firmly and his countenance exhibited not the slightest tremor'. Slender and fair, with a mild, intelligent face, some bystanders were so taken aback with his appearance they were heard to exclaim, 'Can that man be a murderer?' *The Australian* reported that 'he was a well-favoured young man who behaved with becoming modesty and apparent piety'. Indeed when he appeared in court for sentencing, Comerford had told the chief justice after he sentenced him to death that 'I offer up my life to God for the crimes I have committed.' Recalling this, *The Australian* commented that he 'appeared to have entirely changed his nature and to be visited with compunction'.[32]

According to Edward Smith Hall, a Christian of the Anglican faith, the dignity with which Comerford faced death was not unusual. Many years later he wrote, 'I have attended many of these men in the condemned cell, when their career was at an end and they knew that they must die . . . their fortitude on being led out to execution and under the fatal beam has often excited my admiration. I felt that I could not have died so well . . . if I have no doubts for my own salvation, I certainly had none for that of many of these extraordinary men.'[33]

Comerford of course was a Catholic. After spending many hours in prayer with him, it was Father McEncroe who was beside him as he mounted the scaffold. The priest was fulfilling the mission for which he had come to the colony—to bring comfort as well as repentance to prisoners—but whether he foresaw the demands it would make on him is doubtful. By all reports he was already an alcoholic. His colleague Father William Ullathorne described him as being from time to time 'overcast with a terrible melancholy, accompanied by a great internal heat and peculiar twitching of the corners of the mouth; and then came an intense longing for a drink on this really otherwise very sober man. If then I took his shoes and his hat and locked his door to save him from sallying forth, he so far lost his senses as to get out of the window as he was and cross the park to some Catholic house [usually Plunkett's], where he would implore the people for the love of God to put the light wine used in the country down his throat.'[34]

Despite instigating much of the bloodbath Joseph, aka John Dignum, escaped conviction for the murders. Comerford's early confession and guilty plea meant he was an attainted felon whose evidence against Dignum could not be used. However, Dignum was convicted of highway robbery shortly after and transported to Norfolk Island for life with the comment 'not to be returned'.[35]

Henry Lugard was still in Sydney when Comerford was executed. He would have known him well from the ship where, as court-martialled soldiers rather than criminals, Comerford and Edward Robinson would have helped in some minor way to manage the prisoners, even if it was only to act as mess captains. As Comerford went to the scaffold, Lugard would have had his own view on who was the real villain and who the follower. He and his friend, Ensign Abel Best, were already on Norfolk

Island when Dignum arrived there in October 1838. Ensign Best shared the community's fascinated horror, referring in his journal to 'the notorious Comerford' and noting every detail of the murders he and Dignum had committed and the fact that Dignum had escaped execution. When Dignum absconded from the island's settlement, the young ensign was merciless. 'I expect that he will kill some one if they try to take him and if I were Commandant I should seize this opportunity to rid the world of such a Monster for I would send a Sergeant and six, with orders to shoot him like a dog or Wolf when told where he might be found.' He was relieved when a week later, Henry Lugard told him Dignum had been recaptured. The man had offered no resistance when he was discovered, only begged that they would not hurt him. He blamed other prisoners for his escape, claiming they spread a story that he ate his Port Phillip victims and they nicknamed him 'the Cannibal'.[36] Despite his bloody trail, Dignum escaped lightly. A decade after Comerford's execution, Dignum received a conditional pardon.[37]

Back on the mainland, Lugard's shipmates had been distributed across the colony. By 1836 it was official policy to send them to remote areas, removed from sight, away from the temptations of Sydney. Only a few men from the *Hive* were assigned in Sydney, or to other districts on the Cumberland Plain such as Parramatta or Penrith. Most were sent up or down the coast, or west over the Blue Mountains where settlement was expanding further out from the initial township of Bathurst. Within months of the *Hive*'s arrival, prospects for further European settlement in the far south-west beyond Goulburn were being investigated by Major Thomas Mitchell, whose journey to the mouth of the River Glenelg and across to Portland Bay in present-day Victoria created new and dazzling colonial horizons. They would act as a magnet drawing men and masters further into the interior. The Hunter Valley had been the fertile drawcard for settlement during the 1820s. In the thirties, it was displaced by the vast pastures which Mitchell dubbed 'Australia Felix'.

CHAPTER 5
A Question of Fairness

Over 60 of the Irishmen from the *Hive* were assigned to the Hunter Valley. Of those, fifteen went to the Paterson area, another five to the upper reaches at Cassilis and Merton and Dartbrook while the rest were scattered in the centre around Patrick's Plains and Maitland. They may be forgiven for thinking when they first arrived that the egalitarian Sydney culture was a mirage. The social structure that greeted their eyes in the Hunter more nearly resembled Ireland with its Protestant landowners in control of large estates and building mansions to match them. Also obvious was another characteristic from home: prejudice.

'The good folk of the Hunter have a great aversion to the Irish. Indeed many will not have an Irish servant at all,' explained magistrate George Brooks when asking the colonial secretary to assign more women prisoners to the Hunter but only from an *English* ship.[1] The Hunter gentry were not alone in this regard. Brothers Gregory and John Blaxland, who had arrived as early as 1806, felt the same and so did Dr Robert Townson who 'disparaged the Irish convicts he received and insisted Englishmen only be sent in future'.[2] Sometimes lack of skills rather than ethnicity created prejudice against the Irish. For example, in the late 1820s the superintendent of the Australian Agricultural Company referred to 'the little they can do' although acknowledging they 'performed with willingness and their conduct has been orderly and respectful'. However, he was equally critical when another batch of prisoners arrived which 'consisted chiefly of boys from 15 to 18 years of age'.[3]

Sometimes such prejudice was explicitly sectarian. Before 1835, there were no Catholic priests based anywhere in the Hunter Valley, nor for that matter any Presbyterian or Church of England ministers except for the Reverend Middleton in Newcastle. Most services were conducted by employers, from the Church of England Prayer Book. When Catholic priest Father Therry visited the Hunter in 1827 Irish convicts complained to him that they were being flogged if they refused to attend. When called to account by Therry, magistrate James Webber explained that he had been trying to stop it occurring. To the envy of Protestant prisoners, who were also flogged if they refused to attend but had no excuse, Webber declared Catholics exempt from attending Protestant divine service.[4]

Religious services conducted by their masters provided an opportunity for protest which some prisoners took, knowing full well they could reduce the employer to helpless fury. Alan Atkinson found an example of John Mullens, presumably a Catholic from his surname, who refused to utter the responses during Sunday prayers. Furthermore, his master claimed to the bench that Mullens had 'scowled at him' and 'his looks and manner were more aggravating than if he had made use of the worst language'. Fortunately the magistrate Henry Antill, who had been Governor Macquarie's aide, ruled that 'the men need not respond [in prayers] unless they think proper.' When the master tried to substitute a second charge of insolence he refused to hear it.[5]

Protestant convicts protested at in-house divine service just as skilfully as Catholics. Robert Howcroft, for example, was a Yorkshire errand boy who had been convicted of stealing books at the age of thirteen. In New South Wales he worked for solicitor George Allen, who was a devout Methodist. The battle of wills that developed between servant and master began one Sunday when Allen sent the boy to the watch-house for refusing to attend prayers. It was aggravated when he sent Robert a second time for drunkenness. In the following months, Robert protested mutely, but in a way calculated to distress his master intensely. Deeply upset but missing the point entirely, Allen confided to his diary, '[He] makes a point of going to sleep every time we have service. I have spoken to him over and over again. Where it will end I know not but it is really awful to see such depravity in a mere child. If he could not help it, it would be different but to see the lad compose himself to sleep as soon as the sermon or prayer be commenced is really *awful*.'[6]

Reading prayers to your own household was an increasing practice in Britain as evangelical Christianity became more widespread. Reading prayers to a large, coerced workforce, some of whom were Catholics, was quite another matter and not a ritual that many of the free settlers had encountered on either scale or composition. Nor for that matter had many of them been pastoralists on the scale they became in New South Wales. Being appointed an honorary magistrate, a role occupied at home by the aristocracy and its relatives, was the ultimate accolade. As we have seen, the new settlers aspired to the status that all these obligations conferred.

James Webber, along with Newcastle magistrate Alexander Scott and his brothers Helenus and Robert, were among an influx of gentry settlers in the 1820s who were attracted by Commissioner Bigge's recommendation that they be given land grants and convict labour proportionate to the funds they brought to develop their property. They had a choice of locations and many chose sites in the Hunter Valley for which Newcastle was the coastal port, with a short steamer ride from there to the highest river port of Morpeth. Being a contrary Scot, Alexander Berry went south. 'Everyone,' he wrote, 'was flocking to the Hunter River, Bathurst and other places, where there was already a settlement and all were elbowing one another.'[7] But Berry was unusual. Rather than venture much further into the wilderness, many of the gentry who arrived in the twenties settled along the Paterson and Williams rivers, gradually extending into the foothills of the Chichester Range where the towns of Gresford and Dungog developed. Traditionally, the area was part of the lands of the Gringai clan of the Wonnarua tribe. The river itself was named by its indigenous owners as Windang, meaning plentiful and abundant. Attracted by the many cedar trees along its banks, Europeans had been active there from soon after their arrival and convict gangs were deployed to cut the cedar and float its logs down river. In 1811 Governor Macquarie authorised small land grants to emancipist farmers on the lower Paterson and they became the earliest white settlers in the area.[8]

By comparison with the newcomers, some of the older settler families with names like Blaxland and Cox and Bell were now into their second Australian generation. They were not at all daunted by the bush. When the Hunter Valley first opened for free settlement in the twenties they quickly obtained pastoral grants in its far reaches, additional to those they already held nearer Sydney. As we shall see, many of the native born of humbler origin did the same in the south-west. Equally keen to maximise their landholdings, the newer arrivals in the Hunter soon followed the locals seeking extra acreage.

The 1820s were rich pickings for those with the enterprise to emigrate but by the 1830s land from the Crown was only obtainable by purchase and within Governor Darling's limits of settlement known as the Nineteen Counties. Beyond those boundaries, unauthorised squatting was becoming an increasing problem. Richard Bourke had encountered a similar issue when he was governor of Cape Town. His time in South Africa had taught him that raising stock in a dry climate required large tracts of land well beyond the size considered sufficient in Britain or Ireland. A year after he arrived in New South Wales, he wrote to Thomas Spring Rice with a touch of sarcasm: 'Sheep must wander or they will not thrive, and the colonists must have sheep or they will not continue to be wealthy.' Nor, however, did he want rights of possession displacing rights of the Crown. Legislation was passed and commissioners appointed to supervise the process. They were followed by the Crown Lands Occupation Act which became law in 1836 and provided for annual occupation licences on unsurveyed runs beyond the Nineteen Counties.[9] Bourke envisaged the establishment of towns in regional areas to ensure that law and order accompanied the dispersal of stock and people but in 1834 the British government rejected the idea including his proposal for the development of Twofold Bay as a township.[10]

Whatever the means of acquisition, gentry settlers who arrived in the twenties soon joined the older families in obsessively buying, leasing and selling land to one another if they could not get it from government. These activities also meant that convicts assigned to one master by government could find themselves swapped to another as part of a land deal. Sold as an asset in fact.[11]

If prisoners, themselves, wanted to relocate, they needed to change masters. Women convicts were still changing their situation frequently in the 1830s, usually by convincing their master they were useless. It was harder for the men. Employers increasingly hung on to their assigned men whatever the provocation. They knew transportation to New South Wales would soon end, and with it would go the supply of free labour.

Increasingly they watched the convict assignment lists with a jealous eye. 'It is extremely galling to see others getting assigned servants and carrying on their business at half the expense of many others as well as myself,' wrote Richard Scougall, who despite his claims of having followed necessary procedures appears to have realised suddenly in 1840 that his labour force was evaporating without likelihood of replacement.[12]

Some masters congratulated themselves for having arrived just in time. Arthur Wray wrote to his brother, 'It was a most fortunate thing for me that I came out at the time I did. One month later and I should not have got convicts, in which case I must have looked out for a situation, or have been ruined in attempting to settle up the country with free servants at most exorbitant wages.'[13] In this climate assigned servants were too precious to let go easily; at most, employers would swap individuals in order to get someone with the skills they required. Or lend them to bring in a harvest or do some trade work such as carpentry. Some employers did ask the authorities first, particularly after Governor Bourke tightened regulations concerning assignment. Among Bourke's changes, an employer had to obtain permission from the local magistrate in order to borrow, or swap, a servant, who in turn should inform the superintendent of convicts. Nevertheless, unofficial swaps continued to take place, generally without disturbance unless some issue brought them under notice of the authorities in Sydney. If this occurred, it was usually because one of the men complained about his treatment or his food. Then an investigation could result in convicts being taken away and reassigned elsewhere, leaving their master lamenting the hardship inflicted on him.

New South Wales might have been an open-air gaol but food was a constant preoccupation for prisoners all over the colony, and always had been. Sufficient food. Its quality. Freshness. Variety. Food as a symbol of fairness. Food as payment for work done. In this, Australia's convicts were no different from today's prisoners institutionalised behind high walls for whom food is the number one topic.[14] Alan Atkinson's examination of convict protest was based on colonial bench books where he found that complaints about rations were rare, due, he concluded, to fear of punishment. However, other sources demonstrate that complaints about food were frequent and widespread, often involving collective action. Erin Ihde found many recorded in the pages of the *Monitor*. The colonial secretary correspondence is also a rich source.[15] The fundamental role of food in keeping the peace in the penal colony was described by a convict in the final years of transportation. Writing in the 1860s he said 'many of the evils of the system are hardly perceived [by the prisoners], even though insensibly irritated by them. The one great thing with these is to have free intercourse with each other, and so long as they have this, *and can get enough to eat and obtain an occasional chew of tobacco*, other annoyances, even while they irritate, do not trouble them greatly' (emphasis added).[16]

Long-time settlers in New South Wales well understood the importance of food in managing their workforce. Over the years, a system of rewards and punishment had developed involving food. For approximately 30 years, convicts were paid wages with which they could buy some 'luxuries' such as sugar and tobacco—or have the cost deducted at the master's store in the case of rural areas.[17] When wages were officially ended in 1823, prisoners became more dependent on the goodwill of their master. Even so, some masters found it easier to continue paying wages, particularly to old hands who had been around before the change. And the wise master, like Alexander Berry, ensured that items like sugar, tea and tobacco were still supplied even though they were not part of the official government ration. Unless a man misbehaved, he could expect to receive them regularly from Berry, who recalled in his *Reminiscences*, 'We managed our convicts chiefly by moral influence as we had no police. Occasionally we had troubles with incorrigibles, but these were the exceptions.' Rations were deployed as a form of control, as Berry explained: 'There was a stated Government ration which settlers were obliged to give to their convicts, consisting of beef or pork and flour. We increased these rations, and in addition gave tea, sugar and tobacco to all our well behaved servants . . . When they misbehaved or became contumacious, we put them on Government rations.'[18] For a while after wages ended in 1823 precise details of the rations to be given to convicts were dispensed with. Instead, masters were required to supply 'an adequate ration'. Adequacy being left to the eye of the beholder created so many problems that in 1831 Governor Darling returned to a regulated ration which stipulated quantities of wheat or flour, of meat, salt and soap. Tea, sugar and tobacco were again categorised as privileges. Surveyor-general Sir Thomas Mitchell, who understood the importance of rations to his workers' motivation, challenged the Commissariat for providing only the government ration to men in his exploration team. On his insistence, sugar, tea and tobacco were supplied as well.[19]

All this was just the official position. The prisoners had their own view. To them, the so-called 'privileges' were entitlements and they would strike against the master who withheld them. In 1821, an assigned servant was harshly sentenced for 'inciting his Masters' servants to combine for the purpose of obliging him to raise the wages and increase their rations'.[20] The seeds of embryonic unionism can also be seen in the use of the term 'delegate' to describe the man appointed by his prisoner peers to oversee the apportionment of rations on their behalf.[21] To the prisoners their treatment was a question of fairness. A wise employer would have done well to heed advice from the wandering mechanic, Alexander Harris, who warned, 'There is among working men, a strong and ineradicable and very correct sense of what is fair. Unless you act fairly to them, they will assuredly endeavour to right themselves. The sense of the risk they encounter in so doing embitters them against you; and instead of being surrounded by faithful servants, you are in the midst of enemies.'[22] As Harris predicted, some men felt so strongly on the issue they would risk punishment by appealing for justice from the magistrates. Thomas Coleman's master took him to the bench on a complaint of insolence but his testimony reveals the strong sense of grievance and entitlement that the prisoners felt about food. He told the bench 'on account of the prisoner idling away his time . . . [I] ordered his tea and sugar to be stopped for that week. He remonstrated a good deal and insisted that he had as much right to it as anyone else, and when . . . [I] pointed out to him that it was entirely a matter of favour (and not of right) his receiving it at all, he was very impertinent.'[23]

In the Illawarra, convicts on the estate of James Spearing brought work to a standstill over rations. In a pattern that is becoming familiar to researchers, they had quickly got the measure of their recently arrived master. On the first Christmas day at his property, *Paulsgrove*, in what Spearing called 'a state of mutiny' but unionists today would call 'walking off the job', the men left the farm 'in a body with singing and other demonstrations of joy' because he would not increase their wheat ration. Incapable of dealing with this behaviour himself, Spearing turned to authority, but the reaction of magistrate Fitzgerald confirms this kind of power play was common. He declined to act immediately because Spearing's complaint 'was of an ordinary nature between the settlers and their men'.[24] At *Tocal* in the Hunter Valley in 1829 the men also struck, refusing to work in the middle of the harvest until additional sugar or milk was provided in accordance with longstanding tradition at harvest time.[25]

Before 1819, both government and landholders operated a system of rewards and punishments as a management tool but its novelty and effectiveness apparently declined. After 1820, the prisoners regarded items classified as rewards as their entitlement. When John Macarthur returned to the colony in 1819 after a long absence he noticed the change in attitude: 'The Convicts are certainly more difficult to manage; they are less respectful; and now claim many of those indulgences, as a Matter of right, which they used to receive thankfully as the reward of merit.'[26] By the thirties the role of rations had advanced to a new level. For all the official rhetoric, the terms of the rewards were now being dictated by the prisoners.

Shortage of food had an unexpected effect on the prisoners. Contrary to assumptions that it would create dog-eat-dog competition, shortage of rations taught the convicts to share and to do so equally without distinction. In the thirties, Martin Cash, who was later a notorious bushranger, described the men's entrenched ethos of fairness and equality: 'At Captain Pike's farm I have seen the rations of meat for forty men weighed off in the lump, which had afterwards to be divided into individual shares by the men themselves . . . Some of them by this process could not possibly receive the authorised complement of 7 lbs for their week's allowance . . . among Captain Pike's servants were to be found men of all trades: blacksmiths, shipwrights, carpenters, wheelwrights, all of whom shared alike . . . I believe it to be a fair representation of nearly all others throughout the colony.'[27] Cash was right. It was not an isolated case. For example, hundreds of miles to the south-west, five men shared freezing conditions on a mountaintop reconnoitre with surveyor-general Mitchell. Forced by weather to stay out overnight, they carefully divided the remaining rations of one of them into five equal, if tiny, portions.[28]

Among the men from the *Hive* in the Hunter was Maurice Leehy, who took the rap for the massacre at Ballyeagh. He was assigned to James Adair who had arrived in the colony in 1827 following the death of his brother George. Adair inherited the 1600 acres on the Paterson that had been granted to George but he was also granted 1280 acres in his own right which adjoined his brother's property. The two estates employed approximately ten convicts courtesy of government assignment.[29] Leehy was in his late thirties when he joined them. With a sentence of transportation for life, he would not have expected to see his wife, three sons and two daughters again. Desperate to avoid being sent away, he led a violent gaolbreak at Limerick six weeks after his trial, but once in the penal colony he appears to have resigned himself to a new life. He was still with Adair in 1844 when he received a ticket-of-leave to which, as a lifer, he was entitled after eight years.[30] His eventual fate can only be surmised. He appears in official documents as Maurice Leehy but newspapers covering the Ballyeagh massacre, the inquest and subsequent trials, variously reported that a Maurice Leehy of Drummartin had been killed in the riot and the man convicted for taking part in the slaughter was Thomas Leehy. At other times they said it was Maurice Leehy who was convicted. In 1853, a young couple named Thomas and Mary Leehy arrived in Newcastle as free immigrants. Two years earlier, Maurice Leehy of West Maitland who had left five children behind him in County Kerry, had sent £12 to Thomas Leehy of Listowel, County Kerry, by way of the remittance scheme that allowed friends and relatives of immigrants to help them defray costs of preparing and clothing themselves for the voyage. The pair settled on a farm near Maitland and named their first son Maurice.[31] As noted earlier, it was a familiar pattern for adult children (or nephews) of convicts to join them later as free settlers.[32]

By the mid-thirties, relatives were usually separated when they first arrived. Brothers Philip and Michael Ryan were assigned to different ends of the colony, Philip went 150 miles south-west of Sydney to work for Jasper Junn in the district called Inverary, Michael to Robert Coram Dillon at Paterson. Michael's master had arrived in the colony as long ago as 1821 when he was 30 years old. By 1836 his business combined commerce with agriculture. Having established a farm on his original grant at Hinton, he started another enterprise in partnership with settler John Bingle, the same who had unwittingly hastened Governor Bourke's legislation to curb the magistrates. The two settlers obtained permission to establish a boatbuilding business in Newcastle and a regular shipping service to Sydney. The land on which the building stood, plus 400 bricks and 60 bushels of lime, was supplied by the government free of charge.[33]

Michael Ryan's experience as an agricultural labourer meant he was sent to work on Dillon's farm at Hinton. Two years later, in 1838, he suddenly absconded but no records survive to reveal why. Unlike other estates further up the Paterson and Williams rivers, Hinton was within easy reach of Maitland, even for a prisoner. Perhaps Ryan was seeking a government official from whom he could get word of his brother. The two made contact during their servitude and were eventually reunited. In August–September 1844 each had his ticket-of-leave altered from their original district to Maitland. Five years later they collected their conditional pardons together.[34] Just like in Ireland, the Ryans had—or soon made—money. Neither man ever married. They settled in the Maitland district, with Michael taking up the leasehold of a farm at Swan Reach, Hinton, from where he ran cattle and other livestock. He died suddenly in 1859 of a liver complaint which was inexplicably distorted by local folklore into death by drowning. Possibly details of the two brothers became muddled. Five years later, while visiting Newcastle to see the doctor, Philip went for a swim on the beach below the hospital. At that time he was described as 'a respectable settler', well known in the town from his habit of wearing a broad-brimmed hat with a black band and a heavy, rough coat. He was paddling on the water's edge, pouring water on his head, when a large wave knocked him over then swept him out to sea. A Mr Little of the Australian Joint Stock Bank who was swimming nearby nearly lost his own life trying to rescue him. Later a sailor who was watching from on shore recovered Philip Ryan's body. The inquest revealed he had £180 in his pockets, an estate which would have been left to relatives who had emigrated from Ireland.[35]

Thirty-seven-year-old Paddy Cavenagh was also separated from his relatives in the colony. His actions during assignment suggest he was trying desperately to find out what happened to his elder sister Catherine Byrne and her son James who were caught with him in Ireland, along with James' friend John Tuohy. Armed with a pistol, a scythe blade and a pitchfork, they robbed a house near Tullaroan in County Kilkenny. The Byrne/Cavenagh family and its associates may have been working as a gang for some years because this robbery was not their only offence. A constable from Tipperary testified that he had caught James Byrne in another robbery in Nenagh and when asked why he was there, James had replied, 'I came with my uncle, Paddy Cavenagh.' A second Tipperary policeman gave evidence that he had caught Cavenagh in yet another house on the same night. In pronouncing sentence, the judge commented that he recognised Cavenagh as 'an old offender' and referred to a case in Tipperary where two men were hanged on Paddy Cavenagh's evidence.[36] Catherine was transported on the *Thomas Harrison* in 1836, a year after the three men sailed on the *Hive*. As noted earlier, there may have been another family member on board with them. The *Hive*'s crew of young boys included one listed as G. Cavenagh.[37]

Paddy Cavenagh never settled in assignment as so many of his shipmates did. Time and again he absconded from his master Crawford Logan Brown.[38] A sandy-haired man with a swarthy complexion and grey eyes, his height of six feet made him readily identifiable and he was always caught. It is possible he was being ill-treated but tracking individual convicts often reveals that they absconded or in other ways misbehaved for a personal reason that was never publicly revealed, admitted or even suspected, by the authorities. Paddy Cavenagh first ran from his master in December 1836, perhaps driven by the approach of Christmas to find at least one of the family.[39] Even so, Cavenagh's reasons for running are ambiguous because Logan Brown was a master who had what he saw as 'bad luck' with his assigned servants.

In 1838 Logan Brown, whose farm was on the Upper Williams River beyond Paterson, wrote to the Colonial Secretary asking for replacement convicts to be assigned to him as a matter of urgency. Describing himself as the proprietor of 4464½ acres, he explained that he was in great economic distress because his convict labour force was so reduced. 'So many work in irons or are at large.' In other words, he had them punished or they had absconded from his service. Only ten remained from at least twenty men who had been allocated to Mr Brown, who took no personal responsibility for this situation. On the contrary he saw himself as very hard done by. 'In August last, I was assigned a stonemason who was accidentally killed while sinking a well,' he wrote. 'In the same month, two men absconded, one of whom is still at large, the other is in an Iron gang for 12 months which means it will be 7 September next year before he returns.' He continued to list his misfortunes: 'On October 2nd two more men absconded. In April 1838, one more then, in June, another man hurt his head.' Governor Gipps formed his own view of the sorry tale. He declined to intervene in Logan Brown's favour and wrote on the file 'So many accidents and many offences for one Establishment would seem to form *prima facie* evidence of mismanagement.'[40]

The men who absconded together in August 1837 were Thomas Fry and Paddy Cavenagh. When Logan Brown sent his memorial to the colonial secretary, Cavenagh was still at large, but Thomas Fry had already been ordered to an iron gang. Nearly ten years later, in January 1846, when Logan Brown was himself sitting as a magistrate of Maitland

Quarter Sessions, Fry who was still his assigned servant pleaded guilty to assaulting him and was sentenced to two years in an iron gang.[41] While the impetus for Cavenagh to run away may have been prospects of a family reunion, it seems certain that conditions on the Logan Brown farm were unpleasant and unfair.

Like the Ryan brothers, Cavenagh's family were widely scattered when they first arrived. Young James Byrne was sent south-west to the newly developing area of Yass. Catherine Byrne who told the authorities she was capable of 'all work' was assigned to domestic service in Sydney. It seems that they were never reunited. Neither Paddy nor his sister were young when they were transported. Catherine was already 50 years of age. Ten years later, in 1846, she was ailing badly and her then master, the baker James Marks of Sydney, wrote to the colonial secretary to ask if she could be placed in the lunatic asylum.[42] Paddy Cavenagh was 37 when he sailed on the *Hive*. After each escape, he was returned to his master until finally, eight years later, he was entitled to a ticket-of-leave. It was issued in May 1845 for the district of Dungog where he had been in assigned service. Whether the familiar environment worked against him is hard to tell, but in August 1846 his ticket was cancelled on the grounds that he was 'unable to support himself'.[43] The cancellation occurred within weeks of Catherine's admission to the asylum but it is unlikely that the brother and sister, neither of whom was literate, ever knew what happened to each other. What became of a boy called Cavenagh who was among the crew of the *Hive* only his descendants can tell us.

By the mid-thirties some of the large estates in New South Wales had changed hands. Motives varied. Severe drought in the late twenties affected all landholders, some to the point of bankruptcy. Others came to the colony always intending to get rich, then get out. Explorer Ludwig Leichhardt was taken aback by the wives of those who always intended to leave. When he asked the women why they did not establish vegetable gardens, most replied that the effort would not be worthwhile because they expected to be returning to England in a short time.[44] Ambivalence about living in a notorious penal settlement also influenced people's decision to leave. It is a measure of the inducements of land and labour that free settlers came anyway but, knowing what the audience at home thought of their choice, they refrained from identifying with their new land. Nostalgia for Britain was accentuated by feeling displaced in a disreputable, perhaps evil location which would infect you with its 'taint'. Among those who left, for example, was William Panton, a free settler near Camden, who wrote deprecatingly of 'this land of convicts and kangaroos' before returning home after ten years farming in the colony.[45] On the Paterson James Webber farmed *Tocal* for ten years, then left the colony to live in Italy. Gentry settlers like these took with them what might have been a middle-class layer in colonial society. Their decision to leave contributed to a social 'hollowing out' that had later ramifications.[46]

The departure of settlers like Webber could, however, provide opportunity for others. When Andrew Liddy, a prisoner from the *Hive*, was assigned at *Tocal* in 1836 it had changed hands. The new owners, Caleb Wilson and his son Felix, were of humble origin. In fact they were people a convict could aspire to emulate. From much the same socioeconomic group as the prisoners, Caleb Wilson came to the colony as a free emigrant in the early days of settlement when his skills as a tailor were in great demand. He established himself via a 100 acre grant at Richmond and a hardware shop in George Street which he and his son developed into a lucrative business. An urban man at heart, Caleb lived in his comfortable mansion at Potts Point in Sydney but Felix raised the family status to that of pastoralist by purchasing *Tocal* from Webber.[47]

At 40, Andrew Liddy was one of the older men on the *Hive*. Born in Belfast, he was also one of only sixteen Protestants among the 250 men. When he was convicted of stealing cloth he described himself as a 'brewer's labourer and soldier', the latter career probably explaining why he was literate and still single because both were characteristics of the British Army. With a dark, sallow complexion, Liddy was above average height for the period at 5 feet 7½ inches. Scars around his left ear and forehead and two on his right leg suggested he had been in military action at some stage. When he arrived in New South Wales he told the muster clerk that his brother James had been transported in 1819. Records suggest that James was in Melbourne by 1841 and it is possible the brothers were never reunited.[48]

Andrew Liddy's experience in a brewery would have been useful at *Tocal* because James Webber had been one of the pioneers of winemaking in the Hunter Valley. Only two years before Liddy arrived, the estate had been lavishly praised in *The Australian*.

Mr Webber's Grapery at the Hunter, the finest in that part of the Colony has produced an unusual crop of grapes this season of the Oporto description; this gentleman expects next season to produce no insignificant quantity of wine from his vineyard.[49]

Tobacco was also a major crop at *Tocal*. In May 1830, 40,000 pounds of it were grown on the estate, an output which required specialised skills and knowledge. These were supplied by three convicts who were assigned to Webber and were, as Brian Walsh points out in his history of *Tocal*, an excellent example of the adaptability of prisoners once they arrived in the penal colony. On the ships' indents, their occupations would have been shown as errand boy, brush-maker and rope-maker, yet all three developed new skills to become 'tobacconists' capable of handling what would have been to them a completely foreign crop. Coincidentally, all of them had been transported for housebreaking. Equally coincidentally, they were an ecumenical group. The fifteen-year-old errand boy named Daniel Callaghan was Irish, James Logan the brush-maker was a Scot aged twenty, and Richard Hughes aged 25 was English. Their efforts were guided by their master who must have studied up on a crop that was notoriously difficult both to grow and to process. Webber was also clever at marketing his produce. Samples of *Tocal* tobacco were distributed in influential quarters and, soon after, the colonial media were raving about its quality as they had about his wine. The *Sydney Gazette* assured its readers, 'We have tried Mr Webber's tobacco. It fully equals the best Colonial tobacco we have met with, and wants age alone to make it as pleasant as the Brazil.'[50]

The Wilsons' purchase of *Tocal* in 1834 did not mean they resided on the estate. Although Felix Wilson was frequently at Paterson, his residence remained in Sydney. On a daily basis, the property and its workforce were managed by an immigrant superintendent, supported by overseers who had themselves arrived as prisoners and who organised the workforce.[51] It was this team who made decisions about whether to grant a pass or support a ticket-of-leave, whether to return a man to government, or order him before the bench for punishment. Success or failure in managing a potentially recalcitrant workforce came back to their character and judgement. Unlike some estates, the only significant instance of violence at *Tocal* was a fight between two prisoners that left one of them dead. That the relationship of *Tocal*'s leaders and their men resembled that of a team is suggested by the marriage in 1841 of James Clements, a convict, to the superintendent's widow. Clements had been transported aged thirteen. He spent his entire sentence at *Tocal* and subsequently settled in the area.[52]

Andrew Liddy left *Tocal* and moved into Maitland when he received his ticket-of-leave in August 1840. The town was awash with pubs and very likely he returned to his Belfast occupation of 'brewer's labourer'. A year later his ticket was cancelled for 'disorderly conduct' which suggests drunkenness. The magistrate ordered him to the probationary gang at Parramatta, a recently developed punishment designed to warn new ticketholders that they should be careful of their behaviour because they were not free yet. The incident sobered Liddy. Six months later, in February 1842, his ticket was restored on the recommendation of Captain Marsh, assistant engineer, who was then supervising the work of the gang. Six months after that Andrew Liddy received his certificate of freedom and could, once again, control his own life.[53]

Despite prejudice against Irish prisoners, particularly the women, large numbers of them were assigned to the Hunter Valley. For example, *Tocal*'s historian, Brian Walsh, calculated that nearly 50 per cent of that estate's convicts were Irish with most of the others English, a handful of Scots and one man from Sweden.[54] Once free, Irish prisoners had the option of moving elsewhere in the colony to areas that were more welcoming to their countrymen. Instead, many chose to make their lives in the Hunter where, as we shall see, they expected to be treated equally.

Elections were always boisterous affairs in New South Wales, from the first democratic votes taken for the Sydney Municipal Council in November 1842. However, the declaration of the poll at Paterson for the first popularly elected Legislative Council in 1843 exploded into violence which bore a strong resemblance to a political riot in Ireland. Candidates for the area had narrowed down to three—William Ogilvie, a pastoralist from the Upper Hunter; Andrew Lang, who was a landholder on the Paterson; and Richard Windeyer, a Sydney-based barrister. Lang was a younger brother of Reverend John Dunmore Lang, who was intent on importing Protestant free settlers to counter the Catholics in New South Wales. Under his auspices, a large group of Presbyterians from Scotland, many of whom spoke only Gaelic, settled on a section of Andrew Lang's land.[55]

Governor Bourke had left the colony six years before this election was held but his influence on attitudes to religion and education could be detected in the remarks of the candidates. Despite his strong Presbyterian background, Andrew Lang told the electors of Durham, 'I am for entire religious liberty and no political distinctions on account of religion; considering the interests of morality and good government as likely to be best promoted by affording all religious denominations a fair field without favour to any.' A month later, Richard Windeyer matched him, soliciting support because 'I am a steadfast supporter of equality in civil and religious rights, an advocate for any general system of education which will leave parents of every sect to give their children such spiritual instruction as they may think proper . . .' Even the conservative pastoralist, William Ogilvie, said he 'was persuaded that religious freedom and liberty of conscience were essential to good government'.[56]

A large crowd gathered to hear the declaration of the poll on Saturday, 24 June 1843. Gentry, small settlers, emancipists and serving convicts mingled around a platform in front of the courthouse, where a running tally of votes was displayed. By 1 p.m. Richard Windeyer was well ahead. Lang's supporters, many of whom were Scottish, were disappointed. Brawls began to break out on the sidelines. Some of Windeyer's friends were assaulted and Lang's banner was paraded provocatively through their midst. Intent on celebrating the result, Windeyer led the way to the Paterson Hotel but a full-scale riot developed before they reached it. Windeyer himself just managed to enter and barely managed to resist attempts to haul him outside again. Stones were thrown, breaking the hotel windows. Doors were forced as the crowd became angry at being excluded from the pub. A convict named John McDonald who was assigned to Andrew Lang incited the rioters to continue whenever they flagged. Later, his master testified that McDonald had no permission to be there. He was rebuked for not sending his assigned servant home. Some time passed before the magistrate, Major Johnstone, restored order with the help of the chief constable and several policemen, who ejected people from the hotel. Only then, was it discovered that the landlord, a Mr Cook, was severely wounded and several others badly hurt. One man, a Mr Duncan McGilavry, died two days later from injuries received that day.[57]

Michael Kelly, who farmed under leasehold on John Eales' land at Hinton, was charged with McGilavry's murder. According to witnesses, he had used a long, thick stick which he swung at McGilavry's head twice, on the second occasion using both hands—very reminiscent of how the Irish used their hurling sticks, although this was not a comparison made in court. Pastoralist James Phillips saw the lethal blows and was among those who identified Kelly. 'I saw the deceased running away and the prisoner at the bar followed him with a large bludgeon . . . The prisoner was dressed in a frock coat and had on a round black beaver hat with a narrow brim.' Phillips thought Kelly was one of Lang's supporters. Others, including Felix Wilson, who owned both *Tocal* and the hotel, were carefully even-handed. He testified, 'Blows were struck by Mr Windeyer's friends as well as Mr Lang's.' He also described the injured landlord in the thick of the crowd, swinging the back of an old chair. Evidence that it was Kelly's blow which killed McGilavry was tenuous. In the light of character references from John Eales, Andrew Lang and James Robinson that he was an honest, sober and industrious man, the judge decided there were mitigating circumstances. He sentenced Kelly to prison for twelve months, the first week in every alternate month to be in solitary confinement.[58]

It may have been drink that fuelled the crowd. Or just excitement. But it smells also of sectarian rivalry. Kelly v. McGilavry? Catholic v. Presbyterian? At the trial, interpreters were required for witnesses who only spoke Gaelic. Nothing supports the assumption by some that these must all have been Scots from Andrew Lang's community. Irishmen were also numerous throughout the district, many of them Gaelic-speaking, and the template for this kind of violence in an election context was created in Ireland.

CHAPTER 6
Unnecessary Irritation

Martin Ryan was a fair boy with blue eyes, red hair and a temper to match. Assigned briefly in 1836 to William Faithful at Goulburn, by spring 1839 he was on his second employer and in a foul mood too. He had been flogged remorselessly for the previous six months and although the wounds had scarred over since his last 50 lashes in July, his back would have still been stiff and sore. When his master Isaac Shepherd told him to get to his work as a shepherd, his grievance welled up. 'Go to work or go before the Bench,' Shepherd ordered but Martin refused and stalked off to his hut. Shepherd made the mistake of following him inside, repeating angrily, 'Do your duty and get out to your sheep or you'll go before the Bench.' Enraged, Martin pulled a spring knife from his pocket and lunged at him yelling, 'I'll have your life.' He sounded so violent that Shepherd hastily left. 'In that infuriated state I was obliged to leave him,' was how he put it to the colonial secretary. But the morning's drama was not over yet. From within his hut, Martin continued shouting threats to kill his master while his workmates stood around outside, watching. When Shepherd asked them to intervene, they all refused. Finally, Tom Taylor, a convict who had been with Shepherd for eight years, volunteered to risk injury and get control of Martin. 'He was convinced that my life was in imminent danger,' wrote Shepherd. Only after Taylor entered the hut did the other men help subdue Martin, who tried to stab one of them too before he was hauled off to the lock-up.[1]

Shepherd was one of those pastoralists who lived in Sydney and only paid visits to their rural holdings, in his case to *Wheeo* near Goulburn. We don't know how long he had been there although the correspondence implies days rather than weeks. Shepherd himself was the son of two convicts, but if he had any sympathy for those under the constraints of servitude there was no sign of it in his treatment of his servant that morning. It's possible he didn't know that Martin had been flogged so often in the months beforehand. He was almost certainly unaware that the boy, who was only sixteen when he landed from the *Hive*, had been transported for a first offence of stealing sugar for which he was sentenced to seven years. Perhaps he assumed a higher degree of criminality had shaped Martin's character, an assumption fuelled by the volatile, reckless responses of an adolescent.

Martin Ryan's experience as a farmer's boy in Tipperary had not helped him adjust to the new land. He was probably sent first to William Faithful because he was so young and Faithful was a long-established settler whom the Assignment Board thought would induct the boy in a constructive way. However, the exact opposite occurred. Whether he was managed by Faithful himself or left to an overseer is unclear but in May 1836, less than six months after he arrived, Martin received 50 lashes for 'neglect of duty', double punishment for a first offence like this. In October he tried to run away again but was caught and received another 50 lashes for absconding. Two and a half years followed with no sign of him in the surviving records and we cannot be sure whether he received further punishments. It is likely he did, however, because he changed employer during this time, probably after absence through absconding again, followed by sentence to an iron gang.

In April 1839, with Martin now at Isaac Shepherd's station, another cascade of punishments began: on 1 April he received 50 lashes for being absent and drunk (probably visiting the local grog shanty). On 6 July he received another 50 lashes for disorderly conduct, and on 30 July another 50 for the same offence. By the time Mr Shepherd visited his property around 12 October, Martin was physically black and blue and emotionally boiling with bitter resentment. It's hardly surprising that he exploded with rage at his master. Later, he compounded this offence by trying to escape from the lock-up and was given another 50 lashes. Shortly after, the bench sentenced him to an iron gang that was constructing a cattle tank at Campbelltown.[2]

In the iron gang, Martin was flogged again for preparing to escape by 'ovalling' his irons so he could slip his feet out. As punishment he received 50 lashes and was put in double irons. Shortly after, when he was chided by one of the guards who testified that he 'observed [Ryan] idling away and told him to get on with his work', Martin reacted just as he had to Isaac Shepherd. Again enraged and in pain, and convinced that a man named White had betrayed him, he raised his pick to strike White, who was working beside him, yelling, 'You crawling bastard, I'll take your life, I'll murder you.' Warned by the shout of another prisoner, White shifted just as the pickaxe struck him, which saved his life. Martin was tried by the Supreme Court and found guilty of striking John White with intent to murder him. His sentence was execution. The judge told him, 'Your days are numbered. You should not expect any mitigation.' Nevertheless, the sentence was commuted to transportation to Norfolk Island for life.[3]

Were these clashes between Martin Ryan and his master Isaac Shepherd the rebellion some claim is missing from Australian history, the uprising the settlers feared? Hardly. Available evidence supports nothing so dramatic or romantic as rebellion. Poor management by a master faced with a smouldering teenager is a more accurate description. Many similar examples of personal clashes between master and man can be found in the convict records. The background of the prisoner is unimportant and so is their original crime. He—or sometimes she—is just as likely to have been Welsh or English as Irish. They could be a lifer who stole with violence, or a pickpocket.[4] Or occasionally, a woman. For example, a large female convict named Ann Walker was so annoyed by her master at his laundry business where she worked that she dunked his head in a bucket of water and strode off singing

> If I had a bean for a soldier who'd go,
> Do you think I'd refuse him, O' no, no, no!

Women could not be flogged so she was sent to the Female Factory for punishment.[5]

Men could be flogged, however, and the first resort of a poor master—or a poor overseer—was flogging. The jury is still out on whether being Irish meant you were at greater risk of the lash. Tim Causer's comprehensive study of men sent to Norfolk Island found Irish prisoners were only in proportion to their numbers on the mainland.[6] The men on Norfolk Island from the *Hive* amounted to thirteen, or roughly 5 per cent of the 250 men on board. Flogging is harder to estimate. Norfolk Island records often contain prisoners' New South Wales police history, which provides better information than any other source about the cumulative punishment that some male convicts experienced. They also reveal the persistent and escalating nature of the flogging, often over short intense periods, which says much about the vindictiveness of the people who ordered it. Analysing the NSW *Government Gazette* to extract men from the *Hive* who absconded and from that estimating floggings does not suggest that, as Irishmen, they were flogged more than convicts of other ethnicity. On the other hand, Sue Rosen's study of the Bathurst Road found more Irish than other prisoners were sent to hard labour on the road, some of them in irons, and these men would have been flogged before they got there.[7] A systematic study of all sources, including bench books, might get us closer to accuracy.

Meanwhile, we are left with anecdotal examples which are at least effective in helping us imagine the human cost. Somewhere between 20 and 26 per cent of the male prisoners in New South Wales and Van Diemen's Land were flogged but, as Hirst pointed out, all of them would have witnessed floggings. Some modern historiography has interpreted flogging as a feminising process. I would argue that such interpretation confuses the experience of the flogged with the observer. 'I heard awhile after the dull, heavy fall of the cat on the flesh . . . But there was no cry, no groan, no prayer for mercy. It was not long I listened. My heart began to beat chokingly and I got away from the legalised abomination as fast as I could.' Catie Gilchrist concluded that flogging 'reinforced the disciplinary hierarchy' but, once again, probably only in those at the top of the hierarchy.[8] More realistically, it can be argued that being flogged in front of your peers was the ultimate test of masculinity, which many prisoners passed by enduring it in silence. Such an achievement was also a form of defiance towards the authorities who ordered the flogging. 'I can bear it,' declared John Buckley, who had experienced the test several times. And visiting Norfolk Island, James Backhouse discovered that 'It is accounted a mark of bravery among them, to bear the punishment unmoved.' Nevertheless the relentless brutality inflicted on John Black, aged sixteen when he arrived, and John McVey, aged eighteen, says much about those who ordered the punishments. Neither young man had been flogged before. And both very likely reacted during a flogging like one of the men from the sample listed below.[9]

JOHN BLACK
CON 33/1/55 No. 14131
No punishment [i.e. previous offence] prior transportation
Original offence Antrim for stealing clothes on 1 July 1833
   [*sic*]—sentence 7 years
Colonial offence: Robbery Tried Bathurst 4 Mar 1840
Sentence—10 yrs after expiry of 3 yrs in irons but never wore
   irons in NI

On arrival assigned William Lewis Penrith, NSW.

NSW record:
5 May 1832 [*sic*], 25 lashes
11 May 1836, arrested Mudgee
31 May 1836, assigned Sydney—50 lashes absent station
15 June 1836, arrested Penrith
31 August 1836, arrested Bathurst
7 Sep 1837, 12 months irons absconding
30 April 1838, 50 lashes absconding
4 July 1838, 50 lashes neglect of work
28 Feb 1839, 3 yrs irons robbery
16 March [1839], 25 lashes making away with slops
19 Aug [1839?], 100 lashes st[ealing] from FP [fellow prisoner]
2 Sep [1839], 75 lashes striking FP with knife
4 January 1840, 25 ditto [striking?] and a lie
21 Jan 1840, absconded Hassans Walls [with Patrick Bruen per *Hive*]

To Norfolk Island July 1840
19 Mar 1841, 1 month Longridge stealing sugar from cask on wharf
22 Mar 1842, 12 months Longridge and sleep barracks without
   indulgence refusing to go to gang
30 Jan 1844, 100 lashes remitted at surgeon's request and to
   Longridge for insulting free woman

JOHN MCVEY

Connaught Journal, 2 April 1835

John McNey [*sic*] stealing 6 pounds from Lieut Knox 85th
Regiment—7 years transportation.

NSW police history:

(SRNSW 4/2465.6, CSIL 39/7778 and *NSWGG*)

24 Nov 1837, 50 lashes HPB [Hyde Park Barracks] neglect of
work & insolence

27 Dec 1837, 50 lashes HPB absenting

11 Jan 1838, 12 months irons HPB repeat absconding

20 June 1838, sent to Hassans Walls [stockade] to serve 12 months
in irons sentenced by HPB absconding

27 June 1838, arrested near 17 Miles Hollow

15 Aug 1838, 12 months irons, Vale of Clywdd [stockade] for
absconding 4th time

13 Sep 1838, 100 lashes & sent to new gaol stockade
[Wooloomooloo] there to complete all sentences in irons

2 Oct 1838, 25 lashes HPB neglect of work

7 Nov 1838, 36 lashes HPB feigning ill

9 Nov 1838, 100 lashes HPB highly insubordinate conduct

20 Nov 1838, 25 lashes HPB for smoking on the work

5 July 1839, 100 lashes HPB recommends 'such daring character'
be sent to Cockatoo Island. Sent to iron gang to complete
all sentences in irons—for 6th absenting. Governor Gipps
approves this 'most daring character' be sent to some secure
place to complete his various sentences—sent to Wollongong.

13 March 1844, absconded from Wollongong [Record ends]

31 Dec 1850, unclaimed letter at Sydney post office [*NSWGG*]

REPORTS FROM MAGISTRATES 1833—some examples

Alexander Somers, *John*, insubordination and absent without
leave, 25 lashes. This man was never flogged before; skin was
lacerated at the 12 lash; he was sufficiently punished at the 12th
lash. He did not cry out, but he seemed to feel his flogging
very much.

William Gregg, *Norfolk*, absent without leave, 25 lashes. This man was punished with 50 lashes about the end of last month; his back was then sore; the unhealed skin broke at the first lash, and at the 4th the blood appeared. This man did not cry out; he is a stout man and has a thick skin, but the appearance of his back, when the punishment was over, sufficiently proved that he had endured much pain.

William Robinson, *Mary*, drunk and making away with a part of his dress which was given him by his master, 50 lashes. This man was never flogged before; he cried out at every lash; the skin was lacerated at the 12th lash; the blood appeared at the 20th; this man suffered intense agony. Twenty lashes would have been an ample warning to him.

Alfred Shanton, neglect of work, 25 lashes, a hardened youngster about 17 years of age; he was determined to bear his punishment like a man; he was however well flogged; back a good deal lacerated, but he did not seem to suffer much bodily harm.

These records survive today because in his changes to the summary jurisdiction, Governor Bourke insisted masters, who acted as magistrates, observe and report on the floggings they ordered.[10]

The challenges to them by Governor Bourke discomforted the settlers, to say the least. Until then, they had experienced only unquestioning support from Governors Brisbane and Darling, for whom their residence in the colony was testimony that the home government's policies were succeeding. Every gentleman and his family increased the respectable element in a colony that sometimes teetered on the brink of chaos. Furthermore, every convict assigned to a settler was one less expense and one less problem for the colonial government. The settlers came to rely on this attitude and the status it gave them.

By the time the *Hive* convicts arrived in the mid-1830s, the settlers who came in the previous decade were well established. Despite difficulties with their convict workforce and with Aborigines, the 1820s had been a time of adventure and optimism as they selected their land and laid the basis for future riches. They were always frightened of Aboriginal attacks and tragically some of them may have pre-empted the threat by shooting first or, worse, over-reacting with mass killings. In the Hunter in 1827, for example, a neighbour of Edward Gostwyck Cory near Paterson wrote to the *Sydney Gazette* anonymously alleging that twelve Aborigines had been shot on Cory's estate, an accusation that he indignantly denied. 'Although provoked by repeated aggravations, my men have never fired at them,' he wrote but then went on to detail how sheep had been attacked by their dogs, his barn and stacks of wheat set on fire and one of the men speared. Whatever the exact truth of it, warfare plainly existed between Cory and the local tribe, some of whom lost their lives.[11]

Bushrangers were also active in the Hunter. 'Jacob's Irish Brigade', named after their master Vickers Jacob, terrorised the settlers for over three months in 1825, for example, before they were captured. Aaron Price, who was an Englishman and one of the group transported to Norfolk Island, subsequently rose to power and prosperity at the penal settlement.[12] Attack by a convict servant, however, could be just as lethal as any by an Aborigine or a bushranger. In October 1832 Joseph Coleman hit his master, Edward Cory, with a spade after a series of escalating exchanges between them over the whereabouts of a spade, the barking of a small dog at which Coleman threw a stone and Cory's opinion that Coleman was insolent in how he spoke. Sentenced in February 1833 to hang for his attack with the spade, Joseph Coleman was defiant saying he could not stand the tyranny on the farm. He was referring to petty fault-finding rather than some systemically brutal regime.[13]

Violence from their servants was not confined to free settlers. In 1838 an assigned servant William Moore attacked his emancipist master John Hoskins, who was a butcher in Maitland. Despite having been a prisoner himself, Hoskins allowed no leeway. When Moore was absent without permission, Hoskins promptly reported him to the police. Returning home, he discovered Moore was back. One of the witnesses said that the two men quarrelled about where Moore slept and there may have been a history of absence overnight. The next morning, Moore went about his work as usual but, according to another servant, was enticed away 'to get some liquor'. Hoskins forcibly brought him back. Assigned servant Samuel Layton, who was in the salting room, testified that soon after, 'I heard the master cry out, "Oh! Sam, Sam, I am killed."' Hoskins then staggered into the salting room where he fell against a cask. 'The prisoner [William Moore] followed, threw him down, then stabbed him in several parts of the body.' When Layton and others tried to pull him off, they were also threatened with the knife. After chasing them away,

Moore returned to the body. When he reappeared on the street outside, he told the assembled crowd, 'I've settled the bloody cattle stealer,' and scraping the bloodied knife with his fingers he put them to his lips saying, 'Here is his heart's blood, and here is a stomach that can eat it.' He then handed himself over to the constable. He was tried in Sydney but the judge ordered he should be executed in Maitland. To the disgust of *The Australian*, he was taken through the streets of Sydney in a cart, sitting on his coffin, and accompanied by his hangman. Soldiers escorted all three by steamer to the Hunter Valley, where Moore was hanged in front of the townspeople.[14]

Grog fuelled violence between master and man. When Richard Jones was stabbed at his property *Turee* in 1838 the culprit was Edward Tufts, a ticket-of-leave man who had previously been his assigned servant. The men on the farm had washed more than 800 sheep that day and Jones rewarded them with a glass of grog each. He was not unusual in doing this. It was a widespread practice on which male convicts insisted as compensation for the discomfort of hours in the water. Details varied from estate to estate according to the negotiations of the prisoner workforce. At least one employer gave the men in the water three glasses of rum but only one to the men who did not get wet.[15] However, rivers of illicit grog followed the initial dram supplied by Mr Jones. A man named David Gill often brought rum to the farm, apparently condoned by Mrs Jones, if not her husband. Mr Jones also paid his shepherds a £5 bonus for every lamb they successfully reared and many were celebrating their good fortune that night. In his own defence, Tufts claimed he was drunk. But he was also aggrieved. Calling Jones every name under the sun—robber, vagabond, thief—he yelled that his former master had robbed him of 400 sheep. When Jones tried to postpone the discussion, Tufts grabbed a pair of sheep shears and stabbed him, telling the other men, 'I've done for the old sweep at last.' At his trial, magistrate Alexander Busby gave evidence that convicted Tufts, but he was uncomplimentary about Jones who, he said, 'was reputed to be a violent man'. Busby also told the court that someone had reported rum was sold at the farm and Jones' application for more assigned servants had been refused six months earlier. But rum for sheep-washing, even though traditional? A monetary bonus for rearing lambs? Plainly a far more complex power dynamic was operating than just a tyrannical master and helpless servants.[16]

Tension among the pastoralists in the Hunter increased when John McIntyre was murdered by his assigned servant in collusion with several others.[17] After McIntyre's death, the settlers' underlying fear about living among vast numbers of prisoners became more acute. On some estates the position of farm constable was created as an extra precaution. The job was usually held by a serving convict or ticketholder who was empowered by being armed. Private lock-ups were also built as holding pens until accused men could be taken before a bench of magistrates.[18] One traveller described what he called 'a true Botany Bay reception' when he visited pastoralists in the Hunter Valley. 'The dogs made a fearful din as we approached the house. From behind the bolted door only one question was put: who were we? When we announced ourselves as friends, the door was opened and we were received in the most friendly fashion.' Not long after, at *Glendon* on the Hunter River, Robert Scott greeted him with double-barrelled gun, cocked, and calling out for identification before he would let him approach.[19]

The memory of his brother John's death triggered direct repercussions when Donald McIntyre was knocked to the ground only three years later by his assigned servant Edward Gill. Details of the exchange between this master and man were very similar to those between Joseph Coleman and his employer Edward Cory. Aggravated to breaking point by his master's pettiness, Gill punched McIntyre. With an iron bar, alleged his master. With my fists, insisted Gill. Furthermore, he claimed that his employer seized him around the neck calling him a 'convict wretch' and then they struggled until McIntyre fell to the ground when a branch left the mark behind his ear. Additional medical evidence supporting Gill's claim that he only used his fists came too late to save him. The court had already accepted testimony which gave credence to the allegation he used an iron bar. He was convicted for attacking his master with intent to kill and sentenced to hang. On the scaffold, the ex-soldier died with dignity, commenting simply 'I never intended to murder my master. It was just a common assault.'[20] The issue that provoked the fight between master and man in the first place was an argument over the prisoners' traditional claim that Sunday was their day off. Gill had obliged his master by working Sunday for a special job. When he took the Monday off *in lieu,* which he said, he assumed he was entitled to do, McIntyre came to his hut demanding he go to work.

So was being Irish a problem here? Were Irish prisoners being treated with prejudice and discrimination? According to magistrate, George Brooks, the Hunter Valley settlers did not like the Irish. On a daily basis, there were very likely constant, petty displays of prejudice—a tone of voice, a lack of patience, contempt or exasperation. In the larger context, however, Peter Hammond's systematic investigation of workplace violence, murder and manslaughter in the Hunter Valley found that the ethnicity of convicts involved in violence split almost equally 50–50 between Catholic and Protestant. The original crime that resulted in transportation was unimportant, and so was the sentence. Hammond did find youth was a significant factor but added 'there is no reason to believe that, for example, Catholics, Irish or those on life sentences were more prone to violent behaviour than any other national or religious group.' Furthermore, he concluded that 'factors which led convicts to kill are likely to be found within the convict system rather than in their upbringing or collective nature'.[21]

A systematic appraisal of convict masters similar to Hammond's study of their employees would assist in analysing the employer's role in these explosions of violence. Fifty years ago T.M. Perry and, later, Sandra Blair argued that the Hunter was distinctly different in social structure to other settled areas such as Bathurst or the south-west, but nobody has yet attempted to profile the employers in detail.[22] Research for this book confirms some differences. Those who settled on the Illawarra, for instance, were more diverse than in the Hunter. They included not only the large-scale farmer and merchant Alexander Berry, who arrived in 1823, but more men who had been ships' surgeons such as the Osborne brothers. Like the Hunter, some Illawarra settlers were ex-military, such as Governor Bourke's aide, Captain Westmacott, but others were wealthy Catholics of whom Cornelius O'Brien was pre-eminent.

Although absconding convicts notoriously 'infested' the cedar forests, conflict with the Aborigines appears less on the coast. Perhaps the absence of sheep in large numbers contributed to more peaceful relationships. In addition, hunting and gathering fish was an important part of Aboriginal life which the Europeans did not disturb. At the Shoalhaven, some of the local tribe worked for Berry. Around Wollongong, one of the first Europeans, C.T. Smith, recalled that 'the Aborigines were never particularly hostile to the whites.' In Chapter 1, we saw the friendly reception from indigenous people when the *Hive* was wrecked. The most memorable battle on the south coast occurred between two Aboriginal tribes at Fairy Meadow in 1830. The issue was apparently a woman and between 70 and 100 Aboriginal men were estimated to have died.[23]

Settlement on the Illawarra was well established when the *Hive* arrived but, inland from the coast, the south-west was just beginning to expand. Free-settler emigrants to the south-west, such as the Catholic Irishman Terence Aubrey Murray near Lake George, had arrived in the twenties but their numbers were very much diluted by native-born sons of convicts like Isaac Shepherd and William Bradley and of soldiers who chose to settle in New South Wales decades before.[24] The south-west generally, from Appin and Campbelltown outwards, was also distinctive for the number of Catholics who settled there, of which more later, and the Braidwood area was notable for its collection of naval men. Several had been surgeons on convict ships, including Dr Braidwood Wilson himself. Landholders also included an admiral (Hawker) and a ship's master, John Coghill.

Further research may reveal distinctive patterns of interaction according to background; for example, between employers such as ships' surgeons who were experienced in managing recalcitrant, cheeky (or insolent), duplicitous prisoners and those such as a ship's master used to a system of command and obedience from his crew. Between these extremes was the mass of new landholders, many with no experience of managing a large workforce, let alone an unwilling one. Inexperience often meant they assumed coercion was the only solution. Social anxiety made them quick to hear insolence or defiance where a more confident person would have laughed it off. But perhaps there are no patterns. Perhaps it all comes down to individual character. The truth could well lie in an astute observation by the Quaker missionary James Backhouse, who travelled extensively in the colonies during the thirties. Wherever he went, he appraised the settlers' relationship with their servants and drew this conclusion:

> Many persons in the colony complain of continual irritation from their servants, but we find that men *who know themselves* generally get on comfortably with them: they are not unreasonable in what they expect and they do not excite them to make insolent replies by imperious language. (emphasis added)[25]

The impact of fear among the vastly outnumbered free settlers has not been given much credence to date, perhaps because of assumptions the convicts lived as flogged and chained slaves. In fact the settler homesteads were the equivalent of building a house today in the middle of a high security gaol. And opening the doors. Those families who could afford it imported their domestic staff in an attempt to gain some insulation from the contaminating forces—as Emmeline Macarthur explained: 'Although my Father had many convict servants, he at no time allowed any to enter the home establishment. Our maids came from Scotland, our men servants were either free English emigrants, or Indians.'[26] The settlers' fear was palpable, as Baron von Hugel noticed when he visited George Wyndham and his wife in the Hunter. European gentleman that he was, von Hugel found a striking contrast between the beautiful and elegant Mrs Wyndham and her surroundings. 'On seeing her, one might well think oneself in one of the elegant parts of London . . . And where do we find her? In the midst of the wilderness, in an unfinished, unadorned house, in constant daily fear of robbers and murderers, surrounded by criminals.'[27]

The free settlers certainly felt under siege. In their minds, their respectable household resembled an oasis of purity in a sea of criminality. And with reason. The disproportion between settlers and criminals past and present, was enormous. In 1836, the total population of eastern Australia, then called New South Wales, was 77,000 scattered from Moreton Bay in the north to the Port Phillip area in the south. Thirty-two thousand of these were classified as 'free settlers' when in fact they included many children of convicts who had arrived with their parents and all those born in the colony to convict parents. According to James Macarthur, a decision had been taken to include the native-born under 'free' to 'break down their pride', which says something about the stance those born in the colony had been taking to newcomers.[28] However, even those who were strictly free settlers included relatives of people who had been transported. The total number of serving convicts in 1836 was 28,000 plus 17,000 classified as emancipists.[29] If the figures were interpreted according to expected allegiance, the preponderance of 'convicts' would be clearer but the colonists preferred to downplay the 'convict element' whenever possible. At a personal level, a family of, say, five, with a couple of servants they brought from home could find themselves living with twenty or more prisoners, plus a couple of ticket-of-leave men and perhaps an emancipist. Pastoralist Terence Aubrey Murray lived alone for many years with 50 to 60 convicts.[30]

The guard, that is, soldiers based in the colony, numbered 2835 in 1837, which was typical for the period. It usually comprised two regiments, one of which would be based in Sydney with detachments of the second scattered round the colony.[31] From 1826, they were supplemented by mounted police and (ex-convict) constables but in fact the forces of law and order were as outnumbered as the free landholders.

The possibility their convict servants would combine against them always spooked the settlers despite reassurances from people who had lived in the colony for decades that violence from the men was rare. Support for this optimism can be found, for instance, in records of the Newcastle Police from 1823 to 1827 which confirm that all but one offence during this period involved only absconding, absence, neglect of work and some thieving. The exception occurred in 1826 when John Herring Boughton of Tillimby, Paterson, was assaulted by J. McAuliffe, one of his convict workforce, a crime for which McAuliffe was sentenced to three years in a penal settlement.[32]

Fear of the Irish was a factor for some settlers. Lorraine Neate, for example, presents evidence that James Spearing was frightened of his convict workforce. Emigrating from the Isle of Wight, he was always conscious of the isolation of the Illawarra with its scattered settlers and distant medical help, not to mention the several periods when the area lacked both military and magistrate. His anxiety was greatly increased by the preponderance of Irish among his men. He believed they were conspiring against him. 'The whole of my servants both bond and free, amounting to sixteen, are Irish,' he wrote to the colonial secretary. 'Can I solicit that the next be of another country as it will form something like a division which is highly requisite in this situation?'[33] At *Paulsgrove*, fear went hand-in-hand with a master who lacked the skills to manage a recalcitrant workforce. And the Irish were everywhere, including even the magistrate.

Spearing was not alone in seeing Irish bogeymen everywhere he looked. The colonial authorities were always braced for an Irish rebellion. The early boatloads of Irish prisoners arrived in the aftermath of the failed 1798 rebellion, bringing with them its passion and grief. More of them arrived in the next few years and between approximately 1800 and 1807 unrest was barely contained. Anxious free settlers were not a problem then. No one could come to the penal colony without permission and their numbers were few. The officials, however, were another matter. Governors Hunter and King were constantly alert to a rebellion in the colony. When an abortive uprising did occur in 1804 it simply fulfilled expectations. Nicknamed Vinegar Hill after the famous battle in Ireland itself, led by Irish gentry convicts who had been transported for taking part in the 1798 revolt, it has come down in legend as *the* Irish rebellion in Australia. 'Death or Liberty' was the rallying cry, as it had been in Ireland. Its leaders were Irish, one of whom was hanged, and a large number of Irish prisoners took part. But not all. Some, such as 'General' Joseph Holt, chose not to get involved. Furthermore, approximately 300 participants, that is, nearly one-third, were English. According to Anne-Maree Whitaker, who specialises in the period, by 1810 most of the participants had integrated into colonial life.[34]

The nearest thing to the uprising the later settlers feared occurred at Bathurst in 1830. When Ralph Entwistle escaped with four others from a farm near Bathurst, the group soon accumulated firearms, horses and supplies by stealing them from other farms. They called at the local magistrate's farm apparently seeking revenge and when his convict overseer refused to cooperate they killed him. Entwistle's motivation is uncertain, some suggesting that it was grievance at having been flogged 50 lashes for swimming naked in the river when His Excellency passed by, others claiming it was problems with rations that made him take to the bush. Whatever the motive, Entwistle had the ability to attract followers. At its height there were said to be 130 men in his gang, but some joined because they were threatened and just as quickly dropped away until only a core group of twelve to fourteen men remained. In the end, ten men were hanged, including Entwistle, and two died of wounds. Landholder George Suttor led a volunteer force which hunted the bushrangers. During the 1804 rebellion he and his wife had been robbed and their lives were threatened. In the heat of pursuit of the gang at Bathurst he wrote that Entwistle had white ribbons in his hat and immediately the group was nicknamed the 'Ribbon Boys'.

However, evidence it was an Irish revolt is tenuous. Entwistle himself was a brickmaker from Bolton in Lancashire. The ten who were hanged included three English, one American, and six Irish convicts. Any suggestion that Ribbonmen were threatening New South Wales was more in the settlers' fevered imagination.[35]

The fears of the settlers were easily stirred up. Rumours and exaggeration fuelled alarm. In 1833 the *Sydney Herald* ran a story about a supposed 'rockite or incendiary notice' being nailed to the gate of an estate near Goulburn by convict servants. Someone was mischief-making. The suggestion of an Irish insurrection had no foundation in truth, reported Lieutenant Lachlan McAlister of the mounted police, who was also a local magistrate. There had been a notice, however it had nothing to do with Irish convicts. According to McAlister it was pinned to the fence of his fellow magistrate Dr Gibson and 'said something very uncomplimentary about the doctor and myself'. Perhaps not coincidentally, Francis Kenny, who was the Catholic son of a convict and a landholder nearby, angrily described Lachlan McAlister as 'rude, insulting and arrogant'. In return, McAlister alleged Kenny's grievance related to a recent appearance before the bench accused of collecting cattle in the neighbourhood and swapping brands. In an implicit barb at someone, McAlister added, 'upon all well-regulated estates, the convicts have given as little trouble during the present, as in former years'.[36]

In September 1833, a similar although micro version of the dreaded revolution occurred in the Hunter Valley when six assigned servants, most of them English, committed what was described as 'mutiny' at the property of self-styled 'Major' James Mudie at Patrick's Plains. After stealing guns, they then robbed the household, stole horses and threatened death to Mudie (who was absent) and his son-in-law John Larnarch who was also their (free-settler) overseer.[37] Mudie's other son-in-law, George Boyle White, later described Mudie as 'an unprincipled blackguard' but at the time he was regarded as just another respectable landholder and the actions of his servants were treated as an outrage.[38] Rations featured prominently in the mutineers' testimony. Larnarch, however, had been a brutal taskmaster. For example, in one month he charged ten of his servants mainly with offences such as insolence and neglect of work, for which each received a flogging ranging from 25 to 50 lashes. Desperate about the situation on the farm, one young convict absconded, trudging 150 miles to Sydney to plead with Governor Bourke. Unfortunately, the governor was away. His son, Dick, acting as his aide, accepted the petition but sent the man back to Mudie with an apology, which brought down retribution on the prisoner's head.[39] Incensed by these events, Mudie later sought revenge by publishing his account of life in the colony. His chief target was the governor who, according to Mudie, 'encourages the correspondence of convicts with himself and his functionaries, receives the secret accusations of any of the ruffians of the colony against their masters, and even comforts and advises runaways who repair to him for consolation'.[40]

The 'mutineers' themselves gave various reasons for their actions. John Larnarch's tyranny was one and for many years it was the focus of discussion, probably because it fitted assumptions about a slave colony. Most of the men's testimony, however, revealed that, once again, food was the underlying aggravation. To modern researchers, the fundamental role of rations, their quality and quantity, is just as significant as Larnarch, particularly when understood in the greater context of this issue. Governor Bourke sent John Hubert Plunkett and the superintendent of convicts to Patrick's Plains to investigate what happened at Castle Forbes. They cleared Mudie of the charge of systematically reducing the rations to which the prisoners were entitled but Bourke formally reproved both Mudie and Larnarch.[41]

Entwistle's revolt at Bathurst had some trappings of an Irish rebellion but no discernible motive associated with Ireland. It was not, for instance, specifically anti-English. The revolts at Bathurst and Patrick's Plains were protests against penal conditions which were triggered particularly by punishments such as flogging but, just as importantly, by food. Both fit the fourth category of convict protest defined by historian Alan Atkinson, that of protest by violent rejection of the penal system. For many decades it was regarded as surprising that so few such events occurred. In fact, their absence demonstrates that the experience of most prisoners was tolerable, perhaps better than tolerable, but as Charles Darwin put it, 'some become desperate and quite indifferent of their lives'.[42] The men's state of mind was the decisive factor and wise masters recognised its importance. Many years later, a prisoner described the best approach for keeping his fellow convicts peaceful. Talking about disproportionate numbers on the voyage out, he wrote: 'the safety of the vessel really depends on the temper of the men . . . it is therefore an object of primary importance to avoid anything calculated to give unnecessary irritation . . . the Australian system aims at being as far as possible self-acting. Order is sought to be obtained not by a show of force . . . but by an appeal to the good sense of the men themselves and by calling on a certain portion of them to assist . . . The Australian plan of keeping the red rag out of sight will afford you [emigrants] a relief you cannot now estimate.'[43] He might have added, It is always wise to keep supplies of sugar, tea and tobacco flowing. And to allow the men their dignity.

CHAPTER 7
The Power of Numbers

The prisoners were not fools. They could smell their employers' fear. As the Illawarra magistrate wrote about James Spearing, 'He has all along been afraid of his men and they know it.'[1] More generally, the prisoners recognised the power that their numbers conferred, power that was being reinforced weekly during the 1830s, which was the peak decade for convict transportation to New South Wales, power that was particularly deployed in the workplace. Convicts may not have revolted, or shed much blood, but assigned to a man they did not respect or did not like, they knew exactly how to run him ragged until he over-reacted and was censured for his behaviour, or gave up.

One tactic that infuriated the settlers was vividly described by an enraged 'Major' Mudie. His resentment also validates the comments made by James Backhouse about the response of prisoners to 'imperious' treatment by their masters. In *The Felonry of New South Wales*, Mudie wrote:

> From the lenity of the colonial government in the treatment of these ruffians, not only are they insubordinate and mutinous, but they are even full of high notions of their own dignity! Masters

have been *reproved* for speaking with too little respect to the *gentry* assigned to them as servants . . . so high-minded, indeed, under this childishly-foolish system, have the felon population become, that convicts of the very worst and lowest grade are quite indignant at being called convicts and insolently deny the right of any one to treat them with disrespect.[2]

The origin of the prisoners' refusal to accept being called convicts has not yet been pinpointed, but it appears to go back to the start of European settlement, when the need to work cooperatively regardless of rank was at its highest. It may also have developed from the distinction at that time between doing government work, such as clearing and building in a gang or team, compared to working legitimately at private, individual tasks or in one's own time.[3] Hence the common description of convicts as 'government men', that is, working on a government project, which they subsequently adopted generically for themselves. Shame was not the reason for rejecting the term 'convict'. Rather, it was a tactic by which prisoners asserted their equality—more precisely, equal worth, equal value in the early settlement, entitlement to respect for their contribution to the common good. If an employer called his servant a 'convict wretch' as Donald McIntyre did Edward Gill, he broke the unwritten code that prisoners were no different to free men in their entitlement to dignity and self-worth.[4] Two decades later, both their demand for respect and the risk of not observing it, was noticed by a free settler on the Victorian goldfields, who commented, 'A convict is a hardened devil; but treat him as an equal, and you are safe.'[5]

In contrast to Mudie, the Macarthur family managed their men on the principle that 'where a man behaves well . . . make him forget, if possible, that he is a convict'. Alexander Berry, who was always conscious that good management was the only real law and order he possessed, gave strict instructions to his overseers on how to treat his men. They were 'never to call them convicts, but merely Government servants or Government men'. If the men did misbehave, Berry's first line of punishment was to put them on 'government' rations. He must have done this sparingly, or for reasons the men found fair, because his estate is known for its cooperative workforce. Berry believed his management style brought advantages. Decades later, he wrote: 'Some of these Government men are still in my service to the present day, and some are my tenants. A few months ago one of the heroes of Trafalgar died at Shoalhaven. He had been transported for striking an officer when in a state of intoxication, and had been upwards of forty years in my service.'[6]

The prisoners' insistence on respect was facilitated by the sparse information which the British government sent to the colony about its transportees. Initially, only a convict's date of trial and sentence was provided to the colonial authorities. It was not until December 1813, three years after Governor Macquarie arrived, that information about prisoners' trade, age and physical description was added.[7] In 1820, Commissioner Bigge concluded that a convict's previous crime and character were entirely overlooked.[8] And he was right. Details of their crimes were not provided until after his report was implemented in the mid-1820s. Meanwhile people were judged by how they performed and by their character. Even later, when colonial authorities were provided with, usually, a one-word description of the convicts' crimes, it was not passed on to their employer. James Spearing, for instance, would not have known that two of those Irishmen he feared were transported for 'insurrection' and 'mutiny including attempted murder'.[9] Unless, of course, they told him. Generally, however, lack of information about their background suited the prisoners. Many arrived in New South Wales sporting a tattoo which read: 'Speak of me as you find.' Circumstances allowed them to put that aspiration into effect. By the 1830s, the emphasis on merit that began of necessity in the early days had become a defining characteristic of the society they founded.

Withdrawal of labour was the convicts' most powerful tool and they used it far more frequently and effectively than we have realised. Even a commandant with arbitrary power could be reduced to despair. At the remote punishment settlement of Wellington Valley in the 1820s the commandant, Percy Simpson, railed against what he called 'the insolence and treachery' of the prisoners. Unknown to them, his rage was increased by the fact his remuneration was linked to the productivity of the settlement.

Simpson was an Irishman who was born in Canada to a military father. He joined the army himself at the age of twenty but his career was unspectacular. Arriving in 1823, he was immediately appointed commandant of the new Wellington Valley agricultural settlement, persuaded by an offer from Governor Brisbane to defer his claim for a land grant in favour of payment based on the amount of wheat produced.

Simpson suffered financially from this unusual arrangement, both the offer and its acceptance revealing the ignorance of the governor and Simpson about the colony and its unusual workforce. Simpson had built roads using the military as his workers, but managing convicts was an entirely new experience for which his background had not prepared him. Commissioner Bigge's recent report recommending greater severity to make the punishment of transportation fit the crime was being implemented by Governor Brisbane and Simpson approached his task with preconceptions about how the prisoners should be handled. Soon after he arrived at Wellington Valley, he wrote, 'Removed as I am at so remote a distance from the immediate seat of government and the assistance of magistrates, it is most essentially requisite that sternness and perhaps some degree of severity should be adopted for the good order and well being of all here. [N]o humane or gentlemanly conduct . . . nothing but fear will prevent them committing excesses.'[10]

Simpson later described his role at Wellington Valley as combining 'commandant, chaplain, commissary and engineer'.[11] Historian David Andrew Roberts has argued that Simpson was handicapped by insufficient official support from Sydney or even from the Bathurst commandant, plus a location that was so difficult to reach that supplies, including rations, were often delayed. Nor did he have anyone to enforce his orders. He had been assigned one corporal and four privates to control his 80-strong workforce, but with one or two soldiers often engaged pursuing or escorting prisoners the forces of law and order were pitifully small. It didn't help that Simpson had to arrange and supervise his own floggings, which made it a very personal punishment. Like so many other confrontations in the penal colony, the degree to which prisoners would accept punishment was governed by their perception of whether it was fair—fairly awarded and fairly administered.[12]

In the colonial context, however, Simpson's greatest drawback was his personality. People who met him reported that he 'behaved . . . in a very petulant and overbearing manner, so much so as to exhaust the patience of any man'.[13] John Maxwell, superintendent of government stock, found him uncooperative and unreasonable. Maxwell's responsibilities included an outstation at Bell's River ten miles from Simpson's location. When he sent fencers there to build stockyards, Simpson refused to issue them with wheat at the same time as meat, forcing them to walk ten miles into the settlement and back, twice a week. One of Maxwell's stockmen wrote asking him 'to protect me from Mr Simpson's threats and let me be fully made sensible how I am in future to act with him'.[14] Describing Simpson as 'irascible and intemperate', David Roberts likened him to Governor William Bligh, whose manner fostered discontent and hardened opposition.[15] Dorothy Raxworthy was convinced that the underlying chaos at Wellington Valley resulted from his 'eccentric personality . . . and bouts of irrational, excessive . . . [and] and unnecessary anger with subsequent floggings of all and sundry'. And Roberts concluded that 'the strongest evidence comes from Simpson's own pen. When his authority was in crisis the tone of his correspondence turned wrathful and furious as he demanded more powers and a flogger to smash the "vile and disgraceful confederacy" of malcontents and subversives and to keep them "in awe . . . [by] making the most serious, indeed awful example" of the leading troublemakers.'[16]

The prisoners showed Simpson no mercy. Most of them had been in the colony for some years. They understood the hardship that could be inflicted by the nature of the land and its vast distances but all had absorbed the egalitarian colonial ethos and many had experienced a variety of masters, as well as flogging and iron gangs. Simpson's style of leadership was one they would not support. If he flogged them, they absconded. If his demands were unreasonable, or without commonsense, they withdrew their labour. Many deserted, some of them more than once. Furthermore, as Roberts put it: 'They were idle and insubordinate, feigned illness, pilfered food, smuggled and distilled liquor. They sabotaged the construction of buildings and the ploughing of fields. They burnt wheat stacks, drove away livestock, waylaid the supply carts and destroyed accounts.'[17] It is hardly surprising that by August 1823 Simpson had to concede defeat.[18]

The imperious manner of assistant surveyor Granville William Chetwynd Stapylton produced a similar outcome. Stapylton accompanied Sir Thomas Mitchell on his southern exploration in 1836. The black sheep of an aristocratic family, he expected deference and obedience from the lower orders. Like Simpson, he was caught by surprise when the convicts refused to defer, indeed went out of their way to challenge him. And doubly infuriated by comparison with the respect they showed to Mitchell.

The expedition had barely set out before Stapylton was at odds with the men. One of his earliest encounters was with Jones the shepherd, who was known to all as a hero for some past feat as a messenger. Stapylton resented the praise and wrote in his journal, 'A scoundrel of the first water, a rascally tale bearer, a sear, a mischief-maker amongst all hands, and an impudent varlet to boot—very forward and officious. Took him down a peg this morning for thinking it fit and proper to give an opinion. A decided favourite with the Chief [Mitchell] and recommended as "one of the good men" . . . such humbug.' Jones, of course, would have his own view about having his advice rejected, let alone being dressed down, probably in front of the other men since that was a habit for which Mitchell later reproved Stapylton. Throughout the journey Jones continued to provoke the surveyor by 'always giving his advice and opinion in a dammed drawling, nasal tone, a complete lawyer . . . An "old hand" as they call it.' Jones was a London groom who, like many prisoners, had adapted his skills to sheep. Convicted of burglary, he had been in the colony nearly ten years during which his experience included flogging and three months in an iron gang. Becoming part of Mitchell's team changed everything. He had been with the surveyor-general since the first major expedition in 1831, during which Mitchell formed the view he was 'intelligent and trustworthy'. After their return from 'Australia Felix' in 1836, Jones was rewarded with a conditional pardon for his 'entire care and management of [100] sheep'.[19]

The men detected Stapylton's disdain and they tested him to see how far they could go. His journal reveals his lack of insight into how he appeared to them and his inability to recognise what was really going on. Writing the same day that he ticked off Jones, he recorded 'Bullock drivers trying to Gammon me into relieving [abandoning] the morning watch. Let them know that I did not intend to be a cypher or one vested with authority and afraid to execute it. Up occasionally before daylight and challenge them at their posts. This is the camp watch. No good to be done without it. Scoundrels. I wish I had done with them. All quiet and subservient now. So far so good.'[20] One of the bullock drivers, James McClelland, was the only Irishman in the team.

At the request of colonial secretary Alexander Macleay, Mitchell's party included the birdstuffer, John Roach. Convicted in London for stealing a coat, he had been assigned to the Macleay family on arrival three years earlier and soon after started work at the Colonial Museum. He joined the expedition to collect natural history specimens and apparently did a good job, but Stapylton loathed him more than any other man. Roach was only in his early twenties but he was conscious of his powerful mentors and his manner, probably studied insolence, made it plain that he knew the fulminating surveyor could not touch him. In his journal, Stapylton referred to Roach as 'Macleay's protégé' and page after page is peppered with complaints about him. 'This Birdstuffer sets me at defiance. My position is an awkward one. If I chain him to a dray I probably quarrel with the Chief [Mitchell] . . . to tolerate his behaviour is an insult to my feelings.'[21]

The ill-feeling between Stapylton and Roach was highly personal, particularly when the prisoner resorted to mockery. 'He even took to mimicking me as I stand by my fire and using insulting gestures towards me. I told him that I observed his conduct and that he should not presume in such insulting behaviour with impunity. His reply was most audacious: "You are a curious man. You would swear anything. You often have done. You told Alick [Burnett, Mitchell's leading man] things which were false about me. What do I care for you. Major Mitchell has often told you, you've nothing to do with me. You are not going to frighten me are you?"' Stapylton was so furious with Roach he 'could hardly refrain from knocking him down'. He told the birdstuffer, 'If you imagine I have no control over you, you will discover your mistake. You forget your situation.' Roach withdrew, 'muttering something most disgusting but I could not hear the precise words he used. He leered back at me with a look of insulting defiance.' Stapylton was even more affronted when, on complaining to Mitchell about Roach, he was told that it was an 'exhibition of selfishness on my part and of a greater regard for my personal comfort than for the success of the expedition'.[22]

Stapylton's man-by-man description of the team reveals more of the behaviour that incensed gentry settlers. Muirhead and Pickering were two court-martialled soldiers from Scotland and the only men for whom Stapylton had a good word. In the aftermath of Mitchell's rebuke of his deputy, they were almost certainly responsible for ensuring the men were less challenging than usual. 'Doubtless two trumps,' Stapylton called them. 'Without their silent influence, this camp would I verily believe be an anarchy [of] disorder and disgrace.' A decade earlier, Percy Simpson would have recognised how he felt.[23]

By accident or design, the men were a mixture of Scottish and English, plus McClelland. As far as Stapylton was concerned, however, it was those know-alls from his own part of Britain who were the worst. After nearly six months in their company he exploded, 'Audacious vagabonds.

An English convict without exception is the most offensive animal in the creation. So provokingly wise in his ignorance.'[24] It was class rather than ethnicity that mattered to Stapylton who was ever conscious, even with Mitchell, that 'I am better born'.[25] Ultimately, Mitchell was more generous than his deputy deserved. His report about the exploration praised Stapylton for 'his zeal and perseverance'.[26]

Anyone who 'put on side' could expect trouble from the prisoners, as Thomas Stewart discovered as late as 1855. An officer in the Van Diemen's Land Commissariat, Stewart was left to mind Norfolk Island between the end of the penal settlement and the arrival of Pitcairn Islanders to settle there. Stewart was neither an aristocrat, nor a wealthy landholder, just a moderately well-educated middle-ranking official and genuinely religious free settler who arrived in Hobart in 1843. He saw his twelve months caretaking as an opportunity to accumulate some money, to demonstrate the benefits of kind but firm leadership and as a chance for his wife to enjoy living in Government House. He didn't bank on the reaction of his workforce. They consisted of five convicts and four ticket-of-leave constables, an overseer named Rodgers and his wife, who was pregnant, plus an elderly official from the Convict Department named Waterson and his wife. All of them regarded the 'interregnum' as a holiday. They did not want to work, nor were they interested in humouring Stewart's pretensions to acting as a benevolent commandant. When he insisted everyone attend Divine Service, conducted by himself, one of the constables initially tried to change his mind—'The men like to do their washing on Sundays'—but they complied with his wishes. Of his own accord, Stewart excused the two Catholics. Attempts to micromanage their work caused sharp resistance. Overseer Rodgers' resentment increased exponentially with Stewart's assiduous checks on what he was doing. The ticket-of-leave police felt the same, one of them telling Stewart, 'We are paid constables and I think it is a great want of faith or trust on your part to put an overseer over us.' Daniel Farrell, a court-martialled soldier transported for hitting his sergeant, simply revolted.[27] On being told to sleep in Government House, he not only refused but arbitrarily removed himself to a distant hut behind the empty military barracks. On being instructed by Stewart to do the washing at Government House, he exploded. 'Washing!' he exclaimed with what Stewart described in his journal as 'great emphasis'. 'Washing. I'm not going to wash!' The shouting match rapidly escalated, culminating in a manhunt of farcical proportions through the dark bush, until Farrell surrendered not to Stewart but to Rodgers. When Constable Bright arrested him, he did it more as a friend, saying, 'Don't be obstinate, Dan. Put these handcuffs on.'

Since the Irishman resolutely refused to apologise, Stewart faced the dilemma of what to do with him. Eventually he convened a court, although he lacked the powers of a magistrate. A formal trial followed. Farrell cross-examined all the witnesses. Only right at the end did he take pity on Stewart and apologise. 'I am heartily sorry that I have given any offence and allowed my bad temper to get the better of me.' He was admonished and discharged. From their experience of being a prisoner, the convicts recognised the benefits of autonomy and delegation long before modern management theorists discovered them. Left to his own devices in future, Farrell worked productively in the dairy and tending to the gardens.[28]

As Lieutenant Simpson had learned the hard way, the criminal context of the penal colonies created workplace expectations that required nuanced management well beyond the skills of Thomas Stewart. Despite ten years in Australia, Stewart, the free settler, had not yet absorbed the convict-created ethos. He did not know how to generate respect and cooperation without a formal structure to support him. And his attitude was not conducive to success. 'You want too much homage paid to you,' overseer Rodgers told him. A master or overseer's willingness to pitch in was a major touchstone to generating respect from his men. Even Rodgers, who led as 'first among equals', was not immune from the expectation that the boss must be prepared to 'muck in'. When he criticised the work of one of his constables, the man retorted. 'I have done what you would not do yourself.' Stewart could not adjust to the lack of hierarchy. He told the four ticket-of-leave constables that expecting him to work alongside them was unreasonable. Nevertheless they forced him to adopt local ways. Faced with total lack of cooperation or poor workmanship, Stewart turned cooper and made some barrels himself. He also used blacksmith's skills to make a spade. Only in an emergency did the group work as a team. For example, when moving the big launch in raging seas from Ball's Bay to the main settlement everyone, including Stewart, pitched in at risk to their lives.[29]

The prisoners were maddened by what they called 'petty tyranny' and we, today, would term 'micromanagement'. When historians Hamish

Maxwell Stewart and Bruce Hindmarsh investigated conflict on the
McLeod estate in Van Diemen's Land they concluded that the direct
involvement by a master was a contributing factor to conflict with
convict servants. McLeod, it should be noted, was a Scot who emigrated
in 1823. In background, and apparently in character, he was similar to
many of those who went to New South Wales at that time.[30] Excessive
management by a kindly master was no easier to bear than by a tyrant.
John Hirst found an example of mutinous conduct being dealt out to the
Reverend Lancelot Threlkeld, who in theory was on the prisoners' side.
He even described them as 'white slaves' who deserved as much sympathy
as black slaves. When he became a master of convicts for the first time
he discovered that the power of colonial slaveholders was not unlimited,
as Hirst explains: 'They were abusive and lazy; they feigned sickness; the
skilled men pretended not to know their trades; they declared boldly they
would never behave and told Threlkeld to return them to government.'
Threlkeld had some of them flogged. When their behaviour did not
improve, he withdrew their privileges. Deprived of tea, sugar and tobacco,
the men's campaign against their master reached crescendo. A forerunner
of what became the legendary Australian 'go slow' was instituted, but it
was food that provoked the final showdown. Hirst describes how they
dumped their beef ration on Threlkeld's doorstep, claiming it was too
bony and refusing to accept his argument that he had given them extra
to make up for it. When he discovered that they had broken into his
store and stolen pork as a replacement he accepted the inevitable and
returned them to government.[31]

After Commissioner Bigge's report, the policymakers tightened
the system to make it more punitive but, as we have seen, the settlers'
dependence on their men to prosper diluted it in many ways. As it did
on government projects too. When historian Bill Robbins carried out an
analysis of the government lumber yards he concluded that they 'were
not driven by punishment or even reformation . . . they were dominated
by concern about labour productivity. In pursuit of this productivity,
management did not rely on the terror that [Manning] Clark or [Robert]
Hughes suggest characterised the management of convict labour in the
penal colony of New South Wales. The management of the convict labour
process at the lumber yards was an elaborate bureaucratic system, which
utilised sophisticated management strategies and pursued the rational

objective of improving labour productivity. In this way the lumber yard case study confirms the conclusions made by others.'[32]

Like Robbins, Grace Karskens found that the building of the Great North Road from Castle Hill to the Hunter Valley was far more sophisticated than tradition would have us believe. The design, the quality of construction, and the productivity of the workforce under overseers who understood how to motivate their men contradict stereotypes of the road gangs and their work. In 1828 Percy Simpson took over as superintendent of the work, the same Percy Simpson who had struggled to establish the settlement at Wellington Valley. Indeed his predecessor on the road, Lieutenant Jonathan Warner, had experienced similar problems with his workforce to Simpson's at the valley. For example, the scourger created a demarcation dispute about whether he was supposed to do anything more than flog. Even when the Sydney authorities confirmed that his job description involved other duties too, he refused to cooperate, leaving the young lieutenant with no means of punishment. To make matters worse, Warner was also challenged by the local, ex-convict settler, Solomon Wiseman, whose 100 pigs kept rolling in the mud and polluting fresh water needed for the workmen. Wiseman supplied the gangs with meat—oversupplied as it turned out. When one of the overseers refused to take more than they needed, Wiseman threatened that 'he would take his horse, ride off and have his ticket taken'. The man was so shaken that he asked to be transferred elsewhere, which Percy Simpson arranged for him.[33]

The five years since Simpson's arrival at Wellington Valley had educated him in the vagaries of a convict workforce. There was no bastardry he had not seen. No insolence he had not experienced. He had also discovered the productivity that could be extracted by a good overseer. He replaced the intimidated overseer with a better man, 'an active and intelligent man, well-acquainted with the system established here of constructing the roads and possibility to execute orders he receives as well as being a good disciplinarian'.[34] A man's background played no part in selection for promotion. How a man behaved, how he performed on the spot, was more important.[35] Most overseers were convicts who had been sent to the gangs as punishment, or tickets-of-leave men. As Karskens points out, 'they were invaluable and essential to the grand project. Several in particular were valued and praised by Simpson and his successors . . . for their work on the roads and bridges. Today, the massive structures are a striking, rich and direct record of the work of these overseers and the gangs they supervised.'[36]

All the problems that Simpson had experienced at Wellington Valley were present on the road but there were always overseers and superintendents between Simpson and the men. Besides, Simpson understood roads. Years earlier he had built them on the Ionian island of Paxos. The scale of the Great North Road and the grandeur of the scenery inspired him to make his most striking contribution to the colony. With her background in archaeology, Karskens was able to examine remains of the road and establish the quality of workmanship, likely productivity and therefore management skills of the overseers as well as the overall superintendence. 'The walls are . . . manifestations of the approaches of successive surveyors and the supervisory work of their subordinate overseers.'[37] And they revealed that, despite the penal setting, some men found motivation and pride in their work.

In 1828 Governor Darling informed the British government that the settlers could not train the men because they were inherently too bad. For over a century no one considered that the fault might have resided with the settlers themselves. Karskens' work demonstrated that the problem rested with the master rather than the men. As she put it: 'How is it that these gangs, by all accounts unskilled and unwilling, in the end achieved some of the most ambitious and impressive engineering of the colonial period? These were men whom settlers, in spite of their desperate need for labour, could not coax to work for them, who had committed more crimes since their arrival in the colony, and who were unlikely to have been skilled and valued workmen. Moreover, the builders of the ascent of Devine's Hill, the most substantial section, were recaptured runaways from other gangs.'[38] Karskens points out that both Percy Simpson and his successor, Heneage Finch, were inspired by a vision of the Great Road, requiring the best engineering possible and which they hoped would earn them substantial remuneration and acclaim. But it was the overseers who actually supervised the work.[39]

Overseers who understood the prisoners' culture could increase their productivity in a way the lash could not. Inserting an overseer who would act as a conduit between masters and servants seemed the obvious solution. However, it depended on the overseer. Intent on eliminating what he saw as the invidious use of convict or emancipist overseers, Commissioner Bigge recommended that free men should replace them. Accordingly, in

1823 the British government rounded up some of its military pensioners and informed them they were posted to the colonies as overseers or sub-overseers. They were a mixed bunch. William Branch, for instance, was a retired artilleryman who was about 51 years old and had already spent ten years in retirement. He sailed with his wife and infant son on the emigrant ship *Jupiter*, which disembarked one overseer and four sub-overseers in Hobart and a further two overseers and eight sub-overseers, including Branch, in Sydney.[40] Sent initially to Newcastle, he then spent seven years in Port Macquarie after it replaced Newcastle as a secondary punishment settlement. In 1832 he went to Norfolk Island for fifteen months. It soon became plain that age and infirmity combined with the difficult colonial workforce meant he was out of his depth in senior roles. He was reduced to lesser responsibilities. At Port Macquarie, his problems were compounded by a corrupt superior officer. Superintendent of agriculture William Parker installed his mistress, a prisoner named Isabella Hewitt, in the Branch household so she could come to his farm or he could visit her whenever he wished. With Isabella in possession of their best bedroom, Mrs Branch in effect became her servant.[41]

Whatever William Branch's personal limitations, he is an example of free overseers who arrived in the penal colonies as a result of the Bigge report. Many of them would have been of similar age and background. Like Branch, most worked exclusively for government. Private settlers were forced to import their own men, or rely on a relative as Mudie did John Larnach with disastrous results. Caleb Wilson who bought *Tocal* from James Webber made a better choice. He hired a superintendent named Ralph Mills Clarke, a former sergeant in the Royal Marines who emigrated as a military pensioner in 1817. He had accumulated a variety of experience in the colony before taking on responsibility for the *Tocal* estate.[42] Clarke managed the workmen in a way that was productive and kept trouble to a minimum. Perhaps the best testament to his skill is the thirteen-year-old boy convict, James Clements who, in contrast to Martin Ryan and other boys on the *Hive*, spent his entire sentence at *Tocal* protected from brutality elsewhere. Later, when Clarke was killed in an accident, Clements married his widow.[43]

The 'free' superintendents or overseers never displaced convict or emancipist overseers entirely. While the penal colonies existed, emancipists continued in supervisory roles. Furthermore, coming to the colony as a free man was not necessarily an advantage to the job. The difference between the local, usually ex-convict overseer and the imported version was made very plain, for example, on Norfolk Island when both kinds were operating simultaneously.[44] Appraising officials there in 1846, Robert Pringle Stuart reported, 'Superintendent Pilkington may be able to acquit himself with prisoners from England, but [he] is inefficient at the settlement among the colonial convicts.' Pilkington was one of several overseers appointed in England who sailed directly to Norfolk Island. He had no experience of the Australian mainland, let alone its culture, and most likely operated with the 'command and control' style of his experience in English prisons.[45] Overseers like this faced the same subversive resistance as newly arrived military officers such as Percy Simpson and Jonathan Warner and, for that matter, many of the gentry settlers.

The extent to which a single prisoner could reduce his superintendent to helpless fury was demonstrated by John Buckley, alias Denahy, from the *Hive* whose complaints triggered an inquiry into magistrates, masters and their superintendents in the Hunter Valley. Sixty pages of documents were generated relating directly to Buckley's case. From them, one aspect stands out: this was not a simplistic situation of brutal, powerful master and victimised convict. Interaction between the two men was the key and the prisoner was no passive victim. If anything, his behaviour could be interpreted as provoking, even taunting, his superiors. That was certainly how it seemed to them.

Buckley was one of those legendary Irish sheep thieves—caught in a rural laneway, shepherding two sheep that were not his own.[46] Like all the men on the *Hive* who stole livestock, he received a life sentence. In New South Wales his record was already chequered with disciplinary offences when he was assigned to retired naval surgeon, Dr James Bowman, in the upper Hunter. His record by December 1840 included:

Goulburn 11 February 1837: Neglect of duty, 50 lashes
Liverpool 25 March 1837: Improper conduct, six weeks treadmill
Invermein 1 January 1838: Absconding, 50 lashes
Patrick's Plains 17 September 1838: Absconding, 50 lashes
Patrick's Plains 17 October 1839: Disrespect, reprimanded

This last complaint arose when his then overseer at *Segenhoe*, a Mr Dawson, thought Buckley was mishandling his sheepdog. 'I accused him of putting the dog at the sheep, which he denied,' Dawson told Percy

Simpson, who was by then police magistrate at Patrick's Plains. 'I told him if he didn't keep the dog back, I would kill it.' At the threat to his dog, Buckley fired up. 'If you do, I won't shepherd for you. Or anybody.' Dawson was incensed. 'A good flogging would do you good for such insolence.' This threat did not deter Buckley, who had been flogged before. 'I don't care. I'm able to bear it', he retorted. Before the bench, however, he claimed he was 'sometimes not right in the head' and hoped Mr Dawson would overlook his insolence. The excuse worked. Simpson sentenced him to seven days in the cells for impudence, noting 'at the request of Mr Dawson, the prisoner is forgiven'.[47]

When *Segenhoe* was sold, Buckley like other government men was transferred to the new owner. Dr Bowman did not live there. Management of *Segenhoe* and Bowman's other property *Waverley Downs* was left to a superintendent named John Shepherd, with overseers below him.[48] On 11 December 1840 John Buckley lodged a formal complaint against his superintendent. He described how he had gone to Muswellbrook to get treatment for bad eyes. After three days in hospital he was given medicine and told to return to *Segenhoe*. According to Buckley, he asked Shepherd for a pass to continue on to his work station but Shepherd didn't give him one. Shepherd claimed he told Buckley to get it from the overseer George Thorn. In any event, Buckley stayed overnight and testified that, while there, he saw a man being dragged by Mr Shepherd to the farm lock-up. The next day Shepherd told him 'Be off to your station. I thought you would be half way there by now.' Buckley told the magistrate, 'I went 7 miles that day and got as far as a flat on the Iron Bark Range where I stayed overnight. The next day I went 15 miles farther and reached *Waverley Downs*. My station is about 7 miles beyond. While I was getting something to eat in a hut, Mr Shepherd called me outside and asked "Why aren't you at your station?" I told him', said Buckley, 'that I was not well . . . and not in a fit state to take charge of 1200 sheep.' He must have then turned away, at which Shepherd lost his temper. Striding after Buckley, he grabbed him by his braces and dragged him to stand in front of the hut, saying, 'If you stir from there, I'll shoot you as dead as a maggot.' Seizing a gun that was leaning against the hut, he put the muzzle to Buckley's head snapping, 'Get into the hut. There's nothing wrong with your eyes. You're scheming.' An hour later, Shepherd sent the overseer to ask Buckley again if he would go to his station. No doubt sensing a complaint of 'refusing to work' was about to be lodged,

Buckley asked for a pass which he claimed Shepherd started to write, then screwed it up saying he would give no pass. At this point, Buckley walked off and into Scone where he recounted what happened to Mr Robertson, the resident police magistrate. Robertson ordered the case be heard a week later, that Shepherd be summonsed and also Buckley's witnesses, John Allan, a convict, George Swain, son of a convict on the station and the acting overseer whose name was Liver.[49]

After delivering this bombshell, Buckley returned to *Segenhoe*, asked to see Shepherd and with great effrontery asked for a pass to go to his station. Shepherd again lost his temper, grabbed Buckley by the coat and frogmarched him to the farm lock-up. For three nights and two days he was kept there on bread and water until taken before the bench at Muswellbrook charged with 'taking to the Bush'. The acting police magistrate refused to hear the case, saying it belonged to the Scone jurisdiction. However, he kept Buckley in the lock-up for a week before sending him to Scone for the hearing arranged by Robertson. On arrival, Buckley swore yet another affidavit about what happened and a further complaint that the junior superintendent, George Thorn, refused him rations, but this time before two magistrates, Robertson plus John How, JP.[50]

It was Christmas, which may explain why Percy Simpson was covering the Scone bench and why it was he who wrote to recommend that Dr Bowman's convict servants be withdrawn because of 'the tyrannical, unjust and overbearing conduct of Messrs Shepherd and Thorn'. He was defending the police magistrates as much as the convicts, informing the colonial secretary that the two superintendents 'were causing a lot of work at Patrick Plains, Muswellbrook and Scone'. In his opinion, 'Dr Bowman should live there or dismiss the two superintendents'. He enclosed the depositions from Buckley's two complaints and those of another prisoner, William Fitzgerald, noting that Buckley had 'substantiated his charge against Shepherd' and was then deprived of his rations by the other superintendent. Meanwhile, he had 'punished' the two convicts and was holding them in the lock-up 'to prevent any further persecution' while awaiting His Excellency's decision whether to withdraw them. Percy Simpson magistrate was quite a transformation from the wrathful Lieutenant Simpson at Wellington Valley nearly twenty years earlier.[51]

We can't be sure what triggered Buckley's decision to take the risk of complaining. He was certainly an opportunistic young man, and perhaps

Shepherd was right in thinking he was encouraged by the attitude of local magistrates. Certainly their decisions in favour of Shepherd's workforce did not meet the superintendent's 'imperious' expectations. He felt they were empowering the prisoners to do as they pleased. At the end of his tether, he even advised Dr Bowman that if this continued it would be better to do without government men and, feeling vulnerable to attack, he urged his master to visit soon.[52]

Analysis of the behaviour of masters and magistrates in the Hunter Valley has previously focused on the landholders, with the prisoners assumed to be victims. Four decades ago, Alan Atkinson recognised such convict actions as a protest but categorised what they did as an 'appeal to authority'.[53] It was far more than that. Despite their disadvantage in the penal system, despite the hardship, brutality and sometimes terror they endured, this was often an expression of power. As a 21st-century politician put it, 'Real power cannot be given but must be taken.'[54]

CHAPTER 8
Floating Nurseries

In May 1837, barely a year after the drama on the south coast beach, Edward Canney returned to Sydney as master of the *Margaret*, the barque that had brought Governor Bourke to the colony. In seafaring quarters, his appointment would have been hailed with delight. People such as harbour master Nicholson, who had sat on the commission of inquiry, perhaps even Governor Bourke, would have taken the opportunity to congratulate him. Twenty-three years was young to be made a captain, even in those days, young to be entrusted with lives and valuable goods in a journey to the far side of the earth. Canney's quiet pride in the achievement is revealed in a note preserved by his descendants.[1] Probably created as a keepsake for his tiny daughter, it contained details of that momentous first voyage including the information that he 'Took command of the *Margaret* in the 24th year of his age'. Among the passengers on board was paymaster Benson of the 28th Regiment, his wife, and son Thomas. No doubt they were all hugely entertained by stories of Benson's shipwrecked comrades on the *Hive*.[2]

After so many voyages during his apprenticeship and subsequently as mate, Canney was more experienced at managing men than Henry

Lugard, but he too was tested in the early stage of his command. Nine of his crew deserted at their first port of call. Sydney was always a temptation for sailors. Many a desperate master resorted to the magistrate to force his men to sail their ship home. Among those who ran was John Hurst, an eighteen-year-old from Canney's home town of Broadstairs, who may have been on board as a favour to someone Canney knew. Hurst was among those rounded up by the Sydney police and forced to crew the ship back to England.[3] Canney—or perhaps the ship's owners—had taken precautions against his inexperience by appointing 38-year-old William Curry from North Shields near Newcastle as first mate. He could also rely on core support from two sailors who had shared his voyage home after the wreck. Twenty-one-year-old Stephen Norris from Deal in Kent had worked as second mate to Canney when he sailed for London after the shipwreck as chief officer on the *Auriga*. Norris now became second mate on the *Margaret*. Making up the trio from the *Auriga* was eighteen-year-old William Green from Cork, an apprentice who also followed Canney to the *Margaret*. After completing Canney's first voyage with the *Margaret*, which arrived in London in July 1838, both men signed up for the second. Stephen Norris now carried the rank of first mate. But this time, both men deserted when the ship arrived in Sydney.[4]

At first glance it seems a shocking disloyalty but there was often a subtext to desertions by sailors. Examining crew lists for numerous ships reveals that some men were working their passage to Sydney by arrangement either with the captain or a senior member of the crew. Examples under Canney were Thomas Clerk, aged 30, and Charles Clerk, an apprentice, who both sailed on the outward leg of Canney's third voyage to Sydney and were discharged together when they arrived.[5] Stephen Norris and young William Green were another (less legitimate) example, but their official record of 'desertion' obscures a very human story. Norris, it turns out, had fallen in love with eighteen-year-old Augusta Mary Siddons, perhaps while on shore leave in 1836. Augusta was part of the seafaring world through her father, Richard Siddons, who was the pilot based at South Head to escort newly arrived ships up the harbour. When Stephen returned to Sydney in May 1837 on the *Margaret*, he and Augusta were married at St Phillip's church on the hill above the cove.[6] The ship was only in port for a month, just time for the commitment to be made and for a very short honeymoon. Sydney was a small town and the seafaring fraternity was a tight-knit community. Canney must have known his mate was marrying the harbour master's daughter. Very likely, he attended the wedding. Very likely he knew that Norris intended to leave the ship in Sydney when they came back for the second time.

Throughout his life, it was characteristic of Edward Canney to help people in need, people in love perhaps or, more often, people caught in the emotional trauma of separation from loved ones or desperate to protect children who might be left alone and destitute. As first mate on the *Hive*, with a captain more interested in the bottle than the details of his ship, we can be fairly sure that it was Canney who arranged for so many young boys to sail as members of the crew. Some of them were revealed to be the sons of prisoners on board but the true story of other boys will remain hidden until their descendants uncover it.

By the time the *Hive* sailed there was in fact an official reunion scheme operating for convict families. It had begun in 1817 when Macquarie was governor but, as Perry McIntyre points out, it had been operating unofficially since 1790 when six women were allowed to accompany their husbands. *Ad hoc* approval was given for others over the following years, sometimes for large groups of families, such as those who came on the *Broxbornebury* (120) in 1814 and the *Northampton* (110) in 1815.[7] Established officially in 1817, the scheme developed further over time. By 1830 the rules had been formalised with more precise detail, such as the amount of time a convict must serve before he was eligible to apply. Good conduct was essential too, otherwise the application would fail at the first hurdle, that is, the approval of colonial officials including the governor. Printed forms were available for applicants. Names, ages and location of a man's wife and children must be supplied. Referees must be obtained in the colony and nominated at home.[8] Towards the end of the 1830s, another significant effort was made to facilitate family reunion. Several ships carrying female convicts also carried the wives and children of men who had been transported earlier. Among them was the *Margaret*.

As captain of the *Margaret*, Edward Canney probably coped better than most at finding himself, in effect, commanding a mobile nursery: not just female prisoners and their children but wives and children of convicts too. On her first voyage to Sydney she carried 153 Irish women prisoners accompanied by 27 of their children plus 25 free women and their 23 children, some of whom were as young as five years.[9]

For the second voyage, again with Canney as captain, 189 women prisoners with 44 children embarked at Dublin in September 1838. This time 57 wives of convicts joined the prisoners, with 44 children, the oldest of whom was nine years. Totalling up the numbers for prisoners and free immigrants reveals that there were 50 children on the first voyage and 44 under the age of ten on the second.[10]

So many young passengers must have caused bedlam above and below decks. As master, Canney could take refuge on the poop deck, but the surgeon superintendent was exposed to the full onslaught. Doctor Henry Kelsall on the first voyage and Doctor George Todd Moxey on the second were entirely responsible for the welfare of these young passengers as well as their mothers. And there were problems to cope with beyond the sheer numbers. Kelsall was appalled to discover that both his penal and his free charges had been sent on board in a filthy state, the prisoners infected by 'the itch' (*psora*) as well as influenza, the immigrants riddled with lice. The convicts, at least, had been supplied with some spare clothing, however inadequate, but the immigrants were not only sent on board in rags, they were given no change of clothes at all. Many were in poor general health. Some seriously ill. Kelsall disembarked four women on the grounds they were too sick to sail.[11]

Not every woman who had been granted the much-desired free passage turned up. Perhaps the thought of the long voyage was overwhelming. Perhaps the desolation of leaving loved ones obliterated the longing to join the one lost many years before. Just as tragic as those who passed up the opportunity were moral judgements made in the office of the lord lieutenant of Ireland which prevented some families from sailing. One woman's chance of joining her husband was dismissed with the comment 'wife having had an illegitimate child, the family are not to be sent out'.[12]

Once under way, the challenges continued for surgeon Kelsall. Like other surgeons he knew that regular food was not enough. Cleanliness, sunshine and exercise were also crucial to keeping his charges healthy. He had trouble getting them on deck. His journal records that 'most of the convicts, if permitted, pass the whole of the day in bed' and he added that they collected all kinds of 'rubbish' about them (for which we might read 'personal possessions'). He was particularly taken aback to discover the Irish prisoners were washing their linen in putrid urine and hanging it up to dry in the prison deck, a habit developed perhaps in gaol when they lacked water. These intrusive attempts to control their behaviour, however, were probably offset for the women by an unexpected benefit from being transported: health care. The surgeon's presence on board offered the best access to medical attention most of them would ever have experienced. But attending to 178 women and 50 children was asking a lot of the most devoted and professional medical officer, particularly when their health began from such a low base. Kelsall lost four women during the voyage (two prisoners and two immigrants), plus five children. As master, Edward Canney quickly became familiar with his sombre responsibility to read the service for burials at sea.[13]

In addition to his medical duties, the ship's surgeon was required to obtain as many details as possible about the immigrant women's relatives in Australia, including the men's location. This may have been information that they were reluctant to give. In any event, they were not very forthcoming. Driven to exasperation by their vague answers, Henry Kelsall described them as 'a stupid set of people'.[14]

Kelsall bore the brunt of difficulties created by transporting so many women and children without appropriate preparation. By the second voyage, some of the problems that he had to contend with had been improved if not fixed entirely. On that trip, for instance, Captain Canney signed a receipt for a long list of extra clothing supplied by the Irish government. Greater details about the women's husbands, their location and name of sponsors in the colony were also supplied by the lord lieutenant's office. Even a list containing the colonial governor's opinion about which men deserved to have their families sent out was forwarded to the *Margaret*. The surgeon for this voyage, George Todd Moxey, was given some control over who sailed. He inspected the women at the gaol in Dublin before they were embarked and described them as 'clean and healthy'. The prisoners were apparently younger than the immigrants which seems logical since the latter were travelling to join husbands. Moxey lectured them all about the importance of keeping their sleeping quarters clean and dry. During the voyage, he encouraged them by awarding prizes of tea and sugar to the cleanest and best organised mess group. Whether it was the tea and sugar, or Moxey's manner, the women were apparently responsive to his wishes so his final summary was far more positive than poor Dr Kelsall. By the end of the voyage Moxey felt able to describe his charges as having become 'well-behaved and obedient'.[15] It is possible he received some help in managing his charges from passengers Reverend Frederick Wilkinson and Mrs Wilkinson, although they were Protestant and these were mainly Catholic women which might have limited their influence. The Wilkinsons were returning to the colony after extended leave, he having been suspended by Bishop Broughton for supporting Governor Bourke's plan to establish the non-denominational Irish national school system in New South Wales.[16]

On his first voyage as captain, Edward Canney was in town for a month. Walking the streets of Sydney he would have been hailed by many people, from the highest to the lowest, who knew him from the two voyages he sailed on the *Hive* and, earlier, when he came to Sydney in the final year of his apprenticeship on the *Katherine Stewart Forbes* in 1830. The latter ship transported 200 male prisoners. In the late thirties, when Canney was in port as Master, some of these men would have been working in Sydney, in the construction gangs, in the dockyard or assigned to private employers. Those with shorter sentences would have recently become free and they, in particular, would have been keen to reminisce and to get news of home. Many years later, the esteem in which Canney was held in New South Wales became apparent when a local appeal was established to raise funds for his widow.[17]

Canney's floating nurseries would have delighted Governor Bourke who had long supported the idea of immigration to alleviate Irish poverty. It featured often in discussions with his friend Thomas Spring Rice, along with the benefits of a non-denominational school system and ideas about equal recognition for the Catholic religion. The decision to end free grants of land in the penal colonies had been taken before Bourke arrived in New South Wales. From 1831 it was sold, with the proceeds used towards an immigration fund to which British charities also contributed.[18] In Britain, a high-powered committee of six commissioners was established. They began by offering women a bounty of £8 to emigrate to Australia and a small number took up the opportunity. Simultaneously, the committee decided to test the feasibility of mass female emigration on female-only ships. With the committee's blessing, two cargoes of women were organised by committed individuals, one of whom was the brother of prison reformer Elizabeth Fry. In August 1832 the first ship, the *Princess Royal*, sailed from England to Hobart and the second, the *Red Rover*, from Cork to Sydney. In the colonies their reception was mixed. Some saw the free women as competition. Riding on the mail coach from Liverpool to Sydney in 1834, Baron von Hugel overheard an animated discussion between 'a fat old Scottish woman' who had followed her convict husband many years before, an Irishman named Besnard who was a clerk with the police at Goulburn and a smartly dressed woman, still a convict, but married to a Mr Norton who had retired from his position as gaoler of the Sydney prison. Both the women 'railed against the recently arrived free immigrant girls . . . that this was a monstrous injustice against the female convicts, who were now finding it more difficult to get married and were no longer able to get such good places when they had served their time'.[19]

Although the immigrant women were welcomed initially by the gentry, reservations set in later. Convinced that the 'criminal class' had unique qualities, the colonists had deluded themselves that poor but free women would automatically be virtuous and hard-working compared with those 'idle, drunken prostitutes' who were transported as prisoners. Whenever an immigrant girl was caught drunk or disorderly, there was an outcry as realisation dawned that they were much the same as the convicts. Despite this reaction, the scheme was successful. After the first two ships left, the committee in London disbanded but put in place a long-term arrangement with the Refuge for the Destitute to oversee female emigration.[20] Between 1833 and 1836 when the focus solely on female emigration ended, the scheme exported to Australia approximately 2700 single women from Ireland and England.[21] Writing of those who arrived on the *Bussorah Merchant* which brought 200 women to Sydney in 1833, Rusden and McIntyre summed up their contribution: 'Some left no discernible imprint on colonial society . . . Others were "failures" whose criminality, inability to cope with the trials of translocation, or early death prevented them from realising their emigration hopes . . . the vast majority of the *Bussorah Merchant* women were resourceful and independent. They lived married lives of quiet domesticity, many experiencing a degree of social and geographic mobility. Some bore large families before a period of widowhood at the end of their lives.'[22] And like the immigrants on Captain Canney's voyages, some married convict men, thus facilitating the union between bond and free settler that is the story of Australia.

A decade earlier Commissioner Bigge had recommended the end of the longstanding colonial device of assigning prisoners to their free wives, that is, free as settlers or free because they were born in the colony. It was as Governor Bourke later pointed out, a 'virtual release from penal servitude'. Just like assigning women to their husbands, although that comparison was not made. An Act was passed to prevent the practice for men, but its consequence was to deprive a significant number of women and children of essential male support. Wives and families brought to the colony were caught in a similar poverty trap if their husband or father subsequently deserted them or could not be found after they arrived. In the latter case, Governor Darling created regulations governing a man's application for passage for his family that contained a requirement of good behaviour. In a further attempt to screen out unreliable men, Governor Bourke's remedy was to extend the period of good behaviour before they could apply.[23]

Within the colony, employers were usually willing to promote family reunion both from the goodness of their heart but also, in some cases, because they would gain extra and willing hands to work for them—a housekeeper perhaps, or someone reliable to do the washing. At other times family reunion could herald the loss of a valuable employee. In 1831 Sir Edward Parry, who was in charge of the Australian Agricultural Company at Port Stephens, faced such a dilemma when pastoralist William Ogilvie wrote asking him to release Richard Beecher so he could join his wife who was in Ogilvie's service. Parry replied that he was 'on every account desirous that [Beecher] should be reunited with his wife' and that he had agreed to apply for her as soon as Beecher could find out where she was. But he had a problem. Letting Beecher go would be detrimental to the company. 'Richard Beecher is an extremely valuable man,' he wrote to Ogilvie, 'not only on account of his steady good conduct, but also from his Qualifications as a Seaman (by which he saves to the Company, in the Lambton Cutter, between £2 & £3 per month).' He told Ogilvie he could only agree to part with Beecher if an able seaman was supplied in exchange and suggested that Ogilvie pursue it with the superintendent of convicts.[24]

Perry McIntyre's research on family reunion revealed that Irish convicts made up 60 per cent of those who applied to the government for their families to be sent out. Of those, 42 per cent were successful.[25] Thirteen men or 5 per cent who arrived on the *Hive* were among those who applied. Some failed at the first test. John Swaine's application, for example, was rejected on the grounds that he had not served enough of his sentence. Lawrence Crotty, who was the informer against the Connery brothers, was refused the first time for applying too early; however, he persisted and his second request was approved. He must have waited with excitement for news that his wife Catherine McGrath and son Michael, aged six, plus a second child whose sex and name he did not know, were on their way. Sadly, there is no evidence they ever arrived. But mystery surrounds them. From the mid-1850s, about the time 'Catherine' would have arrived under the reunion scheme, a Lawrence Crotty and someone called Mary began having children in the Maitland area where Lawrence Crotty who came on the *Hive* held a ticket-of-leave. No record exists of a marriage between Lawrence Crotty and Mary, which suggests it was either a de facto relationship or she was an immigrant. Could she be 'Catherine' under another name?[26]

All kinds of things could go wrong in the application process. One major trap was created when the family moved and the distant prisoner put the wrong address on his application. Patrick Kelly's wife, Ann, nearly missed out on her free passage because of confusion about her address. When information that she was eligible for a free passage finally reached her, she reacted promptly. 'Anxious to go,' was the answer. The Kellys had no children and Ann arrived on the *Tamar* in 1853, eighteen years after Patrick Kelly left Ireland. Another prisoner whose application we can be certain succeeded was James Dalton, about whom there is more below.[27]

Being transported as late as 1835 meant the men from the *Hive* were lucky a scheme was operating at all. When transportation to New South Wales ended in 1840 the British government, intent as always on saving money, closed it down, overlooking the fact that more convicts than ever had been transported during the 1830s and those men and women were just becoming eligible for family reunion. There were also applications already in the system which had not yet been dealt with. And applications continued to come in regardless. Some prisoners would not have known the scheme had ended. Others perhaps ignored what the rumour mill was saying and applied anyway.[28] The efforts of Caroline Chisholm were vital in reviving family assisted immigration. She travelled to London in 1846 intent on persuading the British government to reverse its decision to end the family reunion policy. Her timing was impeccable. Transportation of convicts to Van Diemen's Land had just been suspended and Earl Grey, who had returned to power as colonial secretary, was trying to find a way to restart it that would be acceptable to the colonists including one idea that involved sending wives and families with each convict. In January 1847 Grey took the decision to revive the scheme for sending wives and families of emancipists and of deserving convicts already in the colonies. Prisoners transported after 1840, which meant those sent to Van Diemen's Land, had to pay a proportion of the family's fare. It took over two years before the first families sailed under this plan and, in the meantime, Caroline Chisholm arranged for small groups of families to be sent to Van Diemen's Land on female convict ships. From there, some travelled on to Sydney by coastal steamer.[29]

As mentioned above, James Dalton's application for his family to be sent out was successful. His father-in-law, 60-year-old James Ryan, and also young Daniel Ryan, who were the instigators of the abduction and rape of Catherine Hartney, had both been assigned (separately) in the south-west of the colony, but Dalton was sent west to Bathurst. Assigned to work on the large pastoral holdings of the Scottish settler Archibald Campbell, JP, Dalton appears to have been a model prisoner. There is no indication that he infringed any regulation or put himself at risk by getting drunk. Five years after his arrival, he received a ticket-of-leave and then took up the popular way for an emancipist to make some money—establish a carting business. In his case, the cartage was initially between Bathurst and what had become a mission to the Aborigines at Wellington Valley. In 1842 Dalton received his certificate of freedom. Not long after, he made the transition from carter to storekeeper at the settlement of Summerhill not far from Blackman's Swamp, which in 1846 became a town called Orange. Three years later, he had gained enough personal status to be referred to in the press as 'Mr Dalton'. Or perhaps the *Sydney Morning Herald* did not know he had arrived as a convict when it reported in 1848: 'On the night of Sunday 27th October, a carrier with a drayload of goods for Mr Dalton, Summerhill, encamped at Evan's Plains, was robbed by two men on horseback.'[30]

The absence of his wife Ellen's name on Dalton's application meant he had heard that she was dead, but when he applied for all three children to come, he was unaware that two of them, Thomas and Margaret, had emigrated to Canada. James junior, however, had stayed in Ireland. When he arrived in 1849 on the *Panama* his father had moved into Orange and established a new and bigger store. The two men ran it together until 1853 by which time James junior was running the business for himself. Meanwhile, James the elder had diversified. Taking out a liquor licence in 1851, he set up as a publican at The O'Connell Inn in Byng Street, only a month after the New South Wales gold rush began. In May, gold was discovered near Bathurst and fields quickly opened up all around Orange. The Dalton family was well positioned to prosper as thousands of diggers poured into the area. No doubt profits from both the store and the pub rose steeply.[31]

The year 1851 proved to be James Dalton's lucky strike in more ways than one. Early in June he married Johanna Hogan, an emigrant from County Limerick whose mother had been a Ryan. Over the following years they had six children but only one, Michael, who was born in 1856, survived to adulthood. He later joined his half-brothers in the business of Dalton Bros. James the elder died on 1 January 1860 having laid the groundwork for a significant family contribution to their adopted country.[32]

Like their father, his sons were enterprising and energetic. James junior expanded the business greatly into pastoral holdings, construction and real estate across New South Wales but he continued also as a merchant and distributor of retail goods. His brother, Thomas, became mayor of Orange, then in 1882–91 represented the town in the New South Wales Legislative Assembly. Subsequently he was appointed to the Legislative Council, a position he held until his death in 1901.[33] In that role he was active in the Illawarra district where his father had landed so abruptly earlier in the century. Today his name, if not his story, is well known as locals flock to major sporting events at the Thomas Dalton stadium or walk their dogs in Thomas Dalton park. The younger generation of Daltons symbolise a broader Australian story too. They are typical of many who arrived in Australia later in the nineteenth century and were categorised as 'free settlers' but who had blood ties to the convict era.

Not all reunions were between parent and child. John Horgen, for example, was reunited with his aunt, Anastasia Cotter, who was a free emigrant. Or she may have been his sister. She described herself as 'aunt' to the colonial secretary but 'sister' to the magistrate at Port Macquarie. Significantly, she emigrated after Horgen was transported and followed him to Port Macquarie. The 1837 muster shows Horgen assigned to Charles Steel in Port Macquarie who, according to Anastasia, 'lent' Horgen's services to her on the understanding he stayed within the district. But the pair were ambitious. In March 1838 Anastasia petitioned the governor telling him of her plan to buy a farm 'contiguous to the Sydney Market'. The key to her success, she told him, would be her nephew's help because of 'his long practical farming acquired in the Mother Country and [his] acquired knowledge of the Colony'. She exaggerated her age to 60, when it was really 50. In passing, she also mentioned the need to protect two young nieces which immediately raises a question:

Were the girls in fact John Horgen's daughters? Governor Bourke asked for a further report on John Horgen, which produced a very positive response from the police magistrate in Port Macquarie. 'The conduct of the prisoner Horgen has been highly satisfactory since his arrival in the District,' he wrote.[34]

Sadly it came to nothing for Anastasia, who died in 1839. Horgen's fate is uncertain. Witnesses at his trial described him as 'a clever man' and the manoeuvring revealed by Anastasia's petition confirms it. They were running their own race but exactly what it was is hard for a researcher to determine. Horgen's trial for swearing a false affidavit about the burning down of his farm's outbuildings, for which he received insurance compensation, also revealed he was a man of substance with money, land and reputation. His former landlord testified that he always paid his rent reliably, managed his crops well, then subsequently bought a farm of his own. He is the only prisoner on the *Hive* who is described as exhibiting some kind of shame in the courtroom, 'endeavouring throughout the trial to conceal his face from the gaze of a very crowded Court'. When he was found guilty, he 'shrank down in the dock to avoid the eyes of all . . . which were turned towards him'.[35] His sister's petition and immigration records suggest that he recognised the chances New South Wales offered and had the means to ensure his family shared them.

Like so much else in the convict era, family reunions defied attempts to manage them systematically. When thwarted by the authorities, determined men and women did what was necessary to rejoin their relatives. Their numbers can never be accurately calculated. Perry McIntyre's work and other detailed studies of shipping records during the nineteenth century are expanding our knowledge immensely, but there remains much to be explored from the original documents rather than taking existing publications, such as R.B. Madgwick's *Immigration into Eastern Australia* as a reliable starting point. While excellent in many ways, Madgwick's work drew heavily on the nineteenth-century statistician Thomas Coghlan, whose analysis was based on published government records which took no account of anomalies. More significantly, Coghlan's interpretations were very much shaped by the assumptions of his day, for example, that free settlers and convicts were separate species who never integrated.[36] Indeed for many decades Australians fostered this idea. The Durack family, for instance, is famous in Australian history but flatly denied any connection to Lawrence Durack who arrived on the *Hive* as a prisoner. Nevertheless,

Patsy and Mick Durack, who founded the Western Australian Duracks, were almost certainly nephews. It is only since descendants have taken up detailed individual research that many connections have been exposed. As McIntyre discovered and my own research supports, the reality was the opposite of Coghlan's assumptions. Most of Australia's nineteenth-century migrants were from the same socioeconomic group as the convicts and many were related to them in some way, or became so after they arrived. A significant number of those described as 'free settlers' to Australia were often driven by the emotional impetus for family reunion. We know now that people did not give up just because the government said 'no'. Some convicts subsequently paid for their families to join them. Sometimes the home parish raised money to assist. One way or another, the small proportion who were officially granted a free passage by the government, or those who emigrated through the assistance of the bounty scheme, were swelled by a significant number who came in an unorthodox fashion, for instance, as sailors working their passage, as babies of prisoners, or as criminals transported for crimes that were deliberately committed.

Edward Canney, who had done his part to help people desperate to reach Australia, sailed for England after his second voyage on 29 June 1838, arriving in London for Christmas. He would return to New South Wales one more time as master of a convict transport, once again commanding the *Margaret* and once again carrying 132 Irish female prisoners accompanied by their 44 children as well as 22 free women with 34 children.[37] On the third voyage, he was in a hurry to get home for an important date in London.

CHAPTER 9
Managing Norfolk Island

The night before he sailed from Sydney, Henry Lugard had been introduced to Ensign Abel Best of the 80th Regiment with the words 'Here's another poor Norfolk Island Devil.' They were to be fellow passengers on the *Governor Phillip* the next morning. The two spent the six-day voyage killing themselves with laughter 'until the tears ran down our cheeks' at the antics of Best's commanding officer, Lieutenant McDonald, and his wife. As Best put it in his journal: 'McDonald was a man weighing from seventeen to eighteen stone and his lady was, as some said, his better half.' Realising they would not both fit in their allocated berth, the lieutenant insisted she stay in the main cabin where, to the young men's amusement, 'when the brig rolled she meandered from one side of the cabin to the other like a huge cask and her servant maid was ordered in to hold her still while she slept'. As the weather worsened, she 'wailed fearfully', seeking loud reassurance every fifteen minutes from the master or her husband.[1] By the time they arrived at the island, Lugard and Best's friendship was cemented by laughter.

Commandant Joseph Anderson was in charge of the island for the first nine months that Lugard spent there. He was the seventh commandant since it reopened in 1825 as a secondary punishment settlement. Before that, Norfolk Island was used during the early years of European settlement to cultivate agriculture in the hope it could produce additional supplies for the settlement at Port Jackson. It was also mentioned in the 'heads of a plan' for settlement of Australia, which was drawn up in Britain and required the colonists to investigate the production of items such as sails and clothing from the flax that grew there.[2]

Settlement on the island was established with a small team under the then Lieutenant King. It soon became a useful place for early governors to send people who were proving a nuisance. By that means, they could break up 'dangerous associations' and, in Governor King's case, isolate Irishmen he feared might create a revolt (that is, who had taken part in the 1804 rebellion). However, as the mainland colony became more sustainable and Europeans spread around the Cumberland Plain, the difficulty of landing at Norfolk Island began to outweigh its benefits. In 1808, families who had made it their home were resettled in Van Diemen's Land at what became known as 'New Norfolk'.

When the island was made operational again in 1825, its purpose was punishment. Commissioner Bigge recommended that secondary punishment settlements be sited well away from Sydney in order to prevent escapes. Charged with implementing Bigge's report, Governor Brisbane decided that putting punishment outposts at Port Macquarie, Moreton Bay and Norfolk Island would meet this goal, although Port Macquarie was changed to a free settlement in 1832. Moreton Bay continued until 1839. Norfolk Island endured as a feared place of further punishment until 1855, two years after transportation ended to Van Diemen's Land.

The government always intended to make the convicts fear being sent to its new punishment settlements and we cannot ignore the extent to which official propaganda shaped their reputation. In Norfolk Island's case this was compounded decades later by scaremongering from, mainly, free settlers who wanted transportation to end.[3] The Gothic melodrama they conjured up held sway until recently, when Tim Causer exploded many myths with his doctoral thesis based on a comprehensive examination of the original sources for the first time.[4]

Five of the commandants who preceded Joseph Anderson were military officers who were in charge of the island for short periods ranging from three to five months to sixteen and eighteen months. However, Anderson's immediate predecessor, James Morisset, was there for five years. During his regime, brutal treatment of the prisoners assumed proportions that matched the government's publicity.⁵ Morisset's rule culminated in a mass revolt by the prisoners in 1834. Governor Bourke chose Anderson, who had just arrived in the colony with his regiment, to restore order and supervise the trials and executions that followed.⁶

Joseph Anderson was a Scot, who had been in the army since he was fifteen. He had seen many battles in Spain during the war against the French and, like other colonial administrators, his ideas of discipline were shaped by military service where, for example, flogging was commonplace. On Norfolk Island, like the mainland, the number of prisoners always far outweighed the military guard. In 1836, for example, 1200 prisoners were guarded by about 150 soldiers of the 50th Foot, plus their officers and civilian officials totalling about 30.⁷ Joseph Anderson would have assessed these odds professionally, particularly in the light of the recent mutiny. On discovering that the Norfolk Island prisoners included about 100 former soldiers who had been transported following court-martial, Anderson mustered them specially and, according to his *Recollections*, warned they were threatened with degradation by associating with 'criminals of the deepest dye'. He would try to save them by separating their work and living quarters. Naturally enough, this announcement was greeted by cheers, but this made Anderson threaten, 'If you ever again speak or associate with your former companions, back you go to remain with them as outcasts of misery.' His real purpose, to increase the forces available for controlling an emergency, was revealed when he told them that 'if I require you, I shall put arms in your hands; for you have been soldiers—as I am now—so I shall not be afraid to trust you if necessary'.⁸

Anderson's five years in charge were relatively peaceful for the prisoners, except for one early misstep. In 1835 he decided that potatoes would be beneficial to the prisoners' diet and obtained approval from the authorities in Sydney. A harmless decision in itself but when he announced potatoes would replace sugar, mayhem resulted. Anderson had misjudged the prisoners' attachment to their sugar ration. Most had rarely, if ever, eaten sugar in their homeland where their poverty made it a luxury they could not afford. Its inclusion in their penal rations, whether called a privilege or not, had given them a taste for it that would not be denied. Along with access to red meat, it was one of the dietary benefits of transportation. When they simply refused to accept potatoes as a substitute, Anderson was taken aback, even riding round the various gangs and explaining to the men why potatoes were a good idea. Nothing he said convinced them. They would not budge. Next, he resorted to an official order that amounted to 'Eat potatoes, or else' and categorised their refusal as 'disobedience and insubordination'. Ultimately the prisoners accepted potatoes as a substitute for maize and the sugar ration continued.[9]

When he wasn't supervising and designing buildings, Henry Lugard was hunting, shooting and fishing with his friends. Ensign Best's diary records their activities together: how he 'went shooting pigeons with Lugard', swam or 'fished with Lugard', went on 'picnics organised by the ladies' and 'rode round the island together'. Best also attended 'the christening of Lugard's summerhouse that he had built in his new garden'. It was all a far cry from the experience of the prisoners who surrounded them. Commandant Anderson sometimes joined them for a ride, or for shooting in the bush. In September 1838, soon after Henry arrived, he went with them on a fishing expedition to Phillip Island. Neither he nor Best were there, however, when Lugard, accompanied by the recently arrived deputy acting commissary-general Turner, went back to Phillip Island intent on some shooting.[10] Returning in rough seas, the boat capsized and they had to be rescued by two prisoners, Michael Donnelly and Aaron Price. Price was the same Aaron Price who had been a member of the Irish Brigade which terrorised the Hunter Valley settlers in the mid-1820s. Twelve years later, he was the powerful overseer of public works at Norfolk Island, such a comfortable position that when he gained a ticket-of-leave in 1840 he chose to stay there. Conscious of how nearly they had drowned, Lugard recommended both men for a remission of their sentences.[11]

In November 1839, Lugard was joined on the island by a prisoner he knew from the shipwreck of the *Hive*. Darby McAuliffe was distinctive because of his sandy hair and reddish whiskers. On assignment in New South Wales he killed and apparently ate part of a sheep, betrayed by a carcase which was found in his hut. Until then his record suggests he had been a useful employee, a gardener and a sheepshearer, a steady man who at 33 was older than some of the tearaways who shared his voyage out. His wife and two children, who were left behind when he was transported for shop stealing in Kerry, were an incentive to manage his sentence so he could get them to the colony and he had no police record in New South Wales. When he was charged with 'killing a sheep with intent

Irish poverty became an increasingly controversial issue in England during the nineteenth century, particularly during the Great Famine of the 1840s. Images of tenants being evicted, such as these, were an attempt to jolt the British authorities into action. *Illustrated London News*

Poverty and despair are etched on the face of a nineteenth-century labourer in Ireland.

Portrait of John Hubert Plunkett around the time he arrived in the colony to become solicitor-general. Edmund Thomas, State Library of NSW, P2 / 161, Digital No. 1528443

Portrait of Roger Therry in 1834. Therry was commissioner for the Court of Common Requests and also a barrister in private practice. Richard Read, State Library of NSW, a3754001

The only statue of a colonial governor erected by people who knew him. Its subject, the Protestant Irish governor, Richard Bourke, sat for the sculptor while in retirement in Ireland. Erected on a hill overlooking the Domain, its unveiling in 1842 by Governor Gipps was the culmination of a festive parade along Macquarie Street.

Photograph by Elizabeth Weiss

Convicts built the breakwater to join Nobby's Island to the coast near Newcastle over approximately twenty years. By the 1840s, working on the breakwater was reserved as 'hard labour' for men who had committed further offences after they arrived in New South Wales. Joseph Lycett, State Library of NSW, a928877

The Royal Hotel in Sydney, 1836. It was destroyed four years later by a spectacular fire on St Patrick's Day. I.H. Berner, State Library of NSW, a1811005

The collision between a steamer and the sailing ship *Josephine Willis* made headlines around the world. *Illustrated Times of London*, 5 February 1856

'Very young and very beautiful': Mattie McHenry around the time she became engaged to Henry Lugard. State Library of NSW, A929-2/M

Illustration of a shako badge found at the Lancer Barracks at Parramatta. It formed part of the headdress of a soldier of the 28th (North Gloucestershire) Regiment of Foot, some of whom were on board the *Hive* when it was wrecked in 1835. Drawing by Tim Smith

One of Henry Lugard's successors would have occupied this comfortable office on Norfolk Island, which was possibly designed by Henry. During his time on Norfolk Island in 1838–39, Henry would have worked in a far less comfortable hut. Author's photo

House built to a template design by Henry Lugard on Quality Row, Norfolk Island. The design was repeated several times to create a streetscape. Author's photo

The four paintings on this spread are by S.T. Gill (1818–80). Historically famous as 'the artist of the Victorian goldfields', he also documented the type of work done by Irish and other convicts. Cattle branding was a regular job, along with sheep washing and shearing. 'Cattle branding', S.T. Gill, *The Australian Sketchbook*, National Gallery of Victoria, an7149193

Splitters were part of a sawyers' gang like the ones who went on strike in 1819. Governor Macquarie was fearful that Commissioner Bigge, who was in the colony, would learn about it. 'Splitters', S.T. Gill, *The Australian Sketchbook*, National Gallery of Victoria, an7150082

Convict stockmen 'set off in search of the cattle, riding in a style later cast as the legendary "man from Snowy River" . . . cracking their whips and riding full gallop . . . through wilds, wood, and plains, up and down steep hills'. 'Stockman', S.T. Gill, *The Australian Sketchbook*, National Library of Australia, an 7149199

Drays were often the target of bushrangers. The bullock drivers, who were usually convicts or ex-convicts, could be the victims and sometime the collaborators in a robbery. 'Bullock driver with wool dray', S.T. Gill, *The Australian Sketchbook*, National Gallery of Victoria, an7150077

Nineteenth-century
Australian men.
State Library of NSW, A&A
Photographic Company,
a2822709

The story of a feisty
Irish protestor is
inscribed on Michael
Ryan's gravestone.
The truth was less
romantic. The tomb-
stone was erected by
his brother and fellow
convict, Philip Ryan.
Both were transported
on the *Hive*.
Photograph by Jack Sullivan,
Newcastle Region Library

to steal it' he was aggrieved although the records don't reveal whether that was because he claimed innocence or because he felt his employer should have overlooked the offence. In court he argued that he had been with Henry Hall of Limestone Plains for four years without incident.[12] Other prisoners would have agreed with him that the charge was unfair. Sheep stealing was widespread among farm workers. In some places, the master or overseer would turn a blind eye when convicts supplemented their rations with a choice piece of lamb or beef from their master's stock. Others would bring down the full penalty of the law if assigned servants were caught doing this. James Phillips at the Paterson River prosecuted two convicts who slaughtered one of his sheep. Their sense of entitlement to supplement their rations was evident when they retorted, 'You should have given us more to eat and these things would not happen.'[13]

Darby McAuliffe became an overseer soon after he arrived, possibly because Henry Lugard recognised him as a useful and reliable man from their time during the shipwreck. From that position, he later managed to get the ear of commandant Maconochie, who wrote to Governor Gipps on his behalf in November 1842. McAuliffe wanted the description of the charge altered—and his sentence too, of course. 'The offence [description] can be amended, but that can make no alteration in the man's position at Norfolk Island,' wrote Gipps. 'It was rather of a higher nature than that of simple cattle stealing.'[14] Most of McAuliffe's stay on the island, to which he was sentenced for ten years, coincided with penal reformer Alexander Maconochie's time as commandant. McAuliffe's continued cooperation with Maconochie paid off in the long term. After being transferred to Van Diemen's Land when management switched early in 1844, he completed a further one year and three months under the probation system. In March 1845 the record notes he received a ticket-of-leave 'for his service on Norfolk Island'. Three years later, along with most other New South Wales lifers he received a conditional pardon for his original sentence.[15]

Studies of penal settlements like Norfolk Island have traditionally focused on crime and punishment. And the human condition in extreme circumstances. There is another angle, however. While the business of a penal colony was containing and managing prisoners, the structure for doing so had many similarities with a small–medium business today. Certainly the human resources deployed to run the operation were similar to those we find in the workforce. A comparison between Moreton Bay and Norfolk Island reveals a couple of differences. First is the absence of female convicts. A few women prisoners were sent to Norfolk Island as domestic servants for officials but, unlike Moreton Bay, no women were sentenced there for colonial crimes. The second difference was the greater prominence of civilian officials at Norfolk Island. At Moreton Bay the military combined acting as a guard with supervising work. Except for the early years on Norfolk Island, the military were not responsible for production and they did not supervise the convict workforce. The military were *only* there as a guard—to protect the officials, prevent escapes and put down any mutiny that might occur. From the early 1830s, civilian officials and civilian overseers, some of them ex-convicts, increasingly supervised the prisoners' work. The power structure was more complex than a single despot, backed up by soldiers. Furthermore, Tim Causer's research revealed that tensions in the ruling *structure* gave rise to disputes more often than the foibles of a commandant. He concluded that 'Acrimonious relationships were a fact of life on Norfolk Island.'[16]

The commandants were in effect chief executive of seven departments, not all of which functioned all of the time. Management of the commissariat or government stores, of agriculture and provision of medical services was continuous as was the penal or convict function of assigning prisoners to work or punishment. And keeping their records. A full-blown medical department with dispensers working under the doctor, the presence of both Church of England and Roman Catholic clergymen developed over time, as did the engineering department. Legal functionaries came and went initially, and only briefly resulted in a stipendiary magistrate residing on the Island.[17] The commandant sat at the head of this structure but in reality the chief executive function was severely undermined by that nemesis of every senior manager—a double reporting line. While the civilian staff, like the military, were obliged to obey the commandant's general orders on a daily basis they had their own superiors either on the island or back at headquarters. If they felt aggrieved by the commandant they would seek to bypass him or, in the case of clergymen, go over his head directly to the governor or the British government. However, Causer found that the commandant always won and the complainants were removed 'to keep the peace'.[18]

Departmental officials also fought each other. Turf wars were frequent and commandants had to adjudicate numerous disputes between senior officials from different sections. Disputes were time-consuming and exhausting for a commandant who had greater emergencies to manage.

Joseph Anderson, for instance, was in almost constant warfare with a succession of officials from most branches of his administration: the superintendent of agriculture, the commissary clerk, the superintendent of convicts and the chaplain. Alexander Maconochie found himself in dispute with clergymen of all persuasion, as well as the deputy assistant commissary-general, and two consecutive superintendents of agriculture. Commandant Joseph Childs clashed with the deputy assistant commissary-general and the Church of England chaplain Thomas Rogers. Following which Rogers, along with the then superintendent of agriculture, became a thorn in the side of commandant John Price.[19]

Status anxiety and demarcation disputes occupied a lot of time in the punishment settlements. As Evans and Thorpe demonstrated at Moreton Bay and Causer has found on Norfolk Island, status was a constant preoccupation.[20] For instance, in late 1842 Father John McEncroe, then the senior Catholic priest, complained that the word 'free' was entered after the names of his two catechists, as if they had once been something else. The commandant John Maconochie explained this was due to the assiduous record-keeping of his clerk, a convict named Levi Abraham who had followed orders that the penal status must be recorded for all people earning more than £100. Despite Maconochie's prompt and what he described as 'ample apology from all concerned', McEncroe and his catechists insisted their honour and standing had been impugned. Offended letters flowed to Governor Gipps in Sydney. Maconochie was dealing with this voluble outrage simultaneously with repercussions of a mutiny only months before when convicts tried to seize the ship *Governor Phillip*.[21]

The medical staff could be just as difficult. Commandant Anderson, for example, clashed volcanically with the island's surgeon, Dr Alexander Gamack. The doctor complained to *his* superiors that relations with the commandant were so strained they only spoke in public. To which Anderson replied to *his* superior, the colonial secretary in Sydney, that it was due to the doctor's close involvement with several officials on the island who opposed his, Anderson's, authority. This was a reference to the commandant's feud with the then superintendent of agriculture Archibald McLeod. Determined to rid himself of the doctor, Anderson noted that Gamack attended church with the convicts rather than his own class. And the commandant then stooped to Island gossip, telling the colonial secretary: '*I am very well informed*, a child begotten in Sin is now the living evidence of Mr Gamack's gratitude.' From which he seems to suggest that the doctor had allowed or promoted a relationship between his assigned female servant and the superintendent. According to Causer, the underlying problem was the commandant's belief the surgeon exempted too many men from work and went easy on malingerers.[22]

Managing staff was as much a challenge for the powerful commandants as any difficulty caused by the prisoners, but the problem was not confined to officials. Power was fluid even in secondary punishment settlements. The Hunter Valley bushranger, Aaron Price, was not the only prisoner who had been transported to Norfolk Island but rose to a position of authority. And some officials, such as Alfred Baldock, were ex-convicts who had completed their sentence on the mainland.[23]

Among prisoners, outwitting the state was a constant preoccupation which, if they succeeded, made them heroes with their peers. This culture also legitimated trafficking. On Norfolk Island a prisoner like bushranger Martin Cash kept himself supplied with tea and sugar by making hats. Other prisoners traded their expertise in carpentry or sold their labour privately. Many cultivated vegetable gardens and traded the produce.[24] Their customers were government officials, the military and other prisoners all taking part in a mutually beneficial exchange which cut across power and status.[25] Visiting ships offered a chance for profit from items made or grown on the island. Goods that the vessels carried, including grog, entered the local black market.[26]

Resisting authority was a matter of pride for the prisoners, even if it only extended to style. Martin Cash described the everyday dynamics when he arrived at Norfolk Island in 1844. '[T]he convict regulations,' he said, 'were not strictly carried out, and . . . a free-and-easy style pervaded the whole establishment.'[27] Deconstructing a disapproving account by an official, Robert Pringle Stuart, two years later supports what Cash had to say. Attending the morning muster, Stuart expected to observe a strictly controlled procedure, precise orderly behaviour, obedience to commands and stentorian, punitive guards who enforced the rules. Instead he saw prisoners strolling out of the barracks at their own pace, leaning against a wall or conversing in groups as they had a morning smoke. And soldiers who were equally relaxed and failed to remonstrate if their orders were ignored or rules were broken. Stuart's description provides a vignette of how prisoners set the style and the guards accommodated them. In fact, disrupting established culture like this could be a serious risk. In 1846 the decision to ban prisoners' gardens and some months later to confiscate their kettles triggered a violent mutiny. Discipline tightened to significant cruelty under commandant John Price but there was no indication, from Cash for instance, that it totally destroyed the prisoners' underground society. Despite their individual vulnerability to punishment by flogging or solitary confinement or the loss of privileges, collectively the prisoners exercised considerable power.[28]

Many examples demonstrate that convicts had reason to expect collaboration from all but the highest officials. The guards were from the same socioeconomic background as the prisoners and frequently sympathetic. Martin Cash recounts how on his voyage to Norfolk Island, 'The first mate appointed me cook, *merely with the object of giving me the privilege of remaining on deck*' (emphasis added).[29] As mentioned earlier, the military had no involvement in productivity. Nor were they responsible for discipline or punishment. For most of the soldiers, Norfolk Island was a boring posting except for occasional emergencies. Causer found what he described as 'ample evidence' that prisoners and soldiers on the island interacted easily, often sharing a mutually beneficial economic exchange. Some even escaped together.[30]

Norfolk Island's reputation promoted the idea that, once sent there, a man never returned. And there was no escape. Causer has disproved both. Many escapes were tried and many failed. Late in 1839 Henry Lugard helped foil a daring, if foolhardy, attempt when a boat waiting to take some military officers fishing inside the reef at Slaughter Bay (in front of the main settlement) was suddenly seized by a gang of prisoners working nearby. They grabbed the boat, forced out the convict boat crew and rowed directly over the reef and into the open sea. Bystanders were briefly stupefied when they survived the reef, which was regarded as likely to rip the bottom out of any boat that tried. Henry Lugard, who may have been one of those intending to fish, led the chase with two boats full of soldiers (no doubt enjoying one of their rare moments of excitement). They caught the fugitives about two miles out. Under fire, the convicts surrendered.[31]

From a total database of 6458 men who passed through Norfolk Island, Causer disproved the legend that all men sent there were doubly-convicted. He established that only 3860 were convicted twice, 2590 in New South Wales and 1270 in Van Diemen's Land. A further 165 men had come free or been born in the Australian colonies.[32] The average time prisoners spent on Norfolk Island was three years, after which men returned to either New South Wales or Van Diemen's Land to continue their original servitude or resume their emancipist status. There was far more traffic to and fro than we have previously understood. As we shall see, however, some men, including some from the *Hive*, got caught by the change of management from New South Wales to Van Diemen's Land in 1844, which removed their chance of an early return to New South Wales. Some men were transported directly from England when Norfolk Island was treated as a Van Diemen's Land 'probation station' in the forties and they are discounted in this analysis. There was also a core group among the colonially convicted, usually known as the 'old hands', who fought the system at every turn and suffered its worst brutality, some of whom spent twenty years on the island.[33]

Spectacular exploits by men such as Martin Cash and the long internment of ex-soldier Denis Dougherty combined with the melodramatic interpretation of Norfolk Island history to leave an impression that Irishmen figured largely in the legend. The facts suggest otherwise. Of the thirteen men executed for the 1834 riot only three were Irish. The 1846 riot included only two Irishmen out of twelve hanged. Causer compared his statistics with those of historian Lloyd Robson and of Nicholas and Shergold in *Convict Workers*. Against those yardsticks, there was a 'slightly larger proportion of Scottish and foreign-born men' and 'just over a quarter were Irish, which is perhaps fewer than might be expected given their prominence'. Two-thirds of the men sent to the island gave their birthplace as England.[34] Predominantly Anglo-Celtic, their numbers were spiced with diversity—too much so according to a visiting clergyman who thought the mix an outrage: 'Chinamen from Hong Kong, the Aborigines of New Holland, West Indian blacks, Greeks, Caffres [Kaffirs] and Malays' along with army deserters and, he added, 'idiots, madmen, pig-stealers and pickpockets'.[35] Tim Causer provided some facts to counter his extravagance. His database included 'five Aboriginal men . . . five Chinese, a few Americans and Europeans, and men from Mauritius, India and the West Indies'. These included two men who were Muslims, and 'Robert Abbott of Demerara whose stated occupation was "slave"'.[36]

Overall, Causer proved that there were only 3680 men who went to Norfolk Island because they had committed a second crime in the penal colonies and the majority of those were there not for violence but for property crimes including sheep stealing like Darby McAuliffe. As Causer says, 'The caricature of Norfolk Islanders as depraved criminals has its roots in their imagined backgrounds.'[37]

Also largely a caricature are the conditions in which the men spent their Norfolk Island sentence. There was a gaol gang for local punishment, and grinding labour, some of it in chains, certainly occurred but most prisoners did not work in irons.[38] Punishments were brutal and sometimes sadistic. Prisoners could be vicious and sometimes murderous to one another. But these circumstances had a remarkable consequence. In an amazing description of what was later called 'Australian mateship', Alexander Maconochie wrote in 1842 about the 'old hands' on the island, who were taking part in his new system of mutual responsibility: 'These men knew each other better than did the prisoners [direct from England]; they thus severally chose their companions better; having previously suffered hardship together, they took a deeper interest in each other's welfare; and they thus exhibited much more patience and forbearance with each other's infirmities of temper and other occasional sources of difference.'[39] He concluded that it was 'suffering together' and forming 'friendships in adversity' that were the key to how they cared for one another. However, Maconochie took too much credit. Unknown to him, those qualities he noticed originated in the trauma of the enforced voyage 'beyond the seas' and were incubated further by hardships experienced in the penal colonies. They may have been displayed while he was at Norfolk Island but they were not created by his changes.[40]

Two anecdotes further illustrate the character of men held on the island. In 1834 the schooner *Friendship* dropped anchor close to the shore so the two owners and their wives could dine with Anderson. The commandant warned them of the dangers of their mooring, saying they should stand out to sea immediately if the weather turned bad during the night. The warning was ignored. A gale blew up and the ship's moorings could not hold against the turbulent sea. As dawn broke the vessel was dragged relentlessly towards the rocks with everyone on board soundly asleep. Frantic attempts from shore to wake them included firing guns across the bows. To no avail. It was not until the ship struck and began to break up that anyone stirred. In a repeat of Edward Canney's rescue operation with the *Hive*, a line was fixed to the shore and a large number of prisoners volunteered to risk their lives by forming a human chain along it. Hanging grimly to the rope, they passed women and children from hand to hand as the sea broke over them. Conditions were so rough that a tiny baby was twice swept out of their arms, but miraculously saved. The men risked their lives again to unload the cargo when it was likely to explode.[41] Sixty-one men were recommended for bravery by the captain of the *Friendship*. Anderson praised the men for 'the exertions the humanity and <u>cheerfulness</u>' (underlined in the original). He said that his 'anxiety to do all justice' was why he forwarded so many petitions with his recommendation.[42] The gratitude of Francis White, the baby's father, was profound. Writing to Governor Bourke, he named three prisoners in particular: John McGuiness, who 'made his way through the surf to the vessel when she first struck and, standing on the Chains, was the chief instrument of saving the children'; James Murray who 'at risk of his life, carried Mrs White from the vessel to the beach' and John Bryant, who 'rescued your memorialist's infant after being repeatedly immersed in the water and ultimately carried it on shore'.[43]

The second anecdote concerns the convicts left on the island in 1855 for the handover to the Pitcairn Island settlers. When the Pitcairners arrived they had little knowledge of livestock and none of transport. The handover men helped the new arrivals get settled. Harnessing a couple of bullocks and a cart to bring up the heavy gear from the pier, they gave twenty Pitcairn boys the chance for their first ride on wheels. According to a naval observer, 'The convicts behaved very well in the fortnight they were with the [Pitcairn] natives, teaching them to manage the stock and to plough, work the mills, drive bullocks etc. and considering the strange things horses, ploughs etc. *are* to people who never saw them before, they learnt a good deal.'[44] Pitcairner John Buffett confirmed that 'We were treated with great kindness by the [ticket-of-leave] constables and the prisoners.'[45]

The diversity of jobs on the island also contradicts traditional assumptions. A majority of prisoners worked much as they would have done on a mainland pastoral estate or the government dockyard in Sydney where specialised trade skills were utilised. A wide range of jobs was available. Men worked as agricultural labourers, in the dairy, abbatoir and orchards, but also as clerks, hospital attendants, domestic servants, tutors, clergymen in two cases, bakers, carters and gardeners. In a system similar to building roads in New South Wales, men's labour was utilised in teams of road and bridge parties who were not ironed, and another smaller group whose punishment for infringements on the island was to work in iron gangs for stipulated periods.[46]

Causer found that the convicts brought to the island their perception of colonial 'rights' including withdrawal of labour, negotiation and entitlement to rations. On the island, as on the mainland, rations were the most constant issue.[47] Taskwork was practised in some areas apparently without argument and private jobs were (illegally) performed too. With occasional variation under different administrations, the usual workplace program of time off for half Saturday and all Sunday was followed. Theoretically, Saturday afternoon was for the men to do their personal chores.[48] In practice, they got up to other pursuits as well. The most feared commandant of all, John Price, was asked to explain how they came to perform a theatrical production of 'Black Eyed Susan' in the lumber yard. In his reply Price revealed the power of the prisoners over an extended period, also implying of course that Maconochie was to blame. He told the colonial secretary that attempting to intervene risked inciting violence as the men were accustomed to 'amuse themselves in any way' within the yard, which he said was due to prior 'very great laxity . . . tacitly sanctioned and countenanced'.[49] It didn't occur to him that perhaps his predecessors had no more choice than he but to sanction the men's activities.

In their own time, the men were enthusiastic gardeners with most having their own plot where they grew vegetables to supplement their rations or to trade with others. As early as 1833, commandant James Morisset noted how they would retreat to their small gardens 'the moment they quit Government Labour'.[50] We know they had playing cards and that gambling was hugely popular but it was regarded as immoral and, if caught, the men were punished.[51] The library which had been on the island from at least 1840 was well patronised. In 1846 it contained 500 books. According to Reverend Rogers, nearly 200 were 'mere collections of penny tracts of a very miscellaneous and paltry description'. He was disappointed that religious books were never borrowed while the large holdings of histories and copies of the *Chambers Edinburgh Journal* and the *Saturday Magazine* were 'sought for and read with avidity'.[52]

Commandant Anderson's term ended in April 1839. He was replaced by two military officers. First was Major Thomas Bunbury who held office from May to September 1839. Bunbury and Henry Lugard were friends. On one of their expeditions they got lost in the bush and spent the whole night there, sitting in the dark smoking cigars until dawn. After Anderson left, Lugard moved into Government House to keep Bunbury company.[53] Bunbury's reign ended abruptly when the soldiers from the 80th Regiment who were guarding the island mutinied over Bunbury's order that the sheds behind their barracks from where they conducted a thriving black market with the prisoners should be destroyed. Known, for reasons undiscovered, as 'Irish Town', the huts were regarded by the lower orders on the island as such valuable commodities that soldiers of the 50th Regiment had sold them to the rank and file of the 80th when they relieved the guard. After their first hotheaded reaction, the soldiers of the 80th thought better of it, but Governor Gipps was alarmed when he heard. In consultation with brigade command in Sydney, he decided that the entire detachment should be replaced with fresh troops.[54] As part of the detachment, Ensign Best left too. It was not farewell, however. He and Lugard, and Major Bunbury too, would meet again in New Zealand.

Henry Lugard worked as hard as he played on Norfolk Island. During his time there he completed a survey of the island and a formal plan for the settlement of Kingston. The plan allowed for two churches, one for Protestants and a second for Catholics, both of which were built. Lugard also designed a template for houses to accommodate officials. Over time, ten were completed to his design and they still stand, known collectively as Quality Row. Under his supervision, work began on the construction of a pier using a natural rocky outcrop to the reef as part of the foundations. The difficult construction meant the work was given to the chain gang who were undergoing punishment. Some of these men worked until the tide rose up to their waists. When it receded, they went back in. The job was a long one and not completed until some years later.[55]

Causer's research revealed that 'malingering' was a contentious issue during commandant Anderson's time. Henry's solution was to install 26 handmills on the upper floor of a store near the pier which could be worked by disabled men or those exempt from hard labour for other reasons. The men would not have thanked him for this arrangement. Within a year they had worked out how to damage the mills to the point where they were broken and repaired so many times that Major Bunbury declared they would have to be replaced by new ones. No doubt, once the new mills arrived, the merry-go-round continued.[56] Next door was the Crank Mill which required 92 men to operate. They were supposed to work in silence. Unfortunately for them, most observers of Norfolk

Island were judgemental people, viewing the scene around them from a gentry perspective and usually highly critical. One humourless visitor was appalled at their disobedience: 'a more disorderly, riotous and unseemly exhibition . . . I have never witnessed, so far from silence being observed, the men are engaged in one incessant alternation of shouting, whistling, yelling, hooting, screeching etc. of the loudest description and the use of the most offensive and disgusting language. They can see through the windows all the passers-by and these, especially the officers, are greeted either by excessive shouting and cheering, or by hooting and yelling . . . and an assistant superintendent who is charged with preserving order appears to satisfy himself with parading in peace outside.'[57] Passing the time while performing a very boring task seems a more charitable interpretation of the men's behaviour.

Major Thomas Ryan, also from the 80th Regiment, arrived late in 1839 with a new detachment of men, but he too only ruled for a short time because the British government decided to appoint penal reformer Alexander Maconochie to the post. Before Major Ryan left in March 1840, he paid tribute to Henry Lugard's hard work, writing in his report that 'Many new buildings were completed late in 1839, mainly because of the planning and supervision exerted by Lieutenant Lugard.'[58]

CHAPTER 10
Resisting Ascendancy

By the 1830s the colonial authorities were more alert to the background of newly arrived prisoners. People such as the Connery brothers from Waterford were noticed. Immediately after he landed from the *Hive*, James Connery was sent to the far south-west of New South Wales near an embryonic town called Yass, but when his brothers John and Patrick arrived three years later the authorities kept them close to hand, appointing them immediately as keepers of the Lachlan Swamp, which was Sydney's water reserve.[1] If this was a strategic move then it worked. In the opinion of the brothers' biographer, Brendan Kiely, these jobs were crucial to ensuring the Connerys 'did not contest the penal system in New South Wales', that they did not take to the bush as they had taken to the mountains of Waterford. Kiely describes how they 'adapted quickly to their marshy wilderness and cleared paperbarks and she-oaks to build a house and fence a vegetable garden'.[2] Wild cattle wandering in the swamp provided an opportunity they were quick to take up. Enticed by the vegetables, the cattle entered their snare, thus providing useful income at the Sydney markets. Self-preservation was their watchword. They did not align themselves with convict bolters who often hid in the swamp and in 1842 actually turned in four men after a fight in which John Connery was stabbed.[3]

While John and Patrick served their entire sentence in Sydney caretaking the swamp, James' servitude was wide-ranging. He was assigned first to William Edward Riley, from an England-based family who were originally Irish. Riley's father, Alexander, made a fortune in New South Wales after arriving as a free settler as early as 1804, but in 1817 he took his family back to England. His son came back, however, and in 1833 inherited the estate.[4]

James Connery went first to the Riley property called *Raby* on Alexander's original grant near Liverpool. Detailed records have survived for *Raby* so we know that James arrived on 13 January 1836. We even know that, like Alexander Berry, the management at *Raby* topped up the government rations with extras. In the first week of February, James was issued with ten pounds of 'second class' flour, eight pounds of beef, two ounces of tea, one pound of sugar, one and a half ounces of tobacco and four ounces of soap. He was not at *Raby* long, however. On 25 February he travelled with twelve other men on foot or by bullock dray to Riley's property *Cavan* nearly 150 miles south-west on the Murrumbidgee River. Part of the 70,000 acre property was beyond the limits of location that the government had vainly been trying to enforce for years. Nevertheless, Riley built a comfortable house which he filled, the records tell us, with 'elegant cottage furniture'. He even installed a cannon to communicate with Yass ten miles away.[5]

James Connery was now in country unlike any he had seen before. As if to emphasise the long journey he had travelled from the Emerald Isle, it was high summer at the 'wrong' time of the year and the land was in the grip of drought. At *Cavan* he joined a workforce of approximately 30 men whose responsibilities included managing sheep and cattle and constantly moving them around in search of fodder. Clearing the land was also one of the tasks. Brendan Kiely points out that James would have found cutting down gum trees hard work despite his experience as a woodranger back in County Waterford.[6]

Within months of James Connery's arrival at *Cavan*, William Edward Riley died. Suddenly, James found himself with a new employer. For a brief period, Riley's estate was managed by his friend Stuart Alexander Donaldson who tried hard to maintain its prosperity. In 1838, he was forced to admit defeat. *Cavan* was leased to Major Edmund Lockyer, who

wanted extra pastures to supplement his home run near Goulburn. Up to
that point James Connery's location had been stable; it was his masters
who changed, three times. However, when the financial depression of
the early 1840s forced Lockyer to contract his pastoral operation back to
Goulburn, James moved on.[7] In 1844 he was granted a ticket-of-leave, but
not for Yass or Goulburn, or for Sydney where he might have reunited with
his brothers. Instead, the district chosen by James in which to work for
himself was Port Macquarie.[8] Once a secondary punishment settlement,
it had been opened to free settlement in the early 1830s. Nevertheless,
the town was still important in the penal system. Its well-established
hospital and accommodation at the local gaol made it a useful repository
for newly arrived convicts who were either physically or mentally impaired
or designated 'special' by the authorities because of their crime.[9] Convicts
who became ill or were injured during their sentence were also sent there.
No record survives to offer any explanation why James Connery was there
and why he chose the district for his ticket-of-leave.

Like several of his shipmates, James Connery earned his living
as a carter while holding a ticket. Brendan Kiely believes he played a
part in building a road between the New England plateau and Port
Macquarie which was designed to facilitate exports from the town's
harbour.[10] Certainly a man with a cart was well placed to ferry supplies
to the road camps. Self-employment palled, however. In August 1848
Connery started working for Stuart Alexander Donaldson again, at his
old employer's new stations in New England: 70,000 acres at Clifton
and 100,000 at Tenterfield, both stocked with sheep and cattle. James
worked as a shepherd for £30 a year until his life sentence finally ended
with a conditional pardon in September 1850.[11]

Meanwhile his brothers were fighting to prevent their eviction from
the Lachlan Swamp. After Sydney became a municipality in 1842 the
newly elected city council chose two free immigrants to replace them as
caretakers of the city's water supply. The decision included taking over
the house they built, which stood opposite the new barracks on South
Head Road. Holding that change at bay lasted some years. Meanwhile
another front opened up when an immigrant named Simeon Pearce
was appointed the first commissioner of crown lands for the city. The
Connerys were soon at loggerheads with him too.

In a land deal of his own, Pearce bought large tracts at Randwick
(formerly known as the Sand Hills) which encompassed the Lachlan

Swamp. On the heights to the south of the swamp he planned a respectable middle-class neighbourhood with elegant sandstone homes in a salubrious location near the sea. The two Irishmen and their operation in the swamp were an obstacle to his plans both as developer and as lands commissioner. They also became a thorn in his side.

John was a masterful tactician who had been cultivating influential contacts since he arrived in the colony. One of them was Colonel Barney, the colonial engineer with responsibility for Busby's Bore, which took water from the swamp to the town. Another, surely by no coincidence, was James' employer Stuart Donaldson. It may have been he who conveyed the news to James that his brothers were in the colony. In his campaign to stay put, John drew on anyone he had met with any influence. Switching effortlessly between effrontery, persuasion, insouciance and duplicity, he used every possible means to make their case to remain custodians of the swamp. Government officials were bombarded with a stream of correspondence. John even took the opportunity to strike up conversation with Governor Fitzroy when he inspected the water reserve. Only when he was finally on the ropes did John accept they must move. Then he engineered a swap from the original 'government' house they had built themselves to another nearby which had been used during the building of Victoria Barracks. With breathtaking effrontery, he let some mates move into huts near the old house.[12]

By this time, Simeon Pearce was at his wit's end. Forced to address the points the Connerys kept raising in piteous tones, he was driven to retort 'the object of Mr Connery is to annoy me for having performed my duty in removing his friends from the huts therein mentioned, and for having on several occasions, prosecuted him and his brother for destroying the shrubs and depasturing their cattle on the Sand Hills. They set me and the law at defiance and they have given me more trouble and annoyance than the whole of the inhabitants in the vicinity of the Sand Hills.'[13]

In July 1851, John was injured in a brawl at Emu Plains when the brothers were travelling to the Bathurst goldfields. They turned back to Sydney for medical attention, but he died within a few weeks. We do not know whether James, who was now free, was with them or whether he arrived too late.

Despite being forced to move, James and Patrick prospered as carters around Sydney during the boom created by the gold rush. In 1855 they considered returning to Ireland. Cost was no obstacle but James Connery's conditional pardon prohibited him from returning to any part of Britain. He petitioned the government for an absolute pardon but his application was refused and as 1856 drew to a close it was obvious his time had run out. He was ill with ever-worsening consumption and on 8 September he died aged 51. Neither James nor Patrick married and neither had children, but John left many descendants from his marriage with immigrant Ellen Conolly. Patrick, the oldest brother, lived to be 83. He spent his final years in Randwick on land bought by John, within spitting distance of the Connerys' old antagonist Simeon Pearce. The latter became mayor when the area received municipality status in 1859 and heritage buildings survive in Randwick from his vision of a place fit for gentry. There is no trace now of those defiant reprobates, the Connerys, but most Australians would agree that their spirit lives on.[14]

Prisoners were kept in Sydney for two other reasons. The need for domestic servants by officials was one, but this did not apply to men from the *Hive*. The second was the government's need for tradesmen. Before prisoners were allocated to private employers, the indent for each ship was carefully examined by officials intent on extracting the best of them for public employment. The *Hive* was no different. Colonial architect Mortimer Lewis was asked to assess the expertise of the mechanics on board and choose who to keep.

Five men admitted to being skilled mechanics.[15] They included Thomas Sullivan, a carpenter and joiner who had nearly completed his apprenticeship under his father in Cork before transportation interrupted. He told Lewis he could frame doors, but could not make window sashes or fix staircases. He was more versatile than he admitted, however. Later, he would reveal a talent for making boats. He did not impress Lewis, who categorised him as 'a second rate hand'. Nor did James Hogan who had been apprenticed four years to a Mr Croker in Limerick before he was caught stealing sheep. Like Sullivan, he said he could make a door, but not sashes or a staircase. 'Second rate hand,' wrote Lewis again.[16]

Neither man was kept by the government. Sullivan was sent north to Michael Henderson's farm at Raymond Terrace, from where he absconded two years later. James Hogan went west to work for Charles Booth at his pastoral estate near Carcoar. After receiving his ticket-of-leave in 1844 Hogan stayed in the area, probably working for his former master as so many convicts did. In 1846 he married Bridget Collins and their first child was born at Carcoar. In 1847 the family moved to Gosling Creek near Orange where James leased a 640 acre farm, an achievement beyond dreams to his countrymen still in Ireland.[17]

In 1851 the gold rush disrupted the lives of everyone in the area, including the Hogan family. With James Hogan's skills, they should have done well, but during the next five years James got into financial difficulties. Perhaps the gold lured him astray from his core business. Perhaps he was simply a bad manager. In any event, by 1856, Bridget was so fed up she placed an advertisement in the local press which read: 'My husband, James Hogan of Gosling Creek, near Orange, not being capable of managing his affairs, I beg that no one will buy anything from him, neither will I be answerable for any debts he may incur.'[18] But James did not mend his ways. In 1860 a warrant was issued for the arrest of James Hogan, alias 'Cranky' Hogan, for assaulting his wife. A full description was published to help people find him. He was said to be 5 feet 8 inches tall, 50 years of age with dark brown hair and hazel eyes . . . 'stoops a little when walking, talks very quickly and loud, very dissipated and, when drunk, generally carries a large stick or bludgeon and is very excitable'. He was believed to be in the Carcoar district where, the notice announced, he was well known to police. When last seen, he had a gun with him and was riding a brown mare. In 1864, Bridget left him for a man named William Dawson, by whom she had several more children.[19] In 1871, when their daughter Mary Ann married Matthew Walsh, James was living in Bathurst and describing his occupation as a carpenter. He died at Bathurst in 1885 aged 72 years.[20]

The colonial architect only conferred the accolade of 'first rate' on two men. One was 27-year-old James Fitzgerald, who trained as a plasterer and slater under his father in County Limerick. He had worked at the trade sixteen years including his apprenticeship and told Lewis he could do 'any kind of plastering including put up enrichments to cornices'. He was also literate. Strangely, Fitzgerald was not retained for government work but assigned to publican Henry Hewitt at Patrick's Plains. His building and decorating skills would have been in great demand by settlers in the Hunter Valley, who had endured primitive accommodation during the twenties, but by the thirties were planning more elaborate housing for themselves. Very likely Fitzgerald was soon making money on the side, like the carpenter in Newcastle. His only recorded offence in the colony was for drunkenness in 1840, which was possibly a celebration for gaining his ticket-of-leave. Three years later he was officially free. The *Hive*'s indent recorded that he was a widower with four children when he was convicted for receiving stolen goods. He did not apply officially for their assisted passage but he had the capacity to earn enough personally. By the time he was free, James was 37. The following year, in Singleton, he married Margaret McConnell who came as a convict on the ship *Diana* in 1833. At 46, she was not young and he later said he was only married to her for four years. Subsequently, he married Margaret Gosling and the couple settled in Maitland where they raised two children. James died in 1867 at the Singleton Benevolent Asylum, aged 69.[21]

Twenty-four-year-old Dan Herlihy from Cork told Mortimer Lewis that he had completed seven years as an apprentice sawyer and then worked for three years in his own right. Lewis noted that he could cut veneers. With such valuable skills, Herlihy's fate was sealed and he was sent to join a team of sawyers at the government dockyard. With his trade union background, his ears would have pricked up when his workmates mentioned the legendary sawyers' strike of 1819—as they surely would have when explaining to the new recruit just how much work he should do. Too much and the remaining traces of taskwork might be obliterated when they were trying to keep the concept alive by carefully weighing their productivity versus the official hours imposed. The strike was sixteen years earlier and occurred not at the dockyard but at the sawyers' camp at Pennant Hills. Ordered to increase the amount of timber they cut by nearly 50 per cent, the men refused. The trigger to this dispute was in Sydney where the opening of Hyde Park Barracks had brought changes to long-term working arrangements. Since the men would now be housed in barracks, Governor Macquarie reasoned they no longer needed to stop government work at 3 p.m. in order to earn money for board and lodging in the town. Accordingly, he increased the sawyers' workload, and their rations too. But as the prisoners had come to regard working for themselves as a right not as a privilege (or a necessity) Macquarie's action infringed on time they regarded as precious and private.

The Sydney sawyers had no choice but to comply with the change. When a similar instruction was issued at Pennant Hills, however, the sawyers downed tools. To add insult to injury, the extra work was valued at £2 16s., money they might have earned for their own account. Three weeks passed. The sawyers refused to compromise. Not a tree toppled at Pennant Hills. Not a single blade was put to a log. Governor Macquarie was in difficulties. Apart from the Sydney team, these sawyers were the only ones in the colony and their timber-getting skills were essential for his building program. Furthermore, Commissioner John Bigge was in town, investigating the colony's affairs. Macquarie did not want news of a strike by prisoners to reach Bigge's ears. Finally, the colonial engineer George Druitt, who was also the supervisor of public works, was sent as emissary to Pennant Hills. He explained to the men that it was a matter of making labour conditions and remuneration in rations consistent with the Sydney workforce. Clever Major Druitt appealed not only to their commonsense, but the obligation of fairness they felt towards their Sydney mates. Reluctantly, they accepted his logic. Nevertheless, as a fallback position, two sawyers complained that the rations, even if increased, were not enough for such a workload. Conscious of the penalties for collective action which was still illegal under the Combination Act of 1799, the two men were careful not to speak for their workmates, just claiming that they 'probably felt the same'. The two complainants were charged with 'insolence' and flogged for their pains. None of the other sawyers felt the lash on their backs but Bigge's report suggests that he was told they had all been flogged. Despite their stand-off, the sawyers eventually accepted that parity with the Sydney men was fair. However, they negotiated an agreement that preserved their most cherished right. Taskwork continued at the Pennant Hills camp even though it was being terminated by the government elsewhere. In return, the men increased productivity. From then on, they performed the same amount of work as those in Sydney but they did so by Thursday each week, after which they were free to work for themselves. Five years before Dan Herlihy joined the sawyers at the Sydney dockyard, the Pennant Hills camp had closed. But its legend lived on.[22]

Patrick Brien was also kept in Sydney, but not just because he was an experienced blacksmith. The wreck of the *Hive* exposed the presence of his sons Daniel and Michael among the crew. He would have argued that his trade skills meant he could support them, but he had no chance of winning this point. By the mid-thirties, children of prisoners were always taken away from their parents if they were over three years of age. In addition to removing them from the 'contaminating influence' of their parents, the aim was to train them in a trade and, when they reached twelve or thirteen, apprentice them to colonial masters. The children were also given basic education in reading, writing and numbers.

In the past, Catholic and Protestant children were mixed together; however, the Brien boys arrived at a time when their church was determined to take every Catholic under its wing. Indeed in the search for Catholics, priests now met every ship, those which sailed from England as well as from Ireland.[23] With the support of Governor Bourke, the Catholic Church was on the verge of gaining equal standing in Australia with the Church of England. Although legislation that would make this status official had not yet been passed, Bishop Polding and his young vicar-general Father William Ullathorne were actively asserting their authority in new areas. Among their initiatives was the founding of a Catholic orphanage for children of convicts and immigrants whose parents were deemed unable to care for them. Previously such children were sent to orphan schools divided only by gender, but now they were separated according to religion. Father Ullathorne was assiduous in keeping the colonial secretary informed of every detail about the schools, including staff problems, pupil numbers and the benefit of establishing a second institution at Parramatta to supplement the original school-orphanage in Kent Street, Sydney.[24] In this climate, it was not surprising that the government readily agreed that the young Irish boys should be handed over to the care of the church.[25]

The boys' father was assigned to work in the government dockyard. In 1837, he, Dan Herlihy and four others asked for permission to live on dockyard premises rather than in Hyde Park Barracks. John Nicholson, who managed the dockyard, wrote on their behalf to the colonial secretary promising to ensure they were locked in at 8 p.m. each night. He was not asking an unusual favour. In supporting the suggestion, the convict office told Governor Bourke that men working for the colonial architect, the town surveyor and the boatmen who worked for Nicholson himself all slept at their workplace. But this was news to the governor. 'I am averse to such a practice,' he wrote and asked why it had been adopted.[26]

Patrick Brien had an urgent motive for wanting to live out of barracks that he did not reveal. The previous month, his wife Mary had arrived in the colony as a prisoner. Furthermore, she had brought with her their two remaining children, one of whom was only two years old. A native of Fermoy in County Cork like Patrick, Mary was 36 when she committed what surely was the deliberate crime of stealing some clothes. Not an educated woman, she was nevertheless smart enough to ensure that she stole just enough to get transported but not so much that her sentence was longer than seven years. Short, with a sallow, slightly pockmarked complexion and brown hair already turning grey, she told the authorities that she was a kitchenmaid but could do all kinds of domestic work. Unfortunately the 1837 muster does not record where she was assigned, nor at first is there any connection with Patrick Brien. It is not until her certificate of freedom issued within months of her husband's in 1842 that she reveals she is 'wife of Patrick Brien per *Hive* free by servitude'.[27]

Patrick Brien did not apply for a ticket-of-leave, from which we can probably assume that he was earning money as well as working for the government at the dockyard. By the time he received his certificate it was too late to resume parenting the boys. Both would have been apprenticed long since. And young Daniel who was eleven when he arrived, was eighteen by the time his father was free. He married two years later, proudly described on the application as 'came free' on the *Hive*. Unknowingly, Edward Canney played cupid. He had brought Daniel's wife, Catherine Kelly, to the colony as a prisoner on the second voyage of the *Margaret*. No trace has been found of Daniel's brother Michael. Their father and mother's fate is uncertain too. A Patrick Brien died aged 60 of exhaustion and *amentia* at the lunatic asylum, Parramatta, in 1868, but there were many Patrick Briens and O'Briens in the colony. To all intents, the family vanished.[28]

When he came to New South Wales, Governor Bourke was dedicated to two great causes, both of which reflected his knowledge of Ireland. The first was to create the groundwork for religious equality that would avoid the pernicious sectarianism in his homeland. The second, which was an extension of the first, was to establish education for all children, regardless of their religion, in a national or state system. Religious education would be handled separately by each church. In 1833 he wrote to Lord Stanley pointing out the vast discrepancy in colonial funding for the Church of England compared with other denominations, particularly the Catholics who were so numerous in the colony, and recommended the funds be equalised according to the number of their parishioners. Stanley was slow replying but, unknown to Bourke, he was seeking feedback within England.[29] By the time a reply was received, a new government was in power and Bourke's friend Thomas Spring Rice was secretary of state for the colonies. Approval for Bourke's plan arrived in Sydney early in 1836, just at the time John Hubert Plunkett's appointment as attorney-general became official.[30]

Plunkett's first task was to draft legislation for New South Wales and Van Diemen's Land which became known as 'the Church Acts'. Meanwhile, Roger Therry, who was not a government official and could therefore speak publicly, was deployed to prepare the community through the colonial press. Writing under the *pseudonym* 'Humanitas', he debated all comers including Dr Polding, prelate of the Catholic Church and later designated Archbishop of Sydney, who of course supported Bourke's legislation, and Dr John Dunmore Lang, a fiercely sectarian Presbyterian who, whatever his doubts, realised that the proposed legislation would benefit his church. Therry's main opponent through the media was William Grant Broughton, who had first come to the colony as archdeacon for the Church of England when the colony's bishop resided in Calcutta. Years later, Therry described Broughton as a man 'of cold temperament' although with 'kindly feelings' who 'performed generous actions'. He summarised Broughton's aim as 'introducing into New South Wales the institutions of England, to use Broughton's own language "in all their integrity", which would have resulted in government funding only being given to the Church of England whose wealth would lead to an inevitable ascendancy over other faiths'.[31] However, it would be misleading to construe Broughton's opposition as motivated only by money and power. According to Bruce Kaye, 'the depth of Broughton's Protestantism ought not to be underestimated. It was a Protestantism which saw Roman Catholicism not only as subversive, in [England], and at first also in [Australia], but also and more enduringly, as a system which was fundamentally erroneous as to Christian truth.'[32] And there was a real 'threat'. In May 1836 Bishop Polding wrote to a friend, 'We only want priests to make this country Catholic.'[33]

In June 1836, Bourke took the legislation to the Legislative Council which at that time consisted of twelve appointed members. The bill was fiercely opposed, resistance coming particularly from conservatives such as the colonial secretary Alexander Macleay, merchant Robert Campbell senior who was an active Presbyterian, and two pastoralists Richard Jones and Hannibal McArthur. Bourke only succeeded in getting the bill through by agreeing to exclude Methodists and other dissenting sects and Jews, all of whom Plunkett had included in his draft.[34] (They were added later due to the efforts of Plunkett and others after Bourke left the colony.)[35] With this amendment in 1836, the eight remaining councillors supported the bill. They included pastoralists Alexander Berry, John

Blaxland and Archibald Bell, as well as auditor-general William Lithgow and chief justice Sir James Dowling, who was an Anglican of Irish stock like the governor. Plunkett as attorney-general was on the council and the only Catholic among them. Bishop Broughton, who had previously been a member of the Council as an archdeacon, was not present to voice his opinion at the crucial moment. Anticipating his opposition, Bourke used Broughton's recent elevation to lord bishop of Australia as an excuse to exclude him until confirmation was received from London that the new appointment did not prohibit him from membership of the council.[36]

Introduced in 1836 (New South Wales) and 1837 (Van Diemen's Land) the Church Acts provided funding, proportionate to their parishioners, for all religious denominations to import clergy and build churches. In the years that followed, particularly 1838–43, clergy of all kinds poured into the colonies. Equal treatment did not, however, result in Christian equanimity. The churches fiercely competed for both funds and parishioners. Sadly, Bourke's good intentions laid the seeds of a virulent sectarianism that would flourish in Australia for over a century. However, it stopped the Church of England from becoming the 'established' church similar to its status in Britain and allowed Catholics, as well as other denominations, to worship on an equal basis according to their own rites and rituals, attended by their own priests.

The heartland of sectarianism in the colony in the 1830s was the Hunter Valley. Nowhere else matched it for prejudice against the Irish and Catholicism. Bathurst, for instance, did not experience the kind of religious stand-offs seen in Maitland, perhaps because the Bathurst area was established when indifference, and in many cases antagonism, towards religion was the prevailing mood of the colony. On the coast and in the inland south-west, the presence of influential wealthy Catholics helped counter expressions of sectarianism.

Many men from the *Hive* settled in Maitland, including James McCabe who was one of only five Protestants on the *Hive*. His crime of malicious assault in an Orange procession in Monoghan indicates he was evangelical about his religion. In New South Wales he was initially assigned to John Lewis, who had a carting business at Maitland. When applying for his ticket in 1840, McCabe chose to stay in the town. By 1845 he had acquired land of his own and accumulated enough money to buy two bullocks in a sale at the Maitland races. A dispute about ownership of the bullocks, which was resolved in McCabe's favour, revealed him using religious justifications for arbitrarily reclaiming his property from another farmer who may have been a shipmate. 'I lent them to John Corcoran who has no land of his own,' he explained. 'I took them back when I found they were being put to work on the Sabbath day.'[37] McCabe lived the rest of his life in the town, dying in December 1876 in Maitland hospital under the pastoral care of a minister who described himself as representing the 'Ireland Church of England'.[38]

Bourke's great legacy was to leave the Catholics in the colony with a sense of entitlement to religious equality. Their determination to preserve it was on display in a sectarian row that occurred in 1845–46 about Maitland hospital. The protagonists were Father Joseph Lynch, a priest who had been living in the town for seven years, and a Protestant minister, Reverend Stack, who believed his membership of the hospital's management committee (and by inference his religion) conferred some oversight responsibilities. Their initial squabble took place at the bedside of a dying man named Bunton, who was in severe pain. At issue was whether the patient wished to die a Protestant or convert to Catholicism. His wife who was a Catholic was anxious that he should save his immortal soul through the Catholic rites. When she told Reverend Stack this, his response was to debate with her the theological differences between the two faiths until, as he put it, he had 'put her into a corner in talking of the Virgin Mary'. Under intellectual siege, she finally brought his inquisition to an end by telling him bluntly that she 'was not larned' and walking off. Hearing of this later, Father Lynch claimed, 'He made the poor woman confess her ignorance.' But Reverend Stack persisted, returning twice to proselytise the issue with the dying man and to pray beside him. On the second occasion the patient ventured to ask the minister to be brief because he was not well. On his third and last visit, the Protestant clergyman walked in to find Father Lynch praying with the patient. Heated words were exchanged. Reverend Stack retired. Mr Bunton died.

Such an intrusion on religious devotions was a grave offence. Reverend Stack maintained that he had been quiet and civil in his manner and apologised for the interruption. For Father Lynch, however, the inter-ruption was an unforgivable incident in a campaign to prevent Catholic ministrations to patients at the hospital. He continued to emphasise its gravity in his complaint to the hospital committee and in public meetings of Catholics that followed. Feelings ran strongly against the hospital attendant, a Protestant who sent for a clergyman when a patient was dying. He was the source of Stack's information that Mr Bunton was a Protestant and it was he who, having failed to deter Father Lynch from visiting the patient, then sent word to Reverend Stack.[39]

The gentry dominated the hospital committee but they did not control the town meeting called by Father Lynch. It was chaired by Thomas Dee, the proprietor of a large general store in High Street. The participants were small farmers and businessmen, publicans, carriers, retailers and tradesmen, many of course ex-convicts. Among their number was a Mr Tierney, very likely the former private of the 28th Regiment who operated a shoemaking business in the town. He seconded the motion that 'This meeting being of the opinion that within the precincts of the Maitland Hospital, as at present constituted, neither their pastor nor people can be secure from uncourteous and unwarrantable conduct, unanimously agree that a respectful petition be forwarded to His Excellency the Governor praying for assistance towards the erection and support of an asylum for sick and indigent Catholics." His motion was carried unanimously.[40]

Nine months later they had to do it all over again. Except for a courteous acknowledgement from Governor Gipps, their petition achieved nothing. Rumour had it that influential people had told the governor it had been 'got up in the heat of the moment' and passions would soon dissipate. But when the new president of the hospital committee, Edward Denny Day, proposed as a peacemaking gesture that clergymen should not be members of the committee, his colleagues would not support the idea. Reverend Stack remained in place. The fury of the Catholics was compounded when a ceremony to lay the foundation stone for a new hospital in February 1846, to which everyone had subscribed, was followed by a ceremonial procession to a Protestant church. It was sectarian provocation of a kind that many Catholics had witnessed in their homeland. 'Everything had been done to establish an ascendancy over us,' raged a speaker at the subsequent meeting, 'an ascendancy which we [the Catholic community] are called upon to resist . . . an ascendancy which I hope will never contaminate the land of our adoption (cheers).' John Harpur, brother of the poet Charles Harpur, followed up with a fiery speech about the alarming spirit of religious intolerance similar to that in Ireland. 'I hope this country will never suffer in like manner from the tyrannical operation of such a spirit,' he thundered. Then he invoked the memory of Sir Richard Bourke, to whom a statue had recently been erected in Sydney. 'When I saw it,' declared Harpur, 'I promised to guard, by every means in my power, the blessing which that great and good man had secured to the colony, the blessing of religious equality.'[41]

CHAPTER 11
Catholic Friendly

Shortly before he left Ireland, Richard Bourke had seen a long-cherished dream come to fruition. For many years, he and his friend Thomas Spring Rice had discussed the possibilities of a non-denominational education system. Both Catholic and Protestant children would attend these 'national' or 'public' schools where all subjects would be taught *except* religion, which would be handled separately by the churches according to their scripture and beliefs. When Spring Rice was elected to the British parliament and the dream became reality, Bourke was involved in drafting the regulations under which the new system would operate.[1]

Richard Bourke was a progressive man with enlightened ideas but with hindsight it is plain that introducing his plan for a state school system in the colony at the same time as the Church Act was a tactical error. Defeat on the religious equality issue only made its original opponents more determined to defeat the schools plan. However, the broader context was also not conducive to success. Barely five months had elapsed since Bourke shocked the magistracy by dropping some who had held the title justice of the peace for many years. Conservatives in the colony, most of them Anglican, were outraged. Consequently, Bishop Broughton found many among his flock only too ready to sign petitions and write letters against both the Church Act and the national schools proposal.

Despite the criticisms of its opponents, the schools plan was not anti-religious. Ecumenical would be a more accurate description. For example, Plunkett's biographer argues that the attorney-general believed society needed to be founded on Judaeo-Christian ethics: a belief in God, the Ten Commandments and the afterlife. Furthermore, 'In the vision [Plunkett] and Bourke shared, non-denominational schooling and religious funding under the Church Act went hand in hand, promoting religion and religious tolerance at the same time.'[2]

Hand in hand theoretically perhaps, but hand in hand politically was a mistake. Roger Therry recounted how, soon after he arrived, Bourke sent several letters to him about the national education system. 'The principal features in the Irish plan, namely the separation of literary and moral from religious instruction, will suit the mixed creeds of our population,' wrote the governor. 'I have set my heart on laying a good foundation whilst I am in office. I dread much even in this reforming age, the blighting influence of religious intolerance.'[3] Presumably other leading citizens received similar correspondence. Therry actively tried to help, taking part in press debates and writing an unsigned pamphlet entitled *Explanation of the Plan of the Irish National Schools*.[4] Generally, however, the ground had not been prepared sufficiently. Cooperation by church leaders of all denominations was crucial to the establishment of the scheme in Ireland. Bourke, Spring Rice and others put in great effort to persuade them to an ecumenical position. Lack of cooperation between the churches in New South Wales caused the similar proposal from Bourke to fail. The Protestant leaders fought hard against the idea and were never persuaded to compromise. Led by Bishop Broughton of the Church of England and actively supported by the Presbyterian, Reverend Lang, they lobbied in England as well as the colony. On this topic, they mustered enough votes on the Legislative Council to defeat the plan. Bourke was bitterly disappointed at what to him was a self-evidently sensible approach to education, particularly when so many Catholics lived in Australia. He did, however, extract one small victory in the form of funds for a school in Wollongong on the same principles as those in Ireland.[5]

Wollongong was an embryonic settlement on the coast south of Sydney, sited in Dharawal country and, specifically, on the land of the

Wodi Wodi people. Bourke had visited this Illawarra coast in 1834, the first governor of the colony to go there. Like other travellers, he was struck by its beauty and its fertility. Baron von Hugel, who went a few months later, was puzzled why almost no settlers with capital had established themselves in 'the most splendid district of New South Wales'. The explanation, he decided, was simple. 'Every "Gentleman" who comes to the colony does so with the sole intention of making his fortune quickly and then returning to England . . . profit is always the prime consideration and, for a landowner, large-scale profits are to be made only from sheep-breeding, to which this fertile district is unsuited.'[6] Having struggled down the cliff to get there, he concluded that it had to be lack of access to Sydney which prevented denser settlement. But the landholders' loss was the small man's gain. On his visit, Governor Bourke would have noticed the great number of his countrymen in the area and they would have taken the opportunity to tell him about the obstacles to getting their produce to market. They had no difficulty convincing Bourke that some other way must be found. He too had experienced the hair-raising steepness of the existing track, which made getting a loaded dray down the hill even more dangerous than getting one up. At the governor's request, Major Thomas Mitchell soon after surveyed a route that would improve communication with Sydney.[7] Bourke followed up by allocating funds through his newly created Board of Works to build a harbour for Wollongong.[8]

In the Illawarra, the governor's 'Catholic-friendly' policies intersected with local landholders who were ecumenical in their attitudes to religion or in fact Catholic themselves. One of the former was Charles Throsby Smith, who could be described as a born real estate entrepreneur. His land grant was sited on the coast near a natural harbour. In the late 1820s he had suggested a swap to the government by which it would receive some of his acres for official buildings and, in return, give him land on Flagstaff Hill which he would use for grazing cattle. The government built a courthouse, lock-up and magistrate's residence on the land it acquired from this deal and, with Bourke's financial aid, subsequently created safe harbour for a steamer service to Sydney. Once Wollongong was surveyed after Bourke's visit in 1834, Smith applied for permission to subdivide some of his land into town allotments. In return for such favourable consideration, he undertook to donate land for an Anglican church.[9] Among Smith's employees was 24-year-old Patrick Reidy aka

Ready, from the *Hive*, who was one of those prisoners chosen by Alexander Berry for the Illawarra. Transported for stealing sheep in County Kerry, he bore the burden of a life sentence. Nevertheless, while still a prisoner he married one of Edward Canney's 'imports', Catherine Daley, aged 29, who arrived as a prisoner on the second voyage of the *Margaret*. When Patrick gained his ticket-of-leave in 1844 he became a farmer. The couple spent the rest of their lives in the Illawarra and produced nine children.[10]

While waiting to hear whether his proposal to the government had been accepted, C.T. Smith continued providing a barn in which church services could be held by any denomination, something he had been doing for many years despite what James Spearing claimed was the neglect of both religion and Sunday on the Illawarra. According to Spearing, the attitude of the mainly Catholic community was expressed by their proverbial saying that 'Sunday never found its way down the mountain.'[11] During the 1820s, an Anglican minister would travel down from Campbelltown at intervals and, similarly, Father Joseph Therry would say mass for the Catholics in the same barn. This ecumenical sharing continued until the early thirties when a Protestant catechist named Layton rented the barn and excluded the Catholics. Undeterred, the Catholics transferred their mass to the military barracks.[12]

In 1836, empowered by the equality it gained under the Church Act, the Catholic Church appointed Father John Rigney as the first parish priest of Wollongong. Wealthy Illawarra pastoralist Cornelius O'Brien, a Catholic, donated land and a wooden chapel was built there, which also served as a school.[13] A schoolmaster named Michael O'Donnell was imported as the first teacher.

It was no coincidence that the first national school was established in the Illawarra. Many Irish had clustered there since the area first opened to settlement, not least perhaps because the fertile soil produced two crops of potatoes each year. Many developed farms where even the poorest among them could live well compared with Ireland. Like Bourke, Lady Jane Franklin, wife of the lieutenant-governor of Van Diemen's Land, noticed the large number of Irish people in the area. After passing through Appin on her way to the coast, Lady Jane commented in her journal: 'The people here are of the same Irish origin as at Campbelltown. They are clean and good farmers.'[14]

By 1839 when Lady Franklin visited the Illawarra, Governor Bourke's involvement had been superseded in memory by his successor, who was credited with building a new schoolhouse in Wollongong 'on the Irish plan' worth £3000. 'It is the first experiment of Sir George Gipps,' wrote Lady Jane in her journal before, as a good Anglican, adding that 'the Bishop's school must be supported all the same.' She was referring to the Anglican school recently built by Bishop Broughton to match the other two. Locally, they were still debating the merits of the national schools. Someone in Lady Jane's entourage, probably the Anglican minister Mr Meares, told her that parents were saying their children would go to the Church of England school anyway. Greatly daring, he added that he approved of schools being open to all without enforcing the catechism of a particular church. Lady Jane recorded that 'a warm discussion [followed] between Mr Meares, Captain Westmacott and myself as to schools, creeds etc. Mr Meares, though a stout churchman, thought the Bishop [Broughton] a little narrow minded. Mr Westmacott abused him and they had a little dispute.'[15] As the party was riding along, Mr Tait, 'the Scotch minister', galloped past. According to Mr Meares, there were too few Presbyterians for a separate school to be created but he told Lady Jane, 'Mr Tait had no objection to letting them go to Anglican schools, but wants to teach the catechism etc. himself.'[16]

Thirty-year-old Edward Nunan/Noonan was another of the men chosen by Berry for Illawarra settlers. He was transported for robbing two houses in Ballyclough, Limerick. On arrival in the colony he described his occupation as a 'farm servant' and was assigned to Michael Grey, a landholder near Kiama.[17] From the evidence at Noonan's trial, his crime was no sudden impulse but a premeditated operation in which an armed gang of four, including his shipmate Daniel Riordan, ransacked houses for anything of value.[18] The professional nature of the crime, as well as the value of the goods they stole, influenced the sentencing and both men were transported for life. It meant a long wait until he could send for his wife Julia and two young children. After receiving his ticket-of-leave in 1840 he continued to work for Mr Grey and was still with him in 1847 when, having been recommended for a conditional pardon, he petitioned for a passage for his family. By the time they arrived on the *Panama* in 1849 both Edward and Julia were in their forties. His son, John, was eighteen and described himself as a farm labourer. His daughter, Catherine, who would have been an infant when he left, was now fourteen years old.[19]

Their convict connection ignored, the Noonan family would in future be categorised officially as free settlers, part of an influx of emigrants into the Illawarra, which started during the thirties. Within three decades a large number of farmers and their families from England, Scotland but particularly from Ireland had settled on the Illawarra in what was in effect chain migration. In his book *Farewell My Children*, Richard Reid wrote that by 1861, Kiama, for example, was a very Irish place. 'Just over a quarter of its population was Irish born . . . dozens of interrelated families from the same region of Ireland settled next to each other and, over the next fifty years, encouraged other members of the family to join them.'[20] Those who lacked relatives already in the colony were often directed to the Illawarra by others, for instance, by the Osborne brothers who were major landholders on the coast. Of Protestant Irish descent, Alick and Henry Osborne had been naval surgeons on convict ships. In the mid-thirties, Alick specifically recruited a boatload of assisted emigrants from his home parish in Ireland.[21]

Not all Irish emigrants were Catholic. According to Patrick O'Farrell somewhere between 10 and 20 per cent were Protestants from Ulster, although the bulk of these came much later in the nineteenth century. He also claimed that their extensive archives revealed they 'had little patience with divisive Irish politics or sectarian animus'. From the 1840s there was, however, a concentration of Irish Protestants around Kiama and over the following 40 years nine Orange Lodges were founded. Occasional sectarian threats were made, particularly in 1868 after a Fenian attempted to assassinate the Duke of Edinburgh in Sydney, but overall, little violence occurred. O'Farrell concluded that a reason for such tolerance was the Australian social environment 'whose temper was such that extremism was unpopular; and the considerable number of Irish-born clergy within Protestant denominations, who had Orange leanings, found their enthusiasms—or fanaticism—unshared in congregations themselves minorities'.[22]

Whatever their religion, many of these new settlers in the Illawarra and Shoalhaven fulfilled the Irish dream of access to a viable farm—by leasehold, if they lacked the capital to buy. As noted, Alexander Berry made a practice of leasing land to ex-convicts and small free settlers who had worked for him. And he was not alone. Others who had received large grants also broke up their holdings. Among them was John Hubert Plunkett. In his *Recollections*, James Gormley revealed that his father purchased land in 1840 from Plunkett, whose original grant consisted of 1280 acres to the west of Wollongong.[23] However, land to the south, notably the Kiama area, was richer and a large number of tenant farmers chose that location instead. Usually densely covered with foliage, their tenancy was called a 'clearing lease' which required backbreaking work from the pioneer tenant in return for possession—rent free until the land became productive.[24] This may well have been the outcome for the Noonan family. If it was, their efforts helped lay the foundation of a high quality dairy industry in the area.[25]

Chain migration by the Irish was also significant elsewhere in the colony. In 1818 Governor Macquarie sanctioned an expedition to the south-west which was led by emancipist James Meehan in his role as assistant surveyor. Transported for participating in the 1798 Irish rebellion, Meehan had been the colony's acting surveyor since 1809 and effectively in charge due to the absence of his superior Charles Grimes. It was he who created a distinctive cluster of Irish by urging his fellow revolutionaries to take up good farming country on the south-west Cumberland Plain.[26] Their presence attracted compatriots to settle there too and before long Irish people dominated the areas called Appin and Airds (later Campbelltown). The skew is very apparent in Anne-Maree Whitaker's analysis of the 1828 census for Appin. In that year, residents of the town and surrounding area totalled 223 people, nearly two-thirds of whom were Catholics. Equally revealing is the extent to which free settlers were surrounded by a community of convicts and ex-convicts. Out of the 223 residents only sixteen people were free settlers. The balance consisted of 119 convicts and emancipists, plus 95 children. In later population figures, these children would be classified with 'free settlers', thus presenting a profile of the colony in which 'the convict element' was insignificant.[27]

According to James Waldersee, convicts and immigrants from Ireland chose the south-west in preference to the Protestant dominated Hunter Valley. As exploration penetrated further inland, they followed again with large numbers of Irish settling in that direction. For instance, country named Burrawa by the Wiradjuri people became known colloquially to Europeans as 'the Kingdom of the Ryans'. Here ex-convict Edward 'Ned' Ryan accumulated vast acreage, built himself a 'castle', and created an Irish community of farmers by leasing them land. Closer to Goulburn, Michael Ryan from Tipperary (no relation to Ned) landed in the colony in 1821 with a seven-year sentence. In an example of the opportunities available, he began to accumulate stock while still a prisoner, possibly with cattle paid as a bonus by his master, similar to others who were given sheep. Within twenty years, 200 cattle had become 1200, which Ryan ran under a squatter's licence. He had also accumulated 4000 sheep. He built himself a brick house and employed a school master to teach his five children. To the delight of Father Michael Brennan, he also built a church with tower and belfry on his land. Eighteen men worked for Ryan, to whom he paid 14 pounds with rations, 'including the allowance of tea and sugar'.[28]

As the colonists fanned out beyond Goulburn, taking their convict workers with them, Governor Darling tried to control where they went. Acting on instructions from London, he divided the colony into Nineteen Counties which were decreed to be the 'limits of location'. Beyond the encircling border of the counties, settlement was unauthorised. But there was no line drawn in the ground and the vast pastures tempted both pastoralists and smallholders. Before long, many were squatting beyond the governor's limits. In 1836 Governor Bourke introduced a Licensing Act under which squatters outside county boundaries were to pay an annual licensing fee of £10. Land commissioners were appointed to issue licences and supervise squatting. These measures proved insufficient and Governor Gipps subsequently increased the powers of the commissioners and backed them up with detachments of mounted police.[29]

Over 50 Irishmen from the *Hive* were assigned across the south-west and south-east. Forty-eight-year-old Daniel Kennedy, for example, was assigned to William Bradley at Goulburn. He had been transported with his 21-year-old son Patrick for joining with hundreds of others who stormed the courthouse at Rathkeale in Limerick.[30] In the colony, Daniel's employer described him as 'a remarkably quiet, orderly and well-conducted man'. Perhaps he always had been and it was the sheer injustice around tithes that made him react with such passion that day. Or once in the colony, perhaps he was grieving the absence of his wife, or beset with anxiety about his son whose whereabouts he did not know. Both men were literate but sending letters around New South Wales, let alone through the convict system, was not easy. Young Patrick was described as 'disabled in the right hand'. A scar marred the right side of his face. Together they suggest that he was not born with the incapacity but had been injured in an accident or brawl. Traditionally, the authorities ignored any disability in a convict, assigning men with gross physical handicaps or limited mental capacity in the normal way. In 1826, for example, the Australian Agricultural Company received four men with disabilities out of its 30 assignees—one with dropsy, one lame from a leg wound, one with a crippled arm and one who was blind in one eye.[31] By the thirties, however, Port Macquarie was a designated place for convicts who were ill or disabled and, on arrival in Sydney, Patrick was sent there and would have been assigned locally to some work he could manage, or otherwise assessed as unfit for assignment.

Beyond this particular worry, Daniel may have been reasonably content. Unlike the Hunter settlers, his employer William Bradley had been born at Windsor, the son of Sergeant Jonas Bradley formerly of the New South Wales Corps and his convict wife Catherine Condon. The large tract of land at Goulburn had been granted to Jonas Bradley in the 1820s and, as a youth, William had worked there as a labourer. He was not daunted by the Australian landscape with its huge distances, potentially volatile weather and relentless solitude. Unlike many of the newcomers who installed a superintendent, then retired to town, Bradley lived on his Goulburn station and was directly involved in its management. This hands-on approach may well explain why he remained solvent when many around him were going broke in the early 1840s. For Bradley, the decade presented an opportunity. During this time, he acquired thousands of extra acres on the high plains of the Maneroo.

In 1840, the colonial secretary advised Bradley that Daniel's wife Johanna had written asking what happened to her husband and son. What should have been a straightforward matter was confused by the existence of two Daniel Kennedys on the *Hive*, the second one assigned to Mr Broughton at Campbelltown. Mr Bradley was asked to check whether the Daniel Kennedy assigned to him was Johanna's husband. Meanwhile, the second Daniel Kennedy proved uncooperative. Working on his master's outstation at the Maneroo, his prevarication about providing any details made it difficult for Broughton's overseer to make any conclusive identification. To complicate things further, both Daniels had been convicted at the Rathkeale Quarters Sessions, at the same sessions in 1835, and their crimes were similar—'violent assault' for one and 'malicious assault' for the other. And there was a second Patrick Kennedy on board the *Hive* who had been caught up in the riot at Rathkeale and also transported for 'malicious assault'. The second Daniel Kennedy claimed this Patrick, who was said to be working for a Mrs Walker at Wallerawang near Bathurst, as his son but, since he was 29 and the so-called son was 30 years old, this must have been an attempt to muddy the waters. Mr Broughton reported his Daniel Kennedy as of 'very indifferent character'. Nevertheless he had recommended him for a ticket-of-leave which was granted a few weeks later.

Meanwhile Daniel Kennedy, husband of Johanna and father of Patrick, received his ticket-of-leave. The following year so did his son. Within a couple of years both also obtained their certificates of freedom. What they did then remains a mystery among a plethora of Daniels and Patricks with the surname Kennedy. It would be nice to learn from descendants that Johanna joined them.[32]

John Smith from the *Hive* also worked for William Bradley but he was sent to the run at Maneroo. His brother Michael was assigned in the opposite direction to the Hunter Valley. Neither of them was literate, although Michael said he could read, but the timing of their certificates of freedom suggests they were in touch somehow. Having received his certificate on 22 April 1842, it is possible that John headed up the Hunter Valley to find his brother whose freedom was also due. He persuaded Michael that the Maneroo was where they should settle and they returned together to Cooma.[33]

The Smiths had been transported for 'aggravated assault', which meant they used more than just their fists. They were part of group who attacked John and Berry Preston in Armagh in January 1835 when the Prestons were driving cartloads of goods home. The attackers outnumbered their prey fifteen to two but this in no way diminished the violence used. It was John Preston they were after and he was severely beaten. Berry Preston made an attempt to help his brother but was driven back during which he, too, was injured. Three Smith brothers, Michael, Hugh and John, were part of the mob, but Hugh escaped capture and only Michael and John were tried. Convicted specifically of violent assault on John Preston, they were also convicted of common assault and riot which suggests that something preceded the attack. Robbery was not their motive—Preston had £106 on him, which was untouched. This was a grudge of some kind, perhaps trigged by some transaction at a fair or by election turmoil that was then occurring around Ireland.[34] No sign of this violent past surfaced in Australia. John Smith worked for William Bradley for the six years of his assignment. At some time he transferred to magistrate Nathaniel Powell of *Turalla* near Bungendore, but after the brothers were reunited they farmed at Big Badja near Cooma. John's daughter Bridget emigrated with her husband and baby daughter Alice in 1856, bringing along her sister-in-law Catherine McDonald who subsequently married Michael Smith's eldest son. Michael's wife Mary arrived in 1849 on the *Panama,* bringing their sons John and Henry. With family life regained, the two emancipist brothers continued to live around the Cooma area until they died within a year of each other in the early 1870s.[35] John Smith's obituary described him as 'an old and well-respected resident'.[36]

It was a far less happy outcome for their shipmate Patrick Rourke who worked at Henry O'Brien's run *Douro* near Yass. The Irish flavour to the south-west country was not confined to the workers. Irish gentry, both Protestant and Catholic, were also prominent. Rourke's employer, Henry O'Brien, was a Catholic, a large pastoralist and the magistrate. He and his brother Cornelius had come to the colony in the 1820s with their uncle, whose estates they managed as well as land grants of their own. Widely known as 'Black Harry', Henry was initially based in the west near Bathurst but moved in the thirties to new land in the far south-west. In 1836 his brother sold his land on the coast, and bought land nearby. Patrick Rourke was one of their long-time government men. Convicted of sheep stealing in County Clare, he had been sentenced to life and did not get a ticket-of-leave until 1847. Well into his forties by then, he applied to bring out his family. His master certified on the application that he was 'a well conducted man' who had 'the means of supporting his family'. Rourke's police record was clean. Altogether, he was the perfect candidate and his application was approved without delay. Then he waited. And waited. Sadly the record simply states 'wife's letter returned 22 March 1849' and on the passenger list for the ship *William Jardine*, where a berth was held for the Rourke family, there is a note 'did not embark'.[37]

Terence Aubrey Murray was another example of a wealthy pastoralist who was Irish and Catholic. Born in Limerick like Governor Bourke, he was also a liberal intellectually and ecumenical in his attitude to religion as his two marriages demonstrate. Both his wives were Anglican. He married for the first time in the Church of England, but for the second two ceremonies were held, one Anglican and one Catholic, and his children from this marriage were baptised Catholics. After arriving with his father and siblings in 1827, Murray cut his teeth in the new land by working and living alone on the family's grant north of Lake George in the Collector Valley. In 1837, in partnership with Thomas Walker, he acquired land called *Yarralumla* on the Limestone Plains. In the late thirties, drought took its toll on his stock and Lake George dried up. Accompanied by two Aborigines and two convict overseers, Murray searched for pasture in the high country where he established another run at *Cooleman*. Two years later he took the ultimate rural test for a European when he 'overlanded' to Melbourne and back in the record time of eighteen days.[38]

Murray lived on his land and was intimately involved in its management. If one of his men transgressed, he was just as likely to turn up himself to give evidence—as 21-year-old Matthew Berry from the *Hive* discovered. He inherited Murray as his employer at *Yarralumla* in 1837, but he didn't stay around to find out what his new master was like. In January 1838 he absconded and remained successfully absent for seven months. What he did during that time is a mystery. Perhaps, like his shipmate George Burns, he succeeded in convincing another employer he was a free man and worked for them on a contract basis.[39] When he was caught and taken before the bench, he revealed nothing and made no defence. Consequently, he was sentenced to 50 lashes. What happened to Berry after that is also a mystery. He was very young and Murray may have tried to change his attitude by taking him overland to Port Phillip.

Victoria was the eventual destination for a number of men from the *Hive*. Bartholomew Williams was working for John Coghill at Braidwood when his master part-financed a fellow mariner's overland expedition to Port Phillip in 1838. John Hepburn described how 'I met another old tar John Coghill of Braidwood [who] was also an old colonist. We entered into partnership and I proceeded to a station of his *Strathallan* to await the arrival of my family, determined to take them with me at all risks.' He set out for Port Phillip in January 1838, taking with him a huge cavalcade of more than 2000 sheep, two drays, eighteen bullocks, cart and horse, plus two more horses, personal property and ten men who had been assigned to John Coghill, one of whom was 'Bart' Williams.[40] We can deduce that they gave Hepburn a hard time. Writing in the sixties, he remembered them as 'bad men and petty thieves'.[41] Williams made his life in Victoria, as did Nicholas White, who was one of the youngest on the *Hive*. White overlanded with the Ryrie brothers, to whom he was assigned when he arrived.[42]

The groundwork for what became a legendary overland journey had been laid by Richard Bourke. From mid-1835, the governor was embroiled in controversy about settlement at Port Phillip after Vandemonians took matters into their own hands and crossed Bass Strait. Some settled around Portland on the coast. John Batman and Joseph Gellibrand explored the Yarra River and signed a 'treaty' with the Kulin people. Briefly, visions of an enlarged Van Diemen's Land danced before Governor Arthur's eyes. He delayed telling Bourke that the Port Phillip Association, as the unauthorised settlers called themselves, had written to London arguing that Port Phillip being much closer to Van Diemen's Land should come under Arthur's control. Eventually they received a flea in the ear from Lord Glenelg, who told them that schemes for new settlements by private individuals and companies were prohibited and no change was contemplated.[43] Despite Arthur's subterfuge, both governors knew that Bourke's domain of New South Wales stretched from north of Moreton Bay to the waters surrounding Port Phillip. Furious when he received Arthur's despatch, Bourke did not wait for London's verdict. First he issued a proclamation which declared Batman's claim to a treaty with the indigenous people null and void. In case there was any doubt, he informed all those eyeing the new pastures that anyone who occupied them 'will be considered as trespassers by His Majesty's Government'.[44]

Second, Bourke despatched Major Mitchell post haste to find an overland route to the disputed territory. Mitchell's previous exploration had reached the Murray. This time he was ordered to go beyond it. The journey, which was successful in so many ways for Europeans, resulted in tragic conflict with the Wiradjuri tribes along the way. Wise to the invasion that was inexorably taking over their land, and being acquainted with Mitchell and his men from an earlier journey, large numbers of the Wiradjuri tracked his every move. Intent on catching them by surprise, Mitchell took a small group of his men, split them into two groups, and backtracked. But it was he who was surprised. Confronting him was a large number of indigenous men with whom he had clashed the previous year. They were seeking revenge. A stand-off lasted overnight, during which the Wiradjuri created five campsites to surround the tense white men for whom it was, as Stephen Foster put it, 'a night of watchfulness'. The exploration party was under instructions not to fire unless Mitchell himself gave the order, but the next morning one of Mitchell's men, Charles King, lost his nerve and fired. In the conflict that resulted casualties are uncertain, but at least seven of the Wiradjuri were killed and four wounded.[45] Governor Bourke had given Mitchell written orders to 'conciliate the goodwill' of the Aborigines and instructions 'that no firearms or force of any kind be resorted to unless the safety of the party should absolutely require it'. Months later, when the governor learned what had happened, he ordered an inquiry and many of the expedition team were called as witnesses. To his indignation, Mitchell was censured for both his conduct and his attitude.[46] Meanwhile, settlers continued to take up land at Port Phillip. Hearing that some of them were shooting Aborigines, Bourke despatched a young Church of England catechist named George Langhorne to the area in a futile attempt to protect them.[47]

The year 1836 was a tumultuous one for Richard Bourke, from the announcement of the new magistrates on 1 January. Port Phillip was an ongoing issue from Batman and Gellibrand's incursion in 1835. Conflict with many of his officials was also continuous, none more disturbing than that with the colonial secretary, Alexander Macleay, who opposed the governor at every turn, setting an example that others followed. As members of the Legislative Council and the smaller Executive Council, officials like Macleay were well placed to frustrate Bourke's plans. Voting to block the Church Act and the non-denominational education system were just two of the more obvious ways in which his senior staff opposed the governor. For some time, Bourke had been urging London to appoint a younger man in Macleay's place, preferably the governor's new son-in-law, Edward Deas Thomson. Taking advantage of an unguarded remark by Macleay about retiring, the governor advised London that the colonial secretary was stepping down. The first Macleay knew about it was the announcement of Deas Thomson's appointment in the *London Gazette*. Further conflict followed when the angry magistrates elected the colonial treasurer, Campbell Riddell, to be chairman of quarter sessions, an appointment he wanted to accept but which Bourke, when asked, had forbidden. Reasoning that Riddell's public office made him unsuitable, Bourke suggested Roger Therry would be more appropriate but Riddell defied the governor by not withdrawing his name. In response, Bourke suspended him from the Executive Council and informed London that it was a matter of principle for which he sought support; otherwise he would resign. Glenelg's reply arrived early in 1837. It criticised Riddell for his disloyalty to Bourke, 'his place as an Executive Councillor was therefore bound to support you', but Glenelg felt the suspension which lasted nearly twelve months was sufficient and instructed Bourke to reinstate him once Riddell had apologised. On receiving the despatch,

Bourke tendered his resignation as he had foreshadowed he would.[48] Then he went for a trip to Port Phillip.

He had already sent Captain William Lonsdale to be police magistrate at Port Phillip. Three surveyors were also in place, including Granville Stapylton who by now was drinking so heavily that he frequently ended the night in the lock-up. On arrival, Bourke named the town Melbourne and, later, confessed to his son how much he enjoyed naming the streets as well. Even Thomas Spring Rice was commemorated, if somewhat disguised, by Spring Street. Bourke's own name on one of the city's major thoroughfares recalls that visit.[49] Curious as ever, Bourke explored the surrounding countryside in a long circular sweep, camping each night, escorted by a small entourage including William Buckley, a convict who had lived with the Aborigines for many years.[50] When he finally sailed for Sydney on 29 March the governor had been at Port Phillip nearly a month. Had he but known, even governors were not immune from prejudice. The ship's captain confided to his diary: 'I had a long chat with the Governor, who is an affable and gentlemanly man—but he is an Irishman—and I don't like Irishmen generally.'[51]

Acceptance of Bourke's resignation arrived in July 1837. As he prepared to sail in December he had mixed feelings, although his biographer John Molony says the dominant one was pleasure at the prospect of home, and relief at leaving behind an onerous job made harder by the rancorous conflict that had dogged his time as governor. At a personal level, he would have been desperately sad to leave Anne behind. Even recognising her happy marriage to Edward Deas Thomson, the prospect that they might be saying goodbye for ever must have weighed heavily.

In the public sphere, Bourke left a colony as divided as the one he inherited. The parties had simply swapped positions. Governor Darling's 'opposition' were now Bourke's strongest supporters while the conservatives who had been such a bulwark for Darling opposed everything Bourke did. He had a few unexpected converts, however. The ageing John Macarthur, bastion of conservatism, approved of Bourke's initiatives on economic and commercial issues, telling his son, 'Never have we had a Governor before, capable of discovering, appreciating and drawing forth the resources of the Colony.'[52] The divisions were striking to young Charles Darwin in 1836, who noted, 'The whole community is rancorously divided into parties on almost every subject.'[53] But this was all at a gentry level. Consolation for the departing governor was provided by an outpouring of praise and regret from ordinary people who understood that Bourke had their interests first and foremost, the interests of all regardless of religion or ethnicity. When news of his resignation first broke in January 1837, native-born Bob Nichols compared him to the only governor whose toast was regularly proposed at the annual anniversary dinner. 'His Excellency General Bourke,' said Nichols in a speech to his fellow Australians, 'has done more, by his upright and manly conduct in the Administration of the Government entrusted to him, to advance the lasting and real interests of Australia, than any Governor we have had since the lamented Lachlan Macquarie.'[54]

In their hearts and minds Bourke was the 'people's governor' and the people were determined to celebrate him, ignoring the disparagement of conservatives who dismissed Bourke's supporters as just 'rags and bones', their farewells as 'the cheers of a felon mob'.[55] Their loyalty to their hero persisted, transforming into substance a decade later with the erection of a statue modelled from life to whose construction many had contributed. The long recital of Bourke's achievements inscribed on its pedestal, acknowledged that

> by these and numerous other measures for the moral, religious and general improvement of all classes, he raised the colony to unexampled prosperity; and retired amid the reverent and affectionate regret of the people; having won their confidence by his integrity, their gratitude by his services, their admiration by his public talent and their esteem by his private worth.

The only memorial of a colonial governor erected by people who knew him, Bourke's statue stands today in Macquarie Street, outside the State Library of New South Wales.

CHAPTER 12
A New Governor

Governor George Gipps replaced Governor Bourke, arriving about eight weeks after his predecessor sailed on a long slow voyage which included revisiting the scenes of his military service in South America. Like Bourke, George Gipps was a soldier. He had joined the Royal Engineers in 1809 and served with Wellington in the Peninsular campaigns. After Napoleon's defeat, he spent some years at the Royal Artillery headquarters in Chatham, followed by an administrative role in the West Indies. After marrying in 1830, his career was mainly in England except for two years with the Gosford commission in Canada which investigated the management of crown lands. His biographer Samuel McCulloch argues that the commission's report revealed Gipps 'as a Whig, liberal and just towards the French Canadians'. He was promoted, knighted and appointed governor of New South Wales soon afterwards. Among the challenges he faced in the colony were confrontation over land tenure with the squatters and political tensions as the penal colony began its transition to democracy with a partially elected Legislative Council. Norfolk Island was the subject of a controversial experiment in penal reform and, in 1843, Gipps became the first governor to visit there. Underpinning everything in his first few years was fallout from the economic depression of the early forties on both gentry landholders and poor immigrants.[1]

Relations with the Aborigines were also a major issue during Gipps' time as governor. One of the most egregious clashes between Europeans and the indigenous people occurred during his first year. And Andrew Burrowes from the *Hive* found himself caught in the middle of the tragedy.

Twenty-two years old, with skills as a groom and an indoor servant, Burrowes had been convicted of highway robbery in Sligo and sentenced to transportation for life.[2] In New South Wales he was sent by his employer, Henry Dangar, to be a stationhand on his property at Myall Creek in north-west New South Wales. In June 1838 he and another stockman were droving a mob of cattle to Dangar's 'lower station' five days ride down the Upper Gwydir River where overseer William Hobbs joined them. While they were away the local Aboriginal tribe, members of which he knew personally, were barbarously massacred. Approximately 28 Aboriginal men, women and children were shot or hacked to death with a sword and knives. Most of the white vigilantes who slaughtered them were or had been convicts, but they were led by John Fleming, who had been born in the colony at the Hawkesbury.[3] Calling them 'white' vigilantes is not strictly correct, however. One of the gang, John Johnstone was of mixed race, distinctive enough to be described as a 'mulatto' on his ship's indent.[4]

A merchant seaman by occupation, Johnstone had been transported nine years earlier for theft at Liverpool in Lancashire. At the time of the Myall Creek massacre he was free by servitude and working for another ex-convict named James Cox at Moree.[5] His presence as an equal member of the murderous gang provides significant evidence about racism in the penal colony. First, his presence was unremarkable. Nobody made anything of it. Not the men themselves, nor the investigating magistrate, nor the press. Among the gang, he was referred to as 'Black' Johnstone. Another member of the gang, James Oates, was identified as 'Hall's Jemmy', a reference to his employer Mr Hall. This was typical practice in the colonial community which was awash with nicknames as diarist William Telfer junior recalled: 'If a man came from Dublin, he was called "Dubbo", from London "Towny" and so on.' Similar examples can be found throughout the convict archives—'Port Macquarie Jack' and a bushranger known to all as 'Jack the Rammer'.[6]

Second, Johnstone's membership of the gang is important also for what it is says about colonial racism more broadly. In 1961, Russel Ward wrote 'there is slight evidence of racist feelings in Australia during the period [1788–1851] and a good deal of evidence of the lack of them'.[7] After examining more than 1200 convict records, reading contemporary newspapers, books and correspondence, particularly for *A Cargo of Women* and *Australia's Birthstain*, I reached the same conclusion. Both of us disagree with Henry Reynolds, who claimed in 1974 that:

> Racism was far more deeply rooted in Australian historical experience than we have usually cared to admit. It was already an important force when gold was discovered, and Chinese and later Melanesian migrants fitted into a well-established pattern of race relations. Events of the early colonial period prepared the community for the ready acceptance of social Darwinism in the last part of the century and influenced the development of colonial attitudes to all non-European people.[8]

Reynolds mistake was to extrapolate racism towards the Aborigines to racist attitudes generally. Ward, who did draw a distinction initially, shifted to combine the two in the late 1970s under pressure from new research into Aboriginal issues.[9] For a realistic appraisal to be achieved, a distinction must be drawn between the treatment of the Aborigines, which was frequently racist, and of those from different races or ethnic background—including, for example, Maori or Tahitians—which was usually not. In my convict research I have found no evidence of racism towards non-Europeans generally and, on the contrary, some evidence of comradeship regardless of race. Despite its tragic context, John Johnstone's membership of the Myall Creek gang supports this argument.

The Myall Creek massacre remains a terrible stain on the reputation of all convicts. Ever since it occurred, they have been tagged as the dispossessors and killers of Australia's indigenous people. But the prisoners were easy scapegoats, then and now. For many years little attention was paid to the role of the gentry, whose morals and behaviour were assumed to be above such acts. Diverted by gentry memoirs and archives, and misled by anti-transportationist propaganda about the brutality and depravity of the prisoners, until recently historians have perpetuated a stereotype that convicts were just the type of people who would commit such an outrage. And, undeniably, at Myall Creek, they did. However, elsewhere, the number of indigenous people killed directly by the prisoners' masters, or by military regiments under orders (such as the 1816 massacre at Appin), has been given less weight than it deserves. In the 1980s, Jan Kociumbas highlighted the 'demonisation of the convicts by the anti-transportationist Reverend John West'.[10] And Norma Townsend challenged the stereotype that convicts were villains because they were convicts and/or because the penal system made them so. After forensically analysing information about the Myall Creek gang, which existed because the men were, or had been prisoners, Townsend concluded that, 'It is not surprising that convicts and ex-convicts predominated in Fleming's group. It would have been more surprising [given their proportionate numbers in the community] if they had not, but it was not necessarily their convictism that was the crucial determinant. Length of time and experiences in the colony were arguably more important.' In other words, with the Myall Creek massacre we are considering a dozen or so outrageous individuals who should not be regarded as representative of 'the convict class'. Furthermore, Townsend added, 'Both masters and men, either directly or indirectly, played their parts in different ways in the Myall Creek Massacre.'[11]

Andrew Burrowes did not take the massacre lightly. Indeed his statements reveal that he was distressed by it. He and Hobbs had been told the news when they stopped at a neighbour's station on their return journey and their reaction reveals their immediate concern was for the Aboriginal people as individuals. Perhaps with the dignified elder known as 'Daddy' in mind—or the lively little boy called Charley—the first question both men asked was whether their informant knew who had been killed. 'Mr Hobbs and I asked Bates [the hutkeeper] did he know the names of those blacks that were killed?' But Bates did not know the names of those who died. He had been told the news directly by the killers who had called at the station for breakfast the day after the murder and the names of those who died were immaterial to them. Overseer William Hobbs' next worry was whether one of his stockmen from Myall Creek had been involved. Bates replied to his question that one, Charles Kilmeister, was with the group who came to breakfast.

Back at Myall Creek, they found the station's hutkeeper George Anderson in a state of high anxiety, afraid that he would be implicated. 'It was a shame you could not stop it,' Andrew Burrowes said to him, but Anderson insisted it was impossible. 'The men came and took the

blacks away. There were nine or ten men and I could not prevent it.'
Kilmeister said much the same when Burrowes remonstrated with him
and he was angry with Burrowes for asking. 'I know nothing about it.
You need not speak to me about it. They came here and I know nothing
more about it.'[12]

Police magistrate Edward Denny Day, who was based in the Hunter
Valley, was sent to Myall Creek to investigate. Kilmeister who had returned
there from down river was the first culprit to be arrested. With amazing
speed, the other offenders were tracked down and sent to Sydney for trial
as Day methodically collected statements that would condemn them. His
witnesses were terrified. In a state of 'intense fear' was how Day described
Anderson and Burrowes, adding 'The whole of the witnesses . . . appeared
to labour under an idea that their lives would not be safe after giving
evidence in the case.' Despite his fear, Burrowes appears to have told the
truth without prevarication although he tried to avoid naming some of
the gang and was recalled to give more extensive identification. George
Anderson's evidence was vital to convicting the murderers, but Burrowes'
testimony was also an essential contribution.[13]

There was no such thing as witness protection for a convict in colonial
Sydney. Burrowes was housed in the same gaol as the condemned men
while their trials took place (twice, because the jury at the first trial
refused to convict). Tension between everyone incarcerated at that time
must have been explosive. As soon as the trials were over, the sheriff
asked if he could move Burrowes and other prosecution witnesses to Goat
Island. It was only a temporary reprieve. Three years later, in 1842, he
was found dead at Cockfighter's Creek near Wollombi. An inquest was
held, but the depositions do not survive and Percy Simpson, who was
acting as coroner, did not follow his usual practice of writing up details
in his bench book. Instead, he simply recorded a verdict that gave no
cause, revealed no motive, explained nothing and blamed no one. Nor,
however, did he describe what happened as 'accidental death'. According
to the inquest, Andrew Burrowes just met 'sudden death'.[14]

Edward Denny Day's investigation laid the groundwork, but some
credit for the conviction of the Myall Creek murderers must be given
to John Hubert Plunkett. As attorney-general he was responsible for
the prosecution of the case. Perhaps his most significant act, however,
was his response to the jury's decision to acquit at the first trial on the
grounds that the dead could not be sufficiently identified. To the outrage

of the prisoners' supporters, many of whom were powerful pastoralists
including Henry Dangar, Plunkett immediately ordered that the men be
retained in gaol rather than released. Meanwhile, he assembled another
charge alleging that they had specifically murdered the little boy named
Charley. This time, with the aid of a small, charred rib bone as exhibit,
the prosecution succeeded in achieving a guilty verdict. Seven of the
nine men were hanged.[15]

•

A year later, in November 1839, Governor Gipps called Henry Lugard
back to Sydney. He wanted to discuss plans for a new gaol on Norfolk
Island. Complaints from officials and from clergymen about the evils
of overcrowding to the management, health and morals of the prisoners
had made their accommodation an urgent issue. Commandant Anderson
had been advocating a new gaol (sometimes called 'barracks'). Now penal
reformer Alexander Maconochie, with ideas of his own about how a gaol
should be designed, was on Gipps' doorstep. At that time, the governor
had never been to Norfolk Island. Before meeting Maconochie, he needed
to hear Lugard's views about an appropriate design. And to ask his fellow
engineer some questions. Should it be constructed at the main settlement
near the existing building? Would locating it at the agricultural centre at
Longridge be a better option? The matter was now urgent because the
island was to receive several thousand extra prisoners annually, direct from
England under the newly established probation scheme. They must not
be allowed to mix with the doubly convicted old hands who currently
populated the island.

Alexander Maconochie sailed to Sydney from Van Diemen's Land as
soon as Sir John Franklin offered him the job on behalf of the British
government. The power of decision lay with Gipps, who had arranged
for Franklin to tell Maconochie as a device (successful as it turned out)
for repairing the estrangement between the two men. Maconochie wasted
no time getting on a ship to the mainland. He hoped to persuade Gipps
to change the venue for his experiment in penal management from
Norfolk Island to some other site in Van Diemen's Land. Gipps listened
but, in the end, deferred to the British government's greater wisdom in
choosing Norfolk Island. He was influenced by discussions with Henry
Lugard. 'I only finally decided against Captain Maconochie's proposal
yesterday, having waited for the return from Norfolk Island of an Officer

of Engineers [Lieutenant Lugard] whom I had called up expressly to give me information respecting it and especially of the facilities which it affords for accommodating an increased number of convicts.' Having talked to Lugard, and heard Maconochie's views, he ordered that temporary wooden buildings be erected at Longridge and an existing barn be converted so it could house 200 men. With his usual efficiency, Henry Lugard had recently completed a detailed survey of the entire island. He had established that the island was smaller than previously estimated, only 9000 acres rather than 14,000. Armed with this information, Governor Gipps tried to inject some reality into London's expectations. After quoting Lugard's survey, he wrote 'I fear that the expense of maintaining convicts on it will be greater than your Lordship appears to contemplate.' He estimated the island could probably sustain between four and five thousand extra convicts but not more than that without increasing costs.'[16]

Maconochie was not deterred sufficiently to give up the appointment. He returned to Van Diemen's Land to collect his family, sailing for Norfolk Island on 23 February and arriving there on 6 March 1840.[17] Henry Lugard was required there to start the building work but he did not live on the island again for any length of time. Meanwhile, he was in Sydney and on leave. In his usual energetic way, he made the most of it.

We don't know where he spent Christmas 1839 but it was almost certainly with some colonial family, very likely on their estate rather than in Sydney. Wherever it was, there would have been parties and picnics, dancing and cards and a flock of colonial daughters to add spice to the company. The men would also have spent much time swimming, fishing, shooting and riding, all activities Henry enjoyed. He was particularly fond of horseracing and later in life was one of the stewards at the Penrith Races. It seems he sometimes acted as a jockey himself. Drawing on personal papers, his descendant Cecil Lugard records that he raced a horse at the Sydney Subscription Steeplechase on 5 March 1840. We do know that at one of those parties or picnics, sometime in the early months of 1840, Henry Lugard met Margaret McHenry. Known as Mattie, she was very young, only sixteen, and very beautiful. Of course, he fell in love with her.[18]

Margaret McHenry had an interesting colonial lineage. Her grandfather the Reverend Henry Fulton was a Protestant clergyman who had been transported (with his own consent) for what was described as 'seditious practices', that is, supporting the Irish rebellion of 1798.

He arrived at Botany Bay in 1800 along with other well-known exiles including 'General' Joseph Holt and Father Harold, a Roman Catholic priest who was transported for the same reason. Reverend Fulton, whose parish in later life was based at Penrith, died in November 1840, so it is likely that Henry Lugard met him, even if only briefly. Mattie's mother was his daughter.[19] If Mattie had any doubts about the relationship with Henry—for example, the ten-year age gap or the prospect of leaving Australia—they would have been banished when the whole town started calling him a hero.

It was 2.30 a.m. on 18 March 1840 when a Mr Skinner raced through the streets of Sydney shouting 'Fire! Fire!' Stables owned by Mr James Blanch, ironmonger, were ablaze and threatening the Royal Hotel whose southern wall formed the back of the stables. Animal fodder such as hay fed the flames, which quickly shot high in the air. By 3.30 a.m. they had caught the overhanging eaves of the hotel which soon was also on fire.

It had been St Patrick's Day but, despite the celebratory excesses of the day before, the town responded to the news with alacrity. Two hundred soldiers raced from the barracks which was only a block along George Street from the fire. They brought with them some kind of horse-drawn fire engine belonging to the Ordnance department. Mr Graham of the Royal Engineers followed with eighteen prisoners attached to Ordnance. Shortly after, Mr Tucker, clerk of Hyde Park Barracks, arrived with 300 prisoners armed with useful implements. In this crowd, they were part of the community, not objects of fear. Subsequently, a prisoner named Robertson and two others named Chiddle and Brown were highly praised by the *Sydney Monitor* which recorded, 'The bravery of these men was admirable, in mounting walls, tearing down buildings and doing all that lay in their power to check the flames. We saw other prisoners whose names we wish we could give, that worked very hard.'[20] One of Mr Blanch's assigned servants, joined later by Captain Collins, spent nearly three hours on the roof of his master's house successfully preventing the fire from taking hold. But the nearby hotel was an inferno. So was the old theatre which adjoined it. Properties all around the hotel were threatened including the new Victoria Theatre, Mr Harvie's bookshop and other business premises. Mr Nash saved his house by covering the roof with blankets which he kept wet. Mr Harvie's shop survived but he suffered from an excess of enthusiasm by some soldiers who rushed into his shop and, over his protests, took the whole of his stock into the street.

There was no shortage of willing helpers but a very great shortage of equipment. The first engine to arrive belonged to the Ordnance department. The Sydney-based insurance companies were very slow to act. Eventually, the small engine of the Australian Assurance Company arrived but it was not until much later that it sent its large engine. The Alliance Insurance Company did have the wit to send its large engine from the start but it was still late arriving.

For some time, lack of water was also a problem. Caps had been inserted into the paved street above the Tank Stream and elsewhere into Busby's Bore, but no one had keys to open them. This dilemma revealed the delayed appearance of 'authority' in any form. They were all still at the St Patrick's Day dinner, presumably nursing their port while listening to John Hubert Plunkett play Irish airs. His violin performances on St Patrick's Day were legendary. In any event, the water did not flow until Colonel Barney, who had been among the dinner guests, turned up with a person who had the right keys.

Because the hoses from the fire engines could not reach the roof of the hotel, the heart of the fire fed on itself. Henry Lugard had arrived by then, most probably having come with Colonel Barney from the dinner. Recognising that the fire must be starved of fuel, Henry led a team onto the roofs of nearby buildings owned by a Mr Wyatt who had recently bought them when he also bought the Royal Hotel. Mr Graham, foreman of works, and his convict workers from Ordnance, and Mr Meredith (writer Louisa Meredith's husband) went with him. They were tearing down a boarded-up building, high on its roof, when the roof fell. The *Sydney Monitor* reported that 'Mr Meredith was much bruised, Lieutenant Lugard fell, as also did Mr Graham, but with a few bruises, they escaped.' Mr Wyatt had no doubt that their efforts prevented further loss. The hotel was ruined but his new buildings were intact. Through the *Sydney Herald* he thanked everyone, many by name, who had taken such risks but singled out for further praise 'Lieutenant Lugard, to whose courage, extraordinary activity and presence of mind, Mr Wyatt considers himself indebted.' A grateful Mr Blanch subsequently took out an advertisement to express his heartfelt gratitude to Major Barney, Captain Collins and Lieutenant Lugard 'for their—almost unparalleled exertions—as also Messrs Graham and Watson and those who assisted them in preventing his residence and shop from being consumed by the fire'.[21]

In the aftermath, there was a post-mortem led by the media. Predictably perhaps, the inferno was started by a drunken servant of Mr Blanch whose celebration of St Patrick's Day had been too enthusiastic. He returned as usual to sleep in the stables and, in his stupor, let his candle fall over. *The Australian* called for a Building Act to be introduced that would prevent any building 'borrowing' the wall of the place next door and, equally, would prohibit overhanging eaves like those of the Royal Hotel which sucked the flames inside itself. It could have been worse. Colonel Barney later declared that if the wind had turned southerly he would have felt obliged to blow up several houses in George Street. *The Australian* lashed the two insurance companies for their inadequate firefighting equipment, to which they replied that if firefighting was to be their responsibility then premiums would have to rise because too many local residents insured with companies in Britain rather than with them. *The Australian* declared that a public subscription should be raised 'for the purpose of procuring a certain number of large and really effective engines, with fire-ladders, pipes, buckets etc.' and for storing them in a central building with a salaried attendant to take charge. 'The said engines, in case of fire, to be placed free of charge, at the public disposal.' It was the beginning of the New South Wales Fire Brigade.[22]

The fire has to be the most significant consequence of the many colonial celebrations for St Patrick's Day which, every year, delivered a litany of drunks and petty criminals to summary justice the next morning. In 1838, for instance, one Patrick Maguire was fined for being the ringleader of a mob who had thrown brickbats at the mounted police 'for the honour of St Patrick'.[23] In 1832, a notable but not illegal encounter was reported in the *Sydney Herald* in a mix of nautical terms and boxing cant. 'A very pretty turn-up took place in Sydney on St Patrick's Day between Boatswain, a native black, and a seaman of a vessel in harbour. The black showed such superior science, that the tar was obliged to strike his colours. Boatswain is open to fight anyone of his weight for £50 a side.'[24] In 1838, a rebellion occurred at the King's School at Parramatta. Determined to take part in the annual celebrations, the boys barricaded headmaster Reverend Robert Forrest in the schoolroom demanding that he grant them a half day holiday because it was St Patrick's Day. A stand-off occurred between teacher and students until threats from Forrest that he would call the police convinced the boys they would be wise to give up.[25]

Marking St Patrick's Day was one tradition unambiguously trans-ported from Ireland to Australia: the wearing of the green and the shamrock, lusty drinking and brawling and dancing and singing. Even its agricultural significance as a date for planting the first potatoes was transferred across the world. United Irishman Joseph Holt wrote that on his Australian farm 'my usual time for commencing to sow was the first Monday after St Patrick's Day; it requiring a few days to get my men sober'.[26] But Patrick O'Farrell argues that references like this to drunkenness disguise the greater significance of St Patrick's Day. For the Irish it was a national holiday in both the north and south of Ireland, celebrated by Protestants and Catholics, by gentry and workers alike. As O'Farrell put it, 'At the end of the eighteenth century, St Patrick was an ecumenical figure, transcending religious and social difference and divisions. He was a symbol wherever the common name of Irishman was spoken.' St Patrick might be a saint but the day was not a religious one. It was a festival, a carnival with, according to O'Farrell, a link to Ireland's 'primitive and pagan past, [which] was not seriously eroded until the famine and what is known as "the devotional revolution"—that is the rise to cultural dominance of the Catholic Church, from the 1850s'. In New South Wales, the church increasingly sought to regulate the celebrants. By the 1870s, 'Saint Patrick's Day was transformed from a recognition of shared national origins, and celebration of the absence in new Australia of those religious differences which impeded and constrained life in old Ireland, to a much more narrow, exclusive, and partisan celebration of Irish Catholic religiosity.'[27]

Celebrations in New South Wales were first referred to in 1795 when judge-advocate David Collins remarked in his journal that 'libations to the saint were so plentifully poured, that at night the cells were full of prisoners'. This kind of class-based, patronising tone continued for some years since the only Irish gentry in the colony were prisoners of the Crown and while, like Joseph Holt, they took part in activities marking the Day, they were not in a position to 'raise the tone' to what might be seen as a respectable level. After he arrived in 1810, Governor Macquarie effectively endorsed the day when he arranged entertainment for government men to mark it, but it was not something with which the gentry involved themselves.[28] Press coverage of celebrations was almost non-existent until 1825 when a report in the *Sydney Gazette* suggests annual revelries had nevertheless been occurring before that.

St Patrick's Day and the Races

Last Thursday was ushered in with the usual testimonies of distinguished regard. Music struck up at an early hour through our streets to arouse the attention of the real Hibernian . . . upon the anniversary of his Patron Saint. In the forenoon every carriage, chariot, curricle, gig, horse and cart was in requisition to attend the races. The new course merits our entire approbation, as we think it one of the most eligible spots in the vicinity of Sydney.

This glowing testimonial was followed by a long list of horses and owners (of some social standing) who took part in the races. They included 'Captain Piper's mare, *Jessy*, Mr Badgery's bay horse *Hector*, Mr James White's mare *Star* etc.'[29] In 1826 these kind of activities probably took place but they were not reported. Nor was a dinner, the absence of which may mean that the community was still getting the measure of their new governor, Ralph Darling. But it was also common for landholders, such as Sir John Jamieson, or lesser social beings who were emancipists or native born, to hold private dinners that were rarely reported. The following year street revels, sporting activities and picnics were once again supplemented by a dinner in Sydney for the respectable. Darcy Wentworth, nearing the end of his days, chaired what was described as 'a sumptuous feast'. Although not himself Irish, the chief justice, Sir Francis Forbes, graced it with his presence, the most senior official yet to publicly celebrate St Patrick.[30]

In 1830, the dinner leapt up the social scale. The numbers were much the same but, perhaps encouraged by Sir Francis Forbes, it was now attended by the colonial secretary Alexander Macleay and Justice James Dowling of the Supreme Court, who was of Protestant Irish background. The high sheriff, Thomas MacQuoid, was in the chair, and Roger Therry, who was vice chair, made what were described as 'several eloquent speeches, characterised by that wit, animation and warm-heartedness for which his country is so renowned'. All was harmony and good fellowship or, as the *Gazette* reported, 'The glass circulated cheerfully, but with moderation. Conversation flowed freely along, and all appeared to be at perfect ease, and on the most cordial and unsuspicious terms with one another.' Except towards the end of the meeting. The increasingly irascible John Macarthur caused consternation when his reply to a toast to *the Agricultural Interest of the Colony* turned into an attack on the press, including the government press, that is, the *Sydney Gazette*, the editor of which was present. It was almost the last speech of a long night and Therry, with the help of others, at length persuaded Macarthur to desist before irreparable harm was done.[31]

Sir Richard Bourke was credited with making the Sydney celebrations of St Patrick's Day more respectable than the raggle-taggle festivities in Hobart, but who awarded him that accolade is uncertain.[32] It may have been Bourke who first suggested that a major public event, like a regatta, be staged each year. Or the Catholic Church saw something wholesome like a regatta as a useful diversion from the traditions of races and gambling and drinking. Regattas were popular in Sydney. Traditionally, the colony celebrated Anniversary Day on 26 January with a regatta in which convicts' children soon became renowned for their prowess on the waters. In 1838, the St Patrick's Day calendar included a regatta but the male-only dinner had been replaced by a ball which ladies could attend.[33]

In contrast to his heroics at the fire following St Patrick's Day, Henry Lugard spent May 1840 defending a charge of aggravated assault. It was hardly a Supreme Court trial—taking place in the 'free' section of the Police Court—but the parties treated it seriously and retained top solicitors and barristers. The plaintiff was a Mr Daniel Aldborough of Bridge Street who alleged that Henry Lugard and his companion, a Mr Scrutton, assaulted him. Unfortunately, only one newspaper reported the case, and then so discreetly that we don't know the details. Too much drink perhaps? An offended sense of honour? Captain Innes, the police magistrate, described the affair as 'a most trumpery charge' and thought there was 'no foundation for the epithet "aggravated"'. However, he said, 'the evidence did prove that an assault had been committed'. Henry and his friend were each fined 5 shillings. Mr Aldborough was awarded costs of 4s 6d but it was speculated that fees for the lawyers employed by Messrs Lugard and Scrutton ran into pounds and pounds.[34]

Only ten days later Henry was receiving public praise again. This time it appeared in a letter to the editor of the *Australasian Chronicle* written, most unusually, by the foreman of works for the Newcastle breakwater who signed his name as 'F. Lawson'. He called for an investigation into corrupt practices by some Newcastle citizens and their servants who were making off with food designated for his prisoner workforce. 'I never witnessed [elsewhere] the enormous abuses or obstructions to the public service that exist here,' he wrote. He had been overseeing the construction work for four years, including the time Henry Lugard was in charge, to whom he appealed for support—'I have always acted to the utmost of my power and experience for the public good as engineer officer Lugard Esq., now at Sydney, can testify. During his residence and superintendence at Newcastle there were no complaints. That gentleman was duly instructed, understood his business, though roughly, and always attended to the duties of his situation.'[35] It is not clear what 'though roughly' meant. It may have been a reference to Henry's inexperience at the time, but the positive tenor of the letter is undoubted.

The year 1840 was the last year Edward Canney brought a convict transport to New South Wales. On 18 August 1840 the *Margaret* docked again in Sydney Cove, this time carrying 130 female prisoners from Ireland and 21 of their children, plus 17 emigrant women.[36] The surgeon was Colin Arrott Browning, who lectured the women about paying attention to the state of their stomach and bowels but told them they must come to him promptly if anything was amiss. The hospital bell was rung each morning and evening to remind them of the rules for good health. His stern regime was aimed at keeping them healthy but on all his voyages Dr Browning showed as much concern for the prisoners' souls as for their bodily ailments. So did other surgeons. But the prisoners were not inclined to listen. Whether Catholic or Protestant, their attitude to religion can be discerned from the hundreds of Bibles, prayer books and testaments they left behind when they disembarked.[37] On the *Margaret*, Dr Browning's earnest evangelicalism caused conflict with one of the passengers, a Mr Swanzy (probably Swansea) who may perhaps have sympathised with the prisoners. Certainly, the surgeon fulminated in his journal that he was 'the cause of unutterable mischief' whose conduct 'attempted to neutralise all my efforts to instruct and reclaim the wretched women who had been entrusted to my care'.[38]

Edward Canney spent minimal time in port. He was returning to England via Ambon in the Dutch East Indies. Special cabins had been created on the *Margaret* when she brought Governor Bourke and his entourage to the colony. Canney turned them to advantage by advertising 'superior accommodation' for passengers who sailed with him.[39] Before Canney left England he had become engaged to twenty-year-old Mary Ann Birch. With marriage in mind, he was keen to get back to her.

Ten days before Canney's arrival, Henry Lugard sailed on the *Victoria* for the Bay of Islands. He was under orders to make a military survey of

New Zealand. Mr Graham, the ordnance clerk of works, sailed with him, taking a handpicked team of 24 soldiers and mechanics, the mechanics, according to the press, only until others could be sent out from England. The *Sydney Herald* reported they were instructed to build 'barracks for two companies of infantry and other necessary buildings at Russell, which is expected to be the capital of the northern island. It is about three miles from the settlement of Kororarikaa.'[40] Mr Graham was expecting a long stay, indeed may have intended to settle in New Zealand, because he took his wife and three children with him. Henry must also have anticipated a long absence. Before he left he became engaged to Mattie McHenry, but it would be two years before they saw each other again.[41]

While 1840 was a significant year for Henry Lugard and Edward Canney, it was no less a landmark to many of the men who had been shipwrecked with them five years earlier. In 1840, most of the 'seven-year men' who arrived on the *Hive* received their tickets-of-leave. Within months some of them persuaded the local bench to change them into 'passports' that allowed the bearer to travel between designated districts in the course of work. James Dalton's carting business between Bathurst and Wellington was one example. James Fitzgerald, in Maitland, also obtained a passport to travel round the Hunter Valley plastering walls of new homes built by pastoralists. Some prisoners never applied for a ticket at all, perhaps because their circumstances were already satisfactory. Andrew Hogan and Robert Graham never applied because they were among those few who died in 1836, Robert aged sixteen at Bathurst 'from taking poison unintentionally', Andrew who was twenty at Sydney Hospital from 'unknown causes'.[42] And some never applied because they were in the bush, or in one case had been executed, or were on Norfolk Island for punishment.

CHAPTER 13
'Infested by Bushrangers'

Those in search of a convict rebellion, let alone an Irish one, will not find it among the men who were reconvicted in New South Wales. Perhaps it felt like a wholesale revolt to the settlers at the time, but most of the crimes for which men were sent to secondary penal settlements were so prosaic no researcher could construe them as rebellious. If any crime was going to seem like rebellion it was surely bushranging, but this too mostly arose not from a conspiracy to overturn the system but from individual circumstances related to the workplace. Threats against a bushranger's master were occasionally made but they were spasmodic and a collective uprising like that against Major Mudie and his overseer John Larnarch was almost unheard of. Workplace strikes were far more common. The men from the *Hive* who committed crimes while bushranging were part of a wave of lawlessness that swelled up in the 1830s in New South Wales. Bushrangers were always active in the penal colonies but the extent varied. Paula Byrne's investigation revealed an upswell in the twenties with peak years between 1825 and 1830.[1] Her sample arose against the first arrival of free-settler pastoralists in significant numbers, whereas the *Hive* bushrangers in the late thirties operated against the backdrop that transportation to New South Wales was ending (officially in December 1840). There is no hard evidence that proves this was a motive for bolting, but anticipation may have made the absconders optimistic they could stay longer in the bush and, as it were, outlast the penal colony. Some may even have mistakenly thought the end of transportation would end their original sentence. Whatever the reason, reports of bushrangers were widespread across the colony, particularly during 1839–40.

From the newspapers it appears as if the south-west settlers were competing with those in the Hunter Valley as to who was having the worse time. 'The country about Goulburn is represented to be in a deplorable state on account of the outrages of the gangs of bushrangers with which the place is infested,' shrieked the *Sydney Monitor* before bemoaning the lack of police. A correspondent wrote to say, 'I have not time to tell you all that the bushrangers are doing, but this much I can say, that the Colony never was in such a state before and so unprotected.'[2] Twelve months later, the focus had shifted to the Hunter Valley. 'In one instance which occurred last week,' reported the *Sydney Gazette*, 'twenty assigned men allowed themselves to be bailed up by four bushrangers.' Governor Gipps had threatened to withdraw assigned servants from another district in similar circumstances, which was regarded as 'arbitrary and unjust' at the time, but now the *Gazette* supported the idea. 'We think His Excellency would do well to withdraw assigned servants such as the twenty mentioned above, and to try them as accessories and to punish them accordingly.' The newspaper, however, qualified these exhortations by paying lip service to recent comments by Gipps that doubted the claims about bushrangers were accurate. 'Our own belief,' the newspaper continued, 'is, that one half the stories told are much exaggerated, and that many accounts are without any foundation; at the same time, we do know that robberies are now very frequent in the Hunter district—whether they be perpetrated by bushrangers, or by the assigned servants themselves. Such things have happened as people robbing themselves, such things may happen again.'[3]

Paula Byrne found that bushrangers acquired a mystique in the eyes of the convicts and smallholders. In their own view, they were not absconders but something special. Bushrangers themselves invented the term 'bushrangers'. Some gangs achieved notoriety not only with the broader populace but with each other, their members specifically referring to other well-known gangs. Every bushranger knew the name of 'bold' Jack Donoghoe. Byrne acknowledges that 'clothing, sentiments,

theatricality all gave bushranging an image which could be aspired to',
but she is clear that bushranging was 'not a popular uprising'.[4]

If the length of time they lasted in the bush was a measure of success,
and the reaction of one of the *Hive* men suggests it was, then Patrick
Bruen aka Brien was the most successful from that ship. Bruen was 'out'
constantly from the time he arrived in 1836 to his final spell in the bush
in 1843 which was an uninterrupted two years. As a bushranger, he
operated initially alone, but at some stage acquired a companion whose
name is never mentioned. We don't know whether it was someone from
the same ship. We don't know whether it was a man or a woman. The
term 'companion' was used several times with no details. No mention,
for example, that the person was another prisoner but we can be sure
that if it had been the press would have named him and he would have
appeared at the next Maitland sessions. It begs the question whether
Bruen's 'companion' was a woman, maybe an Aboriginal woman. Certainly
he cared enough about this person to risk capture in an attempted rescue,
something he revealed as he lay dying.

Back in Ireland, Patrick Bruen was a 'cow boy' from County Leitrim
who was convicted of sheep stealing. On arrival in 1836 he was assigned
to George Rust of Appin in the south-west, but soon absconded.[5] By
January 1840 he was working in a gang on the Western Road out of the
Hassans Walls stockade at Hartley. He absconded from Hassans Walls
with John Black from the *Hive* in January, only to be caught in March,
then absconded again from the lock-up in Hartley in April. Because he
did not go to Norfolk Island, we don't have a record of his New South
Wales punishments but, extrapolating from what happened to others,
we can assume that he was flogged each time he was caught. Nine
months passed before he was caught again; then, in January 1841, he
was sent to work from the stockade at 20 Mile Hollow lower down the
mountains road from where he bolted in March and spent the following
two years as a bushranger.[6] Described in the press as 'a notorious and
daring character', he surfaced publicly again in February 1843 when he
was caught by mounted police after bailing-up Henry Nowland on the
road between Wollombi and Maitland. Nowland, who was the son of a
convict, owned the Royal Hotel in Muswellbrook. He was a rich prize for
Bruen who stripped him of his horse, his saddlebags and their contents,
plus 35 shillings in cash.[7]

Lodged in the Wollombi lock-up in leg irons while the police waited for Mr Nowland to identify him, Bruen managed to escape—hobbling along, carrying his irons. Unfortunately for him, police magistrate David Dunlop soon discovered he had gone. Accompanied by a ticket-of-leave man, he gave chase, following Bruen's tracks as far as Patrick's Plains where they lost him. Before returning home, they put the whole district on alert.

Three days later, Bruen was back on the Wollombi–Maitland road, in the meantime having held up several places including the 'old Red House' at Black Creek from where he took a gun, two pistols and some clothes. Everyone was now watching out for him. When local settler Mr Crawford of Browns Muir at Wollombi insisted against all advice on driving to Maitland, two men, one of them an immigrant and one a ticket-of-leave man, followed him expecting he might be robbed. And they were right. They came up behind Crawford's gig just as Patrick Bruen bailed him up. Bruen spotted them and swung away towards the bush but they fired twice, wounding him in the shoulder and lower back so he fell to the ground. In terrible pain from the shot that entered his shoulder and was lodged in his breast, he was taken back to Wollombi in a cart. One witness reported he was 'in great torture'. In this extremity, Bruen revealed his real name (which one report now described as Brown) and that he arrived on the *Hive*. He also explained that he had hung round the Wollombi–Maitland road because he intended to rescue his companion when he or she was escorted from the Wollombi lock-up to Maitland.

Bruen's activities, most particularly his escape from the lock-up for which the keeper was dismissed, had so antagonised the Wollombi townspeople they treated him appallingly. Someone who discovered his condition wrote to *The Australian* in disgust: 'On Wednesday evening, the bushranger, Patrick Bruen, breathed his last . . . The neglected situation of this man, and the repulsive appearance which he presented during his last days of misery, tempts us to inquire what person had charge of him in his last illness? He was left to die without surgical [aid], or any other [help] . . . in a dilapidated bark hut, his bed clothes saturated with the drenching rain and swarming with vermin. He was buried without any form of judicial inquiry.'[8]

It was John Maguire from the *Hive* who revealed that the length of time you stayed out was important in measuring your achievement as a bolter. Maguire was a twenty-year-old porter working in Dublin when he was transported with a life sentence for robbing a Mr Hanratty of £28.[9] On arrival in New South Wales he was assigned to Aspinall & Brown at Bathurst and worked there five years as a stockkeeper. In December 1840 Maguire was indicted with Joseph Bailey aka Badley and Charles Cannon for having firearms in their possession. All three pleaded guilty and were sentenced to transportation for life. However, Cannon, who was a runaway from the employ of publican George Luck at Carcoar, was charged also with murdering Constable Robert Bulmer who was escorting him to gaol in Bathurst. His defence throws some light on John Maguire's activities. Cannon testified that he and the constable were travelling along the road when a gang of five or six men emerged from the bush and freed him. He claimed they recognised his escort, one of them asking Bulmer whether he remembered flogging them down at the Lachlan. Shortly after this exchange, Cannon said he heard a shot, but of course insisted he did not see who killed the constable. However, some of Bulmer's possessions were found on him and another witness testified that Cannon had told them he knew about the murder. He was found guilty and sentenced to death.[10]

John Maguire was proud of his bushranging pursuits. 'I was out 10 months,' he boasted to the Norfolk Island authorities. 'Three others were with me. We fired on the military near Bathurst. I was the leader of the party.' He kept to himself whether he played a role in freeing Charles Cannon and whether, perhaps, it was he who shot the constable.[11]

Maguire was kept in Bathurst until it was clear he would not be needed as a witness at Cannon's trial. Finally, he was despatched in the prison cart to Sydney escorted by soldiers from the 28th Regiment. During the journey, according to an unnamed person who wrote to the *Sydney Herald*, one of the military gave Maguire money and a handcuff key. That's all we know, but it is credible. Evidence recurs of the bond created among prisoners by the long voyage to New South Wales, which appears to have been the defining event in terms of loyalties. Indeed the enduring Australian custom of calling people 'mate' may well have arisen as a contraction of the word 'shipmate' although it was reinforced by other experiences. There is no reason why that bond should have been confined to prisoners. The soldier who favoured Maguire may well have shared the shipwreck of the *Hive*.[12]

Despite any help he received, Maguire spent three years on Norfolk Island. On arrival he claimed he could do no hard labour because he had been wounded in his fight with the military. Gunshot marks on his left breast and right arm are on his convict record. Wherever they did put him to work, Maguire managed to avoid any punishment. In 1844 he was sent to Van Diemen's Land where he served in a probation gang until October 1845. Two years later, as a passholder, he was in trouble for drinking, followed by even more trouble for 'having sexual intercourse with a female passholder in the police office yard'. He was given six months hard labour to reflect on this encounter. In December 1848 he received a ticket-of-leave and in April 1852 a conditional pardon. The rest of John Maguire's story is silent but, like thousands of others, he probably headed for the Victorian goldfields.[13]

Some men were collateral damage from bushranging activities by others. Patrick Tierney (convict as opposed to soldier) on the *Hive* may have been one of these. Transported for life for shopstealing in Galway, he was assigned to solicitor Henry Pilcher who practised in Maitland but also had a farm at which Tierney worked. Within six months of his assignment he was sentenced to 50 lashes for theft. In June 1839 he received another 25 for absconding and in November yet another 50 for insolence. Bushrangers turned up at the farm that month, led by John Shea whom Patrick Tierney knew from when he was assigned to Pilcher. Inevitably, Tierney was accused of collaboration. He was charged with having firearms in his possession and given a punitive life sentence from local magistrates sitting in quarter sessions. Like others on similar charges, however, Tierney's sentence was later commuted to seven years.[14] On Norfolk Island he committed no offences and in September 1844 he was transferred to Van Diemen's Land with one year remaining under the probation system which he served at Seven Mile Creek. While there, he was commended for intervening to save an official from injury when they captured some 'extremely violent' runaways. Tierney received a ticket-of-leave in March 1846 and a conditional pardon three years later.[15] Thanks to research by his descendant, we know that he made his way back to New South Wales and settled at Jamberoo on the Illawarra. An earlier friendship with Denis Collins, who was transported two months before Tierney and settled there, may have been the reason he chose that area.[16] In 1851 Tierney married Collins' daughter Margaret who had emigrated two years earlier with her three brothers.

The pastoralists felt themselves under siege from a criminal community, but the situation was more complex. Emancipists and native-born

Australians who were the children of convicts, plus small free settlers, were targets for robbery just as often. With utter disregard for background or rank, thieves took what they needed wherever it was available. Furthermore, little solidarity existed among the prisoners. Ticket-of-leave holders and assigned servants were active in the hunt for bushrangers, as the case of Patrick Bruen demonstrates. How this group viewed themselves seems to arise from individual circumstances rather than from class consciousness. The one bond that could transcend all else was obligation to help a shipmate.[17] Despite these qualifications, plenty of evidence exists to demonstrate that large numbers of prisoners did collaborate with the bushrangers. Some assisted in robberies like the case of James Hickey below. Others welcomed a gang's appearance at their master's property and did their best to help or shelter them. This complexity was generally overlooked in the rhetoric of pastoralists, who usually cast bushranging as a threat to a class of respectable and virtuous citizens from vicious criminals. And yet, despite the wealth they possessed and the power conferred on them by law, what they alleged also unconsciously revealed how powerless and fearful they felt.

Truth to tell, criminality permeated the colonial community. Charles Darwin probably had the right of it when he declared in 1836 that the penal colony had succeeded in making men 'outwardly honest' but, as he detected, nobody was averse to accepting a product that 'fell off the back of a dray'. In colonial times, both at home and in the colonies, informers officially became 'approvers' or turned king's evidence to testify against comrades in court. Many informal examples of betrayal exist too, like that of John Black, a young Dublin thief who arrived on the *Hive*. His record in the colony is a litany of endless punishments (see Chapter 6) and it would not be surprising if he was desperate for any advantage. Certainly he had no reservation about telling the police the direction taken by some bushrangers.[18]

Thirteen men from the *Hive* were sent to Norfolk Island for committing another crime while they were prisoners—and it would have been fourteen if Patrick Bruen had not been killed. This number is a fraction over 5 per cent of the total 250 men on the ship. They were mainly boys and younger men, and mainly sent there for theft of property. Only one crime was violent, Martin Ryan's clash with his master Isaac Shepherd and subsequent attack on another prisoner in his iron gang which was examined in Chapter 6. In his thesis about the prisoners on Norfolk

Island,[19] Tim Causer found that far from being, as legend would have it, men respited from death sentences for horrible crimes of deep depravity, most prisoners sentenced to the island were there for property crimes. In this, Causer extended Lloyd Robson's finding that more than 80 per cent of male and female convicts were transported from Britain in the first place for some kind of theft.[20] Some of them just could not stop stealing in the colony. Others stole from necessity. Having bolted into the bush, they needed food and clothing, horses and firearms.

Contrary, however, to John Hirst's conclusion in 1983 that Norfolk Island inmates had all been tried in a court of law,[21] Causer found that 1602 (out of a total of 3860) colonial prisoners who went there had not been convicted in any kind of court. For example, one group of men were sent from Port Macquarie in 1830 when its role as a penal settlement ended. Some of them argued later without success that they had been 'unfairly dealt with'.[22] A significant number of prisoners were simply transferred from Cockatoo Island when management of Norfolk Island passed from New South Wales to Van Diemen's Land in the forties. Among these men, whose fate was determined arbitrarily by an official, was John Ryan from the *Hive*.[23]

Causer's detailed analysis of the crimes of prisoners who were sent to Norfolk Island after reconviction in the colonies resulted in a list of their crimes and the percentage of men sent there for each as follows:

Offence	Number of Men and Percentage	
Miscellaneous	18	(0.8)
Property (non-violent)	1453	(66.5)
Property (violent)	416	(*19.0*)
Offence against person	232	(*10.6*)
Offence against system	32	(*1.5*)
Possessing firearms	26	(1.2)
Unnatural offences	9	(*0.4*)
Total	**2186**	(100)[24]

Twenty-four-year-old Michael McNamara belongs in two categories. He was convicted of 'possessing firearms' but his colonial crime was actually burglary, which was later subsumed by charges relating to bushranging. Recorded on the *Hive*'s indent as 'Mathias', he switched to Michael after arriving. As Michael, he was assigned to pastoralist John Eeles in the

Goulburn area but at some time and without any punishment recorded against him he changed to working for Mr Hillas. Altogether, McNamara passed four untroubled years in assignment until June 1839 when he received 25 lashes for losing sheep. We don't know whether this offence coincided with the change of master or whether being flogged made him decide to get away. Only months later, in October, he was charged with burglary in company with another of Mr Hillas' servants John McQuinn.

The burglary charge meant McNamara was in the Goulburn lock-up when five prisoners broke out. The *Sydney Monitor* greeted the news with outrage: 'The robbers who twice in three weeks plundered the Yass mail recently escaped with other prisoners from Goulburn—as numbers have previously done—these men escape under circumstances which leave little doubt that some officials allowed, or assisted them to do so.'[25] In the weeks that followed, Michael McNamara joined other men roaming widely around the Abercrombie River, over the ridges, among steep gullies and deep in the caves, along the faint track between Goulburn and Bathurst. But they were not free for long. By November they were before the Circuit Court at Bathurst. With his burglary charge entirely disregarded, McNamara and others were charged with 'possessing firearms', for which they were punished severely with a sentence of life on Norfolk Island.[26]

Despite the sentence, McNamara spent only four years on the island. As we saw in Chapter 9, he would have experienced much the same working life there as he did on the mainland, a labourer for building or agriculture perhaps, or as a shepherd, or managing crops or working in a dairy. Halfway through his stay, and while the island was still under Alexander Maconochie's command, he was given 50 lashes as 'a notorious malingerer' but it was not accompanied by a sentence to the chain gang so he spent no time in irons while there. When he left Norfolk Island towards the end of 1844 he was 28 years old. After serving five years labour under the probation system in Van Diemen's Land, in 1849 he gained a ticket-of-leave, which was cancelled and reinstated twice. His colonial crime extended his servitude and it was 1857 before he received a conditional pardon for his original life sentence for stealing sheep in County Mayo.[27] Most of his shipmates on the *Hive* who began with transportation for life had been free for almost a decade.

The men sent to Norfolk Island were among the youngest on the *Hive*. Only Darby McAuliffe who killed a sheep and Patrick Tierney, mentioned above, could be described as mature. Juveniles like Martin

Ryan, Peter Ryan, John Ryan (none of them related), John Black and, as we will see in the next chapter, Tom Kelly predominated. By the late thirties the British government had finally become sufficiently concerned about transporting children to establish Point Puer in Van Diemen's Land, but the young convicts who found themselves in New South Wales were terribly at risk in a system that was larger than ever with little of the earlier personal relationships to soften its worst aspects. In the thirties too, it was at its most punitive. The records suggest some attempt to protect children by assigning them to established settlers who were known to officials, but this was far from foolproof.

Many instances of bushranging occurred in the Upper Hunter in 1839 and 1840. By late 1840 Governor Gipps was exasperated with complaints from the free settlers who he felt should have been able to maintain better law and order in their districts. In fact he thought they were exaggerating the breakdown of control in order to make a case for more police. He sent Major Nunn, commandant of the Mounted Police, to investigate. Nunn's report blamed three prominent pastoralists, Messrs Bettington, Blaxland and Leslie, for letting their assigned servants roam at will. In blaming employers for 'lax supervision', however, he overlooked the brutality that made assigned servants run in the first place. The link between flogging and bolting is evident even in this small sample from the *Hive*. After receiving 25 lashes for neglecting his duty, a servant would run, probably not very cleverly. Brought back, he would be given 50 lashes for absconding and then he would run again, further and longer, and very likely link up with others as part of a gang that survived by robbery. They would soon acquire by theft the necessary horses and firearms that transformed them into the bushrangers of legend. If the process was incomplete and they were caught a second time they were flogged yet again and sent to an iron gang where they might be driven to violence, as happened with Martin Ryan, or they escaped and took to the bush again. And when they ran, they robbed. 'Robberies of all kinds daily occur between this place and Yass,' wrote a correspondent from Queanbeyan, who then attacked the local police, alleging that 'the Commandant of the Mounted Police amuses himself near home, as usual' and added that 'the police could not or would not apprehend robbers'. Much to the writer's frustration, assigned servants could not be flogged more than 50 lashes without taking them on a long ride to Goulburn because the regulations required a surgeon's presence if they exceeded

50. His vindictive urge to punish without restraint justified Governor Bourke's actions to reform the practice of flogging six years earlier.[28]

Norfolk Island was established as a secondary punishment settlement on the recommendation of Commissioner Bigge whose instruction from Lord Bathurst as he departed for the penal colonies was to make transportation 'an object of real Terror'. Obedient to London's wishes, Governors Brisbane and Darling reinforced its terrible reputation in the statements they made. So did the newspapers then and for decades to follow. The universal taste for melodrama meant that by the twentieth century, as Causer puts it, 'Norfolk Island was seen as a place of utter despair.' Propaganda had become reality and journalist historian Frank Clune could write: '"All hope abandon, ye who enter here" was the motto of this man-made hell.'[29] This Gothic legend included the idea that, once there, escape was impossible except by death but two men from the *Hive* were among those who spectacularly proved the legend wrong.

Thomas Sullivan was 23 when he was transported from County Cork. He stood 5 feet 8 inches high, which was tall for the period, with dark brown hair and hazel eyes. His training as a carpenter should have ensured a prosperous future in the colony although, as we saw in Chapter 10, the colonial architect was not impressed with his skills and decided against keeping him for government work. Instead, Sullivan was sent to work on Michael Henderson's farm at Raymond Terrace in the lower Hunter Valley. He lasted two and a half years in service before absconding in May 1838, for which his punishment has not survived but would have been at least a flogging of 25 lashes followed by return to his master. He took to the bush again less than a year later and this time stayed out until June 1839, when he was caught with three others robbing the house of Lieutenant Caswell at Port Stephens. Mrs Caswell gave evidence that they were sleeping when the window of their bedroom was smashed, then the front door forced open. Her husband rushed to wake his servants who slept on the far side of the back yard but members of the gang caught him halfway and beat him with sticks before Duffy, the leader, forced him back into the kitchen at the end of a musket, threatening 'I'll do for you.' Mrs Caswell was also beaten with sticks. Fear made her brave. When she saw the musket being pointed at her husband she grabbed it by the barrel, pushing it to one side. Her risky action calmed the situation. 'I'll not hurt you so long as you remain quiet,' Duffy told her. The gang spent three hours ransacking the house for bedding and food and taking silver plate and jewellery as well. The value of their booty was estimated to be £400. None had bothered to disguise themselves, perhaps because they were far from their usual haunts, but it meant that Thomas Sullivan and Duffy were confidently identified by the Caswells. The judge gave them all a sentence of death recorded, which reflected both the value of what they took and the violence of the robbery, but he told them that he would recommend it be commuted to transportation for life.[30] Sullivan, however, was one prisoner who would defeat the penal system even from Norfolk Island, and he did so in company with his shipmate, James Hickey.

There were two James Hickeys on the *Hive*. The older from Kilkenny was aged 30 when he landed and had left a wife and three children at home.[31] The second James Hickey was aged 21 and single. Born in County Limerick, he had been a farm labourer in Clare where he received a seven-year sentence for stealing clothes. This Hickey was assigned in 1836 to pastoralist Thomas Wilmot who sent him to his run at the Maneroo. By 1839, Hickey was based at Wilmot's head station about four miles south of Berrima. It was a spot which drivers of drays on the slow journey from Sydney found convenient as a resting place for their bullocks, a practice with fatal consequences for Hickey. On 5 May 1839 Andrew Shanley and his wife Ellen were travelling on a dray driven by Joseph Saunders which pulled in there with a load destined for publican and storekeeper Mr Moses in Yass. Saunders had previously lived in the Berrima area and friends including James Hickey, William Burnes and Richard Jones came to the camp. Together they made plans to rob the dray.[32]

After three days, the dray moved on but stopped short of its next resting place. Despite the Shanleys' objections, Saunders insisted on spending the night near the house of a man named Biggs. With darkness closing in, the three travellers stopped arguing, ate their evening meal by the campfire and were making up their beds under the dray when seven armed men rode up. Some had blackened their faces as disguise.[33]

Hickey breaks the mould of men who committed a colonial crime to escape brutality in assigned service. He simply went along with a gang intent on robbery, one of whose number committed murder in the process. A stupid, senseless crime but typical of many others. The crimes of men sent to Norfolk Island do not support the idea they were part of some incipient even though thwarted rebellion against the colonial authorities. While some had been driven to individual protest—or despair—by brutality and some were collateral damage in the jittery milieu created by bushranging, many were simply criminals who returned to crime with no apparent justification. Certainly, no gangs of Irishmen roamed the country shouting 'Death or Liberty' to challenge British redcoats, many of whom were Irishmen anyway, but some individuals pulled off remarkable feats that left the penal authorities with their jaws dropping. Our two Irishmen from the *Hive* were among them.

On the night of 13 December 1843, commandant Maconochie's convict clerk, W.H. Barnard, was woken by a dog barking. Peering through the seaward window of his hut he saw shadowy figures of soldiers who were carrying a whaleboat towards the landing place. At first he thought their actions were legitimate. Then he realised they were behaving in a strangely furtive manner and, furthermore, there were other men milling about near the shore. The figures Barnard spotted were four soldiers from the 96th Regiment which was then stationed as the guard on Norfolk Island. The other six men were a mixture of English and Irish prisoners including James Hickey and Thomas Sullivan.[34]

Their plan was timed for when the four escapee soldiers were on guard and perfectly placed as sentries—outside the guardroom where some colleagues slept, outside the boatshed, and near the landing place. They might have got clean away, complete with a 20 gallon keg of water, tools and other supplies but Barnard's loyalties did not lie with his fellow prisoners. He could have gone back to bed. Instead, he slipped out of his back door to alert the police runner, Stephen Smith, who lived nearby. Smith shouted for help and drew his pistol as he ran towards the harbour. With the alarm sounded, shots fired and people rushing towards them the fugitives leapt aboard their boat, pushing off so violently that one of the soldiers, Private James Brady, of the 96th, fell out.

Thanks to Brady's court-martial, we know the details of what occurred, but the incident was so embarrassing for Maconochie that he might otherwise have tried to minimise it. As it was, he waited three weeks before reporting to the governor. He claimed the escape was hastily conceived, which the evidence of careful planning contradicts, and described how he had two boats circling the island and soldiers posted at potential landing places in case the fugitives sneaked ashore to replenish their supplies. He blamed the soldiers, claiming the prisoners left a letter that confirmed 'it was a military initiative'. But the prisoners had tricked everyone into underestimating them. 'None of the escapees were previously suspected men,' wrote Maconochie, 'on the contrary one or two were thought chicken-hearted. The most valuable man among them, Sullivan, who was a carpenter and boatbuilder, was notoriously a chatterer and considered unable to keep his own counsel.'[35]

We don't know what happened to the escapees. They left behind their keg of water and may have died from thirst. Or from starvation, or exposure. If luck was with them, however, a merchantman or a whaler picked them up, particularly if the captain wanted some extra hands for his crew or thought the whaleboat would be a useful acquisition. They were last seen rowing valiantly on the extreme north-west of the horizon without yet having raised their sail. Five years later, the colonial authorities were still circulating their description in the vain hope they would be recaptured (even though the details of James Hickey were those of the older man who was peacefully droving sheep in the Hartley Valley). The fugitives were never caught. Theirs was not the only escape from the 'inescapable' prison but it was certainly unusual because soldiers as well as convicts were involved.[36]

CHAPTER 14
Beyond the Penal Colony

Many former prisoners settled for life in the district where they served their sentence, which in itself says something about the quality of their experience as convicts. Many former prisoners continued working for their original master after they received their ticket-of-leave. Some continued after they became free. Others farmed or worked as tradesmen or retailers in towns nearby where, collectively, they built the infrastructure and created communities.[1]

Those men who moved away from their original location frequently covered vast distances. Some followed their masters who were taking up new pastures. A common reason for a prisoner to receive a ticket-of-leave passport for example, was because his master wanted the man to go with him to a new property. In the early forties settlers fanned out north-west and later far north to the Darling Downs. Among the men who moved with them was 30-year-old Michael Barry. A farm labourer in Ireland, he had adapted to the rigours of the Australian bush. After obtaining a ticket-of-leave in 1840 he took on jobs that involved long journeys, absent from his base for weeks on end, camping each night in the bush with his solitude occasionally relieved by an evening in a pub or by others who joined his campfire. Initially, he travelled for his then employer, Mr McLean, out of the Hunter Valley, over the Dividing Range, across the Liverpool Plains and up onto the New England plateau. Twelve months later his passport was renewed at the request of a new employer, Mr Thomas Parnell, who employed Barry to travel regularly between Liverpool Plains and Morpeth. He might have been droving sheep or cattle, or he might have been driving a cart or, more likely, a bullock dray. Whatever his transport, he was trusted to deliver his load and return to base similarly laden.[2] During the journey, he experienced freedom, choice and autonomy that was a long way from prisons and dungeons—or even daily life in Ireland. His countryman, Martin Cash, who served his initial sentence in the Hunter Valley, summed up the benefits of what some people would see as a lonely life: 'although a measure cut off from society . . . our calm and undisturbed mode of life [was] free from the daily annoyances and petty tyranny which at that time men of my class were generally subjected to and which has ever been the bane of my existence'.[3] In Australia, an Irishman could find peace.

Like Cash, many of his fellow prisoners took to the saddle as if born to ride. Shaking off the pedestrian confines of life in Ireland, their enthusiasm for the power of a good horse and the freedom of the bush confirmed the truth of Patrick O'Farrell's observation that 'the Irish were liberated by Australian openness and possessed of the belief that all could be aristocrats in Australia, the land of free men'. On the trip south with Mitchell, a sullen surveyor, Granville Stapylton left a glimpse of the exhilaration of convicts who were mounted on horses for the first time. 'These men are spoilt and it is enough to spoil them when I see the vagabonds mounted and cutting capers with the Government horses à *la* mounted policemen.'[4] In Van Diemen's Land in the twenties, a settler came across a group of convict stockmen. Having constructed some stockyards, they set off in search of the cattle, riding in a style later cast as the legendary 'man from Snowy River'. 'The men go out in bodies of four or five and cracking their whips and riding full gallop, they hurry the herds without giving them time to escape . . . through wilds, wood, and plains, up and down steep hills and along the most dangerous passes, until they enclose them in the yard.'[5]

In Australia, an Irishman could also find respect for the man he was rather than the peasant caste that limited him at home. Few masters in New South Wales were higher on the social scale than the Leslie

brothers from Scotland. It says much for their character that they were
not worried at being vastly outnumbered by their criminal workforce.
Furthermore, they recognised that their prosperity depended on the men
who accompanied them on a pioneering trek to the Darling Downs. But
it was not only the men who were challenged to adapt themselves to a
new land. Their masters were tested too and in the shared challenges
and adventures of that journey both sides learned to rely on each other.
Decades later Patrick Leslie could not speak too highly of his men: 'We
had twenty-two men, all ticket-of-leave or convicts, as good and game
a lot of men as ever existed and who never occasioned us a moment's
trouble: worth any forty men I have ever seen since.'[6] Most of these
far-ranging prisoners who began in the Hunter Valley never came back
to New South Wales. If they did not see out their lives in a new rural
location, they settled in Ipswich or the newly developing town of Brisbane
that in 1840, replaced the penal settlement of Moreton Bay. As we saw
in Chapter 11, a similar pattern existed in the south-west.

In April 1842, Henry Lugard returned to Sydney after eighteen
months in New Zealand as commanding Royal Engineer. The Treaty of
Waitangi had just been signed when he arrived there and the Europeans
were intent on laying foundations for a new colony. While his clerk of
works, George Graham, began constructing barracks and other buildings
at Russell, which was expected to be the colony's capital, Henry carried
out a full survey of the North and South Islands. Under his supervision,
official buildings were constructed at the Bay of Islands too.[7] Major
Bunbury and the 80th Regiment were also in New Zealand at this time,
having been sent there after they left Norfolk Island. Soldiers from the
regiment's rank and file provided labour to construct Fort Britomart and
barracks in Auckland to Henry's design. Ensign Best, of course, was with
them. Curious as ever, he was intrigued by the arrival at Auckland of
some early settlers on the *St George* from which, to his astonishment, 90
boys aged between fourteen and twenty years disembarked. Strictly, they
were not free settlers but convicts. Like those sent to Western Australia
during the same period, they were young criminals who had served time
in Parkhurst prison on the Isle of Wight. Best says they volunteered to
come and they may have done in the sense that a soldier 'volunteers' in
the army when an officer tells him to do something. Some were so near
the end of their sentence they were set free when they landed. Others,
according to Best, were still to serve 'a certain term of apprenticeship',

which means they would have been put to work as labourers.[8] Historically, these boys have been described as 'apprentices' in both Western Australia and New Zealand, but they were no different to the convict boys transported to New South Wales and Van Diemen's Land in the 1830s. Only the terminology—and the times—had changed.[9]

When Henry Lugard left New Zealand he farewelled Major Bunbury and Ensign Best for the last time. The 80th Regiment went on to India. Seven months later the Anglo–Sikh War broke out. The 80th moved to the front line. After an exhausting march of 150 miles, they joined an attack on an army of heavily entrenched Sikhs. The battle lasted all night. Well after midnight the 80th was ordered to take a heavy gun. By the dawn they were inside the battery and despite heavy losses briefly thought they had carried the day. But the enemy were playing dead. Catching the British off guard, the apparently lifeless bodies rose up again in a surprise attack. As Bunbury shouted orders and his troops tried to regroup, Abel Best was killed rallying the men.[10]

When Henry left in 1842, his significant role in New Zealand's foundation ended. George Graham and his family stayed behind and according to researcher Philip Heath, Mr Graham and Major Bunbury are usually credited with Henry Lugard's work. There is no listing for Henry Lugard in the New Zealand *Dictionary of Biography*, but there is none in the Australian equivalent either.[11]

His legacy to history would have been the last thing on Henry's mind when he left New Zealand. He was anticipating a reunion with Mattie McHenry. Correspondence flowed back and forth while he was away. The wedding was planned. A dress had been made. Once Henry knew his return was imminent, the date was set. Less than four weeks after he landed in Sydney they were married by Reverend Henry Bobart at St John's church, Parramatta. We don't know where they went for their honeymoon—Solomon Wiseman's inn near the Hawkesbury River ferry was popular with newlyweds and, like Edward Deas Thomson and Anne Bourke, they might have gone there. By September they were settled in Mrs McHenry's house in Bligh Street, Sydney, where in July the following year, their son was born. The baby lived for five months and twelve days, long enough for his mother to become entranced with him, to look for his smile, to feel the grip of his tiny fingers before, two days after Christmas, he died. Eighteen-year-old Mattie was stricken. Almost simultaneously news arrived that Henry's father, Captain John Lugard, had died three months earlier. If he had ever contemplated staying in New South Wales, at Mattie's suggestion perhaps, the combination of the two events decided Henry that it was time to return to England—a change of scene for Mattie and comfort for his mother. They sailed early in 1844.[12]

By the time Henry Lugard departed, most of his shipmates from the *Hive* were free and settling down as citizens of their adopted country. But some were not. Some had come a cropper, too young or too dumb to work the system to their benefit, unlucky, unwise, hotheaded. Or just plain criminally inclined.

Tom Kelly was thirteen and stood only 4 feet 9 inches when he was transported for stealing wool with his older brothers, fifteen-year-old Denis who was a stable boy and Michael, who was 24 and employed as a farm servant. All three ended up in the south-west of New South Wales. Michael was assigned to John Coghill at Kirkham near Campbelltown and subsequently at Braidwood. Tom went to William Faithful near Goulburn.[13] Denis Kelly proved the luckiest brother, being assigned to the Ryrie brothers at the Maneroo. A stablehand in Ireland, he must have taken to the work of a stockman as if in heaven for there is no record of any offence or punishment against his name. He stayed with the Ryries throughout his sentence, eventually droving stock for them down to Port Phillip where he received his ticket-of-leave in 1842.[14]

Tom Kelly was one of the youngest boys on the *Hive*. Only Cornelius Sheehan at twelve was younger.[15] Hoping perhaps to find his brothers, he absconded from Faithful barely six months after he arrived. And when the authorities caught him, they thrashed him with 50 lashes on his unblemished skin. After absconding again in early 1838 he was sent to an iron gang at Bathurst for twelve months. Six months after that ended he was sentenced for two years to another iron gang for larceny. By the end of his second stint in a gang, in June 1842, he received a ticket-of-leave for the Goulburn area. It was followed in 1844 by his certificate of freedom. He had endured nine years to complete his seven-year sentence, years which had brought him nothing but brutality and misery.[16]

Receiving a certificate of freedom usually marked the end of a man's connection to the penal system, but not for Tom Kelly. Briefly, his personal life looked positive when he married an immigrant's daughter, Sarah Cunningham, in 1845. Sadly, disaster followed.[17] Only days later, Tom and two others were charged with 'assault and burglariously entering a home with intent to rob' at the River station, Mummell, where Tom was employed. Wearing black masks, they held up a shoemaker named Bartholomew Sullivan who guarded sheep for the landholder, George Hobbler. Sullivan lived a mile from the main homestead but it was not Hobbler's goods the trio wanted. They believed there was cash in the hut and ransacked the place trying to find it.[18]

They were found guilty despite what their lawyer claimed was tenuous evidence about their identity and an attempt by Sarah to provide an alibi.[19] Tom found himself back in the penal system, sentenced to transportation for fifteen years, three of them to be on Norfolk Island.[20] Prisoners reconvicted in New South Wales or elsewhere, including South Australia, were sent to Van Diemen's Land first where a decision was made about what to do with them. It was February 1846 before Tom arrived at Norfolk Island as directed by the judge. He was now 23 years old and had reached his full height of 5 feet 9 inches. Penal reformer Alexander Maconochie had long gone. Joseph Childs was now commandant but when his decision to withdraw the prisoners' kettles provoked a full-scale riot he was replaced by John Price who became notorious for his psychological warfare against the prisoners. His use of informers among them was also well known. Tom Kelly spent eighteen months under Childs and the early days of Price without punishment. By August 1847, however, he had been noticed. That month he received fourteen days in the chain gang for giving tobacco to another prisoner. A month later, he was punished with 36 lashes for being idle, followed six weeks later by an admonishment for disobeying orders. In June 1848 he received one month hard labour in the chain gang for 'disposing of his rations'. Eight weeks later came another sentence, this time four months in the chain gang for having a dog in his hut. The ability to hide emotion was essential for surviving penal servitude. Losing his dog could well have hurt Tom more than all the other punishments combined, but not a flicker of such feelings would have crossed his face. Tom Kelly spent just under four years on the island before sailing in November 1849 for Van Diemen's Land where he served the rest of his sentence. Like many other prisoners of that time, his record ends in 1852 with the word 'absconded'. No evidence has surfaced to indicate he ever resumed married life with Sarah. In fact she appears to have married someone else. Hopefully Tom, too, found another partner on the Victorian goldfields.[21]

This sample of 250 Irishmen on the *Hive* suggests that more Irish offended after they were free than English or Scottish prisoners. A similar sample of 200 men who arrived on the *John* from England in 1832, which I researched for *Australia's Birthstain*, produced nothing like the number of men who committed a crime and were punished by the courts after they received their certificate of freedom. For example, seven men from the *Hive* are listed in the Darlinghurst gaol entrance book for the years 1850–54 against four men from the *John*, one of whom was Irish anyway.[22] Was this pattern a result of discrimination against the Irish? It would take a larger investigation to be certain, but at first glance the evidence from the *Hive* suggests otherwise. Tom Kelly was employed at the time he returned to crime. Furthermore he was working and making a life for himself in the very Catholic town of Goulburn. If there is a pattern, then it may indicate that Irishmen found it harder to make a living as a result of prejudice. Tom Kelly was not the only prisoner from the *Hive* who continued to commit crimes. Several men served three or five years on the roads in the 1850s when transportation in eastern Australia was a fading memory. Patrick Keys, for example, was convicted of stealing money in Yass in 1854, twelve years after he had received his certificate of freedom. In the process he also committed the sin of betraying a (ship) mate's trust.[23]

Some of the saddest casualties from the *Hive* were men who became town vagrants. Michael Kelly (Tom's eldest brother) was among this group. Whatever his own shortcomings, he had a hard servitude at Braidwood with former ship's master, John Coghill, who was given to describing his assigned servants as 'rogues and fools' and treated them accordingly. Consequently, they responded to their master in ways we have come to recognise. In her comprehensive thesis about Coghill, Christine Wright concluded: 'That Coghill found his workforce recalcitrant and difficult to manage is obvious. Drawing on his many years of seafaring experience, he treated them strictly and with severity . . . however that experience was in a world where flogging and brutal punishment were commonplace.'[24] Unlike his brother Tom, Michael Kelly never committed a crime that resulted in further transportation. Staying around Braidwood, he spent time in Goulburn gaol in 1856 and again in 1867 for 'vagrancy'. He was in Braidwood gaol in 1868 and again in 1872.[25]

Maurice Walsh, who had been assigned with shipmate Moses Howlett to Mr Wright at *Lanyon*, was another town vagrant, the kind of derelict old man at whom townspeople pointed and whispered, assuming he was typical of all ex-convicts. If Maurice Walsh had any family life—and there are records to suggest that he married—it was not obvious by the time he died. He was found on a Queanbeyan street in 1872 and died as he was being taken to hospital. At the inquest that followed, the coroner found his death resulted 'from exhaustion, from want of food and exposure to the cold'. He was 68 years old.[26]

Although the attrition among men from the *Hive* was higher than other ex-convict groups, very likely because they were Irish, many benefited from opportunities they could not obtain at home. The overall numbers who found a new and better life still outweighed those who ended in the sad, worn-out, lonely condition of Michael Kelly and Maurice Walsh. Except for James Dalton, there were no rags to riches stories among them, demonstrating yet again that the big chances for a socioeconomic leap occurred earlier in the convict period. And even so, it was Dalton's sons who greatly increased the family's wealth and status, a pattern typical of many Australian families. Nevertheless, the towns in which Kelly and Walsh staggered around looking for a bed, for a feed or another drink were populated by fellow emancipists who were prospering in every possible occupation: as retailers or farmers, publicans or labourers, stockmen or miners, as nursemaids and sempstresses, and as mothers and fathers, all participating in making a community which they called home.

The free-settler family of former soldier Private Patrick Tierney and his wife Bridget made good lives for themselves in Australia. Sometime between 1845 and 1851, they moved from Maitland to Armidale, where they settled permanently. Their decision to move may have been prompted by the discovery of gold at nearby Uralla which was then called Rocky River. If so, Patrick struck lucky. Lands commissioner Massie confirmed that gold had been found in October 1851. In November, Tierney bought his first parcel of land in Armidale, subsequently adding to it with an adjoining block and building a hut or house which straddled the two. Over the following years he continued his business as a shoemaker but combined it with tin and gold mining. His sons maintained the tradition of being miners but became horse breakers, postmasters and farmers too. No official record exists of Patrick's death, but Bridget described herself as a widow in 1885 shortly before she died.[27]

After Richard Bourke left, the two remaining members of the O'Connellite tail continued their contribution to the penal colonies. When a temporary vacancy arose on the Supreme Court in 1839 it was offered to John Hubert Plunkett, then to Roger Therry, both of whom miscalculated and declined. Not long after, it became a permanent appointment and the incumbent, Alfred Stephen, was confirmed. To achieve permanent appointment to the bench, Therry had first to accept a vacancy in Port Phillip until February 1846 when he returned to Sydney to be sworn in as a judge of the New South Wales Supreme Court. After serving on the court for more than a decade he retired to England in 1859. He had planned to settle in Dublin but after two months concluded, 'I found myself quite a stranger in my native land.' Shortly after, he and his wife moved to Bath where he died in 1874.[28] In Therry's *Reminiscences* he wrote: 'To have been honoured with the friendship and confidence of such a man as Sir R. Bourke—to have battled by his side—and to have been deemed worthy of acknowledgement by him that I rendered him some aid in this good cause in which he triumphed—is the most agreeable congratulation that attends the retrospect of my past public life in Australia.'[29]

John Hubert Plunkett spent the rest of his life in Australia, paying only one visit to Ireland in 1842, perhaps to assess the opportunities for Catholic lawyers. On returning to New South Wales the following year he continued as attorney-general. By right of office, he was also a member of the Legislative Council and participated in many significant debates. During the late forties, his close friend and priest, Father John McEncroe, became a leader of the anti-transportation campaign. Perhaps influenced by McEncroe about the homophobic subtext to that crusade, Plunkett shocked the Legislative Council with an unexpected but fiercely eloquent speech against the resumption of transportation. It made William Wentworth so angry that he left the chamber before Plunkett finished speaking.[30]

Plunkett's presence in New South Wales ensured that Bourke's dream for a national system of schools eventually prevailed although ultimately not in a form he could support. The initial Bourkean compromise where each denomination was funded to run its own schools continued until 1848, when the Legislative Council under Governor Fitzroy instituted a Board of National Education to establish and manage a system of government schools. Plunkett was appointed chairman. A Denominational Schools Board was set up at the same time to oversee subsidies to church schools and to ensure quality.[31] He believed in this dual model and, a decade later, his support for state schools finally ended when it became apparent that churches would lose the right to funding for denominational schools once a national system was in place.[32] Plunkett's final years were marred by financial and other difficulties associated with his twin brother Christopher, who emigrated to Melbourne. On the marital front, Marie Charlotte's recurring melancholia, perhaps triggered by disappointment over their lack of children, was an emotional rollercoaster for Plunkett, although they remained a devoted couple. He died in May 1869 leaving very limited funds to support his wife, who became a governess in order to survive.[33]

In April 1852 Edward Canney returned to Sydney. Now master of the immigrant ship *Lord William Bentinck*, he was carrying a particularly precious cargo in the form of his wife Mary Ann and their toddler daughter. After marrying in 1842, Edward spent three years on short runs across the Atlantic. It was not uncommon for a master's wife to sail with him and Mary Ann may have accompanied Edward to Jamaica when he took command of the *Lady Sarah Bayley* soon after their marriage. A nice short voyage to an exotic location. Six months later, Edward had his bride back in London for the birth of their son.[34] He stayed home with his new family for four months before signing on as master of the *Samuel Baker* in February 1843, in which he confined himself to the Jamaica run for three years. A second son, Richard, was born in 1845. Over the next six years Canney commuted back and forth to East India as master of the *John Oldham*. It was not a short voyage but it was nothing compared with heading further south to the Antipodes. In September 1849 his daughter, Mary Ann, was born.[35] Two years later Edward Canney was ready, probably more than ready, for some global travel. This time he persuaded Mary Ann to leave the boys with family and sail with him, bringing two-year-old Mary Ann along too.

In August 1851 the Canney family set out for New Zealand on the *Lord William Bentinck*, a voyage which for Mary Ann and Edward probably fulfilled a long-cherished dream. Arriving off New Zealand on 12 December, Edward landed immigrants at three ports around the coast—at Auckland where the Canneys spent Christmas, then Wellington, New Plymouth and back to Wellington from where they sailed for Sydney on 30 January 1852.

Arriving at Sydney on 5 April, the Canneys looked up Edward's cousin Eliza, whom he knew well from childhood since she was a similar age and their mothers were sisters. In 1834, aged twenty, Eliza had married surgeon Frederick Harpur and in 1841 they emigrated to Australia, where

Frederick developed a practice that specialised particularly in *accoucheur,* otherwise known as delivering babies. He also carried out post-mortems and frequently testified at coronial inquests. When the Canneys arrived, the Harpurs were living comfortably in Balmoral House at Balmain on the shores of Sydney Harbour.[36]

The next section of the family voyage concentrated on trade rather than passengers, although Edward was never averse to conveying people and this may be why their first port of call was Madras. Singapore was next, then China, after which they sailed for Manila where they collected a cargo of sugar for Sydney. Loading took time and they were in the Philippines over two months.

The *Bentinck* was an unusual ship in more ways than one on this voyage. Ships' crews in the nineteenth century were notoriously mutinous, untrustworthy and violent, frequently brawling, swearing, lazy and drunk. They were also treated appallingly and endured dreadful conditions on board. Furthermore, sailors, like soldiers, were still flogged even longer and harder than convicts.[37] By way of an experiment, the *Bentinck*'s crew had committed to the complete journey, rather than being discharged and rehired, as was customary, at the end of each leg. Nevertheless, the risk of desertion remained—the first mate 'deserted' in New Zealand, probably by arrangement with Edward, and they lost an able seaman in Sydney and another in Madras. But those were small numbers, particularly when the Australian gold rush was an enticement to stay. As a precaution in Manila, and with their consent, the crew's mariners' tickets were held by the British consul while they were in port. Among the crew were men who would serve with Canney during his next two voyages, for example, nineteen-year-old Henry Ray Grey from Kent, who was second mate. Grey was related to the ship's owners, which later caused difficulties.[38] On the *Bentinck*, however, he was too young and too raw to be a problem. As usual, two apprentices were also on board with whom Canney always took particular care. On his next voyage he had to endure two senior officers who were incompetent sailors and also violent and sadistic towards the youngest members of the crew. He recorded in his log: 'About 8.30 a.m., heard Robert Jameson midshipman crying bitterly on the poop. Went on deck [where] Jameson informed me Mr Lewis [second mate] had struck him claiming he told an abominable lie . . . Told [Lewis] I did not allow him to strike anyone . . . if he beat the Boys who were not able to take their own part, I would serve him worse than he could serve the youngsters. He was very impertinent . . . The youngsters are sent on board under my protection, not under the officers. If they require punishment I must be appealed to.'[39]

Edward Canney combined a capacity for heroism and a talent for decisive action with compassion for people. But he was no pushover. More than seamanship was required of a ship's master in the nineteenth century and Canney could be as tough and ruthless in his decisions as the situation demanded. The voyage of the *Lord William Bentinck* was exceptional for its harmony, probably achieving a standard Canney would have wished for every journey. A combination of the crew agreement signed before they left London, his own leadership, and possibly also the presence of his wife and daughter, proved so successful that it created a stir when the ship returned to London. A fortnight after the crew were discharged, 'An Old Shipmaster' wrote to the *Shipping and Mercantile Gazette*:

> Sir—an extraordinary case of good conduct among seamen having of late come under my observation, I think it desirable the same should be published if not intruding upon your valuable columns, to prove that seamen if properly treated are capable of appreciating kindness and good management. The ship *Lord William Bentinck*, belonging to Messrs Fletcher & Co of Union Dock, Limehouse and commanded by Capt. Canney, sailed from London in August 1851 went to three ports in New Zealand and Sydney, from thence to Madras, Singapore and China, across to Manila and took a cargo sugar again for Sydney and finally loaded home from thence to London—the said crew continuing throughout this long period, faithfully, soberly and carefully performing their duty upon the agreement they bound themselves to in London. Upon consideration of such services, the owners handsomely remunerated the crew on arrival here on 2nd October 1853, having been absent upwards of two years. Every possible inducement was held out for them to desert, but to no purpose—they considered they had a good home in their ship, were kindly treated by their captain and every individual became attached to the ship.[40]

With the sugar finally on board, the *Bentinck* sailed for Sydney on 25 November 1852. It was a nightmare passage of three months, during which the ship was battered by high seas and strong winds that tested all Edward's seamanship and the teamwork of his crew. For Mary Ann and their little girl, it must have been a terrifying experience, made worse for Mary Ann by pregnancy. At one stage they encountered a heavy gale that lasted twelve hours, carried away the ship's foreyard and blew the main topsail out of the bolt ropes. The calm waters of Sydney Harbour must have been a welcome change as they sailed through the Heads on 17 February 1853.[41] From the family's point of view, they had made it with two months to spare. On 14 April, presumably attended by Frederick Harpur, Mary Ann gave birth to their third son whom they named Bentinck after their trusty ship. The *Sydney Morning Herald* duly recorded the occasion:

> BIRTH, 14 April 1853
> Circular Quay, Sydney, Australia.
> On board ship *Lord William Bentinck*, lying at Circular Quay, on the 14th instant, Mrs Canney, of a son.[42]

Once sugar had been unloaded and the *Bentinck*'s hold was nearly full with cargo for London the ship's agents were still determined to get the most out of the voyage. Week after week they advertised to top up the load with lightweight but valuable produce from the goldfields. And a passenger or two.

They sailed from Sydney in May, reaching home on 2 October 1853 after a momentous voyage of more than two years. A handwritten note, which is one of the few archives surviving in the Canney family, suggests that Edward helped with childcare during this leg of the voyage by teaching his daughter the rudiments of reading and writing. A childish hand inscribed the back of the paper with the words 'Mary ann 2'. It became her keepsake. Tragically, she was later stricken with consumption and died as a young woman of 25. Baby Bentinck became a wine merchant in London and had three children of his own, none of whom took to the sea. Neither of the elder boys followed their father's profession. However, traces of his character can be discerned in Edward, his firstborn, who became a clergyman and was rector of St Peter's, Great Saffron-Hill, East London, for nearly 40 years. According to this Edward's obituary, 'he was one of the first to provide meals for the underfed boys and girls of his district'.[43]

CHAPTER 15
Creating the Australian Way of Life

It is unlikely that Henry Lugard ever seriously considered staying in New South Wales. He was a man of Empire, whose destiny was always global. Australia was just a posting, memorable because it was his first and because it was where he met Mattie. She would have kept her faraway birthplace alive in their family mind, wistfully sometimes perhaps, but they never returned. Edward Canney's career could have transferred to the Antipodes but he was irrevocably tied by the long seagoing tradition of the Canney family from their base in Kent. Furthermore, neither man chose his career as a means of becoming wealthy. Both were motivated by love of what they did and by duty. Together, however, they represent the kind of settler that Australia did not attract. As Alexander Berry pointed out—and he would have heard the conversations that revealed it—gentry settlers came to Australia to make money. The fact it was a penal colony created immense mental and emotional barriers to adopting the country as their own. Many were frightened of their criminal workforce and despised the community at large. And all of them struggled to overcome the barrier which surgeon superintendent Peter Cunningham described when he said, 'Australia is the only country you are ashamed to admit having visited.'[1] Despite themselves, some settlers fell in love with the place, but many left as planned, usually after ten years. Furthermore, during much of the penal era free settlers could not come to the convict colonies without permission, which also delayed the creation of a middle class. The vacuum allowed the prisoners' ethos to consolidate. As we have seen, even after free settlers began to arrive from the 1820s they were still substantially outnumbered by emancipist families and their descendants, many of whom had intermarried with immigrants, not just for decades but, I would argue, throughout the nineteenth century. The free-settler figures have always been fudged because later generations wanted to promote the idea that convicts were insignificant.

Those who argue that being a convict in Australia was the equivalent of being a slave maintain that slave colonies in the West Indies prove the discrepancy in numbers in Australia between a tiny middle class and a large convict population did not eliminate class.[2] This point demonstrates the danger of applying a remote British Empire yardstick to Australia, carrying within it assumptions of the dominant class in Britain. More than one group participates in the creation of class. It is not simply the product of beautiful Georgian houses, wealth and carriages and lots of sheep. Attitudes count. Self-assertion of class is meaningless, its power circumscribed, if it is not accepted by those excluded from the privileged group. And in Australia it never was.

Evidence for the rejection of class is scattered through the records in a variety of ways, in different situations, at different times and locations. Free settlers did not displace the ethos developed in Governor Phillip's time and sustained thereafter by the intense colonisation which locals inflicted on newcomers. Using humiliation and mockery, and sometimes threats, convict society ensured that social class designators were kept at bay. And the absence of a numerically significant middle class contributed to an egalitarian ethos which the prisoners preserved from the earliest days.

Most Australians nominate 'egalitarianism' as a key value of our society. We are sure it exists, yet we struggle to describe what we mean. Outsiders have not found it difficult. In a pub during the 1830s, emigrant Alexander Harris noticed what he called 'a remarkable peculiarity' common to ex-convicts: 'Every man seemed to consider himself just on a level with all the rest.' In the 1920s a similar self-confidence attracted the notice of visiting novelist, D.H. Lawrence, who wrote, 'There was really no class distinction. There was a difference of money and of "smartness". But nobody felt better than anybody else, or higher; only better off. And there is all the difference in the world between feeling better than your fellow man, and merely feeling better-off.' These comments indicate that the nub of Australian egalitarianism is not money or education, not limited to the superficiality of manners, but something far more profound. Unlike other societies where a *faux* equality of manners might be granted from above, Australian egalitarianism rests on the attitude and self-belief of the workers.[3]

So how did the working man acquire this level of confidence? How did Australian society achieve this unique composition? As this book and earlier work by Alan Atkinson and John Hirst demonstrates, its roots lie in the convict era.[4] I believe that we have never been able to describe it because, traditionally, we lacked detail about that time.

The first major contributor to Australia's egalitarianism was the culture the prisoners brought with them. My research into convicts' crimes in Britain and Ireland revealed our founders were defiantly unrepentant, making a virtue of necessity by boasting about their crimes and ridiculing anyone who appeared self-righteous. In the 1820s, surgeon Peter Cunningham who made several voyages on convict ships wrote: 'Thieves generally affect to consider all the rest of mankind equally criminal with themselves . . . It is their constant endeavour to reduce everyone to the same level with themselves.'[5] This levelling attitude was bolstered by the presence on nearly every ship of a lawyer, or doctor or architect, sometimes a couple of merchants, even the occasional clergyman—middle-class people rendered equal by the criminal conviction. In crowded, hierarchical Britain, the sceptical criminal ethos was scattered through society and had no broad influence. It is our good fortune that Britain put all its bad eggs in one basket, which reinforced their levelling instinct and enabled them to create a community in their own image.

In Australia, events conspired to reinforce the wistful egalitarianism of transported criminals.

Most startling to people used to being disregarded outcasts was Governor Phillip's order in 1788 that rations in the starving settlement were to be shared equally regardless of rank. By this, Phillip made it clear that the humanity of the most lowly convicts was as important as his own. They came from a criminal tradition that shared the booty from crime equally between those who took part, but Phillip's announcement transformed their practice to a virtue. Furthermore, he conferred value on the prisoners in their own eyes as well as others. The significance they placed on Phillip's decision can be judged by its long-lasting effects. Evidence exists that the practice of giving everyone equal worth and sharing equally was cherished from Phillip's day. The convicts made it the pattern for how Australians related to each other. The enduring nature of Phillip's decision was on display in Japanese POW camps during World War II where the Australian practice of sharing resources is well documented. We can see the same influence today in the community consensus that our government should always provide a 'safety net' for the less fortunate.

Another factor in developing Australia's egalitarianism was the sparse information which the British and Irish government sent with its transportees. For over 30 years colonial authorities managed the penal colonies knowing only the date of the convicts' trial and length of sentence. The only exceptions to such relaxed disregard were political prisoners such as the United Irishmen of 1798. Generally, details of the convicts' crimes were not provided until the mid-1820s. Of necessity, a culture developed of judging people by their character and behaviour rather than by their background. What began inadvertently became a defining characteristic of our society.

Try as they might in the early years, the authorities never succeeded in bending the convicts entirely to their will. Sheer weight of numbers combined with the obstreperous nature of the transportees meant the penal colonies had to be largely a cooperative venture with the prisoners. Local society was far more fluid than envisaged by policymakers in London. From 1788, individual relationships broke down what elsewhere would have been ranks of power and status. Officers and convict women became lovers. 'Infatuated soldiers' from the other ranks settled here with their convict partners when the original guard returned to Britain. Pastoralist William Bradley's parents were one such example. In New South Wales, a notorious pickpocket became superintendent of convicts. Prisoners and ex-prisoners became policemen, soldiers in the NSW Corps, farmers on their own land, householders. Many disregarded instructions to do what they wished. James Ruse, for instance, successfully farmed for the government, then dropped his cooperative facade and led a band of convicts and emancipists to farm at the Hawkesbury without authority.

Court-martialled soldiers transported as convicts also blurred discrepancies of power and class: deals were done and liberties taken because so often the gaolers found common ground with the people they guarded. British expectations of hierarchy, control and orderliness were turned upside down. Convicts and emancipists intended to keep it that way.[6]

It was 32 years before a barracks was built in Sydney to house the convicts. Grace Karskens pointed out that until then prisoners lived in their own houses where they developed private lives and private possessions. They operated businesses in their homes. Their households provided board and lodgings, and in many cases employment, for later convict arrivals.[7] Being assigned to work for one of their own kind was a major contributor to our democratic culture. In 1819, when Commissioner Bigge investigated the penal colonies, he found that many ex-convict employers shared their living arrangements with their convict servants and maintained 'little if any Distinction between them'.[8]

From the earliest times, the prisoners pressed otherwise middle-class people to act as if they were equals. In the 1830s, Martin Cash described how he would offer a cup of tea because 'at this time any gentleman travelling through the bush was not above sharing our hospitality, it being a general understanding through the colony.'[9] Hindsight makes obvious, however, that no gentleman who wanted to preserve his safety, not to mention pastoral productivity, would have been foolish enough to reject the invitation.

This pressure for classlessness continued after the convict era. In 1902, when Henry Montgomery returned to England from his post as bishop of Tasmania, it was very clear he had absorbed the enforced democracy of the ex-convict community. Writing a manual for clergymen sailing to the colonies, he told them: 'Make sure to clean your own boots and learn to shoe a horse. Don't use "the affected voice or manner". And never speak about "the lower classes". Australians don't like it.'[10] Observing the same phenomenon in 1974, author Craig McGregor wondered 'why the wealthy feel under some pressure to be accepted by ordinary working Australians rather than the other way round?'[11] In the 21st-century the same pressure—its source unrecognised—makes the prime minister feel obliged to sit beside his driver.

A significant contributor to egalitarianism was work practices and attitudes that sprang from the power the prisoners possessed when the government needed their help to put the colony on a sustainable footing. They continued throughout the convict era. There was always a discrepancy between policy and reality. In Australia, men from the lowest socioeconomic level at home developed the confidence to strike for their entitlements and bargain collectively. And they did so while prisoners, decades before the development of trade unions and the arrival of immigrant union leaders.

In Governor Phillip's day the convicts announced that they would 'sooner perish in the woods' than be obliged to work regular hours, nor anything like a full day. They demanded taskwork instead. This meant that once the daily task was completed they were allowed free time to 'earn money, plant their gardens, play or wander as they chose'.[12] Despite Commissioner Bigge's determination to change it, as we saw in Newcastle and on Norfolk Island, for example, many still worked under the task system 30 years later.

Initially, convicts were paid wages only for *extra* work. By the early 1820s, however, pastoralists were obliged to pay their convict workers a wage set by government regulation. When this policy changed in 1823, many masters continued to pay wages as an incentive and the practice faded slowly. The provision of sugar and tobacco as incentives became entrenched in the system of convict management and were of vital importance to the workforce who regarded them as entitlements and would strike if they were not provided.

The convicts recognised that withdrawal of labour gave them power and used it frequently and effectively. Combined with a refusal to defer, a disregard of rules and a determination to do only what suited them, it could leave even a commandant with arbitrary power at his wits end. At Wellington Valley in the 1820s, commandant Percy Simpson conceded with embarrassment, 'It must appear strange that from the civil and military situation I had held for some years before, I should now find it difficult to manage a few convicts.'[13] The subversive power of prisoners even prevailed at the penal settlement of Macquarie Harbour where, as Hamish Maxwell-Stewart noted, 'The death of the station was the product of many things but most could be traced to the work of the prisoners themselves . . . In the end the only way of making the place work had been to seek the compliance of the convict population, striking off their irons and increasing their levels of incentives until the terror of the place had been reduced to the point when it no longer functioned as a penal station proper.'[14]

Through experience, the prisoners developed a technique of enforcing their wishes from below which extended eventually to the style of leadership they were prepared to accept. One of the clearest examples can be found in the way convict members of Major Mitchell's exploratory party treated his assistant surveyor, Granville Stapylton, who was the black sheep of an aristocratic family and expected deference and obedience. By comparison, Mitchell treated the men according to how they performed and in return they supported him. Meanwhile the perceptive Quaker missionary James Backhouse noticed that self-confident employers 'generally get on comfortably with them' because they did not make unreasonable demands or use 'imperious language' which provoked insolence.[15] In the 1840s squatter Arthur Hodgson described what was required to get the best from his convict workforce when he said: 'They must be led not driven. They must be humoured not ordered; for knowing their own worth they will only exert themselves [according to] the treatment they receive.'[16] Essentially, the convict workforce demanded respect to a degree unknown in their homelands.

Exercising authority in an egalitarian society was not easy. In the 1920s D.H. Lawrence was intrigued by the difference he noticed in New South Wales. 'There is no giving of orders here; or if orders were given, they would not be received as such. A man in one position might make a suggestion to a man in another position and this latter might or might not accept the suggestion according to his disposition. How could a country run like this? . . . But the country *did* run.'[17]

The penal colonies created a dilemma for leaders who were faced with extracting productivity from workers who had no predisposition to cooperation, let alone obedience. In fact, the opposite. They were likely to respond with subterranean ridicule or dumb insolence to someone in command. And they could counter harsh commands or coercion by reducing their productivity. While the lash might punish them, it could not deliver a workplace result. Punishment by the loss of privileges like sugar and tea or tobacco, or their kettles, resulted in wholesale mutinies on Norfolk Island, as it did elsewhere.[18] These workplace characteristics led to the development of a peculiarly Australian style of leadership which it took the rest of the world more than a century to emulate. The standard command and control model of the era that assumed respect for the uniform or the office simply did not work in the prisoners' colony. Overseers imported directly from England to Norfolk Island, for example, ran foul of the local culture. After a visit to the island, Robert Pringle Stuart reported to the controller general in Van Diemen's Land, 'Assistant Superintendent Pilkington may be able to acquit himself with prisoners [direct] from England but is inefficient at the settlement among the colonial convicts.'[19] In response to these challenges, a leadership style that can be summarised as 'first among equals' developed as the only way to motivate the prisoners. It was eloquently described by a digger on the goldfields who wrote, 'that's the style . . . a leading man in a party who consults all his mates how the work is to be done, and then sets his head to work and plans the whole'.[20] As the quote makes clear, the men understood that in the long run someone must decide. Consultation was the key because it acknowledged the worth of each man's opinion. In the 21st-century, management theory replaced 'gang' with 'team' but we can see now that same approach was operating decades earlier in convict Australia.

Dig deep in our penal history and you will find the underlying dynamics of Australian society.

Australia's unique form of mateship, for example, originated in the shared trauma of being transported across the world, which created a bond that extended to military and civilian passengers who travelled on the same vessel. After they landed, mateship was broadened and reinforced by experiences in the penal system. As we saw in Chapter 9, reformer Alexander Maconochie, writing in the 1840s, captured its essence when he wrote about the doubly convicted prisoners on Norfolk Island, 'having previously suffered hardship together, they took a deeper interest in each other's welfare; and they thus exhibited much more patience and forbearance with each other's infirmities of temper and other occasional sources of difference. The [other] prisoners had not previously suffered together; they did not know each other well enough and had not formed "friendships in adversity" and they were less amenable to the system of mutual responsibility.'[21]

Some argue that my claim about egalitarianism is 'too strong to be accepted whole, especially', they say, 'by those familiar with the strict marginalisation of the Irish'.[22] However, we need to resist the habit of drawing conclusions about the first half of the nineteenth century based on evidence from a later period. This applies to the Irish as much as any other aspect of those times. In 1990, Patrick O'Farrell acknowledged the historical difference before and after 1850 when he wrote, 'Historical understanding of the Irish in Australia has been contaminated by stereo-types generated since the 1840s by Irish nationalism and Catholicism. That has left virtually half a century, since 1788, as a kind of pre-history, unexplored.'[23]

Before 1840, little evidence exists of discrimination or marginalisation of the Irish in Australian society. Any perception that there was reflects contemporaneous middle-class opinion that has been taken as fact, or by extrapolating from a later paradigm. The big set pieces that we know so well can certainly be found—the 1804 rebellion including the execution of Philip Cunningham (and the participation of over 300 Englishmen); jittery, disparaging comments from Governors Hunter and King for whom an Irish rebellion was a real prospect; and handwringing by Father Joseph Therry and all writers since, about the lack of priests for Catholics, which is traditionally presented as gross discrimination while the context is ignored. In reality, great tracts of New South Wales lacked clergymen of any persuasion. In most areas, the Irish were no more discriminated against by not having priests than the English and Scots, that is, assuming they yearned for religious consolation at all—which most did not. No doubt some discrimination falls below historians' radar but it is possible to conclude that, pre-1840, discrimination towards one another did not exist between convicts and emancipists. In fact a ticket-of-leave convict asked Caroline Chisholm to arrange for his family to come to this 'comfortable country'. 'Catholics and Protestants live here quiet,' he told her. '[I] never saw a fight between a Catholic and a Protestant here on the score of religion.'[24] Evidence that is put forward for discrimination and, indeed, the practice of discrimination was gentry orientated. It was landholders who said 'Don't send us more Irish.' It was educated men, such as Samuel Marsden, giving evidence to Commissioner Bigge or to one of the endless inquiries in London that declared the convicts depraved because in their view they were 'godless'. But Marsden also said, 'when men become convicts, a difference of religious opinions is hardly discernible among them.'[25]

So how did we come to believe that the story of the Irish in Australia was one of endless discrimination from the beginning? That it was a tale of the Catholic Church beleaguered?[26] Once queried rather than assumed to be true, the answer is obvious. The history of the Irish and of Catholicism in Australia was predominantly written by the Catholic Church. Without discrimination, there could be no heroic struggle in which the church emerged triumphant. 'Catholic historians of the period up to about 1835 have usually cried "Persecution" on the grounds of the same few isolated instances spread over fifty years,' declared James Waldersee.[27] Cardinal P.F. Moran, for example, condemned 'the severe punishment by which men, themselves dead to all sentiments of morality and religion, sought to compel them [the Catholics] to do violence to conscience and join in the Protestant service they abhorred'. The scholarly Catholic historian, Archbishop Eris O'Brien, quoted James Bonwick who supported the anti-transportationists and whose subsequent work virtually created Australian history. Thousands of schoolchildren learned Bonwick's respectable version of history on subjects like The Explorers, The Gold Diggers, The Squatters, Bass and Flinders, Ned Kelly and Captain Cook. To the extent convicts featured at all in Bonwick's history, it was a Gothic tale which was as fictional as novelist Marcus Clarke's *His Natural Life*. Quoting Bonwick, Eris O'Brien wrote:

> Catholics could expect no favour. All had to go to Church; they were driven as sheep to the fold and, whatever their scruples, they had to go . . . If a man humbly entreated to stay behind because he was a Presbyterian, he incurred the danger of a flogging. It is said that upon a similar appeal from another who exclaimed a Catholic, he was silenced by the cry of a clerical magistrate. 'Go to church or be flogged.'[28]

Countering this hyperbole, we saw magistrate Major Antill support a convict against an indignant employer on just such an issue. And James Webber at Paterson called to account over reports from Father Therry that landholders were flogging Catholics.[29]

Many people contributed to a one-dimensional image of the Irish who were transported to Australia, including lawyer Roger Therry, who wrote, 'That a large number of convicts from Ireland were deservedly sent out for outrages that merited transportation cannot be doubted; but it is not less true that very many were transported for the infringement of severe laws, some of which are not now in force and for offences for which a few months imprisonment would, at present be deemed an adequate expiation.'[30] Fathers Ullathorne and McEncroe, too, protected the Irish from their accusations of mass homosexuality. Instead, the English were declared the main offenders. Visiting Norfolk Island,

Governor Gipps was told that the Irish were untainted by what was said to be widespread 'unnatural crime' there.[31] It must also be recognised that the Irish emancipists themselves were not immune to fudging. Nor were their descendants, many of whom automatically cast their Irish ancestor as a 'freedom fighter'.

A classic example of sentiment trumping reality occurred regarding brothers Philip and Michael Ryan. In an old cemetery at East Maitland stands a weathered tombstone which proclaims:

Gloria in Excelsis Deo
Erected by Philip Ryan in memory of his brother *Michael Ryan*
of Swan Reach: a native of Thornback, parish of St Canices,
County Kilkenny, Ireland, who has been circumvented of his
just and legal property, persecuted by wilful and corrupt
perjury, returned guilty by an infamous and bigoted jury for
being a sincere patriot and sentenced wrongfully by the laws
of the land.
Farewell dear Brother for a while. Hoping the Almighty God
has received your soul and on your smile, until his herald
summonses me to be for ever blessed with thee. Amen
Died on the 28th Sepr. 1859, aged 56 years.[32]

Research about the Ryan brothers contradicts nearly every line of this stirring cry. Local history, too, recorded that Philip Ryan was a free settler, who paid this tribute to his convict brother.[33] However, as we saw in Chapters 2 and 5, Philip Ryan was not a free settler. Both men were transported as convicts for an agrarian dispute—which details suggest was not an injustice but a business negotiation that went wrong. At best, we can grant them leeway on the motive because insufficient information remains to be sure about its origin. Certainly, religious discrimination was not a factor because all parties were Catholics. When the Ryans could not achieve the result they wanted, they attempted murder.

Roger Therry's *Reminiscences* have been mined for information about the Irish convicts. When he wrote that 'No provision was made for education in the religion of their parents', it was gold for those who wanted to cast a tale of discrimination. Bourke's Church Act by comparison is often omitted as an inconvenient truth or treated cursorily.[34] The anti-transportation campaign also contributed to our ignorance. Campaigning

from a premise that only brutal slavery and convict depravity preceded
their arrival as immigrants, the anti-transportationists distorted the truth
so effectively that their Gothic myth was accepted as reality. With Father
McEncroe among the leaders of this crusade, it was inevitable that the
Catholic Church embraced their view. And so did historians. Despite
his suspicions of the unexplored decades, Patrick O'Farrell's verdict that
'Catholics were brutalised and depraved with the rest' is a direct echo of
anti-transportation propaganda which he accepted as reality.[35]

In stark comparison, James Waldersee described Catholic history as
'the twin "black and white" legends, of persecution wreaked by bigoted
and vindictive officials on a helpless Catholic minority, who as transportees
were either righteous patriots or innocent farm-boys, and as emancipists were, with the exception of the lucky few, poor and downtrodden'.
After extensive research including detailed analysis of Catholics in the
1828 census, Waldersee concluded 'Both legends have turned out to need
not merely revision, but virtually rejection.'[36]

The penal system subsumed difference. Waldersee also concluded,
'Catholic convicts did not . . . really form a distinctive class.'[37] Indeed,
the researcher looks in vain for evidence of discrimination against the
Irish as prisoners. Difficulties experienced by the Irish in obtaining
documents such as tickets-of-leave are no different to convicts of other
ethnicity or colour. Their prominence in workplace disputes are equalled
by the Scots and the English. Peter Hammond's study of violence in the
Hunter Valley found no greater participation by or against the Irish. Tim
Causer's research into Norfolk Island established that the proportion of
Irish sent there was consistent with their numbers on the mainland. By
comparison, however, Sue Rosen found more Irish prisoners labouring
on the Bathurst Road, the only significant aberration in the pattern.
Most evidence indicates that the penal authorities, whether bureaucrats
or magistrates, acted with little regard to whether a prisoner was Irish,
Scottish or English, black or white. Their status as a prisoner was far
more important. Prejudice where it operated in the convict colony must
have occurred at a personal level between individuals. It seems likely,
for example, that superintendent Shepherd's antagonism towards John
Buckley was aggravated by the fact he was Irish. But prejudice could also
be used as a weapon. The archives suggest that Buckley was playing the
'irritating Irishman' for all it was worth. Innocent bewilderment: What
me? Tell a lie? Dumb insolence on a masterful scale.

Between the prisoners, differences of race, religion and class were irrelevant in a shared struggle to survive their servitude. I have found no evidence of ethnic or religious differences playing a part in disputes between convicts. Resentments, jealousy, betrayal are certainly there, but they originate in particular circumstances involving individuals. A handful of sectarian disputes between ordinary people can be found in Melbourne in the forties. Few details remain about the earliest, which occurred in March 1843 when, emboldened perhaps by St Patrick's Day, a group of men entered the taproom of the Golden Fleece announcing 'they were Irishmen and what had the English to say about them'. In 1846, on 12 July—the anniversary of the Battle of the Boyne—banners supporting the Orange cause were draped from the Pastoral Hotel in Melbourne. They attracted an angry crowd. Shots were fired from the hotel. One grazed a priest who was attempting to disperse the crowd. Eventually, the Riot Act was read but the crowd refused to leave until a man was arrested and charged with shooting with intent to murder.[38] It took decades of colonial sectarianism from about 1850 to create such prejudice between ordinary people that parents were warning their children 'not to mix with those Catholics'. And the children were hurling sectarian epithets at one another on a daily basis. Once begun, though, this kind of behaviour lasted for over a century.

The major issue put forward as an example of discrimination in the convict era has been compulsion to attend divine service. We cannot be sure how aggrieved the Irish prisoners really felt about this, because being Catholic became the perfect excuse for escaping compulsory religion. Any assessment requires acknowledgement that most of the Irish who were convicts left home before 'the devotional revolution' around 1850, when the Catholic Church cemented its grip on Irish society. The prisoners' experience with clergymen for whom they were forced to pay tithes in Ireland or as magistrates in Britain created negative attitudes rather than reverence for their role. Some convicts were transported because a clergyman prosecuted them. Many were committed for trial on a clergyman's say-so. With this background, they were unlikely to turn devotional on arrival at the other side of the world. Furthermore, much evidence exists to confirm that, whatever their ethnicity, convicts resented divine service as an interruption to their day. Visiting a pastoral estate on a Sunday, Alexander Harris, for example, commented, 'nobody here keeps the day as anything more than holiday. Men wash their shirts, and grind their week's wheat, and visit [each other].'[39] Knowledge of the prisoners certainly suggests that at least some of the Irish would have deployed the lack of a Catholic priest to suit their own purposes.

Convict history and its culture explain longstanding puzzles about the Irish in Australia. Many people have wondered, for instance, why they were so disconnected from the troubles in Ireland compared with the continuing involvement by Irish in America. The reason wasn't just distance, as traditionally suggested, but the strength of the culture established by the convicts. Adopting the local ethos required in New South Wales meant leaving behind old associations. While the Irish in America were part of a society founded on religious principles which kept the past alive, the Irish in Australia belonged to a community founded by criminals who made it a condition of acceptance that a person leave behind the strife, the loyalty—and, of course, any criminal conviction. As Patrick O'Farrell commented, 'It was and remains, meaningful to speak of Irish-Americans. Not Irish-Australians.'[40] One notable exception was World War I. As Australians prepared to support Britain in a war against Germany, there were many of Irish Catholic descent who objected fiercely to taking part. Nevertheless, strife over conscription in 1916, which coincided with the Easter Rebellion in Ireland, was memorable because it was so rare.

The Irish were the first 'minority' to benefit from the convict determination that all who settled in Australia should leave the past behind, that they must take on what became known colloquially as 'the Australian way of life'. Except they were not a minority but part of the majority, the prisoner workforce who created such a culture and who became increasingly possessive about preserving it. Traditionally we have been led to believe that Australians fear foreigners, but examination of our convict years reveals that 'foreign' had nothing to do with it. The convicts feared being overwhelmed by the British class system which would return them to outcast status. They waged a relentless campaign that forced free migrants to take on the local ethos. 'New chums', they called them. Or more insultingly, 'Self-imported devils'. This 'colonisation' process which could often be harsh or even cruel to newcomers was well known at the time. James Macarthur commented in 1837, 'They feel the colony is theirs by rights, and the emigrant settlers are interlopers upon the soil.' This was the culture that Irish prisoners from the *Hive* joined on landing in 1836. As prisoners, they were welcomed by their peers into the confident mainstream, a dramatic contrast with their status as feckless peasants in Ireland.[41]

Some free settlers were relatives like James Dalton's sons and Edmund Noonan's wife and children. Most were from the same socioeconomic group as the prisoners—the Tierney family, for example. Many were from the same village. Although sometimes quite ruthlessly indoctrinated, they conformed with the local community to fit in. Middle-class settlers bitterly resented the attitudes of the locals. In 1834 George Bennett wrote: 'It is well known that free emigration is detested by most of the convict party, and a wealthy individual of this class once remarked, "What have the free emigrants to do here? The colony was founded for us. They have no right here."' Twenty years later, Reverend John West declared resentfully 'A community of little more than half a century old cannot be entitled to denounce Englishmen as foreigners or to complain that strangers usurp the rights of the country [i.e. locally] born.'[42]

From very early, locals would put new chums through the hoops to ensure they understood how to behave in Australia. Showing you could take a joke was an important yardstick. Alexander Harris described how he was tested by *being* the joke. Gathered round a fire in a stockman's hut, everyone took their turn at entertaining. 'One sang a song, another told some tale of olden times, another told news of the bushrangers, another described land he had just found for a cattle run . . . My share was to answer all the questions which any and all thought proper to put to me . . . and to pocket with the best grace I could (for most of these men had been convicts) the jokes they not very sparingly but I must say with very good humour, cut on me for having come to the colony "to make a fortune", for being a "free object" or for having "lagged myself for fear the king should do it for me".'[43] A wide-eyed newcomer on the Victorian goldfields recounted a similar experience around the campfire. 'The greater the criminal, the more he is respected amongst his own class,' he wrote. 'Very horrible is some of their stories. Can they be true or are they imposing on our credulity? And yet some of their adventures are droll and laughable and told with such candour as sets us all into a roar of laughter.'[44]

In 2010, researchers Ipsos Mackay found that derisory nicknames were part of 'a withering initiation' applied to each migrant group in turn. New arrivals since World War II have been called 'dagoes' and 'wogs', 'Balts', 'yellows', 'slopes' or 'slanty-eyes', 'Lebs' and 'curry-munchers'. Recently it has been 'towel heads' who are suspected of undermining our way of life. Had Ipsos Mackay looked further back, they would have found a long precedent for this custom. 'Pom', for instance. As in 'Pommie bastard'. As in Englishman straight off the boat who needed acculturating to local ways. History doesn't make it right but, if the tradition was understood it might be less scarifying for 21st-century newcomers. It is the historic requirement to leave the past behind that explains why increasing support for multiculturalism is nevertheless accompanied by a persistent expectation that newcomers embrace 'the Australian way of life'.[45]

Chapter 2 analysed the violent crimes for which Irish men were transported, under four broad categories. As we have seen, elements of those crimes transferred to Australia. Political brawling, for example, occurred around the first democratic elections in New South Wales but with the exception of Paterson in 1843, where a man died from a riot with sectarian elements, it did not generally give rise to violence. Such echoes of Ireland did not continue after the early forties. Politics remained boisterous, but became harmless. The only threat to this equanimity was an alleged Fenian attempt in 1868 to assassinate the visiting Duke of Edinburgh which Robert Travers concluded was more about Henry Parkes' creation of a 'Fenian panic' for political advantage.[46]

Tribal violence did not suddenly vanish once the antagonists were transported, but it certainly dissipated. The vast distances of the new land would have helped counter this longstanding cultural tension. There was space for everyone. No need to argue over issues like fishing rights or play out a neighbourhood ritual that was centuries old. With tragic irony for Aboriginal people, the lack of traditional ownership by Europeans probably facilitated the healing of deep-rooted Irish enmities that had their wellspring in a lush green landscape. Historic associations with landmarks evaporated, taking old conflicts with them. Dead Man's Gully displaced the River Shannon. The high plains of the Maneroo supplanted the Connemara. At an interpersonal level, some old antagonisms still simmered but they were minor in the scheme of things. After all, thousands of miles from Ireland, an Irishman was an Irishman was an Irishman and whether he was from Munster or Connaught became less important than the fact he shared memories of home. Echoes of an Irishman's readiness for a good brawl could, however, always be found on St Patrick's Day. In 1833, there was a fierce encounter in Sydney between traditional adversaries, very reminiscent of scenes on the strands of the Shannon, but without the bloody deaths that so often occurred in Ireland: '[A] scene occurred outside the toll-bar, that out-Donnybrooked Donnybrook Fair, for brutality. A party of choice Emeralders, who had been keeping up St Patrick's day on Sunday, assembled [and] when a fight occurred, one of the combatants struck the other a foul blow; this was the signal for a fight-general; each person chose his side, every paling in the neighbourhood was put into requisition and the two battalions attacked each other with deadly animosity; the road was strewed with the wounded and the battle did not cease, until the last man of the vanquished party had bitten the dust.'[47]

The agrarian injustices of Ireland were not replicated in New South Wales. Despite an outcry from new arrivals that began in the 1840s about the immense landholdings of the squatters, the Irish emancipists gained ready access to rural leases and to town allotments. Some bought farms that were small in the Australian context but far larger than anything they could have acquired at home. The Irish passion for land of their own, whatever the size, infused Australian society. Nowhere was it stronger than the original penal colony of New South Wales where the enduring obsession with real estate is said to be unique globally.[48]

Australia satisfied the hunger for land, and remedied the religious discrimination and injustice under the law which the Irish suffered for centuries in their homeland. But the fourth category of violent crime, that of sexual violence, is not so clear-cut. Stripped of its association with Whiteboy politics, of impetus from dowries and inherited land, of its tradition as a romantic ritual, and with family rivalries no longer relevant, abduction stands revealed as too often condoning violence against women. Back to its original roots, perhaps. James Kelly concluded that, 'Abduction [in its original eighteenth-century form] was not without its religious and political dimensions, but it can be better explained by reference to the economic imperatives of status and the long tradition of male violence against women.'[49]

As noted in Chapter 2, Kiera Lindsey found that of the hundreds of Irish men convicted of abduction in the first half of the nineteenth century, at least 134 were transported to the Australian colonies, the majority Catholics.[50] One of the best known prisoners at Botany Bay was the Irish knight, Sir Henry Browne Hayes, who was transported for abduction. He has been treated indulgently by history. Until Lindsey took up the subject, little consideration was given to what became of the young woman he forced to marry him.[51] The crime of abduction also continued in Australia although it was no longer entwined with politics or religion.[52] Whether the woman's economic circumstances continued to play a role is unclear. Given the ambiguity around abduction, Lindsey took pains to differentiate as far as possible between collusive abductions and coercive ones. Altogether, she identified at least twenty cases of abduction in Australia between 1800 and 1850, of which five appeared to be elopements. During the same period there were 56 abductions in England of which eleven appeared to be elopements.[53] These figures, however, refer to convictions. In Australia, Lindsey discovered 'a dramatic increase in the prosecution of abduction from the late 1840s until the late 1850s',[54] a timeframe that coincides with the virulent anti-transportation campaign run mainly by clergymen intent on reforming the morals of a 'depraved' convict community.[55]

The practice of gangs of men abducting a woman and all or some of them raping her continued sporadically in Australia. A disproportion of men to women during the convict era does not entirely explain its existence although it may have contributed. When committed by prisoners, gang rape was invariably opportunistic rather than premeditated.[56] Gang rape occurred throughout the nineteenth century, however, and to such an extent that, as Frank Bongiorno discovered, 'the impression developed in the late nineteenth century that it was a distinctively Australian crime—indicative, as one judge put it, of "a degraded state of morality here"'.[57] The 1886 trial, for example, of nine youths in Sydney who were involved in gang rape, colloquially known as the 'Mount Rennie case', was the culmination of a series of gang rapes that had occurred over preceding months. Generally, gang rape accounted for a high proportion of all rape charges in the late nineteenth century. And they were not all confined to former convict colonies. Jill Bavin-Mizzi's examination of rape trials in Victoria, Queensland and Western Australia between 1880 and 1900 found that of 190 cases, 70 (almost 37 per cent) were gang rapes.[58]

Analysis of penal society answers the longstanding question about why the prisoners did not rebel. Given their overwhelming numbers, they—and specifically the Irish—were expected to mutiny. When they did not, the gentry had an answer. 'It is a curious fact,' wrote Charles Darwin, who visited in 1836, 'but I was universally told that the character of the convict population is that of arrant cowardice—although not unfrequently some become desperate and quite indifferent of their lives, yet that a plan requiring cool or continued courage was seldom put into execution.'[59] Of course people who held that view took no account of the conditions from which the convicts, including the Irish, had come. They did not understand that the prisoners who came from the lowest, most desperate level of the hierarchical societies at home recognised a chance for themselves and their families in Australia. Furthermore, these commentators failed to perceive the 'mutiny' that was actually occurring. For all the notorious outbreaks on Norfolk Island, Tim Causer concluded that the men there 'contested their captors on the "ordinary battlefield" of day-to-day life.'[60] My research concludes that in this regard Norfolk Island should be seen as a microcosm of what occurred on the mainland. In their way, the male convicts never stopped rebelling, the Irish among them. But their revolution has not been detected because it occurred in the workplace. In an exercise of power, their weapons were the strike, insistence on penalty 'rates' such as sugar and tea and tobacco, time 'in lieu' for working on Sunday, and a weekend that increasingly consisted of half day Saturday and Sundays to themselves. As the sawyers' strike demonstrated, they also deployed the concept of enterprise bargaining. The fact that these same tactics were utilised in what was supposedly the ultra punishment settlement as well as the mainland only emphasises the profound role they played in the life and culture of the New South Wales penal colony. In Australia, the Irish working man acquired power. A prisoner in Western Australia spoke for most of the men who were transported when, referring to their disproportionate numbers, he wrote, 'the bond class . . . are perfectly conscious of their power and only quiet and orderly because they see there is nothing to be gained by a contrary course'.[61] For many, he might have added, 'And much to lose.'

Nevertheless, some kept hoping. When Friedrich Engels heard of trouble on the New South Wales goldfields in 1851 he predicted excitedly to Karl Marx, 'The British will be thrown out and the united states of deported murderers, burglars, rapists and pickpockets will startle the world by demonstrating what wonders can be performed by a state consisting of undisguised rascals. They will beat California hollow. But whereas in California rascals are still lynched, in Australia they'll lynch the gentry.'[62]

Some argue that the clash of arms at Eureka in Victoria in 1854 was the long-expected rebellion by the Irish. Comparing the goldfields of Victoria, however, with those in New South Wales, illuminates what happened at Eureka. The issues over licences in both colonies were the same, but the processes were different. Peaceful negotiation in one colony. Bloodshed in the other. Experienced administrators in New South Wales, who had monitored the temperature of the penal colony for decades quickly recognised it would be fatal to oppose the diggers outright. They must negotiate, just as they had done many times before, when the same men were convicts. In Victoria, La Trobe reached a similar conclusion, but much more slowly. Nevertheless, before ending his term as lieutenant-governor he recommended that the tax on miners should be replaced by a tax on gold similar to New South Wales.

The clash of force at Eureka was not a rebellion, let alone an Irish one. Most of the multicultural leaders who led the 120 rebels had been in the country barely two years. They had not yet been acculturated to the ethos of leaving the past behind and their agenda bore little relevance for Australia. Peter Lalor, for instance, wanted 'Independence'—for Ireland. Like Sir Charles Hotham, the governor, who had been in Victoria less than six months, it can be argued they misunderstood the community to which they emigrated. In Australia, neither the Irish nor anyone else felt the need to rebel. The gentry had been expecting Engels' 'lynch mob' for years and the working man already had the power that Marx theorised could only be achieved by bloodshed. Preserving what they had won was far more significant. For example, we saw in the 1840s, how the Irish Catholics swore to prevent the Protestant Ascendancy of their homeland from ever contaminating 'the land of our adoption'. Hardly a vote for rebellion.

Like other prisoners, the Irish saw Australia as their adopted home, a place where they had access to land, where hard work rather than birth, education or religion, could bring rewards. Roger Therry put their attitude down to the following:

> In a country where abundant means rewarded industrious habits, these men became prosperous. Meat, which they only partook of a few times in each year on festive occasions in Ireland, was now daily and amply supplied to them; and the ready reward of honest pursuits worked a wondrous change for the better in their social condition.[63]

Another factor against rebellion were the strong family ties to the colony which many Irish prisoners had before they were transported. On the

Hive, for example, nine men already had relatives in New South Wales. In addition, she carried six pairs of brothers, two sets of fathers and sons, one group of three brothers. And those are just the ones we know about. Ties of kinship in the colony extended widely to cousins and aunts and uncles, to familiar faces from clans and villages. Good reports about Australia had spread through Ireland, many by word of mouth but some too by letters. For example, in the mid-thirties, three Irish convicts in Australia had this to say to friends and family back home:

This is a very fine country, not a finer in the world and a very wholesome climate.

You may very clearly see what an opportunity there is for well conducted persons.

This is the best country under the sun. I am very thankful to my prosecutors for sending me here to the land of liberty and freedom.[64]

On a visit to Ireland in 1837–38, Father William Ullathorne became aware of such positive views about transportation. In order to disabuse the Irish people about the benefits of life in Australia, he had 20,000 copies of his pamphlet *The Horrors of Transportation* distributed across Ireland.[65] This, rather than the long voyage, may have persuaded some wives that they should not risk their children in the colony. Father Ullathorne's evidence to the Select Committee on Transportation in London did have a detrimental effect on immigration. His testimony that the penal colonies were rife with homosexuality in addition to other alleged depravities was publicised throughout Britain and did untold damage to Australia's reputation.[66] When transportation ended, thousands of Irish still took up the option of assisted emigration to Australia but others from Scotland and England hesitated, or chose Canada, New Zealand or South Africa instead. Most Irish emigrants went to the United States but between 1850 and 1880 a steady 10 per cent continued to migrate to Australia. Waldersee has calculated that 10 per cent of Irish emigrants went to Australia before that date as well.[67]

With Governor Bourke out of the way, the Protestants rallied. Increasingly, long arguments about Catholicism, or popery as it was called then, filled the press. When Father Ullathorne returned from London in December 1838 he was taken aback to find people were now being categorised by religion and ethnicity. 'Hitherto, national distinctions had been instinctively avoided in the colony: all prided themselves on being Australians,' he wrote.[68] In the antagonistic climate, Protestants conflated Catholic and Irish so the ethnicity of immigrants became increasingly contentious. An excess of Irish immigrants between 1839 and 1841 fuelled the increasingly virulent public debate over who should manage migration and how the migrants should be selected. Britain was accused of planning to overwhelm the colony with Irish. When Governor Gipps suggested it was not religion but the quality of labour which was important, the *Sydney Herald* retaliated by accusing him of being 'a miserable apologist of a system of Popish trickery' and claimed that the Irish were now 'special favourites' of the British government.[69] Much debate occurred about immigrants being accepted according to the proportions of English, Irish and Scots already in the colony. Different schemes were tried, from government selection to nomination by families. None quietened the anxiety and the prejudiced angst.[70]

It is usually assumed that prejudice against the Irish in Australia was simply transferred from Britain or was a by-product of general Irish history, but such contention fails to take account of the colonial debate in the 1830s about non-denominational education and equality of religion. Much of what happened in the 1840s and thereafter was a reaction from politics around the Church Act of 1836. Even Patrick O'Farrell fails to take account of the Act, while for Catholic Church historians the actions of a governor detracted from their vision of the church triumphant. Governor Bourke's progressive ideals in fact left a sad legacy of prejudice more vicious, more virulent and more enduring than similar divisions elsewhere. Only Ireland itself preserved sectarian divisions longer than Australia. As we saw in the Maitland Hospital dispute, sectarian prejudice began to develop in the forties. By the following decade the churches had made big inroads towards gathering their flock into particular denominations, transforming the 'live and let live' philosophy of convict Australia. In the sixties, prejudice and discrimination were rife. Toleration diminished.

Despite the efforts of the churches, a visitor to Australia in the 1860s could still write, 'religious convictions sit more lightly upon the people than they do in the old world'.[71] And ordinary people prospered. Adaptability rather than continuity was the key to a prisoner's success in their new land. The Irish who were transported for stealing sheep did not necessarily develop successful careers with sheep in Australia. Although many did continue as labourers or shepherds or shearers, jewel thieves who became stockmen and rope-makers who turned into tobacconists were commonplace rather than exceptional. More predictably, many Irish emancipists became publicans, some of their inns being substantial and prosperous, others little more than disorderly shanties. The proprietor of the fashionable Gill's Hotel in central Sydney was an example of an Irish publican made good.[72]

In a community where penal conditions fostered pragmatism, the Irish brought intangible benefits to the Australian character, not least as Waldersee put it, a 'heightened awareness of the tragic and the wonderful'. In a country where landscape's awesome scope dwarfs human significance, it was a contribution of profound importance towards the newcomers' adjustment to the land. On foot or on horseback or dray, the convicts roamed widely, often alone. Camping under its starry sky, they learned to love the country from the ground up, its red earth, its dry plains, its scarecrow trees and the air and scent of the Australian bush. Their bushcraft developed from adapting their skills to their needs and by watching the Aborigines and copying their methods.[73] In time, convicts provided the template for Europeans' relationship with the bush, becoming legends in their own lifetime to their compatriots and to later generations as well.

The Irish, like the poor Scots and working-class English, recognised that Australia offered them a chance beyond anything achievable at home. Nowhere was this more vividly on display than in the rural townships of New South Wales. Before the great drought of the 1890s places like Maitland and Singleton, Queanbeyan, Cooma and Goulburn, Yass and Burrawa, were built by emancipists and their children with a vision that they would one day become the equivalent of Limerick and Cork, Manchester and Nottingham. Transported stonemasons, carpenters and plasterers built the hotels and the hospitals, the houses and shops. Congregations of Catholics and Protestants built their churches. Emancipist farmers grew produce for distribution by men in business as carters and retailers. Labourers built local roads and bridges. Shoemakers, bakers, blacksmiths, dressmakers and midwives provided services. As literacy spread, their children became teachers, journalists, bank officers and parish clerks. When the townships acquired municipal status in the 1860s, they stood for election to councils and shires some convicts' children became mayors. No aristocracy stood in their way. In the pastoralists' eyes, the towns were convict built and they kept their distance, a culture that was still evident in the 1950s.

Despite increasing sectarian dispute, fundamental attitudes did endure among the people which allowed the legacy of the convict Irish to survive. By their presence in such numbers in the 1830s—and the fortuitous leadership of the O'Connellite tail—the Irish sowed the seed for a philosophy of education that was ahead of its time. Long after the national schools in Ireland had ceased to operate, the Australian version that originated in the 1830s was adopted throughout New South Wales by Premier Henry Parkes.[74] Governor Bourke's plan, nurtured by Plunkett, survived long enough to lay the groundwork for a system of secular education throughout Australia. Under Parkes, however, denominational schools lost their subsidies, triggering a dispute over educational funding that has raged in Australia ever since.[75]

Perhaps more than any other legacy, Australia is indebted to the Irish for religious equality that not even the most pernicious sectarianism could dislodge. Decades after the convict era ended, it was further entrenched as one of the few human rights protections articulated in the Constitution. Such continuity can reasonably be credited to that early attorney-general, John Hubert Plunkett. As a member of the Catholic Association, he kept alive the resolution it passed at Ballinasloe, Connaught, consisting of five principles, the first of which announced forthrightly, 'The State should have no established religion. It should preserve neutrality between them all.'[76] In 2013, one of Australia's leading constitutional lawyers, George Williams, pointed out, 'The framers of Australia's constitution were steeped in the Christian tradition, yet chose to create a nation that could accommodate religious diversity . . . Section 116 prohibits Australia from having a state religion, including Christianity. It also guarantees the right of every person under federal law to exercise the religion of their choice, and says that a person's religion cannot be used to determine their suitability for federal office.'[77] In 2013, the first Muslim elected to a federal ministry swore his oath of office on the Koran under this section. Without 'the Irish factor', the Constitution might well have been far less inclusive. Its endurance is something to celebrate, recognition that, in Australia, 'the luck of the Irish' eventually lost its traditional irony and became simply positive.

CHAPTER 16
The Lives of Men

Shortly after returning to Britain, Henry Lugard was promoted second captain and posted to Limerick. No doubt the move delighted his wife, who must have heard tales of Ireland from her family since she was a toddler. The green beauty of the island, the familiar brogue, would have made her feel welcome beyond anything England could offer. The Lugards spent the next decade in Ireland, moving from Limerick to Dublin in 1847 when Henry was promoted a full captain. Seven years later he was made lieutenant colonel. In Dublin, he held the position of assistant adjutant-general Royal Engineers based at the War Office. Among the many projects he supervised was the planning and construction of a camp at the Curragh of Kildare.[1]

In Limerick, Henry Lugard caught up with Richard Bourke, who was living in retirement at *Thornfield*. Following a rapturous reunion with his daughters Frances and Mary Jane and their families when he arrived in England, Bourke spent time in London with Spring Rice, who was secretary of state for the colonies. He was horrified to discover the calumnies about the penal colonies from the Select Committee on Transportation, which had been widely publicised while he was travelling home. Bourke was forthright in their defence. 'A picture of horrors has lately been drawn in the [Molesworth] report,' he wrote. However, 'the unfavourable representations are manifestly great exaggerations'. Pointing out that the 'vices' nominated by the committee of 'drunkenness and brutal coarseness of speech and manner' had also been described by a recent traveller in Upper Canada, Bourke argued that they were characteristics of any newly formed settlement and not evidence of some extraordinary depravity at Botany Bay. Furthermore, he continued, 'I give it as my deliberate opinion, that not only has transportation administered efficaciously to the wants of the settlers, and raised up a magnificent colony, but it has led to moral improvement of the convicts to the full as much as . . . [penitentiary] discipline in Great Britain and Ireland.'[2]

Declining an official offer to be governor of Jamaica and an unofficial sounding out by Thomas Spring Rice about becoming commander of the British forces in India, Bourke settled happily back into Limerick to the great joy of his tenants and friends in the county. Once again, he was an active patron of the Ahane National School in the grounds of *Thornfield*, his involvement so personal that he presented the prizes every December until his death. He was also chairman of the Limerick Agricultural Society and helped establish an agricultural school in County Limerick. When the local area was hit hard by the Great Famine, Bourke met weekly with the Castleconnell Relief Committee in attempts to alleviate its effects. In his spare time he resumed editing the correspondence of his famous relative, Edmund Burke. He remained well informed about New South Wales through correspondence with Anne and also his son-in-law Edward Deas Thomson, who as colonial secretary was at the heart of Governor Gipps' administration and of his successors. Roger Therry was among those who wrote frequently. He, as well as John Hubert Plunkett and others, called on Bourke when they visited Ireland.

Although Henry Lugard was a junior officer during Bourke's administration, he would have been welcomed as a friend at *Thornfield* for the up-to-date news he could tell of the colony. For example, Henry was still in New Zealand but Mattie was living in Bridge Street in 1842, two blocks down the hill from where Bourke's statue was unveiled in February. It arrived in Sydney 'packed in three heavy cases, together with fourteen pieces of granite for the pedestal'. A public holiday was declared for the unveiling by Governor Gipps. Before the ceremony, a festive parade marched along Macquarie Street, led by mounted police, to the music of the band of the 28th Regiment which was soon to leave the colony. They were followed by groups from six Masonic lodges, the Temperance Society and the Order of Oddfellows. Members of the organising committee marched too, presumably including their secretary, Judge Roger Therry. It was not, however, an ecumenical event. Members of the St Patrick's Society took part accompanied by clergy and hordes of Catholic children but there was no similar representation from the Protestant churches. While the gentry would have found this significant, the people were intent on celebrating and it is unlikely they cared. Donations for the statue had been widespread throughout the colony. Its completion was a popular achievement rather than an official one. Donors to the fund brought up the rear of the parade, many of them humble people such as William Branch, the former overseer (and a Protestant), who had contributed 1 shilling.[3] The statue's subject had sat for the sculptor on several occasions. He would have been interested to know whether the final version was a good likeness.

Richard Bourke had not quite twenty years in retirement before dying peacefully at *Thornfield* in August 1855 aged 78. Henry Lugard would have been among the many luminaries, family and friends who attended his funeral.

The Lugards had several children during their years in Ireland, the first of them a son, Edward, in January 1844. Mattie's mother visited frequently from New South Wales and in 1855 her brother John McHenry convalesced with them after being severely wounded in the Crimean War. Henry's mother also stayed with them for several months. In 1857, Henry was called to duty in his first overseas posting since returning from New South Wales. Appointed Commanding Royal Engineer for what came to be called the Second Opium War, he sailed for Hong Kong on 4 April. The ship's passengers were all senior military commanders who were received with ceremony and hospitality everywhere they dropped anchor. In Gibraltar they were joined by three more luminaries, then sailed on to spend three days in Malta where Henry dined with the governor and attended a Grand Maltese Commercial Ball. Writing home, he teased Mattie that he was 'much disappointed with the beauties'. General Pennefather, who was based there, arranged a grand review of 7000 men which the tiny parade ground could barely contain. Malta also offered Henry a chance to catch up with an old friend, Colonel Harkness, the commanding Royal Engineer, who had been commissioner of public works in Ireland.[4]

After a trek across Egypt from Alexandria, they embarked for Aden. There, Henry was invited by Captain North of the Rifles to ride to the headquarters of the 86th Regiment four miles away. He was struck more by the accommodation than military spit and polish. After the discomfort of their steamer, he relished a real bed. 'Oh! the luxury of the sleep I obtained on a simple couch with matting and mattress and a snow white sheet—the room being open to the air like a birdcage.' Heading for Galle five days later, the ship rolled heavily in a huge gale. During the night Henry fell asleep on a chair that was lashed to a bulwark but in the heavy seas broke free after a violent lurch from the ship. 'I was dashed over with violence on the deck and away to leeward. Brought up with my head against an iron ring.' The collision was severe enough to knock him unconscious for some time. A doctor on board cared for the severe cut on his head. All seemed well. They landed at Hong Kong one day short of seven weeks since leaving Southampton.[5]

Soon after landing, Henry complained of earache. The pain intensified over the next fortnight as doctors tried every possible cure including caustic, leeches, blisters and hot fomentations by syringe. They probed his ear until he was 'half mad with pain'. Increasingly, he had to decline taking part in the grand ceremonies welcoming Lord Elgin to the colony. Soon, his ill-health was obvious to his colleagues and General Ashburnham instructed him to take sick leave. After a short break in Macau he returned to work. Ironically, the 23rd Company of Engineers whose arrival he was eagerly awaiting in Hong Kong, was diverted to India at the last moment for deployment by the now Brigadier-General Sir Edward Lugard, who had just been appointed adjutant-general. Henry wrote to his brother with mock reproach, although it became increasingly apparent that the mutiny in India was serious beyond anyone's expectations. Henry had no option but resort to volunteers from the marines, who he could train in artillery and engineering roles. Despite a heavy workload, he wrote daily to Mattie and everywhere he went he bought her presents: pieces of lace, lace mittens, coral charms from Malta, dresses and bracelets of carved peachstone from Shanghai and two ivory parasol handles which he bought in Macao. But all was not well. In mid-November he suddenly became feverish. Three days later he was dead. The cause was said to be 'hard labour in this treacherous climate' but modern medical knowledge would suggest that the earache and earlier, the heavy blow to his head, had something to do with it.[6]

Back in Ireland, Mattie was devastated. She had received no warning he was ill. The dreadful news waited in a letter from Hong Kong which was on the hall table when she came in from a walk with the children. For days she neither ate, nor drank, nor slept. Her anxious mother-in-law worried that the shock was 'beyond her strength'.[7]

Henry Lugard was eminent, professional and popular and there were many official and personal obituaries. He was buried in the Hong Kong cemetery near the racecourse, with full military honours involving a gun carriage and a long procession of dignitaries from all European nations. Reporting on the funeral, the *Times'* special correspondent wrote: 'Many of those present not only knew him as an officer, whose loss at this critical moment is disastrous to the public service, but loved the man. I was one of those who mourned to think that we shall hear no more his frank hearty laugh and receive no more his manly soldier-like greeting.'[8]

There were many obituaries but none more heartfelt than that of Henry's 83-year-old mother. Writing to her eldest son, Frederick, she had accepted that her youngest died from overwork. 'Dearest Henry . . . his zeal, his love of his profession and the good of his country, obliged him to have such heavy field exercises in so treacherous a climate that his precious life was sacrificed in the prime of manhood, not 43 years old, and you must remember what a fine constitution he ever had, but what a comfort to know that he was a religiously good man and universally loved and respected. I lived under his roof eight months in Dublin and I thankfully admired his worth.'[9]

Nearly two years earlier, in February 1856, Edward Canney set out from St Katherine's dock on the Thames commanding the clipper *Josephine Willis*. She was carrying immigrants bound for New Zealand, ten as cabin passengers and 60 in steerage. With 35 crew, the total number on board was 105. As was now customary in a time of transition to steam, they were towed to Gravesend by a steam-driven tug then handed over to the pilot who took them to the open sea. Throughout this two-day process, Canney was exchanging jocular signals about who was faster with an old school friend who was captain of the *Progress*, a screw steamer that was also making its way downstream. By Sunday evening the *Josephine Willis* was under full sail.[10]

Canney must have had some trepidation about the voyage. His passengers included Henry Ray Grey and his brother, who were relatives of the ship's owners. With Grey's wife, they were emigrating to New Zealand. But the man's presence on board as a cabin passenger, who would eat in the captain's mess, be accommodated close-by, whose company would be unavoidable, was a reminder of the previous voyage when Grey had served under Canney as chief mate and the men clashed. Far from giving leadership to the crew as first officer, Grey spent that voyage taking a rest at every opportunity, smoking against Canney's strict orders that no one should do so while at work, ignoring the drunkenness of the crew who broached casks of brandy in the hold and later got into the gin. Grey was constantly at odds with the crew, at one moment ingratiating himself by, for example, allowing shore leave, at the next enraged by insolence or disobedience. In a bad temper, he would thrash the boys. While Canney was absent from the ship, Grey gave ordinary seaman James Durston 'an unmerciful beating', nearly killing him. When he could speak, Durston told Canney that the chief mate, who was 'very much excited', threw him off the rail, calling him a bugger, and that the doctor who should have intervened was drunk. Relationships deteriorated from then on. Barely three weeks out Grey told Canney that he didn't know how to signal ships. Several captains he had sailed with knew better. The usually amiable Canney grumbled to his log: 'His unwarrantable presumption and assurance in his own abilities is beyond belief. I was thoroughly acquainted with the signals before he was born. It is only on this voyage, he has learnt to know the flags.' He ended his log for that voyage with a complete summary of the dereliction of duty, the rows and the incompetence of Grey. With all this in mind, Canney must have looked forward to the day when he could disembark Henry Ray Grey, passenger, in New Zealand.

Once the ship was under way on this second voyage, Canney went below to chart his course, leaving chief officer Kester Clayton in charge and William Grindle, a seaman he knew well, at the helm. Two lookouts were posted forward to watch for the lighted buoys that managed seagoing traffic through the English Channel. The passengers, many of whom were seasick, had retired to their cabins. As Canney discussed their course with Dr Jarvis, a tremendous grinding crash sent him haring up to the deck. A lookout had mistaken a light on the steamer *Mangerton* for one of the buoys. The mate rushed forward to shout 'Port your helm!'

at the steamer but it was too late. The *Mangerton* crunched into their hull near the main mast with such force that she cut the *Josephine Willis* down to the water's edge. For a few precious minutes, the earth stood still. A handful of crew and some passengers used the pause to scramble onto the steamer.

Edward Canney had been in this situation before. Once again, his brain was in overdrive canvassing the options even as he was shouting 'Man the pumps.' and telling Grindle at the helm to 'Keep her due north.' He knew they were in relatively shallow water, only nine miles out from Folkestone. 'Hoist the mainsail,' he hollered at the crew. 'I'll run her ashore.' Surrounded by panicking people still coming up from below, he tried to reassure them. But his first aim was to get control of the crew. 'Stand by my orders all hands and I'll save you.' It was a futile task. Some of them were already on the steamer. Even as he spoke, the ship's boats were being lowered. The chief officer later claimed that the captain gave the order to lower the boats but no other witness reported that. Given his previous record, Henry Ray Grey behaved much as we might expect. Self-preservation was his only concern. Grey and his brother and wife, with the doctor, a young immigrant woman and one of the crew commandeered the first lifeboat and pulled away from the ship. Shortly after, the pinnace and the second lifeboat followed, leaving 60–70 people standing helplessly by. One boat, containing mainly crew, rowed safely to Deal. The second boat made it to the steamer. One of the surviving crew told the coroner, 'All the boats were gone. They were capable of holding all hands but they were set adrift with only a few people in them.'

When the steamer reversed thrust and pulled back from the hole she had created, Canney realised what would happen. 'Throw the hen coops overboard,' he shouted, 'And hang on to them.' The water was icy but Canney had every reason to expect that rescue would come quickly—from the steamer, from other ships in the Channel. As he shouted, the *Josephine Willis* rolled onto her beam ends, the top-gallant yards lying in the water. Some of the passengers and crew clung to her timbers. Thrown into the water, George Horner obeyed Canney and clung to a hen coop but became so cold he climbed onto the mizzen mast. About two hours later the only boat that set forth from the steamer saved him with five other passengers and crew.

After she rolled, Canney briefly balanced on her hull but a large wave swept him off. He was last sighted helping two women cling to a hen coop. At several points, he might have saved himself but his concern, as always, was for others. Two years later, Grey, whose enmity towards Canney must have been well known in seagoing quarters, gave an interview to the *United Services Magazine* which was both inaccurate and defensive. Grey told the magazine he was 'conversing [with Canney] under the poop awning when the collision took place' but every other source placed the captain plotting his course in the cabin. In evidence Grey claimed that on board the *Mangerton* he had volunteered to return to give help to the wreck. The inquiry obliged him by blaming the crew and charging the captain of the steamer with manslaughter.[11] Announcing its verdict that there were errors on both ships, it added 'there was a great want of humanity on the part of the crew of both ships, in not sending assistance to the passengers of the ship whilst they had it in their power to do so; we believe that if proper efforts had been made, many more lives would have been saved'.[12] What could Grey do but align himself with the view expressed on all sides that Canney deserved high praise for his 'coolness and bravery', for 'his seamanlike and gallant conduct'? William Goodwin, an old colleague and now editor of the *Cornwall Chronicle* in faraway Launceston, summed up the opinion of all who knew him: 'Had Captain Canney been a selfish man—had he been impressed with a less generous sense of duty, there is every probability that by abandoning others, he might have saved himself. But he died like a true-hearted British sailor, endeavouring to save the weak and helpless.'[13]

The dark waters were freezing. As one by one his female companions slipped away unconscious, Canney had time to understand what was happening, to realise there would be no rescue. Perhaps he understood that the steamer too, according to its captain, was in difficulty, but above all he would have recognised what he was losing. At the top of each swell, he could see the lights of Folkestone. Mary Ann and the children were near but impossibly far away. With creeping finality, the intense chill permeated his body, numbing his fingers, loosening his grip on the hutch until, finally, the sea bore him away, laying claim to a man for whom it was friend rather than enemy. It never gave up his body.

On the far side of the world, the sun was climbing the sky to make the water dance with diamonds. At Wreck Bay, as it was now called, the Aboriginal community were trawling their nets, scooping up the mullet that Gundawarra, the west wind, was harassing out of the estuary and through the translucent shallows that fringed the long curve of white sand. The bay was teeming with life. The wooden spars of a wrecked ship no longer intruded. Their remnants had been long hidden beneath the sand. The bay was peaceful—for now.

The sun rose over the coast, waking the ranges. Its early morning rays touched a solitary horseman ambling across the high plains, a black and white dog loping alongside. He was a man who had known suffering and want, who had lived with violence and loss. Ruthless when necessary. Capable of stubborn resistance, particularly when joined with his mates, life had taught him endurance. And solitude. Not necessarily alone though—a 'little mate' as he called her, very possibly farewelled him that morning among the peppercorn trees—but he had learned to keep a still tongue, hide his thoughts, disguise his vulnerability from others for fear they might use it, deflect their attacks with laconic humour. His feelings were buried deep, often incomprehensible even to himself. As the sun rose and the haze increased, his image dissolved beneath the overwhelming light. And the convict bushman rode into legend.

Acknowledgements

Many people helped with this book. Foremost among them was James Canney, one of the few descendants of Edward Canney, in his case from 'Baby' Bentinck who was born on Sydney Harbour. He would be delighted to hear by email from any undiscovered relatives: <jameswbcanney@ hotmail.com>. I owe thanks to Airlie Moore, descendant of Edward Canney's aunt, who put us in touch.

Another source of great support has been Tim Causer, friend and scholar from University College, London, whose doctorate on Norfolk Island is the first based on primary records. Our email discussions have sustained me through the writing.

Other scholars whose recent work contributed significantly included Perry McIntyre, Lorraine Neate, Brian Walsh, and Kiera Lindsey who generously shared her thesis on abduction. Historically, work by John Hirst and Alan Atkinson opened perspectives that are developed further in this work, while Stephen Nicholas and the contributors to *Convict Workers*, Grace Karskens, David Andrew Roberts and the late William Robbins added important details. So did Max Waugh, biographer of Richard Bourke, also Tony Earls and John Molony's work on J.H.

Plunkett. Historians Barrie Dyster, and Robert and Sally O'Neill provided valuable scrutiny. Thanks also to Gregory Young, a fellow researcher in the National Library of Ireland, who gave me a copy of the Irish edition of A.G.L. Shaw's *Convicts and the Colonies*.

My thanks to maritime archaeologists Tim Smith and Sarah Ward from Heritage New South Wales for information about the hunt for wreckage from the *Hive* and for their enthusiasm about my project to use the wreck as a springboard to explore issues relating to the Irish in Australia.

As always, descendants of the convicts themselves made significant contributions through family history scholarship. They included: Gordon Staples (Patrick Tierney, convict), Larry Adams (James Dalton), Ted Russell (Edward/Edmund Conway), Tom Stephens (Lawrence Durack), Anne Rodger and Ron Dunbar (Michael and John Smith), Toni Pomering (Michael Leeny), Linda Combe (James Hogan) as well as Ellen Smith and Adele Tiernan who are descended from Private Patrick Tierney and Bridget and Barry James who has done valuable research on his ancestor, William Branch. Also of enormous value, often from a family history angle, were the publications of the Paterson Historical Society.

I am grateful to librarians and archivists at NSW State Records, the Mitchell Library, the National Library of Australia, the National Library of Ireland, Rhodes House in Oxford and the National Archives of Great Britain at Kew. At Lithgow Library in New South Wales, Maureen Breckell and Kay Shirt saved my life by arranging inter-library loans.

Overseas research can be lonely but Chris Ashton and Ana Pisano provided companionship in Dublin. My sister-in-law Elizabeth Smith came with me to Durham. Meredith Daneman cheerfully tolerated my absences at Kew and provided company in the evening. And I could travel with a light heart because Christina Lincoln was minding Casey.

In Australia, Janine and David Haydon were very supportive. My thanks to John Stephenson, Penny Nelson, Rhonwyn Cuningham and particularly Charlie Brown, who remembered my project despite some wrenching personal circumstances. Lastly but never least, thanks to my family including Robert and Nicole Macfarlan, Rosalinde Kearsley, Graham who came with me on a tour of Tocal, and Josh, who has never known life without a mother absorbed by history but who manages to remain cheerful despite it.

I have been fortunate to have Carl Harrison-Ford edit most of my books and the dedication reflects my appreciation.

A full list of the prisoners who arrived on the *Hive* can be found on my website: <www.babettesmith.com>. I will always be interested to hear from their descendants and to share information with them.

Babette Smith
November 2013

Select Bibliography

Archival Sources (as cited)
Archives Office of Tasmania
NSW State Records
NSW State Library
Mitchell Library
National Library of Australia
The National Archives (UK)
The National Archives of Ireland—Irish Transportation Records,
    The National Library of Ireland

Indexes
Joan Reese Index to Colonial Secretary Correspondence
Phoenix hulk Transportation Entrance Books and Prisoners Received
Vernon Indexes including:
    Goulburn Gaol Entrance Book
    Darlinghurst Gaol Entrance Book
    Berrima Gaol
    Iron Gangs at Scone
    Convict Road Gangs
    Windsor Gaol
Mayberry, Peter, Online Index to Braidwood Gaol, 1870–72
HRA, series I, vols 1–20

Websites

Barrie and Margaret Chapman (creators and editors), *Australia's Red Coat Settlers*, <http://freepages.history.rootsweb.ancestry.com/~garter1/>. Last revised: 7 March 2009

Barry Cubitt, *The Ribbon Gang: The story of the Bathurst Convict Rebellion of 1830*, <http://en.wikipedia.org/wiki/Bathurst_Rebellion>, 1998

Colonial Case Law, New South Wales, <http://law.mq.edu.au/research/colonial_case_law/nsw/cases>

Free Settler or Felon? <www.jenwilletts.com>

Peter Mayberry, *Irish Convicts to New South Wales 1788–1849*, <http://members.pcug.org.au/~ppmay/convicts.htm>

Michael Organ's website, <www.uow.edu.au/~morgan>

The History of Illawarra and its Pioneers, <http://archive.org/stream/cu31924000335707/cu31924000335707_djvu.txt>

Primary Sources (published)

Anderson, Joseph, *Recollections of a Peninsular Veteran*, London: Edward Arnold, 1913

Andrews, Alan E.J. (ed.), *Stapylton, with Major Mitchell's Australia Felix Expedition, 1836*, Hobart: Blubberhead Press, 1986

Baxter, Carol (ed.), *1822 Muster*, Sydney: ABGR in association with the Society of Australian Genealogists, 1988

Baxter, Carol (ed.), *1823, 1824 and 1825 Muster*, Sydney: ABGR in association with the Society of Australian Genealogists, 1999

Berry, Alexander, *Reminiscences of Alexander Berry*, Sydney: Angus & Robertson, 1912

British Parliamentary Papers (BPP), Shannon: Irish University Press, 1969–71

Butlin, N.G., C.W. Cromwell and K.L. Suthern (eds), *1837 General Return of Convicts in New South Wales*, Sydney: ABGR in association with the Society of Australian Genealogists, 1987

Cash, Martin, *The Uncensored Story of Martin Cash, (Australian Bushranger) as told to James Lester Burke*, compiled and edited by Joan Dehle Emberg and Buck Thor Emberg, Launceston: Regal Publications, c.2000

Cook, Thomas, *The Exile's Lamentations*, North Sydney: The Library of Australian History, 1978

Cunningham, Peter, *Two Years in New South Wales, a Series of Letters* [London], 1827, two vols, facsimile edition, Adelaide: Libraries Board of South Australia, 1966

Curr, E.M., *Recollections of Squatting in Victoria* [1883], Melbourne, 1965

Darwin, Charles, *Charles Darwin: An Australian selection*, Canberra: National Museum of Australia, 2009

Govett, William Romaine, *Sketches of New South Wales*, Melbourne: Gaston Renard, 1977

Harris, Alexander, *An Emigrant Mechanic, Settlers and Convicts or Recollections of Sixteen years labour in the Australian Backwoods* [London, 1847], Melbourne: Melbourne University Press, 1964

Historical Records of Australia, series 1, vols 1–20, Frederick Watson (ed.), Sydney: The Library Committee of the Commonwealth Parliament, 1914

Hodgson, Christopher Pemberton, *Reminiscences of Australia, with hints on the squatters life*, London, 1846

Illawarra Pioneers pre 1920, compiled and edited by Illawarra Family History Group, 1992.

Lindsay, Benjamin, *Early Land Settlement on the Illawarra, 1804–1861*, Wollongong: Illawarra Historical Publications, 1994

Macarthur, James, *New South Wales: Its present state and future prospects*, London, 1837

Maxwell, John, *Letters of John Maxwell, Superintendent of Government Stock 1823–1831*, compiled by Bertha Mac Smith and Brian Lloyd, Wangaratta, Victoria: Shoestring Press, 1982

New South Wales Directory for 1839, facsimile, Sydney: Royal Australian Historical Society, 2000

Norfolk Island: The Botany Bay of Botany Bay, Adelaide: Sullivan's Cove, 1979

Parry, Edward, Sir Edward Parry to Colonial Secretary, *In the Service of the Company*, Letter no. 84, 1 May 1830, <http://epress.anu.edu.au>

Polding, Bishop, *Letters of John Bede Polding*, 2 vols, Glebe, NSW: Sisters of the Good Samaritan, 1994

Sainty, Malcolm R., and Keith A. Johnson (eds), *1828 Census*, Sydney: Library of Australian History, 1985

Stewart, Thomas Samuel, *Journal, Norfolk Island 1855, 'Waiting for the Pitcairn Islanders*, Laurel Chambers and Merval Hoare (eds), self-published, 1992

Taylor, Nancy M. (ed.), *The Journal of Ensign Best*, Turnbull Library Monograph, Wellington, New Zealand, 1966

Telfer Jnr, William, *The Wallabadah Manuscript, Recollections of the Early Days*, introduction and notes by Roger Milliss, Sydney: UNSW Press, 1980

Therry, Roger, *Reminiscences of Thirty Years Residence in New South Wales and Victoria*, facsimile edition with an Introduction by J.M. Bennett, Sydney: Sydney University Press, 1974

Ullathorne, W.B., *The Autobiography of Archbishop Ullathorne, with Selections from his Letters* [1891], 3rd ed., London: Burns & Oates

Ullathorne, W.B., *The Catholic Mission in Australasia* [1837], Adelaide: Libraries Board of South Australia, 1963

Newspapers—Ireland

Athlone Independent

Athlone Sentinel

Belfast News

Carlow Morning Post

Carlow Sentinel

Clare Journal

Clonmel Advertiser

Clonmel Herald

Connaught Journal

Cork Constitution

Cork Evening Herald

Drogheda Advertiser

Dublin Observer

Enniskillener Constitution

Erne Packet

Finn's Leinster Journal

Freeman's Journal

Kerry Evening Post

Kilkenny Journal

Kilkenny Moderator

Leinster Express

Limerick Chronicle

Limerick Post

Limerick Times

Mayo and Roscommon Constitution

Morning Post (London)

Newry Examiner

Roscommon Gazette

Roscommon Journal

Sligo Journal

Southern Reporter

Waterford Mail

Newspapers—Australia

Australian

Australasian Chronicle

Colonist

Goulburn Herald

Maitland Mercury

Port Phillip Gazette

Sydney Gazette

Sydney Herald

Sydney Monitor

Sydney Morning Herald

Selected Secondary Sources

Allan, Susan R., 'Irish Convicts: Hampdens or hardened criminals? A review of the work of Lloyd Robson and John Williams: A comparative case study', in *Tasmanian Historical Studies*, vol. 7, no. 2, 2001

Atkinson, Alan, 'Four patterns of convict protest' [1977], in Penny Russell and Richard White (eds), *Pastiche 1: Reflections on 19th century Australia*, Sydney: Allen & Unwin, 1994

Atkinson, Alan, *The Europeans in Australia: A history*, vols 1 & 2, Melbourne: Melbourne University Press, 2004

Atkinson, Alan, and Marian Aveling (eds), *Australians 1838*, Sydney: Fairfax, Syme & Weldon Associates, 1987

Barker, Theo, *History of Bathurst*, vol. 1, *The Early Settlement to 1862*, Bathurst: Bathurst City Council, 1992

'Barney, George (1792–1862)', *Australian Dictionary of Biography*, <http://adb.anu.edu.au/biography/barney-george-1744/text1931> (author unnamed)

Bateson, Charles, *The Convict Ships 1787–1868*, Sydney: Library of Australian History, 1983

Binney, Keith R., *Horsemen of the First Frontier and The Serpents Legacy*, Sydney: Volcanic Productions, 2005

Blair, Sandra J., 'The revolt at Castle Forbes: A catalyst to Emancipist Emigrant Confrontation', *JRAHS*, vol. 64, pt 2, September 1978

Bongiorno, Frank, *Sex Lives of Australians*, Melbourne: Black Inc., 2012

Boyle, Harry F., *George Boyle White 1802–1876*, Heritage Address, Paterson, NSW: Paterson Historical Society, 1995

Bridges, Barry, 'Aspects of the career of Alexander Berry, 1781–1873', PhD thesis, Wollongong: University of Wollongong, 1992

Britts, M.G., *The Commandants: The tyrants who ruled Norfolk Island*, Adelaide: Rigby, 1980

Brown, Barbara, and Shirley Threlfo, *The First Fatal Election, Paterson 1843*, Paterson, NSW: Historical Society, 2001

Byrne, Paula J., *Criminal Law and the Colonial Subject: New South Wales, 1810–1830*, Melbourne: Cambridge University Press, 1993

Campbell, Craig, and Helen Proctor, *A History of Australian Schooling*, Sydney: Allen & Unwin, 2014

Campbell, Malcolm, *The Kingdom of the Ryans: The Irish in southwest New South Wales, 1816–1890*, Sydney: UNSW Press, 1997

Causer, Tim, '"Only a Place Fit for Angels and Eagles": The Norfolk Island Penal Settlement, 1825–1855', PhD thesis and database, London: University of London, 2010

Causer, Tim '"The worst types of sub-human beings"? The myth and reality of the convicts of the Norfolk Island Penal Settlement, 1825–1855', in *Islands of History*, Proceedings of the 25th Anniversary Conference of the Professional Historians Association (NSW), Norfolk Island 2010, Melbourne: Anchor Books, 2011

Causer, Tim, 'Anti-transportation, "unnatural crime" and the "horrors" of transportation', *JACH*, vol. 14, 2012

Clarke, Keith M., *Convicts of the Port Phillip District*, self-published, 1999

Clay, John, *Maconochie's Experiment: How one man's extraordinary vision saved transported convicts from degradation and despair*, London: John Murray, 2001

Clune, Frank, *The Norfolk Island Story*, Sydney: Angus & Robertson, 1981 edition

Coghlan, T.A., *The Wealth and Progress of New South Wales, 1886–87*, Sydney: George Robertson & Co., 1887

Coulthard-Clark, Chris, *Where Australians Fought: The encyclopaedia of Australia's battles*, 2nd edn, Sydney: Allen & Unwin, 2001

Dyster, Barrie, 'The fate of colonial conservatives on the eve of the gold rush', *JRAHS*, vol. 54, pt 4, December 1968

Dyster, Barrie, 'Public employment and assignment to private masters, 1788–1821', in Stephen Nicholas (ed.), *Convict Workers: Reinterpreting the past*, Cambridge: Cambridge University Press, 1988

Dyster, Barrie, *Servant and Master Building and running the grand houses of Sydney, 1788–1850*, Sydney: UNSW Press, 1989

Earls, Tony, *Plunkett's Legacy: An Irishman's contribution to the rule of law in New South Wales*, Macquarie Law Monograph, Melbourne: Australian Scholarly Publishing, 2009

Earnshaw, Beverley, 'The Lame, the Blind, the Mad, the Malingerers: Sick and disabled convicts within the colonial community', *JRAHS*, vol. 81, pt 1, June 1995

Elliott, Rex, *History of Erowal Farm*, researched and compiled by Rex Elliott, Sanctuary Point Printing, 2nd ed., 2010

Evans, L., and P. Nicholls (eds), *Convicts and Colonial Society, 1788–1868*, 2nd ed., Macmillan, 1984

Finger, Hans Wilhelm, *Ludwig Leichhardt: Lost in the Outback*, Sydney: Rosenberg, 2013

Fitzsimons, Peter, *Eureka, The unfinished revolution*, Sydney: William Heinemann, 2012

Foster, Roy, Oxford University, speaking on *The Story of Ireland*, presented by Fergal Keane, DVD disk 3, London: BBC Worldwide, 2011

Foster, William, 'Education in New South Wales under Governor Sir Richard Bourke', *JRAHS*, vol. 47, pt 5, 1961, pp. 255–80

Foster, William C., *Sir Thomas Mitchell and his World 1792–1855*, Sydney: Institute of Surveyors New South Wales, 1985

Frost, Alan, *Botany Bay: The real story*, Black Inc, 2011

Garnsey, Philippa, *Ryansvale: The family, the property, the people*, self-published (available 80 Avenue Road, Mosman NSW 2088), 2011

Gartrell, Glenda, *The Scotts of Mulloon: And the Families who Settled the Long Swamp Near Bungendore*, Artarmon, NSW: the author, 2011

Gent, Lesley C., *Gostwyck, Paterson, 1823–2009*, Paterson, NSW: Paterson Historical Society, 2009

Gilchrist, Catie, '"The relic of the cities of the plain": Penal flogging, convict morality and the colonial imagination', *JACH*, vol. 9, 2007

Gill, Andrew, *Convict Assignment in Western Australia, 1842–1851*, Marylands, WA: Blatellae Books, 2004

Gray, Nancy, 'John Bingle (1796–1882)', *Australian Dictionary of Biography*, <http://adb.anu.edu.au>

Gray, Nancy, 'Helenus & Robert Scott', *Australian Dictionary of Biography*, <www.adb.anu.edu.au>

Hamilton, Pauline, 'No Irish Need Apply: Prejudice as a factor in the development of immigration policy in New South Wales and Victoria, 1840–1870', PhD thesis, Sydney: University of New South Wales, 1979

Hammond, Peter, 'Murder, manslaughter and workplace relations in convict New South Wales, 1824–1838', BA thesis, University of New England, 2003

Hartley, Dulcie, *John Herring Boughton of Tillimby, Paterson*, Heritage Lecture, Paterson, NSW: Paterson Historical Society, 2000

Hawkins, Ralph, *The Convict Timbergetters of Pennant Hills*, Hornsby, NSW: Hornsby Shire Historical Society, 1994

Hill, Myrtle, 'Culture and Religion, 1815–1870', in Donnchadh Ó Corráin and Tomás O'Riordan (eds), *Ireland, 1815–1870 Emancipation, famine and religion*, Dublin: Four Courts Press, 2011

Hindmarsh, Bruce, and Hamish Maxwell-Stewart, '"This is the bird that never flew": William Stewart, Major Donald MacLeod and the Launceston Advertiser', *JACH*, vol. 2, no. 1, 2000

Hirst, J.B., *Convict Society and its Enemies*, Sydney: George Allen & Unwin, 1983

Hirst, J.B., *The Australians: Insiders and outsiders on the national character since 1770*, Melbourne: Black Inc, 2007

Historical Studies of Australia and New Zealand, Eureka Supplement [1954], Melbourne: Melbourne University Press, 1965 edition

Ihde, Erin, 'Monitoring the situation: The "convict journal", convict protest and convicts' rights', *JRAHS*, vol. 85, pt 1, June 1999

James, Barry, *A Branch of the Family: William Branch c.1772–c.1845, gunner, husband, father and overseer of convicts*, privately published by Barry James, 76 Plateau Road, Springwood NSW, 2008

Johnson, Beverley, 'Percy Simpson (1789–1877)', *Australian Dictionary of Biography, Supplementary Volume*, <http://adb.anu.edu.au/biography/simpson-percy-13196/text23891>

Karskens, Grace, 'Defiance, deference and diligence: Three views of convicts in New South Wales road gangs', *Australian Historical Archaeology*, vol. 4, 1986

Karskens, Grace, *The Colony: A history of early Sydney*, Sydney: Allen & Unwin, 2009

Kaye, Bruce N., 'Broughton and the demise of the royal supremacy', *JRAHS*, vol. 81, pt 1, June 1995,

Kelly, James, 'The abduction of women of fortune in eighteenth-century Ireland', *Eighteenth Century Ireland*, no. 9, 1994

Kent, David, and Norma Townsend, *The Convicts of the Eleanor: Protest in rural England, new lives in Australia*, London: The Merlin Press, 2002

Kiely, Brendan, *The Connerys: The making of a Waterford legend*, Dublin: Geography Publications, 1994

Kildea, Jeff, *Anzacs and Ireland*, Sydney: UNSW Press, 2007

Kinealy, Christine, 'Politics and administration, 1815–1870', in Donnchadh Ó Corráin and

Tomás O'Riordan (eds), *Ireland, 1815–1870 Emancipation, famine and religion*, Dublin: Four Courts Press, 2011

King, Hazel, 'Sir Richard Bourke (1777–1855)', *Australian Dictionary of Biography*, <http://adb. online.anu.edu.au/biography/bourke-sir-richard-1806/text2055>

Kociumbas, Jan, '"Mary Ann", Joseph Fleming and "Gentleman Dick": Aboriginal–convict relationships in colonial history', *JACH*, vol. 3, no. 1, April 2001

Lawrence, D.H., *Kangaroo* [1923], Harmondsworth: Penguin, 1950

Lea-Scarlett, E.J. 'James Henry Crummer (1792–1867)', *Australian Dictionary of Biography*, <http:// adb.anu.edu.au/biography/crummer-james-henry-1940>

Lindsey, Kiera, 'A mistress of her own actions: The abduction of Mary Ann Gill, Sydney 1848', *Melbourne Historical Journal*, vol. 37, December 2009

Lindsey, Kiera, 'Taken: A history of bride theft in nineteenth-century Ireland and Australia', PhD thesis, Melbourne: University of Melbourne, 2011

Lindsey, Kiera, '"So much recklessness": Abduction in the colony of New South Wales', *Australian Historical Studies*, vol. 44, no. 3, 2013

Lugard, Cecil, *Monographs about Captain John, Edward and Henry Lugard*, ML A923.2–5

McCulloch, Samuel Clyde, 'Sir George Gipps (1791–1847)', *Australian Dictionary of Biography*, <http://adb.anu.edu.au/biography/gipps-george-2098/text2645>

McGrath, John, 'Riots in Limerick, 1820–1900', in William Sheehan and Maura Cronin, *Riotous Assemblies*, Blackrock, Cork: Mercier, 2011

McIntyre, Perry, *Free Passage: The reunion of Irish convicts and their families in Australia, 1788–1852*, and accompanying database, Dublin: Irish Academic Press, 2011

McIntyre, Perry, and Elizabeth Rushen, *Quarantined! The 1837 Lady Macnaghten immigrants*, Melbourne: Anchor Books, 2007

Macqueen, Andy, *Frederick Robert D'Arcy: Colonial surveyor, explorer and artist, c.1809–1875*, Wentworth Falls, NSW, the author, 2010

McQueen, Humphrey, *A New Britannia*, St Lucia, Queensland: University of Queensland Press, 4th ed., 2004

Maddrell, Roslyn, *Braidwood and District Post Office and People,* Braidwood: Braidwood and District Historical Society, 1996

Madgwick, R B., *Immigration into Eastern Australia 1788–1851* [1937], Sydney: Sydney University Press, 1969

Martin, W.W., *Henry Parkes*, Melbourne: Melbourne University Press, 1980

Mawer, G.A., *Most Perfectly Safe: The convict shipwreck disasters*, Sydney: Allen & Unwin, 1997

Maxwell-Stewart, H., *Closing Hell's Gates: The death of a convict station*, Sydney: Allen & Unwin, 2008

Meredith, David, 'Full circle? Contemporary views on transportation', in Stephen Nicholas (ed.), *Convict Workers: Reinterpreting the past,* Cambridge: Cambridge University Press, 1988

Molony, John N., *An Architect of Freedom: John Hubert Plunkett in New South Wales, 1832–1869*, Canberra: ANU Press, 1973

Molony, John N., *The Native Born: The first white Australians*, Melbourne: Melbourne University Press, 2000

Moore, Clive, 'Colonial manhood and masculinities', *Journal of Australian Studies*, no. 56, 1998

Morrison, Meg, *Aaron Price, the Unsung: A factual convict story of cruelty, rebellion, anxiety, slavery and freedom*, Bellevive, Tasmania: the author, 2008

Mullaly, Paul R., *Crimes in the Port Phillip District, 1835–55, Melbourne:* Hybrid Publishers, 2008

Neate, Lorraine, *Paulsgrove, Illawarra, 1825–1836*, the author, 2010

Nicholas, Stephen (ed.), *Convict Workers: Reinterpreting the past*, Cambridge: Cambridge University Press, 1988

Nugent, Ann, *The Story of Fishing at Wreck Bay, as Told by the People*, [Canberra]: Schools Commission, 1980

Ó Corráin, Donnchadh and Tomás O'Riordan (eds), *Ireland, 1815–1870: Emancipation, famine and religion*, Dublin: Four Courts Press, 2011

O'Farrell, Patrick, *Letters from Irish Australia, 1825–1929*, Sydney: UNSW Press, 1984

O'Farrell, Patrick, *Vanished Kingdoms: Irish in Australia and New Zealand, a personal excursion*, Sydney: UNSW Press, 1990

O'Farrell, Patrick, *The Irish in Australia*, Sydney: New South Wales University Press, revised edition, 1993

O'Farrell, Patrick, 'St Patrick's Day in Australia', The John Alexander Ferguson Lecture 1994, *JRAHS*, vol. 81, pt 1, June 1995

Organ, Michael K. (ed.), *Reminiscences of Illawarra, by Alexander Stewart*, Woonona, NSW: Illawarra Historical Publications, 1987

Organ, Michael, K. (ed.), *The Illawarra Diary of Lady Jane Franklin, 10–17 May 1839*, Woonona, NSW: Illawarra Historical Publications, 1988

Organ, Michael K. (ed.), *Punishments at Illawarra Stockade, 1827–1844*, <www.uow.edu.au/~morgan/stockade.htm>

Parry, Sir Edward, *In the Service of the Company, letters of Sir Edward Parry, Commissioner to the Australian Agricultural Company*, vol. 1, Canberra: ANU E-Press, 2005

Perry, T.M., 'James Meehan (1774–1826)', *Australian Dictionary of Biography*, <http://adb.anu.edu.au/biography/meehan-james-2443/text3257>

Quinlan, Michael, 'Trade unionism and industrial action in Tasmania, 1830–1850', THRA, *Papers and Proceedings*, vol. 33, no. 1, March 1986

Reid, K., *Gender, Crime and Empire: Convicts, settlers and the state in early colonial Australia*, Manchester: Manchester University Press, 2007

Reid, Richard E., *Farewell My Children: Irish assisted emigration to Australia, 1848–1870*, Melbourne: Anchor Books, 2011

Reynolds, Henry, 'Racial thought in early colonial Australia', *Australian Journal of Politics and History*, vol. 20, no. 1, 1974

Ritchie, John (ed.), *The Evidence to the Bigge Reports, New South Wales Under Governor Macquarie*, 2 vols, Melbourne: William Heinemann Australia, 1971

Roberts, David Andrew, '"A sort of inland Norfolk Island"? Isolation, Coercion and Resistance on the Wellington Valley Convict Station, 1823–26', *JACH*, vol. 2, no. 1, April 2000

Roberts, David Andrew, and Daniel Garland, 'The Forgotten Commandant: James Wallis and the Newcastle penal settlement, 1816–1818', *Australian Historical Studies*, vol. 41, no. 1, March 2010

Robbins, William, 'The lumber yards: The management of convict labour, 1788–1832', *Labour History*, no. 79, November 2000

Robbins, William, 'Management and resistance in convict work gangs 1788–1830', *Journal of Industrial Relations*, vol. 45, no. 3, September 2003

Robson, L.L., *The Convict Settlers of Australia*, Melbourne: Melbourne University Press, 1965

Rosen, Sue, *Men at Work: Penal ideology and nation building on the Great Western Road*, Sydney: Heritage Assessment and History, 2006

Rushen, Elizabeth, *Single and Free: Female migration to Australia, 1833–1837*, Australian Scholarly Publishing, 2003

Rushen, Elizabeth, and Perry McIntyre, *The Merchant's Women*, Spit Junction, NSW: Anchor Press, 2008

Serle, Geoffrey, *The Golden Age: A history of the colony of Victoria 1851–61*, Melbourne: Melbourne University Press, 1963

Shaw, A.G.L., *Convicts and the Colonies* [1966], Dublin: Irish Historical Press, 1998

Sheehan, William, and Marian Cronin (eds), *Riots and Revolts in Ireland*, Blackrock, Cork: Mercier Press, Ireland, 2011

Silver, Lynette, *The Battle of Vinegar Hill 1804: Australia's Irish rebellion*, Sydney: Doubleday, 1989

Smith, Babette, *A Cargo of Women: Susannah Watson and the convicts of the Princess Royal*, 2nd ed., Sydney: Allen & Unwin, 2008

Smith, Babette, *Australia's Birthstain*, Sydney: Allen & Unwin, 2008

Smith, Babette, 'The handover: A glimpse of men and management in the penal colonies', in *Islands of History*, Proceedings of the 25th Anniversary Conference of the Professional Historians Association (NSW), Norfolk Island 2010, Melbourne: Anchor Books, 2011

Smith, Babette, 'Beyond Birthstain: Further research into the anti-transportation campaign in Australia', *JACH*, vol. 14, 2012

Stewart, A.T.Q., *The Narrow Ground: Aspects of Ulster, 1609–1969*, first published London: Faber & Faber, 1977, The Blackstaff Press, facsimile edition, Belfast, 1997

Stoneman, David, 'The Church Act: The expansion of Christianity or the imposition of moral enlightenment?' PhD thesis, Armidale: University of New England, 2011

Thompson, M.M.H., *The Seeds of Democracy: Early elections in colonial New South Wales*, Leichhardt, NSW: Federation Press, 2006

Townsend, Norma, 'Masters and Men and the Myall Creek Massacre', in *The Push From the Bush, Myall Creek issue*, no. 20, April 1985

Travers, Robert, *The Phantom Fenians of New South Wales*, Kenthurst, NSW: Kangaroo Press, 1986

Travers, Robert, *The Grand Old Man of Australian Politics: The life and times of Sir Henry Parkes*, Kenthurst, NSW: Kangaroo Press, 1992

von Hugel, Baron Charles, *New Holland Journal, November 1833–October 1834*, translated and edited by Dymphna Clark, Melbourne: Miegunyah Press, 1994

Waldersee, James, *Catholic Society in New South Wales, 1788–1860*, Sydney: Sydney University Press, 1974

Walsh, Brian, *James Phillips Webber: The man and the mystery*, Paterson, NSW: CB Alexander Foundation, 2008

Walsh, Brian, *Voices from Tocal: Convict life on a rural estate*, Paterson, NSW: CB Alexander Foundation, 2008

Walsh, Brian, 'The politics of convict control in colonial New South Wales: "The notorious OPQ" and the clandestine press', *JRAHS*, vol. 96, pt 2, 2010

Walsh, Brian, and Cameron Archer, *Maitland, on the Hunter*, Paterson, NSW: CB Alexander Foundation, 2nd ed., 2007

Walsh, Brian, and Ralph Hawkins, *Convict Tools: Working at Camden Part and Tocal*, Paterson, NSW: CB Alexander Foundation, 2013

Ward, John M., 'Sir Charles August FitzRoy (1796–1858)', *Australian Dictionary of Biography*, <http://adb.anu.edu./biography/fitzroy-sir-charles-augustus-2049/text2539>

Ward, Russel, *The Australian Legend* [1958], Melbourne: Oxford University Press, 1970

Ward, Russel, '*The Australian Legend* re-visited', *Historical Studies*, vol. 18, no. 71, 1987

Waugh, Max, *Forgotten Hero: Richard Bourke, Irish-born governor of New South Wales, 1831–1837*, Melbourne: Australian Scholarly Publishing, 2005

Whitaker, Anne-Maree, *Unfinished Revolution: United Irishmen in New South Wales, 1800–1810*, Darlinghurst, NSW: Crossing Press, 1994

Whitaker, Anne-Maree, 'James Meehan—nearly Australia's third surveyor-general', Society of Australian Genealogists, *Descent*, vol. 24, pt. 2, June 1994

Whitaker, Anne-Maree, *Appin: The story of a Macquarie town*, Alexandria, NSW: Kingsclear Books, 2005

Williams, John, 'Irish convicts and Van Diemen's Land', THRA, *Papers and Proceedings*, vol. 19. no. 3, 1972

Williams, John, 'Irish convicts in Tasmania', Centre for Tasmanian Historical Studies, *Bulletin*, vol. 2, no. 3, 1989

Wilson, Brenda, 'Edward Denny Day's investigations at Myall Creek', in *The Push from the Bush, Myall Creek issue*, no. 20, April 1985

Wilson, Catherine Anne, *Tenants in Time: Family strategies, land and liberalism in Upper Canada 1799–1871*, 2009, <www.mqup.ca/tenants-in-time-products-9780773535237.php#sthash.Kze3Yn5p.dpuf>

Wilson, Gwendoline, *Murray of Yarralumla*, Canberra: Tabletop Press, 2001

Wilson, Gwendoline, 'Sir Terence Aubrey Murray (1810–1873)', *Australian Dictionary of Biography*, <http://adb.anu.edu.au/biography/murray-sir-terence-aubrey-2498>

Wright, Christine, 'Rogues and fools: John Coghill and the convict system in New South Wales', *JACH*, vol. 3, no. 2, 2001, and Christine Wright database

Wright, Christine, *Wellington's Men in Australia: Peninsular War veterans and the making of empire, c.1820–1840*, Basingstoke: Palgrave Macmillan, 2011

Notes

Abbreviations used in the notes

ADB	*Australian Dictionary of Biography*
AJCP	Australian Joint Copying Project
ANU	Australian National University
AOTAS	Archives Office of Tasmania
BPP	British Parliamentary Papers
CSIL	Colonial Secretary In Letters
HRA	*Historical Records of Australia*
HRV	*Historical Record of Victoria*
JACH	*Journal of Australian Colonial History*
JRAHS	*Journal of the Royal Australian Historical Society*
ML	Mitchell Library
NAI	National Archives of Ireland
NLA	National Library of Australia
NLI	National Library of Ireland
NSWBDM	New South Wales Births, Deaths and Marriages
NSWGG	*New South Wales Government Gazette*
PROV	Public Record Office of Victoria
SRNSW	State Records of New South Wales
The Push	*The Push from the Bush, a Bulletin of Social History*, Myall Creek issue, no. 20, April 1985, UNE
THRA	Tasmanian Historical Research Association
THS	Tasmanian Historical Studies
TNAUK	The National Archives, United Kingdom

UNE   University of New England
VPRO   Public Record Office Victoria

Introduction

1 Robson, *Convict Settlers of Australia*, pp. 16, 28.
2 Shaw, *Convicts and the Colonies*, p. 167.
3 Stewart, *The Narrow Ground*, p. 113.
4 See *Australia's Birthstain*, chapter 3, and *A Cargo of Women*, chapter 3.
5 Robson, *Convict Settlers*, at p. 143; Shaw, *Convicts and the Colonies*, chapter 8, numbers transported at p. 166; and Nicholas (ed.), *Convict Workers*, Table A1, p. 204, puts the total sent to New South Wales at 31.7 per cent.

Chapter 1   Beached

1 Nugent, *Story of Fishing at Wreck Bay*.
2 *Sydney Herald*, 17 December 1835.
3 Sandhurst Collection, <collection@rmasandhurst.mod.uk>.
4 Surgeon's Journal, SRNSW ADM 101/34, Reel 3198.
5 Unpublished letter to *Sydney Herald* dated 12 January 1836, ML Ah45, CY 3576; *Hive indent*, SRNSW X637, Reel 907.
6 Inquiry into wreck of the *Hive*, ML 1267/14, Missing NSW Governor's Despatches, [TRANSCRIPTS], 1836–37, AJCP CO 201/252.1, pp. 1653–6.
7 *Hive indent*, SRNSW X637, Reel 907; *Freeman's Journal*, 23, 25, 26 June 1835.
8 *Inquiry*, p. 1652.
9 Ibid., pp. 1655–6.
10 Family history supplied by descendant James Canney.
11 *Inquiry*, passim.
12 Bateson, *Convict Ships*, pp. 50, 38–57.
13 Unpublished letter, ML Ah45, CY 3576.
14 Information from descendant Ellen Smith.
15 *Inquiry*, passim.
16 *Inquiry*, pp. 1653–4.
17 Unpublished letter, ML Ah45, CY 3576.
18 Berry to Colonial Secretary, 14 December 1835, CSIL 35/10071, in SRNSW 4/2282.2.
19 John Lamb to Colonial Secretary, 14 December 1835; Alexander Berry to Colonial Secretary, 14 December 1835, CSIL 35/10071, SRNSW 4/2282.2.
20 *Inquiry*.
21 Nugent, *Story of Fishing*.
22 John Lamb to Colonial Secretary, 14 December 1835, mentions that Kelly was guided to his farm by an Aborigine, as do some newspaper reports, but the exact circumstances in which the Aboriginal tribe encountered the Europeans are not known. My description is an educated guess.
23 Donoghoe to Colonial Secretary, with Berry to Colonial Secretary, 14 December 1835, CSIL 35/10071 in SRNSW 4/2282.2.
24 Elliott, *History of Erowal Farm*.
25 Bridges, 'Aspects of the career of Alexander Berry'.
26 SRNSW 4/2282.2, CSIL 35/9908 within 35/10071.
27 Berry to Colonial Secretary, 14 December 1835, marked 'Private' with 'official' letter in SRNSW 4/2282.2, CSIL 35/10071.
28 Unpublished letter, ML Ah45, CY3576.
29 *Sydney Herald*, 14 December 1835.
30 *Sydney Herald*, 17 December 1835.
31 *Sydney Herald*, 21 December 1835; Harbour Master to Colonial Secretary, SRNSW 4/2278.
32 Colonial Architect, Mortimer Lewis, to Colonial Secretary, 30 December 1835, SRNSW 4/2529.4, CSIL 35/10382.

33   *Hive* crew muster, with covering letter from Captain McCrea, of HM *Zebra*, SRNSW 4/2326.1 CSIL 36/739.

34   *Sydney Herald,* 7 January 1836.

35   *Sydney Herald,* 25 January 1836.

36   *Inquiry.*

37   Ibid., also Harbour Master to Colonial Secretary, 11 February 1836, SRNSW 4/2319, CSIL 36/1292.

38   Mawer, *Most Perfectly Safe,* p. 110; *Sydney Herald,* 4 April 1836; Nutting's letters, SRNSW 4/2322.4, CSIL 36/2378.

39   Bateson, *The Convict Ships,* pp. 351, 353, 355.

40   *Sydney Herald,* 17 March 1836.

41   Ensign Kelly: TNAUK WO12/3438 17th Regimental Musters and Pay 1835–36; *Hart's Army List 1834–1848–49*; *Order of Battle 1845–46* 2nd Battalion 22nd (Cheshire) Regiment of Foot in Madras; marriage, children and death at <http://archiver.rootsweb.ancestry.com/th/read/KELLY/2009–06/1246360797>; GStove9999@aol.com.

42   Lugard, *Monographs,* ML A923.2–5.

43   Sandhurst Collection.

44   Departed per *Bencoolen* for Madras, *Sydney Herald,* 2 June 1836 and *Calcutta Monthly Journal and General Register,* 1836; Marriage of Edward Lugard to Isabella Mowbray, <http://thepeerage.com/p23767.htm>; L.G. Pine, *The New Extinct Peerage, 1884–1971,* London: Heraldry Today, 1972, p. 185; Birth and death of Eliza Jane Lugard, born 20 May 1838 at Dinapore, died 3 October 1840 at Ghazeepore, *India Office Records* N/1/50 fn.79, N/1/58 f.132; death of Travers Lugard, infant son of Lieutenant Lugard, HM 31st Regiment at Ghazeepore, 22 March 1840, *Colonial Magazine and Maritime Journal,* vol. 2 1841; TNAUK Divorce and Matrimonial Causes Court, Emmeline Elizabeth Lugard v. Edward John Lugard, 1886, File no. J 77/357/784.

45   Clarke, *Convicts of the Port Phillip District,* p. 61; John Black, AOTAS CON 33/71, p. 16620.

Chapter 2   A Capacity for Violence

1   Roy Foster speaking on DVD, *The Story of Ireland,* pp. 153–4.

2   Stewart, *The Narrow Ground,* p. 121.

3   McGrath, 'Riots in Limerick', in *Riotous Assemblies,* pp. 153–74.

4   Female violence was vividly described in depositions for another case where, after a man had been knocked senseless into a ditch, 'Bet Healy broke his nose with a large stone, then she caught him by his legs and turned him on his face in the water' so he drowned. Irish Transportation database, *PPC* I 17 Frame 3712.

5   *Kerry Evening Post,* 25 June 1834, 25 March 1835; *Freeman's Journal,* 27 March 1835; *Limerick Chronicle,* 9 May 1835; *The Fiddlers Companion* at <www.ceolas.org./cgi-bin/ht2/ht2-fc/file=tunes/>; <www.lawlorclan.net/history/history.htm>.

6   Robson, *Convict Settlers,* p. 56.

7   Stewart, *The Narrow Ground,* p. 121.

8   Letter from Lieutenant Wray, Sub-Inspector Maryborough, dated 28 May 1835. Research by descendant Kerrie Fitzpatrick, online at <www.monaropioneers.com/delaney-f.htm>, *Leinster Express,* 30 May, 18 July 1835.

9   *Limerick Chronicle,* 14 March 1835.

10   *Waterford Mail,* 21 March 1835; *Kilkenny Moderator,* 18 July 1835; *Kilkenny Journal,* 18 July 1835.

11   *Cork Constitution,* 2 April 1835.

12   Kiely, *The Connerys.*

13   Ibid., p. 22.

14   Ibid.

15   *Waterford Mail,* 14 March 1835; *Cork Constitution,* 28 July 1835; Kiely, *The Connerys.*

16   Hill, 'Culture and religion', p. 44.

17   Ibid., p. 50.

18 Waugh, *Forgotten Hero,* p. 17, citing Bourke to Spring Rice, 26 August 1826, *Bourke Papers,* ML vol. 9.
19 Waugh, ibid., p. 17.
20 King, 'Sir Richard Bourke'; Foster, *Mitchell,* p. 155.
21 Waugh, *Forgotten Hero,* pp. 18–20.
22 Kinealy, 'Politics and administration', pp. 19–32.
23 Ibid., p. 24.
24 *Kilkenny Journal,* 19 July, 29 July, 1 August 1835; *Kilkenny Moderator,* 29 July 1835.
25 Ullathorne, *The Catholic Mission in Australasia,* p. 15; John West, *The History of Tasmania,* Launceston [1852], 1971 edition, p. 518. Both quotes in Williams, 'Irish convicts and Van Diemen's Land'.
26 Hill, 'Culture and religion', pp. 43–57.
27 Descriptions of Orange processions around Ireland including Monaghan in *Limerick Chronicle,* 17 July, 6 August 1833.
28 'Meeting of the Anti-Tory Association', *Clare Journal,* 11 December 1834.
29 *Morning Post* (London), 18 March 1834; *Limerick Chronicle,* 4 April 1835.
30 Hill, 'Culture and religion', p. 46; Waugh, *Forgotten Hero,* p. 35.
31 McGrath, 'Riots in Limerick', pp. 153–74; *Cork Constitution,* 19 February 1835.
32 *Southern Reporter,* 8 August 1835.
33 Earls, *Plunkett's Legacy,* pp. 20–7.
34 McIntyre database: Petition of Mary Murray, CSORP Box 20 [2610–2750] 1835/2701; *Cork Constitution,* 7, 19 February, 2 April 1835.
35 O'Farrell, *Irish in Australia,* p. 153.
36 Lindsey, 'Elopements were common in Britain . . . [but] they rarely involved feigned abductions and were less frequently brought before the courts.' 'A mistress of her own actions', p. 48.
37 Lindsey, 'Taken', chapter 2: 'Across the centuries'.
38 *Cork Constitution,* 19 March 1835.
39 Williams, 'Irish convicts in Tasmania', p. 24.
40 The information in this paragraph is derived from extensive reading of Irish newspapers, 1825–38; titles are listed in the Bibliography. Lindsey's wider research found that multiple rape by the gang was unusual in the early nineteenth century.
41 *The Erne Packet,* 30 July 1835; *Belfast News,* 27 March 1835.
42 *Waterford Mail,* 21 February 1835.
43 Lindsey, 'Taken', chapter 5: 'A rustic romance', pp. 186–94; Lindsey, 'A mistress of her own actions', fn. 13, p. 50.
44 Lindsey, 'Taken', chapter 2: 'Across the centuries'.
45 Ibid., p. 81.
46 *Limerick Chronicle* extract in *Belfast News,* 21 February 1835.
47 *Limerick Chronicle,* 14 March 1835.
48 *Limerick Chronicle,* 14 March 1835; *Cork Constitution,* 19 March 1835; *Cork Evening Herald,* 30 March 1835; *Clare Journal,* 9 April 1835 plus *The Daltons of Orange* and other information from descendant Larry Adams and City of Orange website, <www.theorangewiki. orange.nsw.gov.au/index.php/James_Dalton>.
49 Lindsey, 'Taken', chapter 2: 'Across the centuries', p. 82.
50 Shaw, *Convicts and the Colonies,* p. 181.
51 Williams, 'Irish convicts in Tasmania', p. 24.
52 Allan, 'Irish convicts: Hampdens or hardened criminals?', pp. 94–118.
53 *Cork Evening Herald,* 3 April 1835.
54 *Connaught Journal,* 14 May 1835.
55 *Hive indent,* SRNSW X637, Reel 907.
56 McVey: *Connaught Journal,* 2 April 1835; Brien: *Cork Constitution,* 11 November 1834; Kavenagh and family: *Kilkenny Moderator,* 18 July 1835, *Kilkenny Journal,* 18 July 1835.

Chapter 3 Settling to the Task

1 'George Barney (1792–1862)', *Australian Dictionary of Biography*, <http://adb.anu.edu.au/biography/barney-george-1744/text1931>.

2 *Newcastle Bench Book*, SRNSW, 28 December 1835, 4/5608. See also 4, 15 August 1837, 4/5608, Reel 2722.

3 Robert Scott, *Journal Describing a Voyage from Hunter River to Sydney in company with Reverend Middleton, Mr Bowman and Mr Dixon*, MLMSS A2266.

4 <www.visitnewcastle.com.au/pages/newcastle>; <www.fairhall.id.au/resources/morpeth/morpeth.htm>; Newcastle Bench Book, SRNSW 4/5608, Reel 2722, CSIL 37/36/4628, 17 December 1837.

5 Robbins, 'Management and resistance', p. 369; also Hirst, *Convict Society*, pp. 35–40; Dyster, 'Public employment and assignment to private masters', pp. 127–51.

6 Causer, '"Only a place fit for angels and eagles"', pp. 204–5.

7 Robbins, 'The lumber yards', p. 150.

8 James Brown's evidence available at <www.une.edu.au/arts/ACF/cf1833>; Edward Parry quoted by Meredith, 'Full circle?', p. 16.

9 Edward Parry to Colonial Secretary, *In the Service of the Company*, Letter no. 84, 1 May 1830.

10 Meredith, 'Full circle?', *passim*.

11 Ibid., p. 15.

12 Kent and Townsend, *Convicts of the Eleanor*, p. 197.

13 Stewart, *Journal*, p. 50.

14 Karskens, 'Defiance, deference and diligence', p. 21.

15 Nicholas, *Convict Workers*, p. 187.

16 Smith, *Australia's Birthstain*, p. 187.

17 Mineral Surveyor to Colonial Secretary, 24 March 1836, SRNSW 4/2316.4, CSIL 36/22.

18 Newcastle Bench Book, December 1836–December 1838, SRNSW 4/5607, Reel 2722.

19 E.J. Lea-Scarlett, 'James Henry Crummer'.

20 Research by descendant Ellen Smith with assistance from Adele McKiernan.

21 Newcastle Bench Book, December 1836–December 1838, SRNSW 4/5607–08, Reel 2722.

22 *Sydney Monitor*, 4 May 1838; *Australian*, 4 May 1838.

23 *Kilkenny Journal*, 18 February 1835; *Cork Evening Herald*, 27 March 1835; Hive indent, SRNSW X637, Reel 907; 1837 Muster; SRNSW 4/2371.1.

24 Convict Mathias Maher in David Andrew Roberts, '"A sort of inland Norfolk Island"?', p. 69.

25 According to missionaries Backhouse and Walker 'the black savage' named Francis was a negro convict not an Aborigine, *The History of the Illawarra and Its Pioneers*, <http://archive.org/stream/cu31924000335707/cu31924000335707_djvu.txt>.

26 CSIL 37/3394; 4/2352, CSIL 37/4293; 4/2416.2, CSIL Police Bathurst 1838; 4/2631, CSIL 43/8781 Monthly Report of Gaol Parramatta; 4/2664.1, CSIL 44/7248 Petition of Margaret Donolon; NSWBDM marriage of Edward Robinson and Margaret Donolon no. 214/vol. 44B.

27 Evidence of Charles Newell, R. v Blackhall, Martin alias Stingaree Jack and Watkins, <http://law.mq.edu.au/research/colonial_case_law/nsw/cases/1838>.

28 H.J.J. Sparks of New Farm, Brisbane, 29 June 1939 to the then Lieutenant Colonel R. Grasebrook, 1st Battalion, The Gloucestershire Regiment, Burma, <http://freepages.history.rootsweb.ancestry.com/~garter1/>.

29 <http://freepages.history.rootsweb.ancestry.com/~garter1/>.

30 Research by descendant Ellen Smith.

31 Smith, *Birthstain*, pp. 119, 124. See also Shaw, *Convicts and the Colonies*, p. 234; *Sydney Morning Herald*, 25 May 1835.

32 *Sydney Herald*, 19 April 1837.

33 *Newcastle Bench Book*, January and October 1838, SRNSW 4/5608, Reel 2722.

34 *Hive indent*, SRNSW X637, Reel 907; 1837 Muster.

35 *Berry Papers*, ML 315, CY2172.
36 *Illawarra Pioneers pre 1920*, p. 141.
37 Ibid., p. 113.
38 *Berry Papers*, ML315.41, CY2172.
39 *Punishments at Illawarra Stockade, 1827–1844*, <www.www.uow.edu.au/~morgan/stockade. htm>.
40 Berry, *Reminiscences*, p. 180.
41 Organ (ed.), *Reminiscences of Illawarra*.
42 1837 Muster; *The Wood Family History Page* at <http://freepages.genealogy.rootsweb.ancestry. com/~bobw/wood.htm>; Rawson, in *Illawarra Pioneers pre 1920*, p. 238: Tried: Dublin City, age 19, Employer: George Wood, SRNSW Fiche 715 p. 206; TL 40/1137 Illawarra; CP 43/1691.
43 Neate, *Paulsgrove*, pp. 18–21.
44 Ibid., pp. 5, 69–70.
45 Ibid., pp. 40–50.

Chapter 4   'The O'Connellite Tail'

1   Waugh, *Forgotten Hero*, p. 46.
2   von Hugel, *New Holland Journal*, p. 214.
3   Waugh, *Forgotten Hero*, pp. 46–8.
4   Newcastle Bench Book, SRNSW 4/5608, Reel 2722.
5   *Sydney Monitor*, 19 October 1831.
6   *Sydney Gazette*, 24 December 1831; *Sydney Herald*, 26 December 1831.
7   von Hugel, p. 214.
8   Smith, *Australia's Birthstain*, p. 210.
9   Actual quote in L. Evans and P. Nicholls (eds), *Convicts and Colonial Society*, p. 64.
10 Walsh, *James Phillips Webber*, pp. 29–30.
11 Waugh, *Forgotten Hero*, p. 59.
12 Ibid., p. 61, citing David L. Waugh, *Three Years Practical Experience of a Settler in New South Wales, 1833–37*, p. 12.
13 Waugh, *Forgotten Hero*, pp. 62–8; *Supplement to the Sydney Monitor*, 21, 31 January, 3 February 1834.
14 Walsh, *James Phillips Webber*, p. 30.
15 Earls, *Plunkett's Legacy*, p. 49.
16 *Sydney Herald*, 13 October 1834.
17 Molony, *Architect of Freedom*, pp. 7–10.
18 Waugh, *Forgotten Hero*, pp. 50, 52.
19 NSWBDM V1841327 130/1841 and V1841119 25C/1841.
20 Earls, *Plunkett's Legacy*, p. 53.
21 Ibid., pp. 52–4.
22 Ibid., p. 43.
23 Molony, *Architect of Freedom*, p. 10.
24 Earls, *Plunkett's Legacy*, pp. 70–1.
25 Ibid., pp. 71–2.
26 Ibid., p. 85.
27 T.L. Suttor, 'John Hubert Plunkett (1802–1869)', *Australian Dictionary of Biography*, <http:// adb.anu.edu.au/biography/plunkett-john-hubert-2556/text3483>.
28 King, 'Sir Richard Bourke'.
29 Earls, *Plunkett's Legacy*, pp. 55–6, 60–1.
30 *Sydney Gazette*, 14 January 1834; *Sydney Herald*, 16 January 1834; Earls, *Plunkett's Legacy*, pp. 63–4.
31 Comerford court-martial, 16 April 1835, *Hive* muster and other papers, SRNSW 2/8263 p. 73, Reel 2422.
32 Comerford colonial crime, trial and execution: Paul R. Mullaly, *Crimes in the Port Phillip*

District, pp. 249–51; *HRV*, vol. 1, pp. 458–74; *Sydney Herald*, 31 May 1838; *Sydney Monitor*, 1 June 1838; *Australian*, 1 June 1838; selected archives, SRNSW 4/2374, CSIL 37/9665; 4/2355.2, CSIL 37/8039.

33 BPP, Crime & Punishment, Transportation 1847–50, vol. VIII, p. 717.
34 Clay, *Maconochie's Experiment*, p. 207.
35 Despite this Supreme Court conviction and a subsequent listing on the *Phoenix* hulk, there is no prisoner named John or Joseph Dignum in Norfolk Island records. It appears he used an alias Hugh Jelling or Jennings on the island, for whom AOTAS CON33/1/71 details match Joseph/John Dignum's activities. Research help from Causer database. See also Privy Council (AJCP PC 1/85), correspondence re 'inaccuracies in the sentence of Joseph Dignum'.
36 *Journal of Ensign Best*, pp. 201–3.
37 AOTAS CON 33/1/71.

Chapter 5   A Question of Fairness

1   Police, Newcastle, SRNSW 4/2251.4, CSIL 1834.
2   Dyster, 'Public employment and assignment to private masters', p. 139.
3   Ibid., p. 175.
4   Walsh, *Voices from Tocal*, p. 69.
5   Atkinson, 'Four patterns of convict protest', p. 77.
6   Smith, *Australia's Birthstain*, p. 164.
7   Berry, *Reminiscences*, p. 172.
8   Roberts, *The Forgotten Commandant*; Blair, 'The revolt at Castle Forbes'.
9   King, 'Sir Richard Bourke'.
10 Ibid.
11 See, e.g., Jack Sullivan, *Charles Boydell 1808–1869 and Camyr Allyn, Gresford*, Paterson, NSW: Paterson Historical Society, 1999, pp. 50–1; Walsh, *James Phillips Webber*, chapter 3, pp. 23–5.
12 SRNSW 4/2458.1, Reel 2218, Miscellaneous 'S', 1839–1840.
13 Arthur Way to his brother Benjamin, 11, 24 September 1842, ML Aw120.
14 I have been an Official Visitor to NSW prisons for more than a decade.
15 Atkinson, 'Four patterns of convict protest', p. 67; Ihde, 'Monitoring the situation', p. 24.
16 James Roe, 'Letter from a Convict in Australia to his brother in England', *Cornhill Magazine*, vol. XIII, no. 76.
17 Dyster, 'Public employment and assignment to private masters', pp. 128–34.
18 Berry, *Reminiscences*, p. 180. For the history of convict wages see Dyster, 'Public employment and assignment to private masters', pp. 127–51.
19 Macqueen, *Frederick D'Arcy*, p. 25.
20 R.J. Hibberd, 'The convict origins of the trade union movement', PhD thesis, 2009, <www.eurekacouncil.com.au/5-Australia-History/History-Pages/1791-convict-origin-trade-union-movement.htm>.
21 SRNSW, 4/2399.2, CSIL 38/6400 enclosed in 38/4952, Petition of John Davis relating to evidence given in Supreme Court 1838: R. v Daniel Maloney and Reid, <www.law.mq.edu.au/scnsw/Cases1838–39/html/r_v_maloney_and_reid_1838.htm>.
22 Harris, *Emigrant Mechanic*, p. 231.
23 Atkinson, 'Four patterns of convict protest', p. 68.
24 Neate, *Paulsgrove*, pp. 63–4.
25 Walsh, *Voices from Tocal*, p. 62.
26 Evidence of John Macarthur in Ritchie (ed.), *Evidence to the Bigge Reports*, vol. 2, p. 79.
27 Cash, *The Uncensored Story*, p. 12.
28 Andrews (ed.), *Stapylton*, p. 132.
29 *Free Settler or Felon?*
30 *Limerick Chronicle*, 9 May 1835; *Limerick Chronicle*, 2 July 1834; *Kerry Evening Post*, 25 March 1835; *Cork Constitution*, 31 July 1835; *Freeman's Journal*, 27 March 1835; *Clare Journal*, 18 March 1835.

31 Maurice Leehy, born Maitland 1858, died as Morris Leehy at West Maitland 1874, son of Thomas and Mary Leehy, NSWBDM 5770/1874 and Index of Births 1858.

32 *Hive indent*, NSWBDM; Reid, *Farewell My Children*, pp. 37–9.

33 *Free Settler or Felon?*

34 Tickets-of-leave 44/241 and 253; Conditional Pardons 49/1190 and 44/1191.

35 Michael Ryan, death NSWBDM 1859/004000; Philip Ryan, death, NSWBDM 1864/004875; *Maitland Mercury*, 13 October 1864; research assistance from Brian Andrews, Sir Edgeworth David Memorial Museum, is gratefully acknowledged.

36 *Kilkenny Moderator*, 18 July 1835; *Kilkenny Journal*, 18 July 1835; *Waterford Mail*, 21 March 1835.

37 *Thomas Harrison* 1836, SRNSW X638–39, Reel 908; *Hive indent*, SRNSW X637, Reel 907.

38 1837 Muster.

39 'List of runaways apprehended last week', *Sydney Monitor*, 26 December 1836.

40 CSIL Miscellaneous 'B' 1838, SRNSW 4/2387.1, Reel 2211.

41 *Maitland Mercury*, 14 January 1846.

42 CSIL 46/2669 1846, SRNSW.

43 *Free Settler or Felon?*

44 Finger, *Ludwig Leichhardt*, p. 63.

45 William Panton, papers in the author's possession.

46 James Webber in Walsh, *Voices from Tocal*, pp. 19–21.

47 Walsh, *Voices from Tocal*.

48 *Hive indent*, SRNSW X637, Reel 907; Marriage James Liddy to Mary A. Wall in Melbourne, NSWBDM V18411090 91/1841.

49 *The Australian*, 21 March 1834, in Walsh, *Voices from Tocal*, p. 40.

50 Walsh, *Voices from Tocal*, pp. 38–9.

51 Ibid., p. 54.

52 Ibid., pp. 71, 120.

53 Research by Brian Walsh online at <www.tocal.com/homestead/vandv/convictpdfs/liddy>: Ticket-of-Leave 40/1669, SRNSW 4/4142 Reel 937 and Certificate of Freedom 42/1250, SRNSW 4/4375 Reel 1011; Cancellation of ticket CSIL 41/7378, Police, Maitland, SRNSW 4/2585.9; Restored ticket, Engineers 1842, SR NSW 4/2571.2, CSIL 42/1828.

54 Walsh, *Voices from Tocal*, p. 8.

55 Walsh and Archer, *Maitland on the Hunter*, p. 48; <http://archiver.rootsweb.ancestry.com/th/read/AUS-NSW-Hunter-Valley/1999-12/0945426611>; Nancy Edge, <nancedge@ozemail.com.au>.

56 Brown and Threlfo, *The First Fatal Election*, pp. 1–2, 13.

57 Brown and Threlfo, *The First Fatal Election*, chapters 5 and 6.

58 Ibid.

Chapter 6   Unnecessary Irritation

1 Isaac Shepherd to Colonial Secretary, 22 October 1839, SRNSW 4/438.1, Reel 2218.

2 Assignment in 1837 Muster; NSW flogging in Norfolk Island record, AOTAS CON 37/1/4.

3 *Sydney Herald*, 6 May 1840; AOTAS CON 37/1/4.

4 Peter Hammond found an almost 50–50 split between Catholic and Protestant convicts' involvement in violence in the Hunter Valley. Youth was a significant factor, but Hammond writes: 'there is no reason to believe that, for example, Catholics, Irish or those on life sentences were more prone to violent behaviour than any other national or religious group'. He concluded that 'factors which led convicts to kill are likely to be found within the convict system rather than in their upbringing or collective nature'. Hammond, 'Murder, Manslaughter and Workplace Relations', p. 14.

5 Smith, *A Cargo of Women*, p. 75.

6 Causer, '"Only a Place Fit for Angels and Eagles"', pp. 77–8.

7 Rosen, *Men at Work*, p. 206.

8   Harris, *Emigrant Mechanic*, p. 69; Gilchrist, "'The relic of the city of the plain'", p. 5; Moore, 'Colonial Manhood and Masculinities'.

9   James Backhouse, *A Narrative of a Visit to the Australian Colonies*, London: Hamilton, Adams and Co., 1843, p. 263.

10 Return of Corporal Punishments, Parramatta 1–30 September 1833, p. 404; BPP, Crime & Punishment, Transportation 1810–41, Vol. VI, pp. 315–550; Alfred Shanton in Waugh, *Forgotten Hero*, p. 60.

11 Hartley, *John Herring Boughton*, p. 11; also Gent, *Gostwyck*, pp. 13, 69.

12 *Australian*, 21 July, 11 August 1825; Morrison, *Aaron Price*, pp. 7–18.

13 Gent, *Gostwyck*, p. 16.

14 *Australian*, 5, 27 February 1838; *Sydney Herald*, 5 February 1838; *Sydney Gazette*, 22 February 1838; *Sydney Monitor*, 16 February 1838.

15 Walsh, *Voices from Tocal*, p. 86.

16 *Sydney Gazette*, 22 February 1838.

17 Val Anderson, *The Dorothy Mackellar 'My Country' Paterson Valley Connection*, Paterson, NSW: Paterson Historical Society, p. 7; *Free Setter or Felon?*; R. v. Ryan, Steel, McGrath and Daley, [1832] NSWSupC 95, <www.law.mq.edu.au/researcg/colonial_case_law/nsw/>.

18 Walsh, *Voices from Tocal*, pp. 51–2.

19 von Hugel, *New Holland Journal*, p. 379.

20 Smith, *Australia's Birthstain*, pp. 187–92.

21 Hammond, 'Murder, manslaughter and workplace relations'.

22 Blair, 'The revolt at Castle Forbes'.

23 Organ, History of the Illawarra and Its Pioneers, pp. 17–18.

24 <www.ryde.nsw.gov.au/About+Ryde/Historic+Ryde/Historic+Buildings/ Addington>; 1814 Muster.

25 *Extracts from the Letters of James Backhouse: Now Engaged in a religious visit to Van Diemen's Land and New South Wales, accompanied by George Washington Walker*, first Part, 3rd ed., London: Harvey & Darton, 1838, p. 66.

26 Jane de Falbe, *My Dear Miss Macarthur: The recollections of Emmeline Macarthur, 1828–1911*, Kenthurst, NSW: Kangaroo Press, 1988, p. 20.

27 von Hugel, *New Holland Journal*, p. 378.

28 Macarthur quote in Evans and Nicholls, *Convicts and Colonial Society*, p. 201.

29 G.H. Swinburne, *A Source Book of Australian History*, 1919, p. 50, cited in Waugh, *Forgotten Hero*, p. 50.

30 Wilson, *Murray of Yarralumla*, chapter 4.

31 L.G. Young, *New South Wales under the Administration of Governor Bourke*, cited in Waugh, *Forgotten Hero*, p. 86.

32 Hartley, *John Herring Boughton*, pp. 12, 17.

33 Neate, *Paulsgrove*, pp. 73–4.

34 Whitaker, *Unfinished Revolution*, p. v.

35 Coulthard-Clark, *Where Australians Fought*, pp. 6–8; Barker, *A History of Bathurst*, pp. 80–5; Suttor's background, Silver, *Battle of Vinegar Hill*, p. 83; Byrne, *Criminal Law and the Colonial Subject*, pp. 138, 139; *Sydney Gazette*, 21 October 1830.

36 BPP, House of Commons, Crime and Punishment, vol. XLVII, 1834; Judy Kenny, *A Footprint on the Sands of Time: Francis Benedict Kenny, 1854–1925*, self-published, 2007.

37 *Sydney Herald*, 11 February 1833; *Sydney Gazette*, 9 February 1833.

38 Harry F. Boyle, *George Boyle White*.

39 Waugh, *Forgotten Hero*, p. 62; Blair, 'The revolt at Castle Forbes', pp. 89–107; Evidence at the inquiry published in *Sydney Monitor*, 21, 28, 31 January, 3, 4, 7 February 1834; Trial *R. v Hitchcock and others [1833]*, Colonial Cases, Macquarie Law School.

40 James Mudie, *Felonry of New South Wales*, pp. 114–15, in Evans and Nicholls, *Convicts and Colonial Society*, p. 167.

41 Blair, 'The revolt at Castle Forbes', p. 99.

42 Charles Darwin, *An Australian Selection*, p. 69.

43 Roe, 'Letter from a Convict in Australia to his brother in England', *Cornhill Magazine*, vol. XIII, no. 76.

Chapter 7 The Power of Numbers

1 Neate, *Paulsgrove*, p. 73.
2 James Mudie, *Felonry of New South Wales*, in Evans and Nicholls, *Convicts and Colonial Society*, p. 167.
3 Dyster, 'Public employment and assignment to private masters, 1788–1821', pp. 127–51.
4 Smith, *Australia's Birthstain*, p. 191.
5 Serle, *The Golden Age*, p. 76.
6 James Macarthur in Kent and Townsend, *Convicts of the Eleanor*, p. 196; Berry, *Reminiscences*, p. 180.
7 First ships with information about age, trade and description were: Male convicts: *Fortune*, July 1813 from England, and *Three Bees*, May 1814 from Ireland. Female convicts: first ships with age and trade but no description: *Wanstead* from England January 1814 and *Catherine* from Ireland, May 1814. Information from ships' indents in *Names of Convicts Arriving in Australia*, James McClelland Research, PO Box 153, Gunnedah NSW 2380.
8 Nicholas (ed.), *Convict Workers*, pp. 19–20.
9 Neate, *Paulsgrove*, pp. 6, 74; Lack of information about the convicts' crimes continued until the end of the NSW penal colony. For example, records for Collaroy station at ML contain a small grey booklet titled 'List of Government Men'. It appears to be the original document supplied to the employer by the superintendent of convicts, in this case c. 1839–40. Each convict is allocated a page containing information from the ship's indent with space for further comments. Name, trial, sentence, trade, physical description and age are given but there is no mention of their crime.
10 Roberts, '"A sort of inland Norfolk Island"?', p. 50.
11 Johnson, *Percy Simpson*.
12 Ibid., pp. 21–2; Roberts, cites research done into acceptance of flogging by sailors in the Royal Navy, N.A.M. Rodger, *The Wooden World: An anatomy of the Georgian Navy*, London 1986, pp. 205–52; Johnson, *Percy Simpson*.
13 Roberts, 'A sort of Inland Norfolk Island"?', fn. 26, p. 58.
14 *Letters of John Maxwell*, pp. 20, 36–7.
15 Roberts, '"A sort of inland Norfolk Island"?', p. 58.
16 Ibid., pp. 58, 60.
17 Ibid., p. 59.
18 Ibid.
19 Andrews (ed.), *Stapylton's Journal*, pp. 91–2, 213, 219, 245–6.
20 Ibid., p. 92.
21 Ibid., pp. 203, 255.
22 Ibid., pp. 188–9.
23 Ibid., p. 219.
24 Ibid., p. 200.
25 Ibid., p. 179.
26 William C. Foster, *Sir Thomas Mitchell*, p. 300.
27 Daniel Farrell, born Kingston near Dublin, military career 60th Rifles, then 8th Regiment. A member of the St Helena Regiment and stationed there when court-martialled for striking his sergeant. Sentenced to life transportation to Van Diemen's Land. Convicted Hobart for housebreaking 1850, sentenced to Norfolk Island. AOTAS CON.37/1//2/555 and CON.37/1/6//1989.
28 Smith, 'The handover', pp. 245–60.
29 Ibid., pp. 245–60.
30 Hindmarsh and Maxwell-Stewart, '"This is the bird that never flew"'.
31 Hirst, *Convict Society*, pp. 28–9.
32 Robbins, 'The lumber yards', p. 159.

33   Karskens, 'Defiance, deference and diligence', p. 19.
34   Ibid., p. 18.
35   The same was true on private estates. Brian Walsh, for example, found 'the tasks allocated to *Tocal*'s convict were determined far more by the level of diligence, trust and adaptability they were prepared to demonstrate than by the skills they possessed on arrival in the colony': *Voices from Tocal*, p. 55.
36   Karskens, 'Defiance, deference and diligence', p. 18.
37   Ibid., p. 18, for Darling's comments citing *HRA*, series 1, vol. 14, p. 69, 22 regarding the gangs.
38   Ibid., p. 26.
39   Ibid., p. 26.
40   James, *A Branch of the Family*, pp. 4–6.
41   Ibid.
42   <www.patersonriver.com.au/people/clarkerm.htm>.
43   Walsh, *Voices from Tocal*, pp. 21, 54, 120.
44   Neate, *Paulsgrove*, p. 73, citing Letter of John Fitzgerald, SRNSW, T25 27/88, Supreme Court, *R. v John Hutton*.
45   Robert Pringle Stuart to Controller General, Van Diemen's Land, 20 June 1846, *Norfolk Island: The Botany Bay of Botany Bay*, p. 69.
46   *Cork Evening Herald*, 3 April 1835.
47   SRNSW 4/5662, Reel 680, Patrick's Plains Bench Book, 17 October 1839.
48   SRNSW 4/2532.2, Reel 2246; for James Bowman, see Dyster, *Servants and Masters*; also <www.jenwilletts.com/james_bowman.htm>.
49   SRNSW, 4/2532.2, Reel 2246; for Percy Simpson, see Johnson, 'Percy Simpson', also *Convict Trail, Caring for the Great North Road*, <www.convicttrail.org./history>.
50   SRNSW 4/2532,2, Reel 2246.
51   Ibid.
52   Ibid.
53   Atkinson, 'Four patterns of convict protest'.
54   Anthony Albanese, 13 October 2013, quoting Don Corleone in the film *The Godfather III*.

Chapter 8   Floating Nurseries

1   Copy of the note supplied by James Canney, descendant of Edward Canney.
2   *Australian*, 22 June 1837.
3   Research by descendant James Canney, TNAUK BT/ 98/188.
4   Ibid., TNAUK BT/.
5   Ibid.
6   NSWBDM 1376/ 21, 10 June 1837; 1828 Census for details of Richard Siddons.
7   McIntyre, *Free Passage*, pp. xxi, 36.
8   Ibid., p. xxiv.
9   Indent and Muster papers, *Margaret 1837*, SRNSW X640, Reel 908, 2/8268 p, 29, Reel 2424.
10   *Margaret 1837*: Indent and Muster papers, *Margaret 1839*, SRNSW X642, Reel 908, 2/8268 p. 255, Reel 2424.
11   Surgeon Kelsall's journal, AJCP ADM 101/PRO Reel 3202.
12   *Margaret 1837*.
13   Kelsall's journal.
14   Kelsall's journal; *Margaret 1837*.
15   Surgeon Moxey's journal, AJCP ADM 101/PRO Reel 3202; *Margaret 1839*; a descendant online at <www.users.on.net/~ahvem/page3/page11/page60/page64/page64>.
16   Neate, *Paulsgrove*, p. 197.
17   *Empire*, 15 September 1856.
18   McIntyre, *Free Passage*, pp. 49–50.
19   von Hugel, *New Holland Journal*, pp. 299–300.
20   Rushen and McIntyre, *The Merchant's Women*, pp. 8–9.

21 McIntyre, *Free Passage*, p. 50.
22 Rushen and McIntyre, *The Merchant's Women*, pp. 80–1.
23 McIntyre, *Free Passage*, p. 46.
24 Edward Parry to William Ogilvie, 26 July 1831, Letter no. 461, p. 314.
25 McIntyre, *Free Passage*, p. 74.
26 McIntyre database: NSWBDM various children born and died to Lawrence Crotty and Mary at Maitland; TL.40/447 for Maitland district, SRNSW 4/4137, Reel 935.
27 McIntyre database.
28 McIntyre, *Free Passage*, p. 50.
29 Ibid., pp. 54–5.
30 1837 Muster; *The Daltons of Orange*, privately published, pp. 11, 12, copy supplied by Dalton descendant Larry Adams.
31 McIntyre database: SRNSW 4/2762.1 CSIL 47/6817 in 47/8453, 4/4819, 4/2886, CSIL 50/1098, AJCP Reel 987, CO 201/384, 201/386/154, 201/426; *The Daltons of Orange*.
32 *The Daltons of Orange*.
33 <http://en.wikipedia.org./wiki/James_Dalton_(Orange,_Australia)>.
34 SRNSW 4/2421, CSIL 38/2860.
35 Death of Anastasia Cotter, NSWBDM V1839216 132/1839; trial *Cork Constitution*, 31 March 1835; *Limerick Times*, 2 April 1835.
36 Madgwick, *Immigration*; Coghlan, *The Wealth and Progress of New South Wales*; McIntyre, *Free Passage*; Rushen, *Single and Free*; Rushen and McIntyre, *The Merchant's Women*; Reid, *Farewell My Children*.
37 *Margaret 1840*: SRNSW X642A, Reel 2662, 2/8268 p. 305; Surgeon's journal AJCP ADM 101, Reel 3202.

Chapter 9   Managing Norfolk Island

1   Taylor (ed.), *Journal of Ensign Best*, pp. 180–1.
2   Frost, *Botany Bay*, pp. 224–5.
3   Smith, *Australia's Birthstain*; Causer, 'Anti-transportation'; Reid, *Gender, Crime and Empire*.
4   Causer, '"Only a place fit for angels and eagles"'.
5   Britts, *The Commandants* (list with dates on contents page).
6   Anderson, *Recollections*, pp. 145–8.
7   Clune, *The Norfolk Island Story*, quoting Chaplain Atkins, pp. 151–2.
8   Ibid., p. 154.
9   Hirst, *Convict Society*, p. 48; Causer, "Only a place fit for angels and eagles", pp. 199–200.
10 Aaron Price diary, DLMLMSQ 247–9; Morrison, *Aaron Price*, p. 23; Taylor (ed.), *Journal of Ensign Best*.
11 Taylor (ed.), *Journal of Ensign Best*; Aaron Price diary, DLMLMSQ 247–9.
12 *Hive indent*, SRNSW X637, Reel 907; AOTAS CON 33/1/55, Image 223; SRNSW 4/2567.2, CSIL 42/9588, Reel 2250.
13 Walsh, *Voices from Tocal*, p. 97, citing SRNSW, *Maitland Quarter Sessions*, 4/8409, pp. 111–17, Reel 2407.
14 SRNSW 4/2567.2, Reel 2250, CSIL 42/9588, 25 December 1842.
15 Darby McAuliffe: AOTAS CON 33–1-55, Image 223.
16 Causer, "Only a place fit for angels and eagles", p. 151.
17 Ibid., p. 140.
18 Ibid., p. 149.
19 Ibid., p. 151.
20 Ibid., p. 341.
21 Ibid., p. 149.
22 Ibid., pp. 150–1.
23 Ibid., p. 165.
24 Cash, *The Uncensored Story*, pp. 146–7.
25 Causer, '"Only a place fit for angels and eagles"', pp. 160–2, 171–3, 238–48.

26 Stewart, *Journal*, p. 103.
27 Cash, *The Uncensored Story*, p. 146.
28 Stuart, 'Report to controller general', in *Norfolk Island: The Botany Bay of Botany Bay*, pp. 49, 51.
29 Cash, *The Uncensored Story*, p. 144.
30 Causer, '"Only a place fit for angels and eagles"', pp. 157–62.
31 Taylor (ed.), *Journal of Ensign Best*, pp. 403–4.
32 Causer, '"The worst types of sub-human beings"?', p. 10.
33 Causer, '"Only a place fit for angels and eagles"', pp. 57–60
34 Causer, '"The worst types of sub-human beings"?', pp. 12, 24.
35 *Norfolk Island: The Botany Bay of Botany Bay*, p. 18.
36 Causer, '"The worst types of sub-human beings"?', p. 12.
37 Ibid., pp. 8–31.
38 *Aaron Price Diary*, ML/DLMSQ 247–9; Causer, '"Only a place fit for angels and eagles"', pp. 159–64, chapters 4 and 4 *passim*.
39 Clay, *Maconochie's Experiment*, p. 231.
40 For an example of the obligation between shipmates see *Sydney Gazette*, 11 February 1834, report of the trial of Cavenagh, Serjeant and Chesterfield.
41 Anderson, *Recollections*, pp. 174–8; Nan Smith, *Convict Kingston*, self-published, 1997, pp. 72–3.
42 Causer, '"Only a place fit for angels and eagles"', pp. 206–7; Francis White petition: SRNSW 4/2288, CSIL 35/6074 and 35/9030.
43 SRNSW 4/2288, CSIL 35/6074, 35/9030.
44 Smith, 'The handover', p. 259.
45 Clune, *The Norfolk Island Story*, p. 295.
46 Causer, '"Only a place fit for angels and eagles"', pp. 159–64, plus chapter 4 *passim*.
47 Causer, '"Only a place fit for angels and eagles"', p. 219.
48 Taskwork, in *Aaron Price Diary*, DLMLMSQ 247–9; Causer, '"Only a place fit for angels and eagles"', p. 219.
49 Causer, '"Only a place fit for angels and eagles"', p. 219.
50 Ibid., p. 211.
51 Ibid., p. 211.
52 Ibid., p. 212.
53 Information from Tim Causer. Source: *Memoirs of Major Bunbury*, vol. 2, pp. 298–9.
54 Britts, *The Commandants*, p. 119.
55 Nan Smith, *Convict Kingston*, self-published, 1997, p. 27.
56 Ibid., p. 33, citing Bunbury, *Memoirs*, vol. 2, p. 295.
57 Ibid., p. 34, citing Stewart, *Journal*.
58 Britts, *The Commandants*, pp. 120–1.

Chapter 10   Resisting Ascendancy

1 Kiely, *The Connerys*, p. 22.
2 Ibid., p. 78.
3 Ibid., p. 80.
4 Ibid., pp. 71–2.
5 Ibid., pp. 72–3, citing *Raby Papers Correspondence and Accounts, 1832–1836*, ML MS A146.
6 Kiely, *The Connerys*, p. 74, citing statement by W. Kilpatrick, superintendent at *Cavan*, 1 September 1837, SRNSW CSIL 8604/1837, 4/2507.2.
7 Kiely, *The Connerys*, p. 75.
8 SRNSW 4/4270, Reel 977, TL passport 48/0568 replacing TL 44/0886.
9 Earnshaw, 'The lame, the blind, the mad, the malingers', pp. 25–38.
10 Kiely, *The Connerys*, p. 82.
11 Ibid., p. 86.
12 Ibid., pp. 87–8.

13 Ibid., p. 96.
14 Ibid., pp. 99–100.
15 SRNSW 4/2529.4, Mortimer Lewis, CSIL 35/10382 contains details of all five.
16 Ibid.; James Hogan and Martin McInerheny, convicted of sheep stealing at Ennis Assizes, County Clare, *Roscommon Journal*, 20 March 1835.
17 Information supplied by descendant Linda Combe.
18 Ibid.
19 Ibid.
20 Ibid. Linda Combe is the great-grand-daughter of Mary Ann Walsh.
21 *Hive indent*, SRNSW X637, Reel 907; Mortimer Lewis letter; NSWBDM 1869/005580; <www.jenwilletts.com>.
22 Hawkins, *The Convict Timbergetters*, pp. 54–5; Ritchie (ed.), *The Evidence to the Bigge Reports*, vol. 1, pp. 34–5, 78.
23 Ullathorne, *Autobiography*, p. 112; Therry, *Reminiscences*, p. 150.
24 SRNSW 4/2305.3, Reel 731.
25 SRNSW 4/2310, CSOL 36/974.
26 SRNSW 4/2374, CSIL 37/2907.
27 *Hive indent*, SRNSW X637, Reel 907; SRNSW 4/2305.3, Reel 731; SRNSW 4/22310, CSIL 36/974; *Roslin Castle indent* 1836, SRNSW, X638–39, Reel 908; SRNSW 4/4373, Reel 1011, CF 42/658.
28 SRNSW 4/4371, Reel 1010, CF 42/257; Death of Patrick Brien, NSWBDM 1868/5843 20 June 1868; marriage of Daniel Brien to Catherine Kelly, SRNSW 4/3508, Reel 6010, NSWBDM V18444125 146/1844.
29 Therry, *Reminiscences*, pp. 148–9.
30 Earls, *Plunkett's Legacy*, pp. 74–8; Waugh, *Forgotten Hero*, pp. 74–81.
31 Therry, *Reminiscences*, pp. 151–2; Earls, *Plunkett's Legacy*, p. 84.
32 Kaye, 'Broughton and the demise of the royal supremacy', p. 51.
33 Polding, May 1856, *Letters*, vol. 1, p. 59.
34 Earls, *Plunkett's Legacy*, pp. 78–81; Waugh, *Forgotten Hero*, pp. 83–6.
35 See, for example, report of debate in the NSW Legislative Council about funding for Jews, *Sydney Morning Herald*, 23 August and 4 October 1854.
36 Earls, *Plunkett's Legacy*, pp. 78–81; Waugh, *Forgotten Hero*, pp. 83–6.
37 *Maitland Mercury*, 7 January 1846.
38 NSWBDM 1876/7559.
39 *Maitland Mercury*, 7 June 1845.
40 *New South Wales Directory 1839*; *Maitland Mercury*, 17, 24, 31 May, 7 June 1845.
41 *Maitland Mercury*, 4 March 1846.

Chapter 11 Catholic Friendly

1 Waugh, *Forgotten Hero*, pp. 21–2.
2 Earls, *Plunkett's Legacy*, p. 206.
3 Therry, *Reminiscences*, pp. 156–7.
4 Waugh, *Forgotten Hero*, p. 87.
5 Ibid., p. 91. Also Foster, 'Education in New South Wales', pp. 255–80.
6 von Hugel, *New Holland Journal*, p. 409.
7 *The History of the Illawarra and its Pioneers*, <http://archive.org/stream/cu31924000335707/cu31924000335707_djvu.txt>.
8 Waugh, *Forgotten Hero*, p. 132.
9 Organ (ed.), *Reminiscences of Illawarra*, pp. 19, 31.
10 Applications to marry, Patrick Ready (*sic*) age 35 per *Hive* (2), Life, Bond, to Catherine Daley, age 29, per *Margaret* (2), Bond 1840, Reverend Rigney, Wollongong, SRNSW 4/1789, Reel 6004; TL 44/318, SRNSW 4/4185, Reel 951; CP SRNSW 4/4480, Reel 798 p.102; NSWBDM 1855, vol. 121A.
11 Neate, *Paulsgrove*, p. 42.

12 Ibid., pp. 44–5.
13 Organ (ed.), *Reminiscences of Illawarra*, p. 45.
14 Organ (ed.), *Franklin Diary*, p. 12.
15 Ibid., p. 20.
16 Ibid., pp. 19, 20; Craig and Proctor, *A History of Australian Schooling*, p. 40.
17 1837 Muster.
18 *Limerick Chronicle*, 4 April 1835.
19 McIntyre database.
20 Reid, *Farewell My Children*, p. 214.
21 Ibid., pp. 214–15.
22 O'Farrell, *Irish in Australia*, pp. 100–2.
23 Organ (ed.), *Reminiscences of Illawarra*.
24 Walsh and Archer, *Maitland on the Hunter*, p. 48; <http://archiver.rootsweb.ancestry.com/th/read/AUS-NSW-Hunter-Valley/1999-12/0945426611>; Nancy Edge, <nancedge@ozemail.com.au>; Catherine Anne Wilson, *Tenants in Time: Family strategies, land and liberalism in Upper Canada 1799–1871*, 2009, <www.mqup.ca/tenants-in-time-products-9780773535237.php#sthash.Kze3Yn5p.dpuf>.
25 *Early Land Settlement on the Illawarra, 1804–1861*, p. 54.
26 T.M. Perry, 'James Meehan'; Whitaker, 'James Meehan'.
27 Whitaker, *Appin*, p. 16.
28 Campbell, *Kingdom of the Ryans*, *passim*; Garnsey, *Ryansvale*, p. 174.
29 Waugh, *Forgotten Hero*, pp. 106–7; King, 'Richard Bourke'.
30 *Limerick Chronicle*, 4 April 1835.
31 Earnshaw, 'The lame, the blind, the mad, the malingerers', pp. 25–38.
32 SRNSW 4/2494.1, CSIL Misc. B 1840, Reel 2219; Daniel: TL 40/1253 and CF 44/410; Patrick: TL 41/385 and CF 42/2146. Death of the second Daniel noted on the *Hive indent*, SRNSW X637, Reel 907.
33 John Smith: CF 42/0618 dated 22 April, 1842; Michael Smith: CF 42/0651 dated 30 April 1842; both in SRNSW 4/4373, Reel 1011.
34 Amargh Assize, *Belfast News*, 27 March 1835.
35 McIntyre database, plus research by descendants Anne Rodger and Ron Dunbar. SRNSW Immigration Records 4/4960, Reel 2474 and 4/4793, Reel 2138. See also website: <www.macfamilytree.com/Anne%20M%20M%Rodger/Barry%20and%20Anne's%20Femaily%20Tree/persons.html>, consulted 30 October 2011.
36 *Maneroo Mercury*, 14 October 1874.
37 McIntyre database: SRNSW CSIL 47/7446, 19 October 1847, Application for Wife and Family, SRNSW 4.2762, CSIL 47/9040, AJCP Reel 987, CO386/154.
38 Wilson, *Murray of Yarralumla*; also Gwendoline Wilson, <http://adb.anu.edu.au/biography/murray-sir-terence-aubrey-2498>.
39 George Byrne or Burns, *Hive indent*, SRNSW X637, Reel 907; Matthew Berry, *NSWGG*, 16 January and 15 August 1838.
40 Extract from Hepburn's diary in Roslyn Maddrell, *Braidwood and District Post Office and People*, 1995, p. 24.
41 See Lucille M. Quinlan, *Here My Home: The life and times of John Stuart Hepburn 1830–1860, master mariner, overlander, founder of Seaton Hill, Victoria*, Melbourne: Oxford University Press, 1967, p. 61. Research by Christine Wright.
42 Bartholomew Williams: Research by Christine Wright; Quinlan, *Here My Home*, p. 61; references for Williams and White in Melbourne in Clarke, *Convicts of Port Phillip District*, p. 61.
43 Waugh, *Forgotten Hero*, pp. 108–9.
44 Ibid., pp. 108–9.
45 Foster, *Sir Thomas Mitchell*, pp. 180–1, 274–6.
46 Ibid., pp. 179–86, 274–6.
47 Waugh, *Forgotten Hero*, pp. 134, 135, 137.
48 Earls, *Plunkett's Legacy*, pp. 148–51.

49 Ibid., pp. 111–17.
50 Ibid., pp. 117–19.
51 Ibid., p. 120.
52 Ibid., p. 132.
53 Darwin, *An Australian Selection*, p. 60.
54 *Australian*, 30 January 1837.
55 *Sydney Gazette*, 7 December 1837.

Chapter 12 A New Governor

1   McCulloch, 'Sir George Gipps'.
2   *Sligo Journal*, 20 March 1835; Hive indent, SRNSW X637, Reel 907.
3   Burrowes crime; Hive indent, SRNSW X637, Reel 907; *The Push*, no. 20, April 1985.
4   *Norfolk indent*, 1829, SRNSW 4/4014, Reel 398.
5   Townsend, 'Masters and Men and the Myall Creek Massacre', *The Push*, no. 20, p. 22.
6   Telfer, *The Wallabadah Manuscript*, p. 29.
7   Ward, *The Australian Legend*, p. 1.
8   Reynolds, *Racial Thought*, p. 53.
9   Ward, 'The Australian Legend re-visited', p. 179.
10 Kociumbas, '"Mary Ann", Joseph Fleming and "Gentleman Dick"'.
11 Townsend, 'Masters and Men', p. 25.
12 Andrew Burrowes depositions, 30 July, 14 August 1838, in *Push from the Bush*, pp. 74–7.
13 Burrowes deposition ibid.; Brenda Wilson, 'Edward Denny Day's investigations at Myall Creek', *Push from the Bush*, pp. 35–57.
14 SRNSW Sheriff to Colonial Secretary re transfer of prisoners to Goat Island, 4/2396, CSIL 38/13067, letter missing from box but details revealed in Register of Letters received; SRNSW Register of Coroner's Inquests, 1796–1942, no. 1885, Singleton, 18 August 1842: 'Andrew Burrowes, by P. Simpson, PM, 23rd August 1842. "Sudden death"'; *Singleton Bench Book*, SRNSW 4/5660, Reel 2738, 'Inquiry re Andrew Burrowes, Hive assigned servant to Henry Dangar, inquiry held on 15 August 1842 into his death the night before'.
15 Earls, *Plunkett's Legacy*, pp. 93–102; Atkinson and Aveling, *Australians 1838*, p. 392; *Colonist*, 5 December 1838; <http://law.mq.edu.au/research/colonial_case_law/nsw/cases/case_index> for all Myall Creek trials.
16 Gipps to Marquess of Normanby, 23 November 1839, *HRA*, series I, vol. 20, pp. 400–1.
17 Ibid.
18 Lugard, *Monograph*.
19 Ibid.
20 *Sydney Monitor*, 23 March 1840.
21 *Sydney Herald*, 20 March 1840; *Sydney Monitor*, 23 March 1840; advertisement by Mr Blanch in *The Australian*, 11, 14 April 1840.
22 *Australian*, 21 March 1840.
23 Atkinson and Aveling, *Australians 1838*, p. 11.
24 *Sydney Herald*, 26 March 1832.
25 Atkinson and Aveling, *Australians 1838*, p. 420.
26 O'Farrell, 'St Patrick's Day in Australia'.
27 Ibid., p. 10.
28 Ibid., p. 7.
29 *Sydney Gazette*, 24 March 1825.
30 *Sydney Gazette*, 20 March 1827.
31 *Sydney Gazette*, 20 March 1830.
32 Atkinson and Aveling, *Australians 1838*, p. 11.
33 *Sydney Monitor*, 14 March 1838.
34 *Sydney Herald*, 20 May 1840.
35 *Australasian Chronicle*, 30 June 1840.
36 *Sydney Gazette*, 18 August 1840.

37   SRNSW, 4/2399.2, Engineers (1) 1838.
38   *Sydney Gazette*, 18 August 1840; *Margaret (3) indent*, SRNSW X642A, R2662, Musters and other papers, 2/8268, p. 305, Surgeon's journal, AJCP ADM 101, PRO Reel 3202.
39   *Sydney Herald*, 19 August 1840.
40   *Sydney Monitor*, 7 August 1840, for departure of the *Victoria*; *Sydney Herald*, 14 August 1840, for purpose of the journey.
41   'A two year engagement', in Lugard, *Monographs*.
42   *Hive indent*, SRNSW X637, Reel 907.

Chapter 13   'Infested by Bushrangers'

1   Byrne, *Criminal Law and Colonial Subject*, p. 131.
2   *Sydney Monitor*, 18 November 1839.
3   *Sydney Gazette*, 12 December 1840.
4   Byrne, *Criminal Law and Colonial Subject*, p. 139.
5   *Hive indent*, SRNSW X637, Reel 907; 1837 Muster.
6   Bruen's movements tracked through the *NSWGG*.
7   Binney, *Horsemen of the First Frontier*, p. 281; *Maitland Mercury*, 11 February 1843.
8   *Australian*, 1 March 1843; *Maitland Mercury*, 18 February 1843; *Sydney Morning Herald*, 22 February 1843.
9   AOTAS CON 17–1-1, Image 74 and CON 33–1-55.
10   *Sydney Herald*, 3 May 1841.
11   AOTAS CON 17–1-1, Image 74 and CON 33–1-55.
12   *Sydney Herald*, 23 April 1841.
13   AOTAS CON 17–1-1, Image 74 and CON 33–1-55.
14   SRNSW CSIL 41/5162, 4/2252.2. Research by Patrick Tierney's descendant Gordon Staples.
15   AOTAS CON 33/1/55, no. 14210.
16   Research by Patrick Tierney's descendant Gordon Staples.
17   *Sydney Gazette*, 11 February 1834.
18   John Black, CSIL 36/7942 within CSIL 36/9183, STNSW 42326.1.
19   Causer, '"Only a place fit for angels and eagles"', chapter 3, pp. 100–29.
20   Ibid., pp. 114–15; Robson, *The Convict Settlers of Australia*, p. 179.
21   Hirst, *Convict Society*, p. 118.
22   Causer, '"Only a place fit for angels and eagles"', pp. 102–3.
23   John Ryan, List of men to be removed to Norfolk Island, SRNSW 4/2638.5, CSIL re Cockatoo Island 1844.
24   Causer, '"Only a place fit for angels and eagles"', pp. 114–15, based on analysis of Convict indents AOTAS CON 31, 33, 34, 37, 39 and Australian newspapers.
25   *Sydney Monitor*, 6 December 1839.
26   AOTAS 33/1/55 Image 228; SRNSW 4/2465.4, CSIL 39/11876.
27   Ibid.
28   *Sydney Monitor*, 6 December 1839.
29   Causer, '"Only a place fit for angels and eagles"', pp. 20–1, 45.
30   1837 Muster assigned to Michael Henderson; absconded *NSWGG* 30 May 1838, 22 May 1839; *Monitor*, 20 November 1839; *Australian*, 19 November 1839; *Sydney Herald*, 18 November 1839.
31   James Hickey: TL 1844/1693; TL passport 48/73 dated 31 January 1844; Conditional Pardon 48/0073, Reel 977; Causer, '"Only a place fit for angels and eagles"', pp. 227–8.
32   *Sydney Gazette*, 7 November 1839; *Colonist*, 6 November 1839.
33   Ibid.
34   W.H. Barnard per *Mary* according to Maconochie's letter, although nobody of that precise name can be found on the ship's indent. The 1837 Muster lists a John and also a Sarah Barnes who were transported per *Mary*. The escapees who collaborated with Hickey and Sullivan were: James Monds (*Exmouth*), Cornelius O'Brien (*Blenheim*), William Brown (*Victoria*),

William Cunningham (*Augusta Jessie*) and someone listed as 'an English prisoner' plus the four soldiers, one of whom was named. SRNSW 4/2658, CSIL 44/1427.

35   SRNSW 4/2658, CSIL 44/1427.
36   *NSWGG*, 7 January 1848, p. 32; Causer, '"Only a place fit for angels and eagles"', pp. 227–9.

Chapter 14   Beyond the Penal Colony

1   Sir Edward Parry, Letter no. 606, Port Stephens, 24 April 1832: 'The two Prisoners of the Crown named in the Margin, who have just received Tickets of Leave being desirous of remaining on the Estate of the Australian Agricultural Company, the former as an Overseer of Sheep in the Company's service, the latter to work as a Shoe-maker—on his own account and with my consent, I request on behalf of these Men, that their Tickets of Leave may be altered to the District of Port Stephens.' <http://epress.anu.edu.au>.
2   Michael Barry per *Hive* 1835 TL 49/2170, passport May 1841 for twelve months to New England from Singleton, SRNSW 4/5660 Reel 2738 and a second passport for twelve months from Singleton Bench to travel between Liverpool Plains to Morpeth, 9 March 1842, SRNSW 4/5660, Reel 2738.
3   Smith, *Australia's Birthstain*, p. 153.
4   Andrews (ed.), *Stapylton*, p. 120.
5   James Ross, *Dr Ross's Recollections of a Short Excursion to Lake Echo in Van Diemen's Land 1823* (Hobart, 1992), pp. 36–9, cited in Atkinson, *Europeans in Australia*, p. 68.
6   Cited in Ward, *The Australian Legend*, pp. 82, 166.
7   *Sydney Herald*, 14 August 1840; *Sydney Monitor*, 7 August 1840.
8   Taylor (ed.), *Journal of Ensign Best*, pp. 376–7, 25 October 1842.
9   For Parkhurst boys in Western Australia see Smith, *Australia's Birthstain*, pp. 254–5 and Gill, *Convict Assignment*.
10   Taylor (ed.), *Journal of Ensign Best*, p. 70.
11   Philip Heath, PO Box 99002, Newmarket, Auckland, New Zealand, to David Nutley, Maritime Archaeologist, NSW Heritage Office, 5, 7 March 2002.
12   Lugard, *Monographs*.
13   *Hive* muster; 1837 Muster.
14   Clarke, *Convicts of the Port Phillip District*, p. 34; Denis Kelly: VPRS 110; TL 8/10/42, with W. Ryrie, Port Phillip.
15   NSW Police History in AOTAS CON 39/1/2/, p. 199, Image 226.
16   Ibid.; *Wanderer Indent*, AOTAS CON 16/1/3/, p. 120.
17   NSWBDM 188/vol. 94, 28 April 1845.
18   *Sydney Morning Herald*, 12 September 1845.
19   Ibid.
20   *Sydney Morning Herald*, 12 September 1845; AOTAS CON 39/1/2/, Image 226.
21   AOTAS CON 39/1//2, Image 226.
22   *Darlinghurst Gaol Entrance Book 1850–1854*, Vernon Indexes; *Hive* transported 250 men, the *John* transported 200.
23   SRNSW CF42/647, 30 April 1842; *Sydney Morning Herald*, 18 March 1854.
24   Wright, 'Rogues and Fools', and Box 13, Cash Book, p. 425, *John Coghill Papers* ML Uncat MSS 511.
25   Christine Wright database: *Braidwood Bench Book*, 22 April 1840, 2 December 1840, 5 January 1842; Peter Mayberry's online index to Braidwood Gaol for 1870–72; Vernon Indexes for *Goulburn Gaol Entrance Book*, SRNSW 6/5425.
26   NSWBDM 1872/006282.
27   Information supplied by Ellen Smith, descendant of Patrick and Bridget Tierney.
28   Therry, *Reminiscences*, pp. 47–9.
29   Ibid., p. 144.
30   Smith, *Australia's Birthstain*, and 'Beyond Birthstain' for McEncroe's involvement in the anti-transportation campaign; Earls, *Plunkett's Legacy*, p. 148.
31   Barker, *History of Bathurst*, pp. 112–14.

32 Molony, *Architect of Freedom*, pp. 271–4.
33 Earls, *Plunkett's Legacy*, pp. 211–12; Molony, *Architect of Freedom*, pp. 9–10, 278.
34 TNAUK BT107/90 408/1844 and BT 107/79; plus birth of Edward junior from descendant James Canney.
35 TNAUK BT 98/379 plus birth of children from James Canney.
36 Research by Airlie Moore, descendant of Eliza and Frederick Harpur, <airlie@rmmoore.com.au>.
37 Bateson, *Convict Ships*, pp. 215–16.
38 *Josephine Willis logbook*, 10 November 1854 – 23 October 1855, transcript supplied by descendant James Canney; TNAUK BT98/4231.
39 Ibid.
40 Reproduced in *Sydney Morning Herald*, 21 January 1854.
41 *Maitland Mercury*, 23 February 1853; *Sydney Morning Herald*, 18 February 1853.
42 *Sydney Morning Herald*, 18 April 1853, research by Airlie Moore.
43 Information from descendant James Canney; *Western Australian*, 27 August 1914, research by Airlie Moore.

Chapter 15 Creating the Australian Way of Life

1 Cunningham, *Two Years*, vol. 1, p. 14.
2 Maxwell-Stewart, review of Smith, *Australia's Birthstain*, *JACH*, vol. 11, 2009, pp. 196–9.
3 Harris, *Emigrant Mechanic*, p. 5; Lawrence, *Kangaroo*, 1950 edition, p. 27.
4 Atkinson, 'Four patterns of convict protest'; Hirst, *Convict Society*.
5 Cunningham, *Two Years*, vol. 1, pp. 238–9.
6 Karskens, *The Colony*, chapters 3–7.
7 Karskens, *The Colony*, pp. 7–8.
8 Smith, *Australia's Birthstain*, pp. 119, 124.
9 Cash, *The Uncensored Story*, p. 6.
10 Montgomery in L. Carlyon, *Gallipoli*, Sydney: Macmillan, 2001, p. 114.
11 McGregor in Hirst, *The Australians*, p. 165.
12 Karskens, *The Colony*, pp. 7–8.
13 Roberts, '"A sort of inland Norfolk Island"?', pp. 50–73.
14 Maxwell-Stewart, *Closing Hell's Gates*, pp. 266–7.
15 *Extracts from the Letters of James Backhouse: Now engaged in a religious visit to Van Diemen's Land and New South Wales, accompanied by George Washington Walker*, first Part, 3rd ed., London: Harvey & Darton, 1838, p. 66.
16 Hodgson, in M. Cannon, *Australia in the Victorian Age*, vol. 2, *Life in the Country*, Melbourne: Viking O'Neill, 1973, p. 40.
17 Lawrence, *Kangaroo*, London, 1950 edition, p. 28.
18 Causer, '"Only a place fit for angels and eagles"', chapter 5, particularly pp. 185–95.
19 20 June 1846. Stuart's report in *Norfolk Island: The Botany Bay of Botany Bay.*
20 *Ballarat Times*, 2 September 1854.
21 Clay, *Maconochie's Experiment*, p. 231. See also 'assigned servant Patrick Wallis deposed that "he was a runaway from one of the road gangs & [two other prisoners] being his shipmates harboured & assisted him while in the bush",' *Sydney Gazette*, 11 February 1834; and the clergy's view 'each of these men has from two to three hundred shipmates, who are his bosom companions; that, when arrived, he finds various former intimates from the same town or country; that, after a while, he probably adds to these some hundred, or two or three, of chain-gang mates; that all these are sworn brothers prepared, with true *esprit de corps*, to back each other out of any difficulty'. Ullathorne, *Catholic Mission in Australasia*, p. 31. Report on the Assize at Goulburn in 1850 confirms the term 'mate', that is, the prisoner's mate, was in use before the gold rush began. *Sydney Morning Herald*, 9 August 1850, p. 3.
22 Chad Habel, review of Smith, *Australia's Birthstain*, *Journal of the Association for the Study of Australian Literature*, vol. 9, 2009.
23 O'Farrell, *Vanished Kingdoms*, p. 20.

24 Waldersee, *Catholic Society*, p. 180.
25 Ibid., p. 9, citing O'Farrell, *The Catholic Church in Australia*, 1968, p. 10. See also Molony, *Architect of Freedom*, p. 200, and Dyster, 'The fate of colonial conservatives', on sectarian attitudes among the gentry.
26 Waldersee, *Catholic Society*, p. 1.
27 Ibid.
28 Ibid., p. 4, quoting O'Brien, *Life of Archpriest Therry*.
29 See Chapter 5; Walsh, *Voices from Tocal*, p. 69.
30 Therry, *Reminiscences*, p. 146.
31 Ullathorne evidence to Select Committee on Transportation, BPP, Crime & Punishment, Transportation, 1837–61, Vol. III, pp. 16–33; *HRA*, series 1, vol. 27, p. 623.
32 Research by Brian Andrews, Sir Edgeworth David Memorial Museum, Kurri Kurri, New South Wales.
33 Ibid.
34 Therry, *Reminiscences*, p. 147.
35 O'Farrell in Waldersee, *Catholic Society*, p. 70.
36 Waldersee, p. viii.
37 Ibid., p. 70.
38 Mullaly, *Crimes in the Port Phillip District*, pp. 745–6, 749–50.
39 Harris quote in Walsh, *Voices from Tocal*, p. 69.
40 O'Farrell, *Vanished Kingdoms*, p. xxii.
41 Macarthur, *New South Wales*, p. 27.
42 John West, *The History of Tasmania*, Launceston, 1852, facsimile edition, p. 525.
43 Harris, *Emigrant Mechanic*, pp. 23–4.
44 Serle, *The Golden Age*, pp. 77–8.
45 *Weekend Australian*, 18–19 December 2010.
46 Travers, *Phantom Fenians*, *passim*.
47 *Sydney Monitor*, 20 March 1833.
48 'The Aussie home dream lives on—social demographer, Mark McCrindle, said Australia's passion for home ownership was unique globally.' *Sunday Telegraph*, 18 August 2013. See also Waldersee, *Catholic Society*, pp. 99–100.
49 Kelly, 'The abduction of women of fortune in eighteenth-century Ireland', p. 8.
50 Lindsey, 'Taken', chapter 3: 'Rebellion, revenge and remorse', p. 82.
51 Lindsey, 'Conjugal wrongs', *The Age*, 5 December 2009.
52 Lindsey, 'So much recklessness', pp. 443, 438–56.
53 Lindsey, 'A mistress of her own actions', p. 50.
54 Lindsey, 'So much recklessness', *passim*.
55 Smith, *Australia's Birthstain*, particularly chapters 7–11, and 'Beyond Birthstain'; Causer, 'Anti-transportation'.
56 Smith, *A Cargo of Women*, p. 89.
57 Bongiorno, *Sex Lives*, p. 97.
58 Ibid.
59 Darwin, *An Australian Selection*, p. 65.
60 Causer, '"Only a place fit for angels and eagles"', pp. 185–95, particularly p. 189, citing James C. Scott, *Domination and the Arts of Resistance: Hidden transcript*, London: Yale University Press, 1990, p. 193.
61 James Roe, 'Letter from a Convict in Australia to his brother in England', *Cornhill Magazine*, vol. XIII, no. 76.
62 Peter Fitzsimons, *Eureka: The unfinished revolution*, Sydney: William Heinemann, pp. 95–6.
63 Therry, *Reminiscences*, p. 146.
64 O'Farrell, *Letters from Irish Australia*, chapter 2.
65 See Smith, *Australia's Birthstain*, pp. 199, 214–19.
66 Ibid., chapter 7.
67 Waldersee, *Catholic Society*, p. 161.
68 Ullathorne, *The Autobiography of Archbishop Ullathorne*, p. 171.

69 Hamilton, 'No Irish need apply', p. 166.
70 Ibid.
71 John M. Ward, *James Macarthur: Colonial Conservative*, p. 282, citing C. Dilke, *Problems of Greater Britain*.
72 Lindsey, 'A mistress of her own actions'.
73 Smith, *Australia's Birthstain*, p. 153.
74 Martin, *Henry Parkes*, pp. 223–30; Travers, *Grant Old Man*, pp. 160–1.
75 Earls, *Plunkett's Legacy*, p. 210. State funding to religious schools ended in 1862.
76 Ibid., pp. 71–2.
77 George Williams, Anthony Mason Professor of Law, University of New South Wales, *Sydney Morning Herald*, 16 July 2013.

Chapter 16   The Lives of Men

1 Lugard, *Monographs*.
2 Smith, *Australia's Birthstain*, p. 210.
3 Waugh, *Forgotten Hero,* pp. 165–90.
4 Lugard, *Monographs*.
5 Ibid.
6 Ibid.
7 Ibid.
8 Ibid., *Times* (London), 1 December 1857.
9 Lugard, *Monographs*.
10 Log of the *Josephine Willis*, TNAUK BT98/4231.
11 The wreck and subsequent inquiry were reported around the globe, including in the Antipodes. Most reports were syndications of British newspapers but they vary in the amount of detail included. Some of the best are *The Times* (London), 15 February 1856 and subsequent days, *Southern Cross* (New Zealand), 13 May 1856, *Otago Witness*, 31 May 1856, *Sydney Morning Herald*, 19 April 1856.
12 *United Service Magazine*, vol. 84, May–August 1857.
13 *Cornwall Chronicle*, 24 September 1856.

Index